The Philosopher Responds

Volume Two

Letter from the General Editor

The Library of Arabic Literature makes available Arabic editions and English translations of significant works of Arabic literature, with an emphasis on the seventh to nineteenth centuries. The Library of Arabic Literature thus includes texts from the pre-Islamic era to the cusp of the modern period, and encompasses a wide range of genres, including poetry, poetics, fiction, religion, philosophy, law, science, travel writing, history, and historiography.

Books in the series are edited and translated by internationally recognized scholars. They are published as hardcovers in parallel-text format with Arabic and English on facing pages, as English-only paperbacks, and as downloadable Arabic editions. For some texts, the series also publishes separate scholarly editions with full critical apparatus.

The Library encourages scholars to produce authoritative Arabic editions, accompanied by modern, lucid English translations, with the ultimate goal of introducing Arabic's rich literary heritage to a general audience of readers as well as to scholars and students.

The Library of Arabic Literature is supported by a grant from the New York University Abu Dhabi Institute and is published by NYU Press.

Philip F. Kennedy
General Editor, Library of Arabic Literature

الهوامل والشوامل

أبو حيّان التوحيديّ

وأبو عليّ مسكويه

المجلّد الثاني

LIBRARY OF
المكتبة
ARABIC
العربية
LITERATURE

The Philosopher Responds

An Intellectual Correspondence from the Tenth Century

Volume Two

Abū Ḥayyān al-Tawḥīdī

Abū ʿAlī Miskawayh

Edited by

Bilal Orfali and Maurice A. Pomerantz

Translated by

Sophia Vasalou and James E. Montgomery

Volume editor

Devin J. Stewart

NEW YORK UNIVERSITY PRESS

New York

NEW YORK UNIVERSITY PRESS
New York

Library of Congress Cataloging-in-Publication Data

Names: Abū Ḥayyān al-Tawḥīdī, ʻAlī ibn Muḥammad, active 10th century, author. | Ibn Miskawayh, Aḥmad ibn Muḥammad, -1030 author. | Urfah'lī, Bilāl, editor. | Pomerantz, Maurice A., editor. | Vasalou, Sophia, translator. | Montgomery, James E. (James Edward), 1962- translator.
Title: The philosopher responds : an intellectual correspondence from the tenth century / Abū Ḥayyān al-Tawḥīdī, Abū ʻAlī Miskawayh ; edited by Bilal Orfali and Maurice Pomerantz ; translated by Sophia Vasalou and James E. Montgomery.
Other titles: Hawāmil wa-al-shawāmil. English
Description: New York : New York University, [2019] | Includes bibliographical references and index.
Identifiers: LCCN 2019012621 (print) | LCCN 2019017484 (ebook) | ISBN 9781479886999 (v. 1) | ISBN 9781479831203 (v. 1) | ISBN 9781479865444 (v. 2) | ISBN 9781479841196 (v. 2) | ISBN 9781479871483 (v. 1, hardcover : alk. paper) | ISBN 9781479834600 (v. 2, hardcover : alk. paper)
Classification: LCC PJ7750.A26 (ebook) | LCC PJ7750.A26 H313 2019 (print) | DDC 181/.6--dc23

LC record available at https://lccn.loc.gov/2019012621

New York University Press books are printed on acid-free paper, and their binding materials are chosen for strength and durability.

Series design by Titus Nemeth.

Typeset in Tasmeem, using DecoType Naskh and Emiri.

Typesetting and digitization by Stuart Brown.

Manufactured in the United States of America
c10 9 8 7 6 5 4 3 2 1

Table of Contents

Letter from the General Editor iii
Map: Buyid and Neighbouring Lands xii

The Philosopher Responds, Volume Two 1
On the influence of companions on a person's character and on the benefits of companionship 2
On why people scorn certain forms of ostentatious demeanor and why individuals aren't simply allowed to do as they please 4
On what the soul seeks in this world and on the nature of human beings 6
On the nature and attributes of God 10
On why people experience fear in the absence of an apparent cause 10
On why people fly into a rage when they can't open a lock 12
On why people with small heads have light brains 14
On certain beliefs concerning the relation between a person's facial hair and his character 16
On why people racked by suffering find it easy to face death 18
On why people denigrate things they fail to attain and are hostile to things of which they are ignorant 20
On why it is easier to make enemies than friends 22
On why atheists act morally 24
On why some people willingly become the butt of other people's jokes 26
On why people love to occupy positions of eminence 28
On why we honor people for the achievements of their ancestors but not those of their progeny 32
On why the progeny of illustrious people evince an elevated sense of entitlement and self-importance 32
On whether it would be more consistent with the true order of things if all people were honored equally 36
On different forms of divination 38
On why some people dislike being addressed as "old man" while others relish it 42
On why people take comfort from knowing they are not alone in their misfortune 44

On the virtues of different nations, such as the Arabs, Byzantines, Persians, and Indians 48
On why intelligent people are more susceptible to grief 50
On why intrinsic merit and worldly fortune do not coincide 54
On the meaning of coincidence 64
On the nature of compulsion and choice 66
On the reason for the wanderlust experienced by certain people 74
On why people desire knowledge, and on the benefits of knowledge 78
On why people and other animals respond so powerfully to certain kinds of sounds and musical effects 82
On why older people are more liable to hope; on the meaning of "hope" and related terms 86
On why women are more jealous than men; on the nature and moral status of jealousy 88
On why more people die young than die old 92
On why people seek likenesses 96
On why we find it easier to represent extreme ugliness in our imagination than exquisite beauty 98
On why sudden joy affects people so violently 102
On why we experience states of suffering more intensely than states of well-being 104
On why seeing someone laughing causes others to laugh 106
On why human beings are so attached to the world despite the misfortunes and suffering they experience in it 108
On why people say the world would fall to ruin if it weren't for fools 110
On the anxiety experienced by people who have something to hide 116
On why we are more likely to heed a preacher who practices what he preaches 116
On why people regret their failure to honor and benefit from great men during their lifetime 120
On why Arabs and non-Arabs declare their pedigrees in times of war 120
On why people distinguish between different kinds of air, water, and earth, but not different kinds of fire 122
On why people feel happier when they unexpectedly obtain something they weren't seeking than when they obtain what they were seeking 126

On why fine edifices fall to ruin when left uninhabited 128
On why men of sublime character beget knaves 130
On why our longing for home grows more intense the nearer we come to it 130
On the meaning of the dictum that judgement sleeps while passion keeps watch 134
On a remark concerning logic made by the dialectical theologian Abū Hāshim to the philosopher Abū Bishr Mattā 136
On why some Arabic words are feminine and others masculine 138
On whether a human being could know everything 140
On why new incumbents are harsh toward the officials they replace 142
On why human beings are considered to be orphans after losing their father rather than their mother 144
On why chess is so hard to master 146
On why people dislike changing their name or patronymic, and why they have a sense of aversion toward certain names and titles 148
On the mannerisms of people whose mind is preoccupied, and on why people have so many different ways of behaving when they feel anxious or unhappy 150
On different ways of approaching God's attributes 154
On why we find it easier to remember what is correct than what is defective 158
On why prosodists tend to produce flat poetry 160
On the meaning of the dictum that the learned live longer than the ignorant 164
On why it is harder to speak eloquently than to write eloquently 166
On the significance of the fact that human beings are the only animals to stand upright 168
On why certainty is less enduring than doubt 170
On why we laugh harder when a person keeps a straight face 172
On the meaning of the scholars' proposition that a rare instance attracts no ruling 172
On the possibility of certain kinds of coincidences obtaining 176
On the role of analogical reasoning in the linguistic sciences 178
On whether God created the world for a cause 180

On why a life of comfort makes people feel oppressed and leads them to behave wantonly 182
On why some things are best when they're new and others are best when old 184
On why people who display great piety are prone to arrogance 186
On why a warm manner is more pleasing than a cold benefaction 188
On why those closest to a king are less inclined to prattle about his person than those at the farthest remove from him 192
On Ibn Sālim al-Baṣrī's claim that God perceived the world while it was nonexistent 194
On why the poets love to dwell on the apparitions that come to them in their sleep 196
On why people are reluctant to advertise their merits 198
On the relative merits of verse as against prose 200
On why people feel oppressed when things are prohibited to them 203
On why preachers are affected by stage fright when addressing large audiences 204
On the anxiety that affects onlookers when they see preachers affected by stage fright 206
On why we hate hearing the same thing twice 208
On whether the religious Law can conflict with human reason 210
On a remark made by Aḥmad ibn ʿAbd al-Wahhāb concerning the possibility of uttering something that is completely false versus something completely true 218
On why excellent souls find repose in the truth and find falsehood repugnant 220
On a question put by Aḥmad ibn ʿAbd al-Wahhāb concerning why animals are generated inside plants but plants are not generated inside animals 222
On the nature of alchemy and why people are so enamoured of it 224
On a question put by Aḥmad ibn ʿAbd al-Wahhāb concerning the difference between the words "indeterminable" and "impenetrable" 230
On the disagreements between jurists 230
On why people despise kings who are governed by pleasure and fear kings governed by reason 238

On the physical reactions people exhibit when listening to music 240
On why liars often tell the truth but not the reverse, and on whether habits can change 244
On certain popular sayings 246
On the distinction between different forms of divination 248
On why there are four categories for inquiry: whether, what, which, and why 250
On the nonexistent 254
On why a physician rejoices at the recovery of his patient 256
On why money is made of silver and gold and not other substances 258
On the specific time when the soul attaches itself to the body 264
On whether souls can recollect what they used to know after leaving the body 268
On why mountains exist 270
On why there are three souls 274
On why the sea is located on a particular side of the earth 276
On why seawater is salty 278
On how we can see things in our sleep without an organ of sense perception 278
On a puzzle concerning the possibility of seeking something we do not know 280
On why it does not snow in the summer 282
On the proof for the existence of angels 284
On what justifies the suffering of children and non-rational animals 286
On why it takes us longer to hear thunder than to see lightning 288
On the possibility that a person may abandon every belief he adopts ad infinitum 290

Notes 295
Glossary 299
Bibliography 304
Further Reading 308
Index 309
About the NYU Abu Dhabi Institute 318
About the Typefaces 319
Titles Published by the Library of Arabic Literature 320
About the Editor–Translators 324

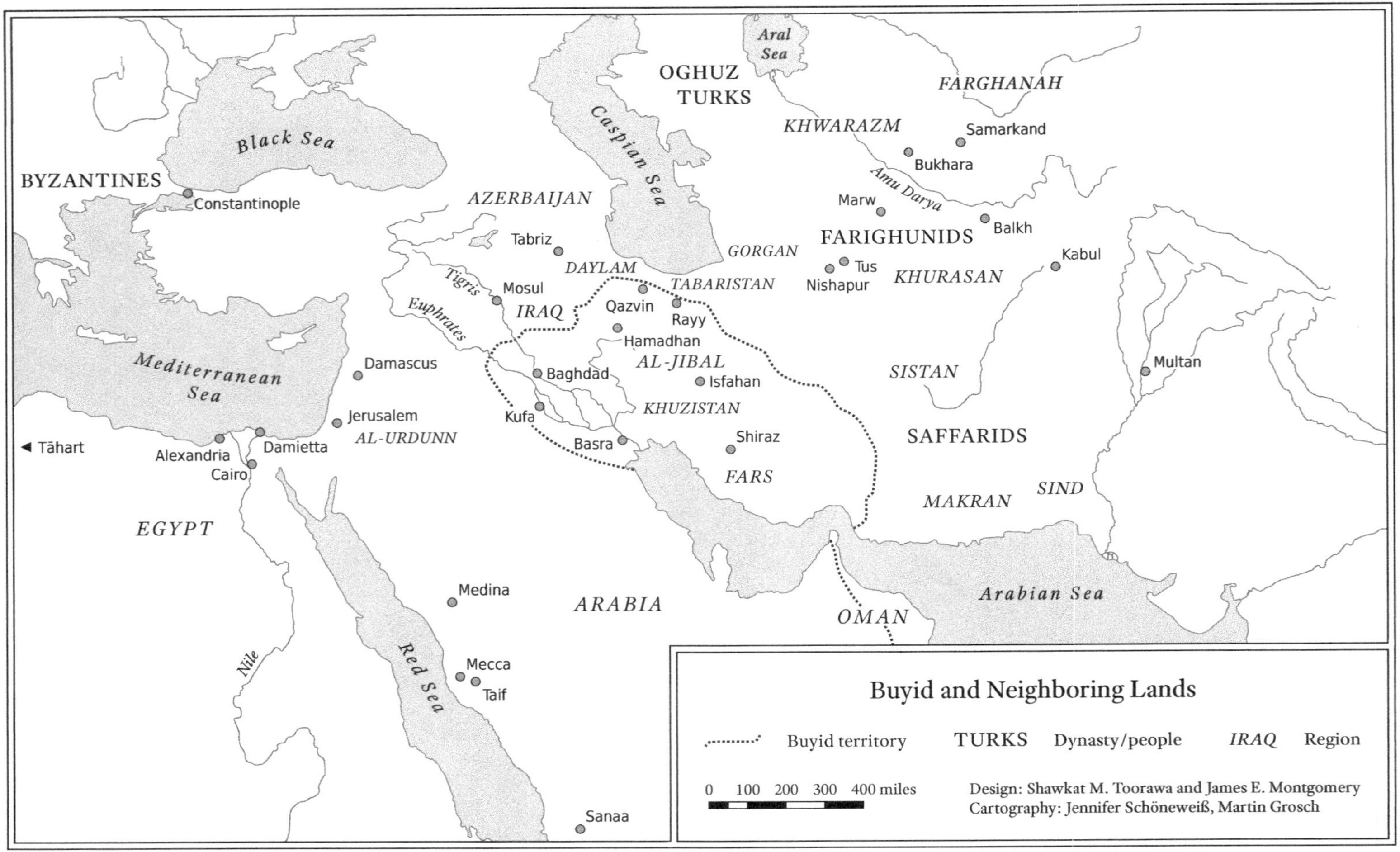
Buyid and Neighboring Lands
Buyid territory
TURKS Dynasty/people
IRAQ Region
0 100 200 300 400 miles
Design: Shawkat M. Toorawa and James E. Montgomery
Cartography: Jennifer Schöneweiß, Martin Grosch
BYZANTINES
Black Sea
Constantinople
Mediterranean Sea
Caspian Sea
Aral Sea
OGHUZ TURKS
FARGHANAH
KHWARAZM
Samarkand
Bukhara
Amu Darya
Marw
Balkh
FARIGHUNIDS
GORGAN
Tus
Nishapur
KHURASAN
Kabul
AZERBAIJAN
Tabriz
DAYLAM
TABARISTAN
Tigris
Mosul
IRAQ
Qazvin
Rayy
Euphrates
Hamadhan
AL-JIBAL
Damascus
Baghdad
Isfahan
SISTAN
Multan
Jerusalem
Kufa
KHUZISTAN
AL-URDUNN
Tāhart
Alexandria
Damietta
Basra
Shiraz
SAFFARIDS
Cairo
FARS
SIND
MAKRAN
EGYPT
Arabian Sea
Medina
ARABIA
OMAN
Nile
Red Sea
Mecca
Taif
Sanaa

الهوامل والشوامل

المجلّد الثاني

The Philosopher Responds

Volume Two

مسألة

ما يصيب الإنسان من قرينه في خيره وشرّه وكيف صار يؤثّر الشرّير في الخيّر أسرع ممّا يؤثّر الخيّر في الشرّير وما فائدة النفس في المقارنة؟ ١،٦٦

الجواب

قال أبو عليّ مسكويه رحمه الله ينال القرين من قرينه الاقتداء والتشبّه وكما أنّ كلّ متجاورين من الأشياء الطبيعيّة فلا بدّ أن يؤثّر أحدهما في الآخر فكذلك حال النفس وذاك أنّ الطبيعة متشبّهة بالنفس لأنّها شبيهة بظلّ النفس ومن شأن الشيء الأقوى في الطبيعة أن يحيل الأضعف إلى نفسه ويشبّهه بذاته كما تجد ذلك في الحارّ والبارد والرطب واليابس ولأجل تأثير المجاور في مجاوره حدثت الأمراض في البدن وبسببه عولج بالأدوية. ولمّا كانت النفس التي فينا هيولانيّة[١] صار الشرّ لها طباعاً والخير تكلّفاً وتعلّماً فاحتجنا معاشر البشر أن نتعب بالخير حتّى نستفيده ونقتنيه ثمّ ليس يكفينا تحصيل صورته حتّى نألفه ونتعوّده ونكرّر زماناً طويلاً الحالة التي حصلت لنا منه على أنفسنا لتصير ملكة وسجيّة بعد أن كانت حالاً. ٢،٦٦

فأمّا الشرّ فلسنا نحتاج إلى تعب به وتحصيله بل يكفي فيه أن نخلّي النفس رسومها ونتركها على طبيعتها فإنّها تخلو من الخير والخلوّ من الخير هو الشرّ لأنّه قد تبيّن في المباحث الفلسفيّة أنّه ليس الشرّ بشيء له عين قائمة بل هو عدم الخير ولذلك قيل الهيولى معدن الشرّ وينبوعه لأجل خلوّها من جميع الصور فالشرّ الأوّل البسيط هو عدم ثمّ يتركّب وسبب تركّبه الأعدام التي هي مقترنة بالهيولى. ٣،٦٦

وشرح هذا الكلام طويل إلّا أنّ الذي يحصل لك من جواب المسألة فيه أنّ النفس تتشبّه بالنفس المقارنة لها وتقتدي بها والشرّ أسرع إليها من الخير لما ذكرناه ٤،٦٦

---

١ الأصل: لاهوتيّة.

On the influence of companions on a person's character and on the benefits of companionship

How is a person affected in his good and evil qualities by his companion? Why is it that an evil person is swifter to exert influence on a good person than a good person on an evil one? What benefit does the soul derive from companionship? 66.1

Miskawayh's response

What we gain from a companion is the possibility of following his example and imitating him. Two natural objects that are physically contiguous must inevitably influence one another. The same applies to the soul, for nature imitates the soul, being like a shadow to it. In nature, stronger elements tend to transmute weaker elements into themselves and assimilate them to their being, as we notice with things that are hot and cold and those that are moist and dry. Illnesses arise in the body on account of the influence exercised by one contiguous object on another, and it is through this means that they are treated by medications. The soul in us is material, so evil comes naturally to it, whereas good comes to it through effort and learning. We human beings thus need to toil at the good in order to acquire it and bring it into our possession. It is not enough for us to realize its form, but we must grow familiar with and habituated to it, and spend a long time reproducing the condition it has generated in us, before it can pass from being a transient condition to being a stable state and an ingrained trait. 66.2

By contrast, we do not need to toil at evil to acquire it. All we need to do is let our soul follow its bent and leave it to its nature; for it is lacking in good, and lack of good constitutes evil. As has been established by philosophical inquiries, evil is not something that has a subsisting essence, but rather consists in the privation of good. That is why it has been said that matter is the origin and wellspring of evil insofar as it lacks all forms. Simple primary evil consists in privation and then enters into compounds. What causes it to enter into compounds are the privations associated with matter. 66.3

A full exposition of these points would take too long, but what you can retain for the purpose of answering your question is that the soul imitates and follows the example of the soul it keeps company with, and that evil comes to 66.4

وهو أنّ النفس التي فينا هي هيولانيّة وأعني بهذا القول أنّها قابلة للصور من العقل فالمعقولات إنّما تصير معقولات لنا إذا ثبتت صورها في النفس ولذلك قال أفلاطن[1] إنّ النفس مكان للصور واستحسن أرسطوطالس[2] هذا التشبيه من أفلاطن[3] لأنّه استعارة حسنة وإيماء فصيح إلى المعنى الذي أراده فيجب على هذا الأصل أن نتوقّى مجالسة الأشرار ومخالطتهم ومقارنتهم ونقبل قول الشاعر [طويل]

عَنِ ٱلْمَرْءِ لَا تَسْأَلْ وَأَبْصِرْ قَرِينَهُ   فَإِنَّ ٱلْقَرِينَ بِٱلْمُقَارِنِ مُقْتَدِ

وينبغي أن نأخذ الأحداث والصبيان به أشدّ الأخذ فقد مرّ في مسألة ما يحقّق هذا المعنى ويؤكّده وينبّه عليه.

مسألة

١،٦٧ ما وجه تسخيف من أطال ذيله وسحبه وكبّر عمامته وحشا زيقه قطناً وعرّض جيبه تعريضاً ومشى متبهنساً وتكلّم متشادقاً ولم شُنّع هذا ونظيره وما الذي سمّج هذا وأمثاله؟ ولم لم يُترك كلّ إنسان على رأيه واختياره وشهوته وإيثاره؟ وهل أطبق العقلاء المميّزون والفضلاء المبرّزون على كراهة هذه الأمور إلّا لسرّ خاف وخبيئة موجودة؟ فما ذلك السرّ وما تلك الخبيئة؟

الجواب

٢،٦٧ قال أبو عليّ مسكويه رحمه الله ينكر ممّا ذكرته كلّه التكلّف وذاك أنّ من خالف عادات الناس في زيّهم ومذاهبهم وتفرّد من بينهم بما يباينهم ثمّ احتمل مؤونة ما يتجشّمه

١ ط: أفلاطون. ٢ الأصل: أرسطوطاليس؛ ط: أرسططاليس. ٣ ط: أفلاطون.

it more swiftly than good for the reasons we have mentioned—namely, that the soul that is in us is material. By this I mean that it receives forms from the intellect. Intelligibles become intelligibles for us once their forms are fixed within the soul. That is why Plato said that the soul is a place of forms. Aristotle admired this comparison of Plato's because it is a fine figure of speech and an eloquent way of indicating the idea he had in mind.[1] Therefore, on the basis of this principle, we ought to avoid associating with evil people, mingling with them, and cultivating their company, and we should listen to the words of the poet who said:[2]

> Ask not about a man, but consider his companion:
> we follow the example of those whose company we keep.

We must also warn young people and children against that as forcefully as possible; as was established, confirmed, and highlighted in the discussion of an earlier question.

On why people scorn certain forms of ostentatious demeanor and why individuals aren't simply allowed to do as they please

Why do people scorn those who keep the lower end of their garment long and drag it behind them; who wear their turbans very large, puff up their collars with cotton, and have their shirt openings very wide, swaggering about and belaboring their speech? What makes these people and their ilk repulsive? What renders them and their cognates unseemly? Why isn't everyone left to his opinion and choice, his desire and predilection? Surely there must be a secret reason that unites men of reason and discrimination, and men of excellence and distinction, in deeming these things repugnant? So, what is this secret and reason? 67.1

Miskawayh's response

It is affectation that renders these things objectionable. The only reason someone diverges from how people customarily dress and act, setting himself apart from them by behaving differently, and being prepared to shoulder the cost of his actions, is that he has a purpose that conflicts with their purposes and an aim that is different from their aims. If his goal is to acquire fame and 67.2

فليس ذلك منه إلّا لغرض مخالف لأغراضهم وقصد لغير ما يقصدونه فإن كان غايته من هذه الأشياء أن يشهر نفسه وينبّه على موضعه فليس يعدو[1] أن يوهم بها أمراً لا حقيقة له ويطلب حالاً لا يستحقّها لأنّه لوكان يستحقّها لظهرت منه وعُرفت له من غير تكلّف ولا تجشّم لهذه المؤن الغليظة فإذن هو كاذب فعلاً ومزوّر باطلاً وما تعاطى ذلك إلّا ليغرّ سليماً[2] ويخدع مسترسلاً وهذا مذهب المحتال الذي يُتحرّز منه ويُتباعد عنه هذا إلى ما يجمعه من بديهة المخالفة والمخالفة سبب الاستيحاش وعلّة النفور وأصل المعاداة. وإنّما حرص الناس وأهل الفضل وحرص لهم الأنبياء عليهم السلام بما وضعوه لهم من السنن والشرائع لتحدث بينهم الموافقة والمناسبة التي هي سبب المحبّات وأصل المودّات ليتشاركوا في الخيرات ولتحصل لهم صورة التأحّد الذي هو سبب كلّ فضيلة ولأجله تمّ الاجتماع في المدينة الذي هو سبب حسن الحال في العيش والاستمتاع بالحياة والخيرات المطلوبة في الدنيا.

مسـألة

ما ملتمس النفس في هذا العالم وهل لها ملتمس وبغية؟ وإن وُسمت بهذه المعاني خرجت من أن تكون عليّة الدرجة خطيرة القدر لأنّ هذا عنوان الحاجة وبدء العجز ولولا أن يتّسع النطاق لسألت ما نسبتها إلى الإنسان وهل لها به قوام أو له بها قوام؟ وإن كان هذا فعلى أيّ وجه هو؟ وأوسع من هذا الفضاء حديث الإنسان فإنّ الإنسان قد أشكل عليه الإنسان ثمّ حكيت حكايات ليس لها غناء في المسألة فلنشتغل بالجواب. ١،٦٨

الجواب

قال أبو عليّ مسكويه رحمه الله لولا أنّ لفظة الالتماس توهّم غير المعنى الصحيح في حال النفس وظهور آثارها في هذا العالم لأطلقتها ورخّصت فيها لك كما أطلقها ٢،٦٨

١ الأصل: يعدوا. ٢ الأصل: تسليما؛ وصوابه من الهامش.

call attention to himself, the only possibility is that he is seeking to create an impression ungrounded in reality and to demand a status he does not merit. For had he merited it, it would have been clear and manifest, and would have been acknowledged without any need for affectation or incurring such steep costs. He is thus in fact a lying counterfeiter, and his only reason for engaging in this is to deceive the good-natured and cozen the unwary—the characteristic behavior of impostors, whom we should guard against and keep our distance from. Additionally, our instinctive response to divergence is involved: Divergence causes alienation, excites repulsion, and generates animosity. What people and men of merit seek, and what prophets also seek through the norms and laws they have imposed on them, is to establish the concord and harmony that generate relations of love and affection, so that all may share in the good and acquire the unified form that is the cause of every virtue, for the sake of which people come together in polities, as it enables them to live well, enjoy life, and attain the goods desired in the mundane world.

On what the soul seeks in this world and on the nature of human beings

What does the soul seek in this world? Does it have something it seeks and 68.1
desires? If these elements attach to it, it can no longer be thought to occupy a lofty rank and possess a momentous standing, for this is the hallmark of need and the first ingredient of powerlessness. But for the fact that it would widen the scope to excess, I would have asked: What is the soul's relation to human beings? Does it subsist through them, or do they subsist through it? And if that is so, in what way is it so? A wider topic yet, a veritable ocean of discussion, is the subject of human beings. For man is a mystery to man. Then you adduced various quotations that contribute nothing to the question, so let us occupy ourselves with our response.

Miskawayh's response

Were it not that the term "seeking" suggests the wrong idea regarding the con- 68.2
dition of the soul and how its effects are manifested in this world, I would have applied it and permitted you to apply it, as others have. But I have seen

قوم ولكنّي رأيت أبا بكر محمّد بن زكريّا الطبيب وغيره ممّن كان في طبقته قد تورّطوا في مذهب بعيد من الحقّ سببه هذه اللفظة وما أشبهها ممّا أطلقته الحكماء على سبيل الاتّساع في الكلام بل لأجل الضرورة العارضة للألفاظ عند ضيقها عن المعاني الغامضة التي أطلقوا عليها. ولكنّي سأشير لك إلى ما ينبغي أن تعتقده في هذا الباب وهو أنّ الطبائع إذا امتزجت ضروب الامتزاجات بضروب حركات الفلك حدثت منها ضروب الصور والأشكال التي تعملها الطبيعة وتقبل من آثار النفس بوساطة الطبيعة ضروب الآثار لأنّ النفس تظهر آثارها في كلّ مزاج بحسب قبوله وتستعمل كلّ آلة طبيعيّة بحسب ملاءمتها في كلّ[1] ما يمكن أن تستعمل فيه وتنهيه إلى أقصى ما يمكن أن تنتهي إليه من الفضيلة.

وهذا الفعل من النفس لا لغرض أكثر من ظهور الحكمة وذاك أنّ ظهور الحكمة من الحكيم لا يكون لغرض آخر فوق الحكمة لأنّ أجلّ الأفعال ما لم يُرد لشيء آخر بل لذاته وكلّ فعل أريد لغاية أخرى ولشيء آخر فذلك الشيء أجلّ من ذلك الفعل. ولا يمكن أن يكون ذلك مارًّا بلا نهاية فالغاية الأخيرة والفعل الأفضل ما لم يُفعل لشيء آخر بل هو بعينه الغاية والغرض الأقصى ولذلك ينبغي ألّا[2] يكون قصد المتفلسف بفلسفته شيئًا آخر غير الفلسفة ولا يجب أن يكون قصد فاعل الجميل شيئًا آخر غير الجميل أعني أنّه لا يجب أن يُقصد به نيل منفعة ولا طلب ذكر ولا بلوغ رئاسة ولا شيئًا[3] من الأشياء غير ذات الجميل لأنّه جميل. وقد أشار الحكيم إلى أنّ النفس تكمل في هذا العالم بقبولها صور المعقولات لتصير عقلاً بالفعل بعد أن كانت بالقوّة فإذا عقلت العقل صارت هي هو إذ من شأن المعقول والعاقل أن يكونا شيئًا واحدًا لا فرق بينهما وهذا يتّضح بعد النظر الطويل في أجزاء الفلسفة والوصول إلى آخرها. ٣،٦٨

فأمّا حديث الإنسان الذي شكوت طوله وما حكيت من الكلام المتردّد الذي لم يفدك طائلاً فالذي ينبغي أن تعتمد عليه هو أنّ هذه اللفظة موضوعة على الشيء ٤،٦٨

---

[1] الأصل: أكمل. [2] الأصل: أن لا. [3] الأصل: شيء.

the physician al-Rāzī and others of his stripe become ensnared in a doctrine remote from the truth as a result of this and similar words that philosophers apply loosely—or rather on account of the contingent need for words, when the words are too narrow to encompass the subtle meanings to which they apply them. Yet I shall indicate the views you should follow on this topic. For when the elements enter into different kinds of mixtures through the celestial sphere's different kinds of movements, they generate the different kinds of forms and shapes that nature fashions, and through the medium of nature receive different kinds of effects from the soul. For the soul manifests its effects in every mixture according to its receptivity; it puts every natural instrument, according to its suitability, to every use it can possibly be put to, and brings it to the utmost state of excellence possible for it.

The soul performs that act for no other purpose than the manifestation of 68.3
wisdom. For the wise agent manifests wisdom for no other purpose beyond wisdom, since the grandest acts are those that are not desired for the sake of something else, but rather for their own sake. Whenever an act is desired for the sake of another end and another objective, that objective has a higher status than the act. This comparative chain cannot extend ad infinitum, and thus the last end and the most excellent act will not be the one that is performed for the sake of some other thing, but rather the one that itself constitutes the ultimate end and purpose. That is why someone who practices philosophy must have no other aim in practicing philosophy than philosophy itself, and why someone who does something fine must have no other aim than the fine. That is, he must not be looking to obtain a benefit, secure an honorable reputation, attain preeminence, or anything else besides doing the fine itself, simply because it is fine. The Philosopher has indicated that the soul is perfected in this world by receiving the forms of intelligibles in order to become an actual intellect after having been a potential intellect. It becomes identified with the intellect when it intellects it, for it is in the nature of that which is intellected and that which is intellecting to form a single indistinguishable thing. One grasps this clearly after one has spent a long time studying the different parts of philosophy and has come to its final part.

On the topic of human beings whose breadth you lamented and on which 68.4
you recounted faltering views that availed you nothing, what you need to take as your mainstay is that this term has been appointed to designate the entity composed of a rational soul and a natural body. For everything composed

المركّب من نفس ناطقة وجسم طبيعيّ لأنّ كلّ مركّب من بسيطين أو أكثر يحتاج إلى اسم مفرد يعبّر عن معنى التركيب ويدلّ عليه كما فعل ذلك بالصورة التي تجتمع مع مادّة الفضّة فسمّي خاتماً وكما تجتمع صورة السرير مع مادّة الخشب فيصير اسمه سريراً وعلى هذا أيضاً يُفعل إذا اجتمع جسمان طبيعيّان أو أجسام طبيعيّة فتركّب منها شيء آخر فإنّه يسمّى باسم مفرد كما يُفعل بالخلّ إذا تركّب مع العسل أو السكّر فيسمّى سكنجبيناً[1] وكما تسمّى أنواع الأدوية والمعجونات من الأخلاط الكثيرة وأنواع الأغذية والأشربة المركّبة ينفرد كلّ واحد منها باسم خاصّ وكذلك يُفعل بالمادّة التي تستحيل من صورة إلى صورة كعصير العنب الذي يسمّى عصيراً مرّة وخمراً مرّة وخلاًّ مرّة بحسب تبدّل الصورة على الموضوع الواحد فالإنسان هو النفس الناطقة إذا استعملت الآلات الجسميّة التي تسمّى بدناً لتصدر عنها الأفعال بحسب التمييز.

مسألة

١،٦٩ حكيت أيّدك الله حكايات بين سائل ومتكلّم ولم تتوجّه إلى مطلوب ينبغي أن نبحث عنه لأنّ المسألة من باب الأسماء والصفات وقد تكلّمنا عليه فيما مضى كلاماً مستقصًى لا وجه لإعادته فينبغي أن تعود إلى ما مضى وتطلبه لتجده كافياً بمعونة الله.

مسألة

١،٧٠ ما سبب استشعار الخوف بلا مخيف؟ وما وجه تجلّد الخائف والمصاب كراهة أن يوقف منه على فسولة طبعه أو قلّة مكانته أو سوء جزعه هذا مع تخاذل أعضائه

١ ط: سكنجبنا.

of two or more simple elements requires a singular name that expresses and conveys the notion of composition, as happens when the form joined to the matter of silver is called a "ring," and the form of a bed joined to the matter of wood assumes the name "bed." Something similar happens when two or more natural bodies are joined and compose another thing that is designated with a singular name. This is what happens in the case of vinegar when it is compounded with honey or sugar and is then called "oxymel"; likewise with the way one designates the different types of medicine or electuaries that blend many ingredients and the different types of composite foods and drinks; each is designated using a specific name. The same thing happens when matter passes from one form to another, as in the case of inspissated grapes called "juice" at one time, "wine" at another, and "vinegar" at yet another, depending on the transformation the form has undergone within a single substrate. Man is thus the rational soul when it uses the corporeal instruments called a "body" to perform actions in accordance with discrimination.

On the nature and attributes of God

Here—God grace you with His support—you quoted various exchanges 69.1
between a questioner and a dialectical theologian, but did not direct yourself to any topic we should make the subject of inquiry. For the question pertains to the names and attributes of God, and we discussed that topic thoroughly earlier so there is no need to rehearse it again. So you should go back to the earlier discussion and look it up, and, God willing, you will find it adequate to the purpose.

On why people experience fear in the absence of an apparent cause

Why do people experience fear in the absence of anything fearful? Why do 70.1
people thus frightened and affected feign hardiness to prevent others from discovering their base disposition, inadequate strength, and lowly anxiety, even as their limbs buckle, they cry out in commotion and are visibly changed, their heart pounds, and they exhibit the effects of what would be plain in the

وندائه على ما به واستحالة أعراضه ووجيب قلبه وظهور علامات ما إذا أراد طيّه ظهر على أسرّة وجهه وألحاظ عينيه وألفاظ لسانه واضطراب شمائله؟

الجواب

قال أبو عليّ مسكويه رحمه الله سبب ذلك توقّع مكروه حادث فإن كان السبب صحيحًا ٢،٧٠
قويًّا والدليل واضحًا جليًّا كان الخوف في موضعه وإن لم يكن كذلك وكان من سوء ظنّ وفساد فكر فهو مرض أو مزاج فاسد من الأصل. ثمّ بحسب ذلك المكروه يحسن الصبر ويحمد احتمال الأذى العارض منه ويظهر من الإنسان أمارات الشجاعة أو الجبن. وأثبت الناس جنانًا وجأشًا وأحسنهم بصيرة ورويّة لا بدّ أن يضطرب عند نزول المكروه الحادث به الطارئ عليه لا سيّما إن كان هائلًا فإنّ أرسطوطالس[1] يقول من لم يجزع من هيج البحر وهو راكبه ومن الأشياء الهائلة التي فوق طاقة الإنسان فهو مجنون وكثير من المكاره يجري هذا المجرى ويقاربه. والجزع لاحق بالمرء على حسبه ومقداره فإن كان المكروه والمتوقّع ممّا يطيق الإنسان دفعه أو تخفيفه فذهب عليه أمره واستولى عليه الجزع ولم يتماسك له فهو جبان جزوع مذموم من هذه الجهة ودواؤه التدرّب باحتمال الشدائد وملاقاتها والتصبّر عليها وتوطين النفس لها قبل حدوثها لئلّا ترد عليه[2] وهو غافل عنها غير مستعدّ لها. وإذا كانت الشجاعة فضيلة وكان ضدّها نقيصة ورذيلة فمن الذي لا يحبّ أن يستر نقيصته ويظهر فضيلته مع ما تقدّم من قولنا فيما سبق إنّ كلّ إنسان يعشق ذاته ويحبّ نفسه؟

مسألة

ما سبب غضب الإنسان وضجره إذا كان مثلًا يفتح قفلًا فيتعسّر عليه حتّى يجنّ ١،٧١
ويعضّ على القفل ويكفر وهذا عارض فاش في الناس؟

---

١ الأصل: أرسطوطاليس. ٢ الأصل: عليها.

expression of their face, the look in their eyes, the words on their tongue, and their disturbed behavior, even if they tried to conceal it?

Miskawayh's response

The reason is the expectation of an untoward occurrence. The sense of fear is 70.2
appropriate if its cause is sound and its ground is clear. If it is not, and fear results from misjudgment and impaired thinking, it indicates a malady or a humoral mixture with original impairment. Depending on the nature of the unwelcome event, fortitude is proper, endurance of the harm it causes is praiseworthy, and human beings exhibit the effects of courage or cowardice. Even the most steadfast and self-possessed, the most perspicacious and keen-minded are unavoidably disturbed when something untoward suddenly happens to them, particularly something terrible. Aristotle says, "He who does not feel anxious at sea when faced with a raging storm and confronted with terrors that exceed the limits of human power is a madman."[3] Many untoward occurrences follow this pattern and approximate to it. The anxiety a person experiences depends on the extent and measure of these occurrences. Even if the expected or the untoward event is such that it is within human power to repel or alleviate it, yet one becomes overwhelmed by anxiety and loses self-control, failing to face it with composure; prone to excessive anxiety, he is cowardly, and from this perspective merits blame. The remedy is to train oneself by confronting and undergoing hardships, by enduring them patiently, and by bracing the soul prior to their occurrence, so that they do not catch one unawares and off guard. If courage is a virtue and its contrary a deficiency and defect, given what was said earlier regarding the passionate sense of attachment people feel toward themselves and the love they have for their own soul, is there anybody who does not wish to conceal his deficiency and display his virtue?

On why people fly into a rage when they can't open a lock

Why do people get angry and annoyed if, for example, they are trying to open 71.1
a lock but it won't open, and then they fly into a rage and bite the lock and curse? This is a phenomenon that is widespread among people.[4]

الجواب

قال أبو عليّ مسكويه رحمه الله هذا العارض وشبهه من أقبح ما يعرض للإنسان وهو غير معذور إن لم يصلحه بالخلق الحسن المحمود وذلك أنّ الغضب إنّما يثور به دم القلب لمحبّة الانتقام وهذا الانتقام إذا لم يكن كما ينبغي وعلى من ينبغي وعلى مقدار ما ينبغي فهو مذموم فكيف به إذا كان على الصورة التي حكيتها. فأمّا سؤالك عن سبب الغضب فقد ذكرته وأجبت عنه وإذا ثار في غير وضعه فواجب على الإنسان الناطق المميّز أن يسكّنه ولا يستعجله ولا يجري فيه على منهاج البهيمة وسنّة السبع فإنّ من أعانه بالفكرة وألهبه بسلطان الرويّة حتّى يحتدم ويتوقّد فإنّه سيعسر بعد ذلك تلافيه وتسكينه والإنسان مذموم به إذا تركه وسوم الطبيعة ولم يظهر فيه أثر التمييز ومكان العقل. وجالينوس قد ذكر في كتاب الأخلاق حديث القفل بعينه وتعجّب من جهل من يفعل ذلك أو يرفس الحمار ويلكم البغل فإنّ هذا الفعل يدلّ على أنّ الإنسانيّة يسيرة في صاحبه جدّاً والبهيميّة غالبة عليه أعني سوء التمييز وقلّة استعمال الفكر. وليس هذا وحده يعرض لحشو الناس وعامّتهم بل الشهوة والشبق وسائر عوارض النفس البهيميّة والغضبيّة إذا هاج بهم وابتدأ في حركته الطبيعيّة لم يستعملوا فيه ما وهبه الله تعالى لهم وفضّلهم به وجعلهم له أناسيّ أعني أثر العقل بحسن الرويّة وصحّة التمييز والله المستعان ولا قوّة إلّا به. ٢،٧١

مسألة

لم صار من كان صغير الرأس خفيف الدماغ ولم يكن كلّ من كان عظيم الرأس رزين الدماغ؟ ١،٧٢

Miskawayh's response

71.2 This phenomenon and its like are among the most repugnant things that affect people, and they deserve blame if they do not rectify it by means of a good and praiseworthy character. For anger makes the blood of the heart swell, out of a desire for revenge, and this revenge is blameworthy if it is not carried out in the right manner, against the right people, and in the right measure. How much more, then, if it takes the form you have described. I have provided a response to your question about the cause of anger. Rational and discriminating human beings must subdue it when roused on the wrong occasion and not accelerate its progress; they must not behave like beasts, adopting the habits of wild animals. For those who aid it through thought, and, through the power of reflection, inflame it so that it burns and blazes, will later struggle to remedy and subdue it. Human beings deserve blame for it if they leave it to the biddings of nature and do not make the effect of discrimination and the power of reason manifest in it. In his book on ethics, Galen mentioned this very case regarding the lock, and he expressed his amazement at the ignorance of people who act like this, or who kick donkeys and punch mules. Such kinds of actions indicate that the individual in question has only a very small quotient of humanity and is dominated by beastliness, which is to say that he has poor discrimination and makes little use of thought. This is not the only phenomenon to affect the common people and the rabble. When appetite, lust, or any of the other expressions of the irascible and beastly soul flare up in them and commence their natural movement, they fail to use the resources with which God endowed them, by which He distinguished them, and on account of which He rendered them human—I mean the effect of reason through good reflection and sound discrimination. It is to God that we turn for help; strength comes from Him alone.

On why people with small heads have light brains

72.1 Why do people with small heads have light brains? And why is it that not everyone with a large head has a weighty brain?

الجواب

قال أبو عليّ مسكويه رحمه الله يحتاج الدماغ إلى اعتدال في الكيفيّة والكمّيّة فإن ٢،٧٢
حصل له أحدهما لم يغن عن الآخر فإن كان جوهره جيدًا في الكيفيّة وكانت كمّيّته ناقصة فهو لا محالة رديء وإن كانت كمّيّته كثيرة فليس هو لا محالة رديئاً فقد يكون كثيرًا وجيّد الجوهر إلّا أنّه يجب أن يكون مناسباً لحرارة القلب ليحصل بين برد هذا ورطوبته وحرارة ذلك ويبوسته الاعتدال المحبوب المحمود. ومتى حصل على الخروج من هذا الاعتدال تبعه من الرداءة قسطه ونصيبه إلّا أنّ التفاضل بين أنواع الخروج من الاعتدال كثير ولأن يكون جيّدًا وكثيرًا زائدًا على قدر الحاجة خير من أن يكون جيّدًا وناقصاً عن قدر الحاجة فإن جمع رداءة الكيفيّة والكمّيّة كان صاحبه معتوهاً مخبّلاً بحسب ذلك.

مسألة

لم اعتقد الناس في الكوسج أنّه خبيث وداهية وكذلك في القصير ولم يعتقدوا العقل ١،٧٣
والحصافة فيمن كان طويل اللحية كثيف الشعر مديد القامة جميل الإمّة ولم رأوا خفّة العارضين من السعادة؟

الجواب

قال أبو عليّ مسكويه رحمه الله هذه المسألة من باب الفراسة والممدوح المحمود من كلّ ٢،٧٣
أمر يتبع مزاجاً ما هو الاعتدال فأمّا الطرفان اللذان يكتنفان الاعتدال أعني الزيادة والنقصان فهما مذمومان مكروهان فإن كان وفور اللحية وطولها وعظمها وذهابها في جميع جهات الوجه دليل السلامة والغفلة فبالواجب صار الطرف الذي يقابله من الخفّة والنزرة[١] والقلّة دليل الخبث والدهاء وهما جميعاً طرفان خارجان عن الاعتدال

---

١ الأصل: والنزارة.

Miskawayh's response

The brain requires balance with respect to both quality and quantity, and realizing one does not render the other dispensable. If its substance is excellent in terms of its quality, but its quantity is deficient, it will necessarily be bad. If it is extensive in quantity, it will not necessarily be bad, for it may be extensive and have an excellent substance, yet it must also have a good relation to the heat of the heart, so that the coldness and moisture of the one and the heat and dryness of the other, taken together, may produce the praiseworthy, desirable balance. When it departs from this balance, it is attended by a corresponding share and portion of badness. Yet there are a number of unequal ways of departing from balance, and it is better that it should be excellent, extensive, and in excess of the amount required than that it should be excellent and fall short of the amount required. If it combines bad quality and bad quantity, the individual will accordingly be an idiotic imbecile. 72.2

On certain beliefs concerning the relation between a person's facial hair and his character

Why do people believe that men with no hair on the sides of their face, and those who are short, are malicious and cunning, yet they do not believe that men with long beards and thick hair, a tall frame, and a handsome appearance have a good mind and sound judgment? Why do they deem a sparse beard felicitous? 73.1

Miskawayh's response

This question pertains to physiognomy. In all things, what is praiseworthy and commendable follows on a particular elemental mixture that constitutes the balanced state. By contrast, the two extremes that stand on either side of the balanced state—excess and deficiency—are blameworthy and repugnant. If an abundant, long, and large beard that grows all over the face is a sign of sound intentions and guilelessness, it necessarily follows that the light, sparse hair that represents the opposite extreme should be a sign of malice and cunning. Both of these are extremes that depart from the commendable 73.2

المحمود وأحسب أنّ للاختيار السيّء مدخلاً وذلك أنّ الرجل إذا كان وافر إضاعة اللحية فهو قادر على أن يخفّف منها بأيسر مؤونة حتّى يحصل على القدر المعتدل والهيئة المحمودة فتركه إيّاها على الحال المذمومة مع تعبه بها وإصلاحها دائماً أو تركه إيّاها حتّى تسمج وتضطرب دليل على سوء اختيار ورداءة تمييز فأمّا عدم اللحية فليس يقدر صاحبه على حيلة فيها فهو معذور.

مسألة

لم سهل الموت على المعذّب مع علمه أنّ العدم لا حياة معه وليس بموجود فيه وأنّ الأذى وإن اشتدّ فإنّه مقرون بالحياة العزيزة؟ هذا وقد علم أيضاً أنّ الموجود أشرف من المعدوم وأنّه لا شرف للمعدوم فما الذي يسهّل عليه العدم وما الشيء المنتصب لقلبه وهل هذا الاختيار منه بعقل أو فساد مزاج؟ ١،٧٤

الجواب

قال أبو عليّ مسكويه رحمه الله هذه المسألة وإن كان الغرض فيها صحيحاً فالكلام فيها مضطرب غير مسلّم المقدّمات وذلك أنّ الإنسان إذا مات فليس يعدم رأساً بل إنّما تبطل عنه أعراض وتعدم عنه كيفيّات فأمّا جواهره فإنّها غير معدومة ولا يجوز على الجوهر العدم بتّة لما تبيّن في أصول الفلسفة من أنّ الجوهر لا ضدّ له ومن أشياء أخر ليس هذا موضعها. فالجوهر لا يقبل العدم من حيث هو جوهر وأجزاء الإنسان إذا مات تنحلّ إلى أصولها أعني العناصر الأربعة وذلك بأن يستحيل إليها فأمّا ذوات الجواهر فهي باقية أبداً وأمّا جوهره الذي هو النفس الناطقة فقد تبيّن أنّه أحقّ بالجوهريّة من عناصره الأربعة فهو إذن دائم البقاء أيضاً. ٢،٧٤

ولمّا لم تكن مسألتك متوجّهة إلى هذا المعنى وإنّما وقع الغلط في أخذ مقدّمات غير صحيحة وإرسال الكلام فيها على غير تحرّز وجب أن ننبّه على موضع الغلط ثمّ نعدل ٣،٧٤

balance. I reckon that poor choice also has a bearing on the matter. For a man who leaves his beard greatly untended is capable of trimming it down with a minimum of effort in order to arrive at the correct balance and praiseworthy appearance. Thus, leaving it in a blameworthy state even though it wears him out and he is always trying to fix it, or leaving it until it becomes unseemly and disheveled, is a sign of faulty choice and poor discrimination. The one who lacks a beard, by contrast, can do nothing about it, and is exempt from blame.

On why people racked by suffering find it easy to face death

Why do people tormented by suffering find it easy to face death even though they know that nonexistence means a lack of life and being, and that however acute the evil one suffers might be, it is conjoined to this cherished life? They also know, moreover, that existents are nobler than nonexistent things, and that nonexistent things have no dignity. So, what makes it easy for them to face nonexistence? What is it that comes over their heart? Does their choice come about through reason or a corrupt humoral mixture? 74.1

Miskawayh's response

This question makes a valid point, though it is expressed in a confused manner and contains premises that are not conceded, for when human beings die, they do not become nonexistent tout court. Certain of their contingent aspects are nullified, and certain of their qualities cease to exist, but their substances do not cease to exist. It is absolutely impossible for substance to cease to exist, in view of the fact that substance has no contrary and in view of other facts established within the fundamentals of philosophy that do not belong to the present context. Substance qua substance is not susceptible to nonexistence. When a person dies, his parts dissolve into their original components, that is, the four elements, which they do by changing into them. The four substances themselves endure in perpetuity. It has been established that the substance of human beings that consists in the rational soul is even worthier of substantiality than the four elements; therefore, it also endures eternally. 74.2

Your question did not center on this issue, and there was a mistake in the use of unsound premises and the unguarded use of words, but it was necessary 74.3

إلى جواب الغرض من المسـألة فنقول إنّ الحياة ليست بعزيزة إلّا إذا كانت جيّدة وأعني بالحياة الجيّدة ما سلمت من الآفات والمكاره وصدرت[١] بها الأفعال تامّة جيّدة ولم يلحق الإنسـان فيها ما يكرهه من الذلّ الشديد والضيم العظيم والمصائب في الأهل والولد. وذلك أنّ الإنسـان لو خُيّر بين هذه الحياة الرديئة وبين الموت الجيّد أعني أن يُقتل في الجهاد الذي يذبّ به عن حريمه ويمتنع به عن المذلّة والمكاره التي وصفناها لوجب بحكم العقل والشريعة أن يختار الموت والقتل في مجاهدة من يسومه ذلك. وهذه مسألة قد سبقت لها نظيرة وتكلّمنا عليها بجواب مقنع وهو قولك ما سبب الجزع من الموت وما سبب الاسترسـال إلى الموت فلترجع إليه فإنّه كاف.

مسـألة

لم ذمّ الإنسـان مـا لم ينله وهجن ما لم يحزه؟ وعلى ذلك عادى الناس ما جهلوا حتّى ١،٧٥
صار هذا من الحكم اليتيمة وقد عادى الناس ما جهلوا كما قيل فلم عادوا؟[٢] ولم لم يحبّوه ويطلبوه ويفقهوه حتّى تزول العداوة ويحصل الشرف ويكمل الجمال ويحقّ القول بالثناء ويصدق الخبر عن الحقّ؟

الجواب

قال أبو عليّ مسكويه رحمه الله هذا من قبيح ما يعتري الناس من الأخلاق وهو ٢،٧٥
جار مجرى الحسد وذاهب في طريقه. وصاحب المثل الذي يقول المرء عدوّ ما جهل إنّما أخرجه مخرج الذمّ والعيب كما قيل الناس شجرة بغي وحسد والسبب في محبّة النفس أوّلاً ثمّ الغلط في تحصيل ما يزيّنها وذلك أنّه إذا أحبّ الإنسان نفسه أحبّ صورتها والعلم صورة النفس ويعرض من محبّة صورة نفسه أن يبغض ما ليس له

١ الأصل: صدر. ٢ ط: عادوه.

to call attention to the mistake before turning to address the point of the question. Life is only cherished if it is excellent, and by an excellent life I mean a life free from evils and adversities, in which the acts performed are complete and excellent, and in which a person is not afflicted by undesirable events such as extreme disgrace, grave injustice, or calamities affecting his family or children. For were a person to be given the choice between this bad life and an excellent death—that is, to be killed in battle while defending his womenfolk and resisting the humiliation and adversities we have described—both reason and the religious Law would mandate that he choose to die and be killed while doing battle against the people who inflict those things on him. A similar question came up earlier, and we provided an adequate reply thereto. That was the question you posed about "why we fear death but sometimes welcome it."[5] So please consult that, for it meets the purpose.

On why people denigrate things they fail to attain and are hostile to things of which they are ignorant

Why do people denigrate the things they fail to attain and disparage the things 75.1
they do not possess? In the same vein, people are hostile to things they do not know, so that "People are hostile to the things they do not know" has become a venerable adage. Why this hostility? Why don't they love them and seek them out and try to comprehend them, so that the hostility may cease and so that honor may be established, beauty perfected, words of praise justly uttered, and statements of the truth veraciously made?

Miskawayh's response

This is one of the repugnant traits of character that afflict people. It is akin 75.2
to envy and tends in the same direction. The person who coined the proverb "Man is an enemy of what he does not know" meant to express blame and reproach, as with the saying "People are a tree that sprouts injustice and envy." The reason for it is, first, the love of one's own soul, and second, an erroneous approach to the acquisition of the things that serve to embellish it. For when a person loves his soul, he loves its form, and knowledge is the form of the soul. One of the consequences of loving the form of our soul is that we hate whatever we do not have as our form. So, if we possess a certain type of knowledge,

بصورة فمتى حصل له علم أحبّه وإذا لم يحصل له أبغضه ويذهب عليه أنّ التماس ما جهله بالمطلب وإن كان فيه مشقّة أولى به ليصير أيضاً صورة أخرى له جميلة ولعلّ المانع له من ذلك كراهة التذلّل لمن يتعلّم منه بعد حصول العزّ له في نوع آخر وبين طائفة أخرى.

فأمّا قولك فلم لم يحبّوه حتّى يطلبوه ويفقهوه فهو الواجب الذي ينبغي أن يُفعل ٣.٧٥
وعليه حضّ صاحب المثل بالتنبيه على العيب ليتجنّب بإتيان الفضيلة. وسمعت بعض أهل العلم يحكي عن قاض جليل المحلّ عالي المرتبة أنّه همّ بتعلّم الهندسة على كبر السن قال فقلت له ما الذي يحملك على ذلك وهو يقدح في مرتبتك ويطلق ألسن السفهاء عليك وأنت لا تصل إلى كبير حظّ منه مع علوّ السن وحاجة هذا العلم إلى زمان طويل وذكاء لا يوجد إلّا مع الحداثة واستقبال العمر؟ فقال ويحك أحسست من نفسي بغضاً لهذا العلم وعداوة لأهله فأحببت أن أتعاطاه لأحبّه ولئلا أبغض علماً فأعادي أهله. وهذا هو الانقياد للحقّ وتجرّع مرارته حرصاً على حلاوة ثمرته ورياضة للنفس على ما تكرهه فيما هو أزين لها وأعود عليها وحملها على ما يصلحها ويهذّبها.

مسألة

لم كان الإنسان إذا أراد أن يتّخذ عدّة أعداء في ساعة واحدة قدر على ذلك وإذا ١.٧٦
قصد اتّخاذ صديق ومصافاة خدن واحد لم يستطع إلّا بزمان واجتهاد وطاعة وغرم؟ وكذلك كلّ صلاح مأمول ونظام مطلوب في جميع الأمور ألا ترى أنّ الفتق أسهل من الخياطة والهدم أيسر من البناء والقتل أخفّ من التربية والإحياء؟

we love it, and we hate it if we do not possess it. We fail to understand that it is better for us to solicit what we do not know through active pursuit, even if it entails effort, in order that this become another beautiful form we possess. Perhaps what prevents us from doing so is our aversion to humbling ourselves before a teacher once we have attained eminence in a different subject and among a different set of people.

You ask: "Why don't they love them and seek them out and try to comprehend them?" This is what one ought to do, and what the author of the proverb sought to encourage by calling attention to the fault, so that it might be avoided by doing what is better. I heard a scholar saying that an illustrious and high-ranking judge set out to learn geometry at an advanced age. He said: I asked him, "What is it that drives you to this, even though it detracts from your status and sets fools' tongues wagging, and even though you will not attain a great share of it, given your age and given the fact that mastery of this knowledge requires a long time and a sharp mind that is only found during youth and the early part of life?" He replied, "Watch your words! I realized I nursed a sense of hatred for this knowledge and a sense of hostility toward its possessors, and I desired to pursue it in order to love it and not to hate a form of knowledge or be hostile to its possessors." This is what it means to submit to the truth and swallow its bitterness, in keenness to taste the sweetness of its fruit and out of a desire to train the soul to endure what it finds repugnant when this redounds to its beauty and profit, compelling it to do those things that reform and refine it. 75.3

On why it is easier to make enemies than friends

Why is it that if a person wanted to, he could make multiple enemies in the space of a single hour, whereas if he tried to make a friend and establish cordial relations with a single companion he could only achieve this over a long period of time and with great effort, much trouble, and financial loss? The same holds true for every good we hope for and every matter we desire, in all domains. Don't you see that it is easier to rend than sew, simpler to destroy than build, less difficult to take life than to nurture and give it? 76.1

الجواب

قال أبو عليّ مسكويه رحمه الله جواب مسألتك هذه منها. وما أشبهها بحكاية سمعتها ٢،٧٦
عن الأصمعيّ وذاك أنّه بلغني أنّ قارئًا قرأ عليه [منسرح]

وَٱلْأَلْمَعِيُّ ٱلَّذِي يَظُنُّ بِكَ[١] ٱلظَّنَّ   كَأَنْ قَدْ رَأَى وَقَدْ سَمِعَا

فقال يا أبا سعيد ما ٱلْأَلْمَعِيُّ؟ فقال ٱلَّذِي يَظُنُّ بِكَ[٢] ٱلظَّنَّ كَأَنْ قَدْ رَأَى وَقَدْ سَمِعَا. فأنا قائل في هذه المسألة أيضًا إنّما صار الإنسان قادرًا على اتّخاذ الأعداء بسرعة وغير قادر على اتّخاذ الأصدقاء إلّا في زمان طويل وبغرامة كثيرة لأنّ هذا فتق وذاك رتق وهذا هدم وذاك بناء وسق باقي كلامك فإنّه جوابك.

مسألة

مـا الذي حرّك الزنديق والدهريّ على الخير وإيثار الجميل وأداء الأمانة ومواصلة البرّ ١،٧٧
ورحمة المبتلى ومعونة الصريخ ومغوثة الملتجئ إليه والشاكي بين يديه؟ هذا وهو لا يرجو ثوابًا ولا ينتظر مآبًا ولا يخاف حسابًا. أترى الباعث على هذه الأخلاق الشريفة والخصال المحمودة رغبته في الشكر وتبرّؤه من القرف وخوفه من السيف؟ قد يفعل هذه في الأوقات لا يظنّ به التوقّي ولا اجتلاب الشكر ما ذاك إلّا لخفيّة في النفس وسرّ مع العقل وهل في هذه الأمور ما يشير إلى توحيد الله تبارك وتعالى؟

الجواب

قال أبو عليّ مسكويه رحمه الله للإنسان بما هو إنسان أفعال وهمم وسجايا وشيم قبل ٢،٧٧
ورود الشرع وله بداية في رأيه وأوائل في عقله لا يحتاج فيها إلى الشرع بل إنّما

١ الأصل: لك. ٢ الأصل: لك.

Miskawayh's response

Your question answers itself. It reminds me of a story I heard about al-Aṣmaʿī. 76.2
I was told that a student read out the following verse to him:

> The canny man is suspicious of you,
> as if he has seen and heard things about you.

The student asked, "Abū Saʿīd, what does 'canny' mean?" He responded, "Someone who is suspicious of you, as if he has seen and heard things about you." I also say regarding this question: The reason people are able to make enemies quickly but can only make friends after a long time and at great cost is that the former involves rending, the latter mending; the former involves destroying, the latter building. Apply this to the rest of your question, and you have your answer.

On why atheists act morally

What drives unbelievers and materialists[6] to do what is good and choose what 77.1
is fine, to return deposits given in trust, persist in kindness, take pity on the afflicted, help those who cry out, and assist those who seek refuge with them and place their grievances before them? They behave this way even though they anticipate no reward, expect no return, and fear no judgment in the next life. Would you say that what motivates these noble traits and praiseworthy characteristics is their desire to be thanked and spared repugnance, or their fear of the sword? Yet they may act this way at times when they cannot be supposed to be taking precautions or seeking to secure gratitude. This can only be for some secret reason that lies in the soul and some mystery that lies with reason. And do these things contain something that points to the unity of God?

Miskawayh's response

There are certain acts, aims, natural attributes, and dispositions that human 77.2
beings possess qua human beings prior to the advent of the religious Law. Their judgment contains certain rudiments and their reason contains certain basic principles for which they do not require a religious Law. Rather, the Law

تأتيه الشريعة بتأكيد ما عنده والتنبيه عليه فتثير ما هو كامن فيه وموجود في فطرته قد أخذه الله تعالى عليه وسطّره فيه من مبدأ الخلق فكلّ من له غريزة من العقل ونصيب من الإنسانيّة ففيه حركة إلى الفضائل وشوق إلى المحاسن لا لشيء آخر أكثر من الفضائل والمحاسن التي يقتضيها العقل وتوجبها الإنسانيّة وإن اقترن بذلك في بعض الأوقات محبّة الشكر وطلب السمعة والتماس أمور أخر. ولولا أنّ محبّة الشكر وما يتبعه أيضاً جميل وفضيلة لما رغب فيه ولولا أنّ الخالق تعالى واحد لما تساوت هذه الحال بالناس ولا استجاب أحد لمن دعا إليها وحضّ عليها إذا لم يجد في نفسه شاهداً لها ومصدّقاً بها ولعمري إنّ هذا أوضح دليل على توحيد الله تعالى ذكره وتقدّس اسمه.

مسألة

١،٧٨ ما الذي قام في نفس بعض الناس حتّى صار ضحكة؟ أعني يُضحك ويُسخر منه ويُعبث بقفاه وهو في ذاك صابر محتسب وربّما خلا من النائل وربّما نزر النائل. فكيف هُوّن عليه الأمر القبيح؟ ولعلّه من بيت ظاهر الشرف منيف المحلّ. وبمثل هذا المعنى يصير آخر مخنّثاً مغنّياً لعّاباً إلى آخر ما اقتصّه من حديث الرجل الذي نشأ على طريق مذمومة وهو من بيت كبير.

الجواب

٢،٧٨ قال أبو عليّ مسكويه رحمه الله مرّ لنا في مسألة الفراسة أنّ لكلّ مزاج خلقاً[١] يتبعه والنفس تصدر أفعالها بحسب تلك الطبيعة والمزاج وأنّ الإنسان متى استرسل للطبيعة وانقاد لهواه ولم يستعمل القوّة الموهوبة له في رفع ذلك وتأديبه نفسه بها كان

[١] الأصل: خلق.

comes in order to call attention to and confirm what they already possess, enlivening what is latent within them and present in their natural constitution, which God bound them to and inscribed within them from the beginning of creation. So everyone naturally endowed with reason and a share of humanity possesses a drive to acquire excellent traits and a longing for good qualities that is simply grounded in the excellent traits and good qualities necessitated by reason and mandated by humanity. Sometimes, to be sure, it may be conjoined with a desire to be thanked, to acquire a good name, or to obtain other things. The desire for gratitude and its concomitants would not have been commended, were it not a fine thing and an excellent quality. If the Creator were not one, this condition would not be universal among people, and no one would have responded to those who urged it and exhorted him to it, had he found nothing within himself to attest to it and corroborate it. Upon my life, this is the clearest proof of God's unity.

On why some people willingly become the butt of other people's jokes

What comes over certain people so they become a laughingstock? People laugh at them, ridicule them, and slap them about, and they submit to such treatment with patience and contentment, though they have little or nothing to gain. How do they acquiesce to this unseemly state of affairs without demur? Sometimes the person in question may even belong to a family of great eminence and lofty standing. Similarly, someone else may adopt effeminate manners or become involved in singing or games—and so on, to the end of the story he recounted regarding a man who grew up following a blameworthy path, though hailing from a great family. 78.1

Miskawayh's response

As we mentioned earlier, in the question regarding physiognomy, every elemental mixture is attended by a specific character, and the acts of the soul issue in accordance with that nature and mixture. People are beasts in the guise of men when they abandon themselves to nature, yield to their blind desires, and fail to use the power they were endowed with in order to remedy this and discipline their soul. The character trait you mention in this question is one of the 78.2

في مسلاخ بهيمة. وهذا الخلق الذي ذكرته في هذه المسألة أحد الأخلاق التابعة لمزاج خارج عن الاعتدال التي متى ترك الإنسان وسوم الطبيعة فيها جمحت فيه إلى أقبح مذهب وأسوأ طريقة وحُقّ على من بُلي بها أن يجتهد في مداواتها ويُجتهد له فيها. فقد تقدّم قولنا في هذا الباب إنّه ممكن ولولا إمكانه لما حسن التقويم والتأديب عليه ولا الحمد والذمّ فيه ولا الزجر والدعاء إليه ولا السياسة من الآباء والملوك وقوام المدن به. ومتى لم يستجب إنسان لمعالجة هذه الأدواء كانت معالجته بالعقوبات[1] المفروضة واجبة فيه. وما أشبه الأمراض النفسانيّة بالأمراض الجسمانيّة فكما أنّ مرض[2] الجسم متى لم يعالجه صاحبه بالاختيار والإيثار وجب أن يُعالج بالقهر والقسر فكذلك مرض النفس إلى أن ينتهي إلى حال يقع معها اليأس من الصلاح فحينئذ ينبغي أن يُراح من نفسه ويُستراح منه وتطهر الأرض منه على حسب ما تحكم فيه الشريعة أو السياسة الفاضلة.

مسألة

١،٧٩ ما سبب الإنسان في محبّة الرئاسة ومن أين ورث هذا الخُلق وأيّ شيء رمزت الطبيعة به؟ ولِم أفرط بعضهم في طلبها حتّى تلقّى الأسنّة بنحره وواجه المرهفات بصدره وحتّى هجر من أجلها الوساد وودّع بسببها الرقاد وطوى المهامه والبلاد؟ وهل هذا الخلق[3] من جنس من امتعض في ترتيب العنوان إذا كوتب أو كاتب؟ وما ذاك من جميع ما تقدّم؟ فقد تشاحّ الناس في هذه المواضع وتباينوا وبلغوا المبالغ.

الجواب

٢،٧٩ قال أبو عليّ مسكويه رحمه الله قد تبيّن أنّ في الناس ثلاث قوى وهي الناطقة والبهيميّة والغضبيّة فهو بالناطق منها يشتاق إلى المعرفة والأدب والفضائل التي

١ الأصل: الأدواء بالعقوبات. ٢ الأصل: مريض. ٣ ط: الجنس.

traits that attend an unbalanced mixture and that become unruly when people are left to the biddings of their nature, leading them to follow the foulest paths. It is imperative that those so afflicted strive to treat them, and that others strive for this on their behalf. Apropos this topic, we have already remarked that this is possible, and were it not possible, there would be no value in reforming and disciplining character, in praising people or blaming them for it, in restraining them from it and urging them to it, or in the exercise of governance by parents and rulers. Indeed, polities are founded on this basis. If someone fails to respond to treatment using such therapeutic means, it will be necessary to treat him through the imposition of punishments. The illnesses of the soul and the illnesses of the body are very similar to each other. A person must be treated through force and coercion when he fails to treat his bodily illness voluntarily and by his own preference. The same applies to the illness of the soul, until we reach a point when we despair of the person ever reforming; then he needs to be relieved of himself and others relieved of him, in order to purify the earth from his existence in accordance with the dictates of the religious Law and virtuous governance.

On why people love to occupy positions of eminence

Why do people love to occupy positions of eminence? Whence was this trait instilled into them? What did nature intend to signify through it? Why do some people take their quest for eminence to extremes, taking spear thrusts and sword strokes in their chests, spending sleepless nights, bidding rest adieu, and crossing sprawling desert wastes? Is this trait of a piece with the rancor a person feels about the way they are addressed when receiving or sending correspondence? And how does that relate to the preceding discussions? For people are extremely competitive over these points, severing relations with each other and taking things to the limit. 79.1

Miskawayh's response

It has been demonstrated that people have three powers: the rational, the beastly, and the irascible. Through the rational power they long for knowledge, fine conduct, and the excellent traits that lead them to wisdom; its effect manifests itself from the brain. Through the beastly power they are driven 79.2

تؤدّيه إلى الحكمة ويظهر أثر هذه من الدماغ وبالبهيميّة منها[١] يتحرّك نحو الشهوات التي يتناول بها اللذّات البدنيّة كلّها ويظهر أثرها من الكبد وبالغضبيّة منها يتحرّك إلى طلب الرئاسات ويشتاق إلى أنواع الكرامات وتعرض له الحميّة والأنفة ويلتمس العزّ والمراتب الجليلة العالية ويظهر أثرها من القلب. وإنّما تقوى فيه واحدة من هذه القوى بحسب مزاج قوّة هذه الأعضاء التي تسمّى الرئيسيّة في البدن. فربّما خرج عن الاعتدال فيها إلى جانب الزيادة والإفراط أو إلى ناحية النقصان والتفريط فيجب عليه حينئذ أن يعدّلها ويردّها إلى الوسط أعني الاعتدال الموضوع له ولا يسترسل لها بترك التقويم والتأديب فإنّ هذه القوى تهيج لما ذكرناه فإن تُركت وسَوْمَها وترك صاحبها إصلاحها وعلاجها بالأعقال واتّبع[٢] الطبيعة تفاقم أمرها وغلبت حتّى تجمح إلى حيث لا يطمع في علاجها ويؤيس من برئها وإنّما يُملك أمرها وتأديبها في مبدأ الأمر بالنفس التي هي رئيسة عليها كلّها أعني المميّزة العاقلة التي تسمّى القوّة الإلهيّة فإنّ هذه القوّة ينبغي أن تستولي وتكون لها الرئاسة على الباقية.

٣،٧٩ فمحبّة الإنسان للرئاسة أمر طبيعيّ له ولكن يجب أن تكون مقوّمة لتكون في موضعها وكما ينبغي فإن زادت أو نقصت في إنسان لأجل مزاج أو عادة سيّئة وجب عليه أن يعدّلها بالتأديب لتتحرّك كما ينبغي وعلى ما ينبغي وفي الوقت الذي ينبغي وقد مضى من ذكر هذه القوى وآثارها في موضعه ما يجب أن يقتصر بها هنا على هذا المقدار.

٤،٧٩ ونقول إنّه كما يعرض لبعض الناس أن يلقى الأسنّة بنحره ويركب أهوال البرّ والبحر لنيل الشهوات بحسب حركة قوّة النفس البهيميّة فيه وتركه قمعها فكذلك يعرض لبعضهم في نهوض قوّة النفس الغضبيّة فيهم إلى نيل الرئاسات والكرامات أن يركب هذه الأهوال فيها. ومدار الأمر على العقل الذي هو الرئيس عليها وأن يجتهد الإنسان في تقوية هذه[٣] النفس لتكون هي الغالبة وتتعبّد القوّتان الباقيتان لها حتّى تصدرا[٤] عن أمره وتتحرّكا[٥] لما ترسمه وتقف عند ما تحدّه. فإنّ هذه القوّة هي التي تسمّى الإلهيّة ولها

---

١ ط: بالناطق منها. ٢ الأصل وط: واتّباع. ٣ الأصل: هذا. ٤ الأصل وط: تصدر. ٥ الأصل وط: وتتحرّك.

toward the appetites by which they obtain all bodily pleasures; its effect manifests itself from the liver. Through the irascible power they are driven to seek positions of eminence, long for all kinds of honor, experience zeal and pride, and solicit power and illustrious status; its effect manifests itself from the heart. The relative strength of each of these powers depends on the mixture of these organs, designated as the principal organs of the body. This mixture may depart from the balanced state, either toward increase and excess or decrease and deficiency. In that case, they need to adjust them and lead them back to the mean—that is, to the balance appointed for it—and not give themselves up to them by abandoning their efforts to rectify and discipline, for these powers flare up for the reasons we have mentioned. If left to their own devices and no effort is made to reform them and treat them by imposing restraints, and nature is followed instead, conditions deteriorate and they gain the upper hand, growing so unruly that we despair of treating and curing them. We control them and are able to discipline them in the first instance through the soul that presides over all of them, that is to say, the discriminating power of reason that is called "divine." It is this power that ought to be in command and to preside over the rest.

So it is natural for human beings to love eminence, but this love must be regulated in order to be appropriate and as it ought. If it runs to excess or to deficiency in someone as a result of a particular mixture or bad habit, he must rectify it through discipline, so that it may move in the right manner, under the right conditions, and at the right time. These powers and their effects have already been discussed at the relevant juncture, so we will confine ourselves to these remarks. 79.3

Furthermore, just as some people, as a result of the movement of the power of the beastly soul within them and their failure to bridle it, take spear thrusts in their chest and confront terrors by land and sea in order to satisfy their appetites, so too other people confront these terrors when the power of the irascible soul goads them to attain honors and positions of eminence. Everything depends on reason, which presides over these powers, and on the effort a person makes to fortify this soul so that it may dominate and subjugate the other two powers, with the result that they proceed at its command, move in the directions it prescribes, and stop at the limits it sets. For this is the power that is called "divine," and it has the insight to treat and reform them, and the capacity and an exclusive title to preside over them fully. But as Plato said, 79.4

قوّة على رئاسة تلك الأخر وهداية إلى علاجها وإصلاحها واستقلال بالرئاسة التامّة عليها ولكنّها كما قال أفلاطن في لين الذهب وتلك في قوّة الحديد وللإنسان الاجتهاد والميل إلى تذليل هذه لتلك فإنّها ستذلّ وتنقاد والله المعين وهو حسبنا ونعم الوكيل.

مسألة

ما السبب في تشريف من سلف له أب أو جدّ منظور إليه مكثور عليه في فعال ١،٨٠
مجّد وشجاعة وسياسة دون تشريف من كان له ابن كذلك؟ أعني كيف يسري الشرف من المتقدّم في المتأخّر ولا يسري من المتأخّر في المتقدّم؟[1]

الجواب

قال أبو عليّ مسكويه رحمه الله إنّ الأب علّة الولد وعرقه يسري فيه لأنّه معلوله ولأنّه ٢،٨٠
مكوّن من مزاجه وبزره فهو من أجل ذلك كجزء منه أو كنسخة له فغير مستنكر أن يظهر أثر العلّة فيه أو ينتظر منه نزوع العرق[2] إليه فأمّا عكس هذه القضيّة وهو أن يصير المعلول سبباً للعلّة حتّى يرجع مقلوباً فشيء يأباه العقل وتردّه البديهة ويسير التأمّل يكفي في جواب هذه المسألة.

مسألة

ولم إذا كان أبو الإنسان مذكوراً بما أسلفنا نعته وبغيره من الدين والورع وجب أن ١،٨١
يكون ولده وولد ولده يسحبون الذيل ويختالون في العطاف ويزدرون الناس ويرون من أنفسهم أنّهم قد خوّلوا الملك ويعتقدون أنّ خدمتك لهم فريضة ونجاتك بهم

١ الأصل: المتقدّم في المتأخّر. ٢ ط: العروق.

the former is as pliant as gold, whereas the latter are as strong as iron, and human beings need to have the will and strive hard to subject them to it—for they will indeed be subjected and submit. God is our helper; He is sufficient for us, and an excellent guardian is He!

On why we honor people for the achievements of their ancestors but not those of their progeny

Why does one honor people who have a father or grandfather who was highly regarded, with many glorious deeds and acts of courage and leadership to his name, whereas one does not honor people who have such a son? I mean, why is it that honor flows from ancestors to descendants and does not flow from descendants to ancestors? 80.1

Miskawayh's response

Fathers are the cause of their children's existence, and their disposition flows into them because the latter represent their causal effect and are constituted from their elemental mixture and their seed. For that reason, children are like parts or copies of their fathers, so it is not strange that the cause should manifest its effect in them or that they should be expected to incline toward the ancestral disposition. The opposite proposition—namely, that the effect should serve as grounds for the cause, reversing the process—is one not countenanced by reason and rejected by basic intuition. The merest reflection suffices to answer this question. 80.2

On why the progeny of illustrious people evince an elevated sense of entitlement and self-importance

And why is it that if someone's father is known for the attributes we have mentioned or for other attributes such as being devout and God-fearing, his children and his grandchildren must swagger about, dragging the hems of their garments along the ground, comporting themselves haughtily and holding people in contempt, thinking that they have been granted the power to rule and presuming that you are obliged to serve them and your salvation 81.1

متعلّقة؟ ما هذه الفتنة والآفة وما[1] أصلها؟ وهل كان في سالف الدهر وفيما مضى من الزمان من الأمم المعروفة هذا الفنّ؟

الجواب

قال أبو عليّ مسكويه رحمه الله قد ذكرنا في جواب المسألة الأولى ما ينبّه على جواب ٢،٨١
هذه التالية فإنّ المعلول إنّما يشرف بشرف علّته فإن كان ذلك الشرف ديناً وعلّته إلهيّة[2] حصل للعرق الساري من الافتخار به ما لا يحصل لغيره ولكن إلى حدّ مفروض ومقدار معلوم فأمّا الغلوّ فيه إلى أن يعتقد أنّهم كما حكيت عنهم فهو كسائر الإفراطات التي عددناها فيما تقدّم. وأمّا قولك هل كان في سالف الدهر شيء من هذا الفنّ فلعمري لقد كان ذلك في كلّ أمّة وكلّ زمان ولم تزل النجابة على الأكثر سارية في الأولاد ومتوقّعة في العرق حتّى إنّ الملك يبقى في البيت الواحد زماناً طويلاً لا يرتضي الناس إلّا بهم ولا ينقادون إلّا لهم وذلك في جميع الأمم من الفرس والروم والهند وسائر أجناس الناس وكذلك العرق اللئيم والأصل الفاسد يهجى بهم الأولاد وينتظر منهم النزوع إليه فيُذمّون به وتُتجنّب ناحيتهم له. ولكن مسألتك مضمّنة ذكر الدين وله حكم آخر كما قد علمت من علوّ الرتبة وشرف المنزلة وإن لم تكن النبوّة نفسها سارية في العرق ولا هي متوقّعة فما[3] يتبع النبوّة من التعظيم والتشريف ونزوع[4] الناس لها بالطبع والتماس أهل بيتها مرتبة الإمامة والتمليك أمر خارج عن حكم العادة ولا سيّما إن كان هناك شريطة الفضيلة موجودة والاستقلال حاضراً فإنّ العدول حينئذ عمّن كان بهذه الصفة ظلم وتعدّ والسلام.

١ الأصل: وما ما. ٢ الأصل وط: الهيئة. ٣ الأصل وط: فيما. ٤ الأصل وط: نجوع.

depends on them? What scourge, what bane is this, and what is its origin? Did such behavior exist in bygone times and among the peoples of earlier eras we know about?

Miskawayh's response

Our answer to the previous question indicates the answer to this. For the honor that attaches to a causal effect depends on the honor that attaches to its cause. So if that honor is due to religious devotion and its cause is divine, the descendants who issue from it feel a sense of pride in it that others do not, though within determinate limits and to a specific degree. To overdo this and to end up regarding themselves in the ways you report are of a piece with the other forms of excess we enumerated earlier. You ask, "Did anything of the kind exist in bygone times?" Upon my life, this has existed among every people and in every era. Noble descent is still for the most part passed on to children, and one expects to see it reflected in their dispositions, so that rulership remains within a single family for a long time, and people refuse to accept anyone else and will only submit to them. This is found among all peoples—Persians, Byzantines, Indians, and the other races. Similarly, children are reviled for their ignoble stock and corrupt origin, and are expected thus to incline; so they are disparaged and eschewed on its account. But your question includes a reference to religion, which, as you know, has a different status with respect to elevated rank and dignified standing, even if the capacity of prophethood itself does not, and is not expected to, flow into offspring. For the glory and honor that attend prophethood, the inclination that people naturally feel toward it, and the interest in serving as leaders and rulers taken by members of the family in which it appears depart from the customary order, particularly if there is an exclusive claim and the condition of excellence is met. Turning away from persons with such attributes will then constitute an injustice and a transgression. And that is all I have to say. 81.2

مسـألة

هـل يجوز أن تكون الحكمة في تساوي الناس من جهة ارتفاع الشرف دون تباينهم؟ ١،٨٢
فإنّه إن كانت الحكمة في ذلك لزم أن يكون ما عليه الناس إمّا عن قهر لا فكاك لهم منه أو جهل لا حجّة عليهم به ولست أعني التساوي في الحال وفي الكفاية وفي الفقر والحاجة لأنّ ذاك قد شهدت له الحكمة بالصواب لأنّه تابع لسوس العالم وجارٍ مع العقل وإنّما عنيت تساوي الناس من جهة النسب[1] فإنّ التطاول والتسلّط والازدراء قد فشا بهذا السبب[2] والحكمة تأبى وضع ما يكون فساداً أو ذريعة إلى فساد ولهذا قال النبيّ صلّى الله عليه وسلّم المؤمنون تتكافأ دماؤهم ويسعى بذمّتهم أدناهم وهم يد على من سواهم.

الجواب

قال أبو عليّ مسكويه رحمه الله إنّما يُشرّف الإنسان بنفسه وبما يظهر فيه من آثار ٢،٨٢
الحكمة وما أحسن قول الإمام عليّ عليه السلام قيمة كلّ امرئ ما يحسن وإنّما حكينا ما تقدّم من سريان النجابة في العرق لأجل أنّ الطمع يقوى فيمن كانت له سابقة في فضيلة أن تظهر فيه أيضاً ولا سيّما إن كانت علّته قريبة منه. وكيف يتساوى الناس في ارتفاع الشرف؟ ولو تساووا فيه لما كان شرف ولا ارتفاع وإلّا فعلى ماذا يرتفع ويشرف والمنازل متساوية؟ ولكن الناس يتساوون في الإنسانيّة التي تعمّهم وفي أشياء تتبع الإنسانيّة من الأحكام والأوضاع ويتفاوتون في أمور أخر يزيد بها بعضهم على بعض.

١ الأصل وط: السبب. ٢ الأصل وط: النسب.

On whether it would be more consistent with the true order of things if all people were honored equally

82.1 Could true wisdom possibly lie in people's enjoying an equally high degree of honor instead of occupying disparate levels within it? If that is where true wisdom lies, then what actually obtains among people must be the result either of a compulsive force they cannot elude or of ignorance that cannot be held against them. By "equality" I am not referring to people's equality in terms of estate and adequacy of means, or poverty and need; the propriety of this has been certified by wisdom, as it follows the natural bent of the world and accords with reason. I am referring, rather, to people's equality in pedigree, for this has led to widespread insolence, domineering manners, and contemptuous behavior. Wisdom rejects the imposition of anything that is evil or that leads to evil. That is why the Prophet said, "The lives of believers are valued alike; the least among them may make covenants in their name, and they will stand as a single man against other parties."[7]

Miskawayh's response

82.2 People command honor through their own account and through the effects of wisdom that manifest in them. How apt are the words of the Imam ʿAlī, peace be upon him: "A man's worth lies in his proficiency." Our earlier remark regarding the nobility that runs in one's pedigree was based on the fact that there is a strong hope that people with a prior connection to excellence will also manifest it themselves, particularly if its cause is near to them. How could people command an equally elevated degree of honor? For were they equal in this regard, this would constitute neither honor nor an elevated degree of it. What would they be elevated and honored above, if all stations were equal? But with regard to the humanity that extends to all of them alike, and with regard to the principles and conditions that attend humanity, people are equal; they differ with regard to other elements, in which some are more endowed than others.

مسـألة

مـا التـطيّر والفأل؟ ولمِ أولع كثير من الناس بهما؟ وكيف نُفي عن الشريعة أحدهما ورُخّص الآخر؟ وهل لهما أصل يُرجع إليه ويوقف لديه أو هما جاريان مرّة بالهاجس والاستشعار ومرّة بالاتّفاق والاضطرار؟ والخبر عن النبيّ صلّى الله عليه وسلّم فاش في هذا المعنى وليس طريقه محدثًا للعلم ولا متنه مجيلاً للرأي إذ يقول لا عدوى ولا طيرة. وقد قيل في مكان آخر كان يحبّ الفأل الحسن. وزعم الرواة أنّه حين نزل المدينة عند أبي أيّوب الأنصاريّ سمعه يقول لغلامين له يا سالم يا يسار فقال لأبي بكر سلمت لنا الدار في يسر. فكيف هذا وما طريقه؟ وهل يطّرد ذلك في تطايره أم يقف؟ ثمّ حكيت الحكاية عن ابن اسماعيل في قصّة الزعفرانيّ. وحكيت أيضاً عن ابن الروميّ قوله الفأل لسان الزمان وعنوان الحدثان وقلت ما أكثر ما يقع ما لا يُتوقّع ممّا لم يتقدّم فيه قول ولا إرجاف حتّى إذا قارن ذلك شيء صار العجب العجاب والشيء المستطرف. ١،٨٣

الجواب

قال أبو عليّ مسكويه رحمه الله الإنسان متطلّع إلى الوقوف على كائنات الأمور ومستقبلاتها ومغيّباتها كما وصفنا من[١] حاله فيما تقدّم فهو بالطبع يتشوّقها[٢] ويروم معرفتها على قدر استطاعته وبحسب طاقته فربّما أمكنه التوصّل إلى بعضها بطبيعة موافقة في رأي صائب وحدس صادق وتكهّن في الأمور لا يكاد يخطئ فيها فهو من أعلى درجة في هذا الباب وأوثق سبب فيه فربّما تعذّر[٣] في بعضها ذلك فيروم التوصّل إليه بدلائل النجوم وحركات الأشخاص العلويّة وتأثيرها في العالم السفليّ ٢،٨٣

١ الأصل: هنّ. ٢ ط: يتشوفها. ٣ الأصل وط: تعدّد.

On different forms of divination

What is the form of divination called "augury," and that called "taking omens," all about? Why are so many people obsessed by them? And why was one of them excluded from the religious Law while the other was licensed? Do they rest on a foundation that we use as our reference point and depend upon? Or are they sometimes based on what people suspect and perceive, and at other times on chance and compulsion? The statement on the topic transmitted from the Prophet is well known, but is not framed in such a way as to produce certainty, and its text does not provide substance for a considered opinion. He says, "Let there be no transmitting of illness and no augury."[8] But it was said on another occasion he was fond of good omens. Those who transmit reports about the Prophet have claimed that when he was staying in Medina at the house of Abū Ayyūb al-Anṣārī, Abū Ayyūb heard him calling two servants of his, saying, "O safety!" and "O prosperity!" They also report that he said to Abū Bakr, "May this house be safe for us and enjoy prosperity." How can this be, and how is it to be understood? Does it confirm that he approved of augury, or does it stop short of that? Next, you quoted what Ibn Ismāʿīl said in connection with al-Zaʿfarānī's story.[9] You also quoted Ibn al-Rūmī's words, "Omens are the tongue of time, and the sign of the accidents of fortune." And you said: How often something occurs unexpectedly, without a statement or prediction to precede it, so that when a prediction accompanies it, it is held to be the greatest wonder and the most remarkable thing. 83.1

Miskawayh's response

As we have already noted, human beings yearn to discover things that exist, things that will exist in the future, and things concealed from their view. They have a natural longing and desire to know about them, depending on their ability and according to their capacity. Occasionally they can attain knowledge of some of them through a suitable nature combined with sound judgment and accurate intuition, and they exercise divination with regard to certain matters such that they hardly ever get them wrong. They then are on the firmest footing in this domain and are practitioners of the highest rank. Occasionally for some matters this is not possible, and, through the medium of astral indications and the movements of the heavenly bodies and their influence on 83.2

ويصدق حكمه أو يكذب بحسب قوّته في أخذ الدلائل ومزجها بعد ذلك. ولهذه الصناعة أصول كثيرة جدًّا وفروع بحسب الأصول وخطأ المخطئ ليس من ضعف أصول الصناعة ولكن من ضعف الناظر فيها أو لأنّه يروم من الصناعة أكثر ممّا فيها فيحمل عليها زيادة على الموضوع منها وربّما فاتته هذه الأسباب ونظائرها من الدلائل الطبيعيّة.

٣،٨٣ وليس من شأن النفس أن تعمل عملاً بغير داعٍ إليه ولا سبب له فيصير كالعبث فإذا سنح له أمران ولم يرجح أحدهما على الآخر طلب لنفسه حجّة في ركوب أحدهما دون الآخر فيستريح حينئذ إلى الأسباب الضعيفة ويتمحّل العلل البعيدة بقدر ما يترجّح أحد الرأيين المتكافئين في نفسه على الآخر حتّى يصل إليه ويأخذ به. وسبيل الرجل الفاضل أن يكون حسن الظنّ قويم الرجاء جميل النيّة فيتفاءل حينئذ. والفأل قد يكون بأصوات بسيطة ليس فيها أثر النطق ولكن أكثره بالكلام المفهوم وقد يكون بصورة مقبولة وأشكال مستحسنة ولكنّ معظمه في خلق الإنسان وقال النبيّ صلّى الله عليه وسلم إذا أبردتم إليّ بريدًا فاجعلوه حسن الاسم حسن الوجه.

٤،٨٣ فأمّا أصحاب الطيرة فلأنّهم أضداد لأصحاب النيّات الجميلة والرجاء الحسن فطريقهم[١] مكروهة وتطيّرهم من الأمور أكثر وأنواع دلائلهم أغزر وأبسط وذلك أنّهم يأخذون بعضها من الخيلان في الناس والدوائر في الخيل وأصناف الخلق الطبيعيّة وبعضها من الأمزجة المتنافرة[٢] والخلق المكروهة كالبوم والهامة والعقرب والفأر وما أشبهها وبعض من الأصوات المنكرة كنهيق الحمير وأصوات الحديد وما أشبهها وبعضها من الأسماء والألقاب إذا اشتقّوا لها ما يوافقها في بعض الحروف أو في كلّها كاسم الغراب من الغربة والبان من البين والنوى نوى التمر من البعد وبعضها من العاهات كالأعور من اليمين والمقعد من الرجل وبعضها من الحركات والجهات كالسانح والبارح والمعوجّ والمائل وجميع ذلك لضعف النفس والنحيزة واستيلاء اليأس

١ ط: فطريقتهم. ٢ الأصل: المنافرة.

the lower world, they judge rightly or wrongly depending on their ability to gather, and then to combine, indications. This craft contains a great number of general principles and subsidiary rules that stem from these principles. Errors are not due to any weakness in the principles of the craft, but rather to the weakness of the person inquiring into it, or to the fact that he wants more from this craft than it incorporates, so that he refers to it things that exceed its purview; and sometimes he may fail to grasp these grounds and other similar natural indicators.

It is not in the nature of the soul to perform an action without motive or grounds, pointlessly, as it were. Thus, if we are confronted with two possibilities, one of which does not preponderate over the other, we try to give our soul an argument for undertaking one course of action rather than the other. We then have recourse to weak grounds, and labor to find improbable causes that might enable one of the two equivalent views to acquire preponderance over the other within our soul, so that we can attain it and adopt it. It is the way of virtuous men to harbor good opinions, sound hopes, and fine intentions, and in such cases they tend to see things as good omens. Omens may be expressed through simple sounds with no trace of articulate language, but they are usually expressed through intelligible speech. They may be conveyed through pleasing images and agreeable shapes, but mostly they are conveyed through the physical features of human beings. The Prophet said, "If you send me a messenger, let him have a beautiful name and beautiful face."[10] 83.3

Those who engage in augury, by contrast, are the opposite of those who nourish fine intentions and good hopes, so their approach is repugnant; they generally tend to augur from things, and the sorts of indicators they use are simpler and more copious. Some they draw from people's moles, from horses' spots, and from different kinds of physical features. Others they draw from incongruous mixtures and repugnant creatures, such as owls, vermin, scorpions, rats, and the like. Yet others they draw from disagreeable sounds, such as the braying of donkeys, the grating of iron, and the like. Some they draw from names and nicknames, deriving words from them that share some or all of their letters; for example, deriving the term "raven" from the term for "estrangement," the term "ben tree" from the term for "separation," and the term "date pits" from "distance."[11] Some they draw from physical defects, such as when a person is missing his right eye or has a crippled foot, and others from movements and directions, as when a bird passes from left to right or from 83.4

والقنوط عليها. وهذه الاستشعارات تزيدها سوء الحال فلذلك نهي عنها وكانت العرب خاصّة من بين الأمم أحرص على هذه الطريقة وألزم لها على أنّ شاعرهم يقول وقد أحسن [وافر]

تَخَبَّرَ طِيرَةً فِيهَا زِيَادُ   لِتُخْبِرَهُ وَمَا فِيهَا خَبِيرُ
أَقَامَ كَأَنَّ لُقْمَانَ بْنَ عَادٍ   أَشَارَ لَهُ بِحِكْمَتِهِ مُشِيرُ
تَعَلَّمَ أَنَّهُ لَا طَيْرَ إِلَّا   عَلَى مُتَطَيِّرٍ وَهُوَ ٱلثُّبُورُ
بَلَى شَيْءٌ يُوَافِقُ بَعْضَ شَيْءٍ   أَحَايِينًا وَبَاطِلُهُ كَثِيرُ

مسألة

ما السبب في كراهة بعضهم إذا قيل له يا شيخ على وجه التوقير والإجلال وهو لا يكون شيخًا؟ وآخر يتمنّى أن يقال له ذلك وهو شابّ طرير؟ بل أنت تجد ذلك في شيخ على الحقيقة يكره ذلك إلّا أنّ هذا علّته ظاهرة ولكنّ الشأن في شابّ يُشيّخ تعظيمًا فيكره وشابّ لا يُشيّخ فيتكلّف وفقد الشباب موجع ووجه الشيب مفظع. ١،٨٤

الجواب

قال أبو عليّ مسكويه رحمه الله إنّما يختلف الناس في ذلك باختلاف نظرهم لأنفسهم وبحسب ملاحظتهم أغراض مخاطبيهم وذلك أنّه ربّما أحبّ الإنسان أن تظهر فضيلته في ابتداء زمانه واستقبال عمره فإذا[1] قيل له يا شيخ ظنّ أنّه قد سُلب تلك ٢،٨٤

[1] الأصل: إذا.

right to left, and when something is crooked or inclining. This is due to a weakness of the soul and the natural disposition, and to its succumbing to despair and despondency. These perceptions exacerbate its condition, and this is why they were forbidden. Of all the nations, the Arabs in particular were extremely keen on this method and clung to it very tenaciously. Yet their own poet put it well when he said:[12]

> Ziyād asked his augurs to inform him
> about it, but no one could.
> He stayed behind as if someone had offered him
> a piece of Luqmān ibn ʿĀd's wisdom.
> He learned that the only omen to be had from augury
> is the augur himself—he is destined for perdition.
> Indeed, things do coincide at times,
> but augury is rife with false predictions.

On why some people dislike being addressed as "old man" while others relish it

Why do some people hate it when others address them as "old man" out of respect and veneration even though they are not old, while others wish to be addressed that way even though they are in the flush of youth? Indeed, we encounter such reactions among people who are actually old and who hate that mode of address, though in this case the reason for their dislike is evident. Our question, however, is about young men who hate being addressed as "old man" when it is meant as an honorific, and about young men who are not addressed as "old man" but affect that status, even though the loss of youth is painful and gray hair is a heinous sight. 84.1

Miskawayh's response

People differ in this regard as a result of the different ways in which they view themselves and the ways in which they perceive the aims of those addressing them. For a person may want to manifest his virtue at the beginning of his life, in his early years; so, if he is addressed as "old man," he may think he has been deprived of that virtue and has been assimilated to those who acquired that 84.2

الفضيلة وأُلحق بمن حصّل تلك الفضيلة في الزمان الطويل والتجربة الكثيرة وربّما كره ذلك أيضاً لأرب له في الشباب وميل إلى اللعب والهوى اللذين يُستقبحان من الشيخ فإذا قيل له يا شيخ رأى هذا اللقب كالمانع له والزاجر وأنّ مخاطبه[1] ينتظر منه ما ينتظر من المشايخ ولا يعذره على ركوب ما يهمّ به ويعزم عليه. وربّما نظر الإنسان إلى مرتبة حصلت له من الوقار الذي لا يحصل إلّا من المشايخ وهو في سنّ الشباب فيُسرّ بالإكرام وسرعة بلوغه مبلغ المحنّكين وأهل الدربة فبحسب اختلاف النظر تختلف وجوه الرضا بهذا الوصف والسخط له.

مسـألة

١،٨٥ مـا عـلّة الإنسان في سلوته إذا كانت محنته عامّة له ولغيره؟ وما علّة جزعه واستكثاره وتحسّره إذا خصّته المساءة ولم تعده المصيبة؟ وما سرّ النفس في ذلك؟ وهل هو محمود من الإنسان أم مكروه؟ وإذا نزا به هذا الخاطر بم يعالجه وإلى أيّ شيء يردّه؟ ولم يتمنّى بسبب محنته أن يشركه الناس؟ ولم يستريح إلى ذلك؟ وأصحابنا يروون مثلاً بالفارسيّة ترجمته من احترق بيدره أراد ان يحترق بيدر غيره.

الجواب

٢،٨٥ قال أبو عليّ مسكويه رحمه الله الجزع والأسف والحزن من عوارض النفس وهي تجري مجرى سائر العوارض الأخر كالغضب والشهوة والغيرة والرحمة والقسوة وسائر الأخلاق التي يُحمد الإنسان فيها إذا عرضت له كما ينبغي وبسائر الشروط التي أحصيناها مراراً كثيرة ويُذمّ بها إذا عرضت بخلاف تلك الشرائط. وإنّما تُهذّب

[1] الأصل: مخلّطيه.

virtue over a long period of time and after extensive experience. It may also be hateful because there may be a particular motive for wanting to be young or there may be a penchant for amusements and blind desires, which are deemed reprehensible in old people. So, if a person is addressed as "old man," he views this appellation as a hindrance and restraint, and assumes that the individual uttering this form of address expects him to act the way he expects old people to act, and will not excuse him for venturing to do the things he has set his mind on. Sometimes a person may take into account the level of respect that has accrued to him, which only accrues to old people, whereas he is still young, and he may rejoice at the honor bestowed and the speed with which he has achieved the status of a seasoned and experienced man. So the pleasure or anger with which one responds to this qualification differs depending on the way one views matters.

On why people take comfort from knowing they are not alone in their misfortune

What causes people to take solace when others share the troubles they are experiencing? What causes them to feel anxious, oppressed, and disconsolate when misfortune singles them out and calamity is confined to them? What secret quality of the soul is expressed therein? Is it praiseworthy or reprehensible for people to respond that way? How should they treat this reaction if it carries them away, and to what should they impute it? Why do our troubles make us wish other people shared in them, and why do we find comfort in that? Our companions report a Persian saying that runs: "If your threshing floor has been burned, you want the threshing floor of others to burn." 85.1

Miskawayh's response

Anxiety, sorrow, and grief are among the contingent effects the soul is subject to, and they resemble other effects such as anger, appetite, jealousy, mercy, cruelty, and all the other ethical characteristics human beings are praised for adhering to in the right manner and in accordance with the other conditions we have enumerated many times, and blamed for adhering to in a way that conflicts with those conditions. The soul is refined through the acquisition of character traits so that these contingent effects affect it as they ought, under 85.2

النفس بالأخلاق لتكون هذه العوارض تعرض له في مواضعها على ما ينبغي في الوقت الذي ينبغي فالحزن الذي يعرض كما ينبغي هو ما كان في مصيبة[1] لحقت الإنسان لذنب اجترحه أو لعمل فرّط فيه أو كان له فيه سبب اختياريّ أو لسوء اتّفاق خصّه دون غيره وهو يجهل سببه. فإنّ هذا الحزن وإن كان دون الأوّل فالإنسان معذور به. فأمّا ما كان ضروريًّا أو واجبًا فليس يحزن له عاقل لأنّ غروب الشمس مثلاً لمّا كان ضروريًّا لم يحزن له أحد وإن كان عائقًا عن منافع كثيرة وضارًّا بكلّ أحد ومنع النظر والتصرّف في منافع الدنيا وكذلك هجوم الشتاء والبرد وورود الصيف بالحرّ لا يحزن له عاقل بل يستعدّ له ويأخذ أهبته.

٣،٨٥ وأمّا الموت الطبيعيّ فليس يحزن له أحد لأنّه ضروريّ وإنّما يجزع الإنسان منه إذا ورد في غير الوقت الذي كان ينتظره أو بغير الحالة المحتسبة ولذلك يجزع الوالد على موت ولده لأنّ الذي احتسبه أن يموت هو قبله فأمّا الولد فيقلّ جزعه على والده لأنّ الأمر كما كان في حسابه إلّا أنّه تقدّم مثلاً بزمان يسير أو كما ينبغي فأمّا ما يعرض للمسافر ولراكب البحر أن يُخصّ دون من يصحبه بمحنة في ماله أو جسمه فإنّما حزنه لسوء الاتّفاق ورداءة البخت فإنّ هذا النوع مجهول السبب ولذلك يُعذر فيه أدنى عذر وأمّا من يتمنّى لغيره من السوء مثل ما يحصل له فهو شرّ في طبعه لا سيّما إذا لم يجد عليه شيئًا ولم يعد له بطائل وحينئذ يحسن توبيخه وتأديبه وقد أحسن الشاعر في قوله [خفيف]

لَيْسَ تَأْسُو[2] كُلُومُ غَيْرِي كُلُومِي[3] مَـا بِهِمْ مَـا بِهِمْ وَمَـا بِي مَـا بِي

١ الأصل: فمصيبة. ٢ الأصل: تأسوا. ٣ الأصل: كلمي.

the right conditions, and at the right time. The sorrow that affects a person in the right manner is the one that arises in response to a calamity that befalls him on account of a wrong he committed or an action he was remiss in or made some voluntary contribution to, or an unhappy chance that singled him out among other people and whose cause he does not know. Even though this kind of sorrow is inferior to the first, it is not held against people. By contrast, no reasonable person feels sorrow over things whose occurrence is necessary or inescapable. Nobody feels sorrow at the setting of the sun since it occurs necessarily, for example, even though it prevents the realization of many benefits, causes harm to everyone, and stops people from seeing and from pursuing their daily business. Similarly, no reasonable person feels sorrow when winter and cold set in or when the summer heat appears; instead, we gear up for it and make preparations.

Nobody feels sorrow over natural death, because it is necessary. It is only 85.3
when it appears at an unexpected time or takes an unanticipated form that people are aggrieved by it. Thus, parents are aggrieved by the deaths of their children, because they had anticipated that they would die before them. By contrast, children are not greatly aggrieved by the death of their parents, for matters follow the course they had anticipated, though it might occur slightly earlier, for example, or when it ought. In the case of the traveler or seafarer who happens to be the only one of his companions to suffer some hardship relating to his property or body, his sorrow is due to suffering misfortune and bad luck. The cause of this type of event is unknown, and one excuses him most readily on that account. Those who wish others to suffer the same kinds of evil that have afflicted them have a wicked nature, especially if this brings them no profit and avails them nothing; in that case, it is right to reprimand and discipline them. The poet put it well when he said:

> The wounds of another do not heal my wounds;
>   let them have their sufferings, and me my own.[13]

مســألة

مـا الفضيلة السارية في الأجناس المختلفة كالعرب والروم والفرس والهند؟ وزعمت ١،٨٦
أنّك حذفت الترك لأنّ أبا عثمان لا يعتدّ بهم إلى ما يتّصل به من كلامك ممّا لم أحكه
إذ كانت المسألة هي في قدر ما خرج من حكايتي.

الجواب

قال أبو عليّ مسكويه رحمه الله لمّا كانت هذه المسألة متوجّهة إلى خصائص الأمم ٢،٨٦
والتعجّب واقعاً ممّا تفرّد به قوم دون قوم أقبلت على البحث عن ذلك وتركت تهذيب
ألفاظ المسألة وهذه سبيلي في سائر المسائل لأنّ صاحبها يسلك مسلك الخطابة
ولا يذهب مذهب أهل المنطق في تحقيق المسألة وتوفيتها حظّها على طرقهم.
فأقول وبالله التوفيق قد تقدّم فيما مضى من كلامنا أنّ النفس تستعمل الآلات البدنيّة
فتصدر أفعالها بحسب أمزجتها وحكينا عن جالينوس مذهبه ودللنا على الموضع
الذي يُستخرج منه ذلك وضربنا له مثلاً من الحرارة الغريزيّة وغيرها إذا كانت حاضرة
كيف تستعملها النفس الناطقة حتّى تكون كما ينبغي وعلى من ينبغي وفي الوقت
الذي ينبغي فإنّ[1] الرياضة وحسن التقدير والترتيب ولزوم ذلك حتّى يصير سجيّة
وملكة هي الفضيلة والخلق المحمود فإذا كان هذا الأصل محفوظاً فما أيسر الجواب عن
مسألتك هذه.

وذاك أنّ لكلّ أمّة مزاجاً هو الغالب عليهم وإن كان يوجد في النادر وفي الفرط ٣،٨٦
ما هو مخالف لذلك المزاج وذلك لأجل التربة والهواء والأغذية والمزاج التابع لذلك
ولما كرهته أنت أيضاً من آثار الفلك والكواكب فإنّ ذلك العالم هو المؤثّر في هذا
العالم بالجملة. أمّا أوّلاً فبتمييز العناصر بعضها عن بعض ثمّ بمزجها[2] على الأقلّ والأكثر

---

١ ط: وإنّ. ٢ والأصل: بعضه عن بعض لم يمزجها؛ صوابه من ط.

On the virtues of different nations, such as the Arabs, Byzantines, Persians, and Indians

What is the virtue that runs in the different nations, such as the Arabs, the Byzantines, the Persians, and the Indians? You then asserted that you omitted the Turks because Abū ʿUthmān al-Jāḥiẓ does not take them into consideration. You went on to make a number of related points that I have not quoted, because the question at hand is fully contained in what I have quoted. 86.1

Miskawayh's response

As this question addresses itself to the special characteristics of different peoples, and as wonder is aroused by the characteristics a given group possesses to the exclusion of others, I have made this the subject of my inquiry, and have not sought to rectify the terms of the question. This has been my approach with all the other questions, because their author follows a rhetorical style, and does not proceed the way the logicians do in investigating a question and applying their methods fully to it. So I respond as follows—God grants success. In our earlier discussion, we explained that the soul uses bodily instruments and that its acts issue in accordance with their mixtures, reporting Galen's view and indicating the location where that discussion can be traced. We illustrated this through the example of innate heat and other elements, explaining how, when they are present, the rational soul uses them such that they obtain in the right manner, for the right people, and at the right time. We also stated that virtue and praiseworthy character are realized through training and the correct determination and ordering of actions, and by persistence until it becomes an innate trait and stable state. If this principle has been retained, there could be nothing easier than to reply to this question. 86.2

In every nation a mixture prevails, even if on rare and unusual occasions certain mixtures may be found that conflict with it. This is due to the type of soil, air, and foodstuffs, and the mixture attendant upon those aspects, and to those influences of the celestial sphere and the stars that you find so odious. For that world is what influences this one on a general level, first by distinguishing the elements from each other, then by mixing them in different proportions, and then by imparting forms and shapes to them. Your demand to be reprieved from the truth has no merit, and you have no means to grant 86.3

ثمّ بإعطائها الصور والأشكال وليس لاستعفائك من الحقّ وجهٌ ولا لإعفائك إيّاك منه طريق فالتزمه فإنّه واجب ولولا أنّ مسألتك وقعت عن غير هذا المعنى لاشتغلت به ولكنّ هذا أصل له فلا بدّ في ذكر الفرع من ذكر الأصل. وإذا كان هذا على هذا فحيث يعتدل مزاج ما من الأمزجة الشريفة أعني في الأعضاء الشريفة وهي القلب والكبد والدماغ وأضيف إلى ذلك ما ذكرناه من أخلاق فاضلة أعني ترتيب الأفعال الصادرة بحسب[1] المزاج وتهذيبها ولزومها بتكرّر[2] الفعل وإدمان العادة فهناك تحصيل الفضيلة الصادرة عنها وسواء أكان ذلك في أمّة أو شخص أو كان ذلك عن ابتداء أخلاق شريفة أو تأديب شيئاً فشيئاً بعد أن يكون المزاج مسعداً والبغية قابلة والعادة مستمرّة فإنّ الفضيلة حاصلة غير زائلة.

مسألة

١،٨٧ ما علّة كثرة غمّ من كان أعقل وقلّة غمّ من كان أجهل؟ وهذا باب موجود في واحد واحد ثمّ تجده في الجنس والجنس كالسودان والحمران فإنّك تجد السودان أطرب وأجهل والحمران أعقل وأكثر فكراً وأشدّ اهتماماً. هذا ويقال إنّ الفرح من الدم والحمران أكثر دماً وأعدل مزاجاً وأوجد لأسباب الفرح وآلات الطرب وأقدر على الدنيا بكلّ وجه وأنت ترى أيضاً هذا العارض في رفيقين خليطين أحدهما مهموم بالطبع وآخر متفكّه بالطبع.

الجواب

٢،٨٧ قال أبو عليّ مسكويه رحمه الله الغمّ يعرض من جهتين مختلفتين إحداهما جهة الفكر والأخرى جهة المزاج فأمّا الفكر فإنّه يعرض منه الغمّ إذا كان المرء ينتظر به مكروهاً وأمّا المزاج فهو أن ينحرف مزاج الدم إلى السواد[3] أو الاحتراق فيتكدّر به الروح الذي

١ الأصل: الضامرة وبحسب؛ ط: الغامرة وبحسب. ٢ ط: يتكرّر. ٣ الأصل: السود.

yourself reprieve from it. So adhere to it, because it must be accepted. Were it not that your question concerns a different topic, I would have devoted my attention to this one; but this constitutes one of the principles on which it rests, so one must mention the principle in discussing its subsidiary. On this basis, when one of the noble mixtures is balanced—that is to say, in the noble organs: the heart, the liver, and the brain—and to this are added the virtuous traits of character we have mentioned, which means ordering the acts that issue in accordance with the relevant mixture, refining them, and adhering to them through repeated action and sustained habit—this leads to realizing the virtue that arises from them. Whether that is found in a nation or an individual, and whether it is due to noble character traits existing from the beginning or to gradual discipline once a felicitous mixture, a propitious aim, and a continued habit are in place, virtue is realized and does not disappear.

On why intelligent people are more susceptible to grief

Why do people with greater intelligence experience much grief whereas those who are more ignorant experience little grief? This phenomenon is encountered among different individuals and among different races, such as the blacks and the fair skinned. For black people are evidently merrier and more ignorant, whereas fair-skinned people are more intelligent and reflective, and more strongly given to worry. This is the case even though it is said that joy comes from the blood, and fair-skinned people have a greater amount of blood,[14] more balanced humoral mixtures, readier access to what brings joy and is conducive to merriment, and greater mastery over worldly things in every respect. This phenomenon is also observable among intimate companions, one of whom is naturally prone to worry, while the other is a natural jester. 87.1

Miskawayh's response

Grief arises from two different quarters: one is reflection, and the other is humoral mixture. Grief arises from reflection if a person expects some evil to happen. Grief arising from the humoral mixture occurs when the mixture of the blood deviates toward blackness or burning, roiling the spirit that is produced by the vapor of the blood in the passageways of the arteries. How clear the vapor is, how well it expands, and how swiftly it moves and courses in that 87.2

سببه بخار الدم في مجاري الشرايين وبحسب صفاء ذلك الدم يكون صفاء بخاره وانبساطه وسرعة حركته وجريانه في ذلك التجويف. وإذا كان سبب الغمّ معلوماً فمقابله الذي هو سبب الفرح والسرور معلوم أيضاً فالعاقل لأجل جولان فكره يكثر انتظاره مكاره الدنيا ومن لا يكثر فكره ولا ينتظر مكروهاً فلا سبب له يغمّه. وأمّا المزاج الذي ذكرناه فقد أحكمه جالينوس وأصحابه وسائر الأطبّاء ممّن تقدّمه أو تأخّرعنه. وهذا المزاج ليس يخلو أن يكون طارئاً أو حادثاً أو طبيعيّاً في أصل الخلقة فإن كان حادثاً فهو مرض وينبغي أن يُعالج بما تعالج به أصناف المالخوليا[1] وأنواع الأمراض السوداويّة التي سببها فساد الدم بالاحتراق وانحرافه إلى السوداء وإن كان أصليّاً وخلقة فلا علاج له لأنّه ليس بمرض فأجيال[2] من الناس وأمم أمزجتهم كذلك.

٣،٨٧ فأمّا ما حكيته عن السودان فإنّ الزنوج خاصّة لهم الفرح والنشاط وسببه اعتدال دم القلب فيهم وليس ما ظننت أنّ أمزجتهم تابعة لسواد ألوانهم وذلك أنّ سبب سواد ألوانهم هو قرب الشمس منهم وممرّها في حضيض فلكها على سمت رؤوسهم فهي تحرق جلودهم وشعورهم فيعرض فيها أعني في شعورهم التفلفل الذي هو بالحقيقة تشييط[3] الشعر ولأجل أنّ الحرارة تستولي على ظاهرهم فهي تجذب الحرارة الغريزيّة من باطنهم إليها لأنّ الحرارة تميل إلى جهة الحرارة فلا تكثر الحرارة الغريزيّة في قلوبهم لأجل ذلك وإذا لم تكن الحرارة الغريزيّة في القلب قويّة لم يعرض للدم الذي هناك احتراق بل هو إلى الصفاء والرقّة أقرب ودماء الزنوج رقيقة أبداً صافية ولذلك تقلّ الشجاعة أيضاً فيهم.

٤،٨٧ فأمّا الحمران فأكثرهم في ناحية الشمال والبلدان الباردة التي تبعد الشمس عنها[4] وتقوى الحرارة الغريزيّة في قلوبهم ولاشتمال البرد على ظاهرهم تبقى جلودهم بيضاء وشعورهم سباطاً وتعود حرارتهم إلى دواخل أبدانهم هرباً من البرد الذي في هوائهم لبُعد[5] الشمس عنهم فهم لذلك أشجع وأقوى حرارة قلوب ودماؤهم لأجل ذلك إلى

١ ط: الماليخوليا. ٢ الأصل وط: كأجيال. ٣ ط: تشيّط. ٤ الأصل وط: عنهم. ٥ الأصل: ببعد.

cavity all depend on the clarity of the blood. Once the cause of grief is known, its counterpart, the cause of joy and happiness, is also known. People of intelligence often expect worldly evils to happen because of how their thought roves, whereas those who do not reflect much and do not expect any evil to happen have no reason to feel grief. The type of humoral mixture we mentioned has been firmly established by Galen, his disciples, and other physicians who came before or after him. The humoral mixture in question will be either adventitious or contingent, on the one hand, or natural and original to one's constitution, on the other. If it is contingent, it constitutes an illness, and must be treated through the means used to treat the various kinds of melancholy and the different sorts of atrabilious illnesses that are caused by the blood's degeneration through burning and by its deviation toward black bile. If it is originally present and part of one's constitution, then it cannot be treated, because it does not constitute an illness; one thus finds entire generations of people and nations whose humoral mixtures are like that.

As for what you have said regarding the blacks, East Africans in particular 87.3
are characterized by joyfulness and animation; the reason for that is the balanced state of the blood of their heart. It is not the case, as you supposed, that their mixtures follow upon the blackness of their skin, for the blackness of their skin is caused by the sun's proximity to them and by its passing vertically above their heads at the lowest point of its orbit, so that it burns their skin and hair, producing in it—their hair, that is—that frizzy quality which in fact signifies that their hair has been singed. As heat overwhelms their exterior, it draws the innate heat out of their interior toward itself; for heat inclines in the direction of heat. As a consequence, the innate heat in their heart does not become too great. If the innate heat in the heart is not strong, the blood found there is not exposed to burning, and instead it tends toward clarity and fineness. The blood of East Africans is always fine and pure, and that is why courage also is rarely found among them.

Most fair-skinned people, by contrast, live in the northern climes and in 87.4
the cold countries, where the sun is distant and the innate heat grows strong in their heart. Because their exterior is encompassed by the cold, their skins remain white and their hair lank, and their heat returns to the inside of their bodies in order to escape from the cold in the air around them as a result of the sun's distance. That is why they are more courageous and why the heat of their heart is stronger; as a result, their blood tends toward turbidity, blackness,

الكدورة والسواد والخروج عن الاعتدال. وأهل الاعتدال الذي يبعدون عن الشمال وعن الجنوب ويسكنون الإقليم الأوسط هم أسلم من هذه الآفات وأصحّ أمزجة وأقرب إلى الاعتدال.

مسألة

١،٨٨ حدّثني عن مسألة هي ملكة المسائل والجواب عنها أمير الأجوبة وهي الشجا في الحلق والقذى في العين والغصّة في الصدر والوقر على الظهر والسلّ في الجسم والحسرة في النفس وهذا كلّه لعظم ما دهم منها وابتلي الناس به فيها وهي حرمان الفاضل وإدراك الناقص ولهذا المعنى خلع ابن الراونديّ ربقة الدين وقال أبو سعيد الحصيريّ بالشكّ وألحد فلان في الإسلام وارتاب فلان في الحكمة. وحين نظر أبو عيسى الورّاق إلى خادم قد خرج من دار الخليفة بجنائب تقاد بين يديه وبجماعة تركض حواليه فرفع رأسه إلى السماء وقال أوحّدك بلغات وألسنة وأدعو إليك بحجج وأدلّة وأنصر دينك بكلّ شاهد وبيّنة ثمّ أمشي هكذا عارياً جائعاً نائعاً ومثل هذا الأسود يتقلّب في الخزّ والوشي والخدم والحشم والحاشية والغاشية. ويقال هذا الإنسان هو ابن الراونديّ ومن كان فإنّ الحديث في هذا الباب بيّن والإسناد فيه عال والبحث عن هذا السرّ واجب فإنّه باب إلى روح القلب وسلامة الصدر وصحّة العقل ورضا الربّ ولو لم يكن فيه إلّا التفويض والصبر حسبما يوجبه الدليل لكان كافياً.

٢،٨٨ والمنجّمون يقولون إنّ الثامن من مقابلة الثاني فكأنّ المناظر والمقابل يدلّان على العداوة. وحدّثنا شيخ عن ابن مجاهد أنّه قال الفضل معدود من الرزق كما أنّ النقص[١] معدود في جملة الحرمان. وقال لي شيخ مرّة اعلم أنّ القسمة عدل والقاسم منصف لأنّه بإزاء ما أعطاك من الأدب والفضل واللسان والعقل أعطى صاحبك المال والجاه

١ الأصل: الخفض؛ وصوابه من الهامش.

and imbalance. The balanced people, who dwell in the intermediate climes, far from both the north and the south, are those freest from these flaws, who have the soundest mixtures and are closest to a balanced state.

On why intrinsic merit and worldly fortune do not coincide

Speak to me about the queen of all questions whose answer is the prince of all answers; a question that forms the lump in one's throat and the mote in one's eye, the morsel one chokes on and the dead weight on one's back, the malady that wastes one's body and the pained sigh one heaves, such is the immensity of the affliction and suffering it visits upon people. The question: Why are excellent men left deprived, while deficient men attain success? This is the reason why Ibn al-Rāwandī threw off the bonds of the faith, why Abū Saʿīd al-Ḥaṣīrī professed himself a skeptic, why some people disbelieved in Islam and others cast doubt on divine wisdom. When Abū ʿĪsā al-Warrāq saw a eunuch coming out of the residence of the caliph with horses driven before him and a throng of people running around him, he lifted his eyes to the heavens and said, "I proclaim your unity in many languages and tongues, I summon people to believe in you through many arguments and proofs, I buttress your religion through every kind of testimony and evidence, and then I walk about like this, naked, hungry, and thirsty, while a black man like that luxuriates in silk and embroidery, surrounded by servants and attendants, with his retinue and entourage." Some say that this was Ibn al-Rāwandī. Whoever it might be, the account of this topic is clear, the chain of transmission reaches far back to bygone ages, and inquiry into this mystery is obligatory. For it is a gateway to securing a tranquil heart, a peaceful breast, and a sound mind, and to obtaining God's approval. Were it to turn out that the only thing one can do in this connection is to entrust things to God and patiently endure according to what the proofs dictate, that would suffice. 88.1

The astrologists say: The eighth mansion is in opposition to the second mansion; it seems that it indicates hostility when a mansion is counter and in opposition to another. An established scholar reported that Ibn Mujāhid said: Excellence is to be counted as part of the sustenance granted by God, and deficiency is to be counted as part of the deprivation inflicted by God. 88.2

والكفاية واليسار فانظر إلى النعمة كيف انقسمت بينكما ثمّ انظر إلى البلاء كيف انقسم عليكما أيضاً أبلاك مع الفضل بالحاجة وأبلاه مع الغنى بالجهالة. فهل العدل إلّا في هذه العبرة والحقّ إلّا بهذه الفكرة ولعمري إنّ هذا المقدار لا يصير عليه الدهريّ ولا التناسخيّ ولا الثنويّ ولكنّ على كلّ حال فيه تبصرة من العمى. ولو قد أفردنا الجواب عن مسائل هذه الرسالة لكان للمعترض والمتشكّك في ذلك مشبع ومروى والله المعين على ما قد اشتمل الضمير عليه وانعقدت النيّة به.

الجواب

قال أبو عليّ مسكويه رحمه الله هذه المسألة كما حكيت ووصفت من صعوبتها على ٣،٨٨
أكثر الناس والتباس[1] وجه الحكمة فيها على أصناف أهل النظر حتّى صار الكلام فيها مشبهاً بقائم الشطرنج الذي يتنازعه الخصمان إلى أن يقطعهما الكلال والسآمة فيطرحونها قائمة ثمّ يعودون فيها مجلساً بعد آخر فتكون صورتهم فيها واقفة بحالها. وكنت أحبّ أن أفرد فيها مقالة تشتمل على جملة مستقصاة تشفي وتكفي عند ما سألني بعض الإخوان ذلك فإنّ أمثال هذه المسائل المتداولة بين الناس المشهورة بالشكّ والحيرة ليس ينبغي أن يقنع فيها بأمثال هذه الأجوبة التي سألت أنت فيها الإيجاز الشديد وضمنت أنا فيها الإيماء إلى النكت لا سيّما وأنا لا أعرف في معناها كلاماً مبسوطاً لأحد ممّن تقدّمني حتّى إذا أومأت بالمعنى إليه أحلت بالشرح عليه ولكنّي لمّا انتهيت إليها بالنظر لم يجز أن أخليّها من جواب متوسّط بين الإسهاب والإيجاز وأنا مجتهد في بيانها وإزالة ما لحق الناس من الحيرة فيها ومن عند الله استمدّ التوفيق وهو حسبي.

---

[1] الأصل: والتماس؛ وصوابه من الهامش.

An established scholar once told me: Be assured that the distribution of different lots in life is just, and that the Distributor acts fairly. He gave you erudition, excellence, eloquence, and discernment, and He gave your fellow wealth, high standing, sufficiency, and a life of comfort. So consider how the blessings were distributed between you, and then consider how the afflictions were also distributed between you. He granted you excellence, but afflicted you with poverty; He granted him plenty, but afflicted him with ignorance. Isn't justice to be found in this reflection, and doesn't the truth lie with this thought? Upon my life, a view of this kind would not command assent from materialists, believers in metempsychosis, or dualists,[15] but in any case it replaces blindness with insight. Were we to devote separate responses to the questions of this epistle, it would sate the objector and slake the skeptic. God is our helper in carrying out what we have in mind and intend.

Miskawayh's response

This question is just as you have stated and described in terms of how difficult 88.3
most people find it and how inscrutable the underlying rationale has appeared to different kinds of inquirers, to the point that discussions of the topic have come to resemble a drawn game of chess. The players contest it until fatigue and weariness overtake them and they let it end in a draw; they then return to it on successive occasions, but from the outside everything always looks the same. I was keen to devote a separate treatise to this topic when asked to do so by a close friend—a treatise incorporating a general and thorough discussion that would fit the purpose and meet the need. For with these kinds of questions, which make the rounds among people and are notorious for the doubt and perplexity they provoke, one should not content oneself with these kinds of answers, which you asked to be delivered with the utmost conciseness and in which I have incorporated only allusions to subtler points—particularly as I do not know of any extensive account of the issue by earlier thinkers, so that I might have adumbrated the main points and referred to that work for a more detailed exposition. Yet, having made it the object of my inquiry, it is impermissible that I should leave it without a discussion midway between the dilatory and the succinct. I shall expend my utmost effort to set it forth clearly and dispel the perplexity it has produced in people. I draw my hope of success from God; God is my sufficiency.

٤،٨٨ فأقول إنّ من الأصول التي لا منازعة فيها وهي مسلّمة من ذوي العقول السليمة أنّ لكلّ موجود في العالم طبيعيّ كان أو صناعيّ غاية وكمالاً وغرضاً خاصّاً وُجد من أجله وبسببه أعني أنّه إنّما أوجد ليتمّ به ذلك الغرض وإن كان قد يتمّ به أشياء أخر دون ذلك الغرض الأخير والكمال الأخير وقد يصلح لأمور ليست من الغرض الذي قُصد به وأريد له في شيء ومثال ذلك المطرقة فإنّها إنّما أُعدّت للصانع ليتمّ له بها مدّ الأجسام إلى أقطارها وبسطها إلى نواحيها وهي مع ذلك تصلح لأن يُشقّ بها وتُستعمل في بعض ما تستعمل فيه الفأس وكذلك أيضاً المقراض إنّما أُعدّ للخيّاط ليُقطع به الثوب وهو مع ذلك يصلح لأن يُبرى به القلم ويُستعمل مكان السكّين وكذلك الحال في سائر الآلات الصناعيّة.

٥،٨٨ وهكذا صور الأمور الطبيعيّة فإنّ الأسنان إنّما أُعدّت مختلفات الأوضاع والأشكال لاختلاف كمالاتها أعني الأغراض التي تتمّ بها والأفعال التي وُجدت من أجلها فإنّ مقاديمها حادّة بالهيئة التي تصلح للقطع كالحال في السكّين ومآخيرها عريضة بالهيئة التي تصلح للرضّ والطحن كالحال في الرحا وقد تتمّ بها أفعال أخر. وكذلك الحال في اليد والرجل فقد يتعاطى الناس أن يعملوا بكلّ واحدة منهما غير ما خُلقت له وعُملت من أجله على سبيل الحاجة إلى ذلك أو على طريق التغريب به كمن يمشي على يده ويبطش ويكتب برجله. ولكنّ هذه الأفعال وإن ساغ صدورها عن هذه الآلات وتمّ بها غير ما هو كمالها وخُصّ[١] بها فإنّ ذلك منها يكون على اضطراب ونقصان عن الآلات التي تتمّ بها أعمالها الخاصّة بها المطلوبة منها الموجودة من أجلها. وإذا كان ذلك مستمرّاً[٢] في جميع الآلات الصناعيّة والأشخاص الطبيعيّة فكذلك الحال في الأنواع كلّها فإنّك إذا تأمّلت نوعاً منها وجدته مستعدّاً لكمالات وأغراض خاصّة بواحد واحد منها. وهكذا يجري الأمر في أجناس هذه الأنواع فإنّ الناطق وغير الناطق من الحيوان ليس يجوز أن يكون غرضهما وكمالهما واحداً أعني

١ الأصل: وخاصّ. ٢ الأصل: كان مستمرّا.

I thus respond as follows. It is an incontrovertible principle acknowledged by all right-minded people that every existent in the world, be it natural or artificial, has a proper end, perfection, and purpose for the sake of which and because of which it was brought into existence. That is to say, it was brought into existence in order to accomplish that purpose, even though it might be used to accomplish other things besides that ultimate purpose and ultimate perfection, and even though it might be good for things that have no relation to the purpose for which it was intended and willed. For example, a hammer is designed to be used by a craftsman for pounding and flattening physical objects in the directions required, yet at the same time it can serve to break things apart, thus being used for some of the functions for which an axe is used. Similarly, a pair of scissors is designed to be used by a tailor for cutting clothes, yet at the same time it can serve to sharpen reed pens, in place of a knife. The same applies to all other artificial implements. 88.4

Natural entities follow a similar pattern. Thus, teeth were designed in different positions and with different forms because of their different perfections, that is to say, the different purposes they are used to accomplish and the different acts for the sake of which they exist. The front teeth are sharp and have the kind of shape that is good for cutting, as is the case with knives, whereas the rear teeth are broad and have the kind of shape that is good for crushing and grinding, as is the case with millstones. They can also be used to accomplish other acts. The same applies to the hands and the feet. For people may venture to put each of these to a use other than the one for which it was created and for the sake of which it was made, whether because they have a need for that or because they wish to provoke astonishment and admiration, the way some people walk on their hands or use their feet to knock people down or to write. Yet even though it is permissible for these acts to issue from these instruments and they are used to accomplish something other than what constitutes their perfection and what is proper to them, this will be marked by disorder and deficiency when compared with the instruments that are used to accomplish the works that are proper to them, that are required from them, and for the sake of which they exist. If that holds true for all artificial implements and individual entities of a natural kind, the same applies to all species. For when we contemplate any given species, we find that each species is disposed to perfections and purposes that are proper to it. It is similar with the genera of these species. For rational and nonrational animals cannot have the same 88.5

أنّه لا يجوز بوجه ولا سبب ألّا يكون للإنسان الذي مُيّز بهذه الصورة وخُلق على هذا الشكل[1] وأعطي التمييز والرويّة وفُضّل بالعقل الذي هو أجلّ موهوب له وأفضل مخصوص به غرض خاصّ وكمال خُلق لأجله ووُجد بسببه.

٦،٨٨ وإذا كان هذا الأصل موطّأً ومقرّاً[2] به وكان على غاية الصحّة وفي نهاية القوّة كما تراه فهلمّ بنا نبحث بحثاً آخر عن هذه الآلات الصناعيّة والأشخاص الطبيعيّة فإنّا نجدها قد تشترك في أشياء وتتباين في أشياء أعني أنّ المطرقة تشارك السكّين والإبرة والمنشار وغيرها في الصورة التي هي الحديدة ثمّ تنفرد بخاصّ صورة لها تميّزها من غيرها والإنسان يشارك النبات والبهائم في النموّ والاغتذاء[3] وفي الالتذاذ بالمأكل والمشرب وسائر راحات الجسد ونفض الفضول عنه ونريد أن نعلم هل هذا الاختصاص الذي لكلّ واحد منها بغرضه الخاصّ به وكماله المفروض له هو بما شارك به غيره أو بما باينه به؟ فنجده الصورة الخاصّة به التي ميّزته عن غيره وصار بها هو ما هو أعني صورة الفأس التي بها هو فأس هي التي جعلت له خاصّته وكماله وغرضه وكذلك الحال في الباقيات.

٧،٨٨ ثمّ نصير إلى الإنسان الذي شارك النبات والحيوان في موضوعاتها فنقول إنّ الإنسان من حيث هو حيوان قد شارك البهائم في غرض الحيوانيّة وكمالها أعني في نيل اللذّات والشهوات والتماس الراحات وطلب العوض ممّا يتحلّل من بدنه إلّا أنّ الحيوانيّة لمّا لم تكن صورته الخاصّة به المميّزة له عن غيره لم تصدر هذه الأشياء منه على أتمّ أحوالها وذاك أنّا نجد أكثر الحيوانات تزيد على الإنسان في جميع ما عددناه وتفضله فيها بالاقتدار على التزيّد وبالمداومة وبالاهتداء. ولمّا كانت صورته الخاصّة به التي ميّزته عن غيره هو العقل وخصائصه من التمييز والرويّة وجب أن تكون إنسانيّته في هذه الأشياء فكلّ من كان حظّه من هذه الخصائص أكثر كان أكثر

---

١ ط: بهذه الصورة. ٢ الأصل وط: ومقرورا؛ وصوابه من الهامش. ٣ الأصل وط: والاعتلال.

purpose and perfection. That is to say, it is in no wise and by no means possible that human beings, who were distinguished through this form, created according to this pattern, endowed with discrimination and reflection, and rendered preeminent through reason—the most glorious gift given to them and the most excellent feature specifically granted to them—should not have a purpose proper to them and a perfection for the sake of which they were created and because of which they exist.

If this principle has been set in place and secured assent—and it could not 88.6
be sounder or stronger, as you can see—we can now investigate these artificial implements and natural individuals from another direction. For we find that they converge in some aspects and diverge in others. Thus, a hammer has in common with a knife, a needle, and a saw the form of a tool made of iron, but it is then set apart through a form that is proper to it and distinguishes it from other tools. Human beings have in common with plants and beasts growth and nourishment, the pleasure taken in food and drink and all other bodily comforts, and the excretion of superfluous substances. What we wish to know is: Is each entity's exclusive possession of a purpose that is proper to it and a perfection that is assigned to it due to the aspects it has in common with, or to the aspects where it diverges from, other entities? We find that this is due to the form that is proper to it and that distinguishes it from other entities, and through which it is what it is. That is to say, it is the form of an axe, which constitutes it as an axe, that determines its specific property, perfection, and purpose; and the same applies to all other entities.

Next, we turn our attention to human beings, which share in the substrate of 88.7
plants and animals, and we say as follows. Insofar as human beings are animals, they have in common with beasts the purpose and perfection of animality, that is, the pursuit of pleasures and appetites, the quest for physical comforts, and the drive to replace the parts of their body that dissolve. Yet, as animality is not the form that is proper to human beings and that distinguishes them from other beings, these things do not issue from them in the most complete manner. For we find that most animals outstrip human beings in all the features we enumerated and surpass human beings in their ability to locate them, devote themselves to them, and obtain greater amounts of them. As the form that is proper to human beings and distinguishes them from other beings consists in reason and its special attributes, discrimination and reflection, these are the features in which their humanity must be vested. So the person with a

إنسانيّة كما أنّ الأشياء التي عددناها كلّما كان منها حظّه من صورته الخاصّة به أكثر كان فضله في أشكاله أظهر.

٨،٨٨ ثمّ نعود إلى شرح مسألتك ونبيّنها بحسب هذه الأصول التي قدّمتها فأقول لعمري إنّه لو كان غاية الإنسان وغرضه الذي وُجد بسببه وكماله الذي أُعدّ له هو الاستكثار من القنية والتمتّع بالمآكل والمشارب وسائر اللذّات والراحات لوجب أن يستوفيها بصورته الخاصّة به ولوجب أن تكثر عنده ويكون نصيب كلّ إنسان منها على قدر قسطه من الإنسانيّة حتّى يكون الأفضل من الناس هو الأفضل في هذه الأحوال من القنية والاستمتاع بها ولكن لمّا كانت صورته الخاصّة به هي التي ذكرنا علمنا أنّ القصد به والغرض فيه هو ما صدر عنها[١] وتمّ بها[٢] كحقائق العلوم والمعارف وإجالة الرويّة وإعمال الفكرة فيها ليصل بذلك إلى مرتبة هي أجلّ من مرتبة البهائم وسائر الموجودات في عالم الكون والفساد كما أنّه في نفسه وبحسب صورته أفضل منها كلّها وهذه المرتبة لا يوصل إليها بغير الرويّة وبغير الاختيار الخاصّين بالعقل.

٩،٨٨ ولا يجوز أن يقال في معارضة ما قلناه إنّ هذه الرويّة وهذا الاختيار إنّما ينبغي أن يكونا في اللذّات لأنّا قد بيّنّا في هذا الموضع وفي مواضع أخر كثيرة أنّ تلك الموجودة للحيوانات الخسيسة أوفر وأكثر بغير رويّة ولا عقل وإنّما تشرف الرويّة وتتبيّن ثمرة العقل إذا استُعمل في أفضل الموجودات وأفضل الموجودات ما كان دائم البقاء غير داثر ولا متبدّل وغير محتاج ولا فقير إلى شيء خارج عنه بل هو الغنيّ بذاته الذي فاض بجوده على جميع الموجودات ونزّلها منازلها بقدر مراتبها وعلى قدر قبولها وبحسب استحقاقاتها. فالرويّة والفكرة والاختيار إنّما تكمل بها صورة[٣] الإنسانيّة إذا استُعملت في الأمور الإلهيّة ليرتقي بها إلى منازل شريفة لا يمكن النطق بها ولا الإشارة إليها إلّا لمن وصل إليها وعرف إلى ما يشار وعلم لأيّ شيء عرض الإنسان من الخيرات ثمّ هو يطلب الانتكاس في الخلق والرجوع إلى مرتبة البهائم

١ الأصل وط: عنه. ٢ الأصل وط: به. ٣ الأصل وط: صور.

greater share of these attributes has a greater degree of humanity, just as, when a person has a greater share of the form proper to him as a result of the features we enumerated, his merit is in starker evidence in all its varieties.

Now let us return to the specifics of the question you raised, to expound it on the basis of the principles set out above. I therefore say as follows: Upon my life, were it the end of human beings, the purpose on account of which they exist, and the perfection to which they were disposed, to accumulate as many possessions as possible and to enjoy food and drink and all other pleasures and comforts, it would be necessary that they exact them fully through their proper form, that they acquire them in great quantities, and that each person's portion of them be commensurate to his share of humanity, so that the most excellent human beings would be the ones who excel most with respect to possessions and their enjoyment. But, as the form proper to them is the one we have mentioned, we know that their aim and purpose is what issues from that form and is accomplished through it, such as to acquire true knowledge and learning, and to deliberate and reflect on them, so that through such means they may attain a rank loftier than that of the beasts and the other beings in the world of generation and corruption, reflecting the superiority they have over them intrinsically and on the basis of their form. This is a rank that they can only attain with the reflection and voluntary choice that pertain to reason. 88.8

No one could possibly object to what we have stated by arguing that this reflection and choice must rather relate to pleasures, for we have shown at this juncture and many others that lowly animals possess the latter in greater abundance and larger quantities without reflection or reason. The dignity of reflection in fact emerges, and the benefit of reason stands out, when it is used in relation to the most excellent beings. The most excellent being is the one that has a permanent existence and does not cease to be or undergo change, and does not need or require anything external to it but is, rather, self-sufficient, diffusing its generosity over all beings and assigning them to their proper stations according to their rank and receptivity, and depending on their merit. Thus, the form of humanity is perfected by reflection, thought, and choice when they are used in relation to divine things, elevating one to noble stations that none can speak of or refer to save those who have reached them, who have grasped the object of reference, and who have come to know the blessings extended to human beings. If one then seeks to sink down in creation and return to the level of the beasts and of those that are ranked with them, who 88.9

ومن هو في عدادها ممّن خسر نفسه كما قال الله تعالى ﴿قُلْ إِنَّ ٱلْخَاسِرِينَ ٱلَّذِينَ خَسِرُوا أَنفُسَهُمْ﴾ فهذا لعمري هو الخسران المبين الذي يُتعوّذ بالله منه دائماً.

١٠،٨٨ ولقد أعجبني قول امرئ القيس مع لوثة أعرابيّته وعجميّة ملكه وشبابه وذهابه في طرق الشعر التي كان متصنّعاً به وهائماً في واديه منغمساً في معانيه [وافر]

أَرَانَا مُوضِعِينَ لِحَتْمِ غَيْبٍ ... وَنُسْحَرُ بِٱلطَّعَامِ وَبِٱلشَّرَابِ

فما هذا الإيضاع منّا؟ وما هذا الحتم من الغيب؟ لقد أشار إلى معنى لطيف[1] ودلّ من نفسه على ذكاء تامّ وقريحة عجيبة ألا تراه يقول وَنُسْحَرُ بِٱلطَّعَامِ وَبِٱلشَّرَابِ أي المراد منّا والمقصود بنا غيرهما وإنّما نسحر بهذين. فقد تبيّن أنّ الإنسان إذا لم تكن غايته هذه الأشياء التي تسمّيها العامّة أرزاقاً ولم يُخلق لها ولا هي مقصوداته بالذات فليس ينبغي له أن يلتمسها وأن يتعجّب ممّن اتّفقت له وإن كان يتشوّقها ويحبّها فليس ذلك من حيث هو إنسان عاقل بل هو من حيث هو حيوان بهيميّ وقد أزيحت علّته في الأمور الضروريّة التي يتمّ بها عيشه ويصحّ منها سلوكه إلى غايته ولم يُظلم أحد في هذا فتأمّله تجده بيّناً إن شاء الله.

مسألة

١،٨٩ ما الاتّفاق؟ وما يتلوه من الكلام.

٢،٨٩ هذه المسألة مكرّرة وقد مضى الجواب عنها مستقصى على شريطة الإيجاز وبعدها مسألة التوفيق وقد مرّت أيضاً فليُرجع إلى الأجوبة المتقدّمة عنهما.

---

١ الأصل وط: الطيف.

have lost themselves—as God said, «Surely the losers are they who lose themselves»[16]—upon my life, this is the manifest loss that one always asks God to preserve one from.

I have been impressed by the words of Imru' al-Qays, for all the crudeness of his Bedouin style, his foreign kingship and youth, and his pursuit of the poetic forms he cultivated and lost himself in, immersing himself in its notions: 88.10

I see us hurrying toward an unknown fate,
beguiled by food and drink.

What is this hurry we are in? What is this unknown fate? He is making a subtle point, revealing a fine intelligence and remarkable gifts. Don't you see that he says we are "beguiled by food and drink"? That is to say: What is willed and intended for us is something else, yet we are beguiled by them. So it has emerged clearly that, since those things the common people call "sustenance" do not constitute the end of human beings, the purpose for which they were created, or their intrinsic aim, they must not pursue them and marvel at those who happen to receive them, even if they long for them and desire them. For they do so not in their capacity as rational human beings but in their capacity as beastly animals. With regard to those necessities on which their life depends and which allow them to proceed toward their end, the impediments have been removed and nobody has been wronged. If you ponder these points, you will find them plain, God willing.

On the meaning of coincidence

What does "coincidence" mean? And the remarks that follow. 89.1

This question has already appeared, and it has received a thorough response 89.2
that nonetheless fulfills the proviso of brevity.[17] After that appears a question about the meaning of "granting a favorable outcome," which has also come up before. So one may consult the answers provided to both questions earlier.

مسـألة

١،٩٠ الجواب أن تفـرد مسألة الجبر والاختيار فيقال ما الجبر وما الاختيار وما نسبتهما إلى العالم؟ وكيف انتسابهما وانتماؤهما؟[١] أعني كيف اختلافهما في ائتلافهما؟ وذلك أنّك تجدهما في العالم مضافين إلى الذين يجمعون بين العقل والحسّ كما تجدهما مضافين إلى الذين ينفردون بالحسّ دون العقل.

الجوابـ

٢،٩٠ قال أبو عليّ مسكويه رحمه الله إنّ الإنسان تصدر عنه حركات وأفعال كثيرة لا يشبه بعضها بعضاً وذلك أنّه يظهر منه فعل من حيث هو جسم طبيعيّ فيناسب فيه الجماد ويظهر منه فعل آخر من حيث هو نامٍ مع أنّه جسم طبيعيّ فيناسب بذلك الفعل النبات ويظهر منه فعل آخر من حيث هو ذو نفس حسّاس فيناسب بذلك الفعل البهائم ويظهر منه فعل آخر من حيث هو ناطق مميّز فيناسب بذلك الفعل الملائكة ولكلّ واحد من هذه الأفعال والحركات الصادرة عن الإنسان أنواع كثيرة وإليها دواع ولها أسباب ويُنظر أيضاً فيها من جهات مختلفة وتعرض لها عوائق كثيرة وموانع مختلفة بعضها طبيعيّة وبعضها اتّفاقيّة وبعضها قهريّة. ومتى لم يفصل الناظر في هذه المسألة هذه الأفعال بعضها من بعض ولم ينظر في جهاتها كلّها اختلطت عليه هذه الوجوه والتبس عليه وجه النظر فيها فعرضت له الحيرة وكثرت عليه الشبه والشكوك ونحن نبيّن هذه الحركات ونميّزها ثمّ نتكلّم على حقيقة الجبر والاختيار فإنّ الأمر حينئذ يسهل جدّاً ويقرب فهمه ولا يعتاص بمشيئة الله تعالى.

٣،٩٠ فأقول إنّ الفعل مع اختلاف أنواعه وتباين جهاته يحتاج في ظهوره إلى أربعة أشياء أحدهما الفاعل الذي يظهر منه والثاني المادّة التي يحصل فيها والثالث الغرض الذي ينساق إليه والرابع الصورة التي تقدّم[٢] عند الفاعل ويروم بالفعل

١ ط: والتئامهما. ٢ ط: تتقدّم.

On the nature of compulsion and choice

The answer to this question lies in devoting a separate discussion to the question of compulsion and choice, to thus ask: What is compulsion, and what is choice? What is their relation to the world? How do they relate and fit together? That is, how do they diverge in their convergence? For you see them in the world attributed to those who combine reason and sense perception, yet you also see them attributed to those who possess sense perception but not reason. 90.1

Miskawayh's response

There are many movements and acts that issue from human beings but that do not resemble one another. For there are certain acts that they manifest insofar as they are natural bodies, and through which they exhibit an affinity to inanimate objects. There are other acts that, besides being natural bodies, they manifest insofar as they grow, and through which they have an affinity to plants. There are other acts that they manifest insofar as they have a sensitive soul, and through which they have an affinity to beasts. Then there are other acts that they manifest insofar as they are rational and discerning, and through which they have an affinity to the angels. Each of the above acts and movements that issue from human beings has many varieties and is grounded in different motives and causes. It can also be considered from different aspects, and it is affected by a large number of impediments and different hindrances, some of them natural, some of them a matter of chance, some of them coercive. When a person considering this topic fails to distinguish these acts from each other and to consider them from every aspect, he is confused by these facets and cannot discern the right way to consider them. As a result, he is overwhelmed by perplexity and his uncertainties and doubts proliferate. On our part, we shall set out these movements clearly and discriminate between them, and then we shall discuss the basic nature of compulsion and choice. The issue will then become much simpler and accessible to understanding, and it will not seem abstruse, with God's will. 90.2

I therefore say as follows. Whatever the different varieties and discrete aspects an act admits, it requires four elements in order to be manifested. The first is the agent who manifests it. The second is the matter in which it is 90.3

اتّخاذها في المادّة وربّما كانت الصورة هي الفعل بعينه فهذه الأشياء الأربعة هي ضروريّة في وجود الفعل وظهوره وقد يحتاج إلى الآلة والزمان والبيئة الصحيحة ولكن ليست بضروريّة في كلّ فعل. ولمّا كانت مسألتك عن الفعل الإنسانيّ الذي يتعلّق بالاختيار وجب أن نذكره[1] أيضاً. ثمّ إنّ كلّ واحد من الأشياء التي هي ضروريّة في وجود الفعل ينقسم قسمين فمنه قريب ومنه بعيد. أمّا الفاعل القريب فبمنزلة الأجير الذي ينقل آلات البناء في اتّخاذ الدار والفاعل البعيد بمنزلة الذي يهندس الدار ويأمر بها ويتقدّم بجميع آلاتها. وأمّا الهيولى القريبة فبمنزلة اللبن للحائط والخشب للباب والهيولى البعيدة بمنزلة العناصر الأولى[2]. وأمّا الكمال القريب فبمنزلة السكنى في الدار والكمال البعيد بمنزلة حفظ المتاع ودفع أذى الحرّ والبرد وما أشبه ذلك.

٤،٩٠ وأمّا أنواع الأفعال التي ذكرناها فإنّما اختلفت بحسب أنواع القوى الفاعلة التي في الإنسان وذلك أنّ لكلّ واحدة من القوى الشهويّة والقوى الغضبيّة والقوى الناطقة خاصّ فعل لا يصدر إلّا عنها. وأمّا الأسباب والدواعي فبعضها الشوق والنزوع[3] وبعضها الفكر والرويّة وقد تتركّب هذه أيضاً. وأمّا العوائق التي ذكرناها فبعضها اتّفاقيّة وبعضها قهريّة وبعضها طبيعيّة. فالاتّفاقيّة بمنزلة من يخرج لزيارة صديقه فيلقاه عدوّ لم يقصده فيعوقه عن إتمام فعله وكمن ينهض لحاجة فيعثر أو يقع في بئر. والقهريّة بمنزلة من يشدّ يديه اللصوص ليعوقوه[4] عن البطش بهما أو كمن يقيّده السلطان ليمنعه من السعي والهرب منه. والطبيعيّة بمنزلة الفالج والسكتة وما أشبههما.

٥،٩٠ وههنا نظر آخر في الفعل ينبغي أن نتذكّره وهو أنّا ربّما نظرنا في الفعل لا من حيث ذاته ولكن من حيث إضافته إلى غيره مثال ذلك أنّا قد ننظر في فعل زيد من حيث هو طاعة لغيره أو معصية ومن حيث يحبّه عمرو ويكرهه خالد ومن جهة

---

١ الأصل وط: نذكرها. ٢ الأصل: الأوّل. ٣ الأصل: والنزاع. ٤ الأصل: ليعوقه.

realized. The third is the purpose to which it is directed. The fourth is the form that exists in advance in the mind of the agent and that he seeks to produce in matter by acting; and sometimes the form may be the act itself. These four elements are necessary for an act to be realized and manifested. There may also be a need for an instrument, for time, and for a sound structure, but these are not necessary for every act. As your question concerns the type of human action that is connected to choice, we must also mention that. Furthermore, each of the above elements necessary for an act to be realized divides into two categories, proximate and remote. An example of a proximate agent is the wage laborer who wields the building tools when making a house. An example of a remote agent is the person who designs the house, who gives instructions to build it, and orders all of the required tools to be brought. An example of proximate matter is the bricks used for the walls and the wood used for the door. An example of remote matter is the primary elements. An example of proximate perfection is the inhabiting of a house. An example of remote perfection is the preservation of material goods and the deflection of the harmful effects of heat and cold and the like.

As for the varieties of acts we mentioned, they differ according to the vari- 90.4
eties of active powers present in human beings. For the appetitive power, the irascible power, and the rational power each have a specific act that issues only from it. Some of the causes and motives consist in longing and desire, and others consist in thought and reflection; and these may form compounds. Some of the impediments we mentioned are a matter of chance, others are coercive, and still others are natural. An example of those due to chance is when a person goes out to visit a friend and comes across an adversary who had not been looking to find him, and who impedes him from completing his action, or when a person gets up to do something and stumbles or falls into a well. An example of the coercive is when thieves tie a person's hands in order to prevent him from striking them, or when a person is shackled by the authorities to prevent him from running away and fleeing. Examples of natural impediments are semi-paralysis, apoplexy, and the like.

There is a further way of considering acts that needs to be called to mind. 90.5
For we may sometimes consider an act not as it is in itself, but under the aspect of its relation to another person. For example, we may consider Zayd's action under the aspect of its constituting an act of obedience or disobedience toward another person, under the aspect of its being loved by ʿAmr and hated by

ما هو ضارّ لبكر ونافع لعبد الله وهذا النظر ليس يكون في ذات الفعل بل في إضافته إلى غيره.

٦،٩٠ وإذ قد نظرنا في الفعل وأنواعه وجهاته وحاجته في ظهوره ووجوده إلى الشرائط التي عددناها فإنّا ناظرون في الاختيار ما هو. فنقول إنّ الاختيار اشتقاقه بحسب اللغة من الخير وهو افتعال منه. وإذا قيل اختار الإنسان شيئاً فكأنّه افتعل من الخير أي فعل ما هو خير له إمّا على الحقيقة وإمّا بحسب ظنّه وإن لم يكن خيرًا له بالحقيقة فالفعل الإنسانيّ يتعلّق به من هذا الوجه وهو ما صدر عن فكر منه وإجالة رأي فيه ليقع منه ما هو خير له. ومعلوم أنّ الإنسان لا يفكّر ولا يجيل رأيه في الشيء الواجب ولا في الشيء الممتنع وإنّما يفكّر ويجيل رأيه في الشيء الممكن ومعنى قولنا الممكن هو الشيء الذي ليس بممتنع وإذا فرض وجوده لم يعرض عنه محال.

٧،٩٠ ولمّا كانت هذه الجهة من الفعل هي المتعلّقة بالاختيار وهي التي تُخصّ بالفعل الإنسانيّ وكانت محتاجة في تمام وجود الفعل إلى تلك الشرائط التي قدّمناها كان الناظر فيها أعني في هذه الجهة يعرض للغلط[1] والوقوع في تلك الجهات الأخر التي ليست متعلّقة بالإنسان ولا مبدؤها إليه وربّما نظر بحسب جهة من جهات الفعل وخلّى النظر في الجهات الأخر فيكون حكمه على الفعل الإنسانيّ بحسب تلك الجهة وذلك بمنزلة من ينظر في الفعل من جهة الهيولى المختصّة به التي لا بدّ له في وجوده منها ويتخلّى عن الجهات الأخر التي هي أيضاً ضروريّة في وجوده كالكاغد للكاتب فإنّه إذا نظر في فعل الكاتب من هذه الجهة أعني تعذّر الكاغد عليه ظنّ أنّه عاجز عن الكتابة من هذه الجهة ممنوع عن الفعل لأجلها وهذه جهة لم تتعلّق به من حيث هو كاتب ومختار للكتابة وكذلك إن عدم القلم والجارحة الصحيحة أو واحداً من تلك الأشياء المشروطة في وجود كلّ فعل إنسانيّ فحينئذ يبادر هذا الناظر بالحكم على الإنسان بالجبر ويمنع من الاختيار.

---

١ الأصل: الغلط.

Khālid, and from the perspective of its being harmful for Bakr and beneficial for ʿAbd Allāh. This way of considering things does not pertain to the act itself, but rather to its relation to another person.

Having considered acts, their different varieties and aspects, and the conditions required for them to be manifested and realized, we may now consider the nature of choice. So we say as follows. The term "choice" linguistically and morphologically derives from the term "good." When one says that a person chooses something, it is as though he does himself some good, that is, he does what is good for him, whether in fact or according to his opinion, even if it is not in fact good for him. So human action connects to it from this facet, and is what issues from a person as a result of thought and deliberation, in order that he should do what is good for him. We know that people do not think or deliberate about things that are necessary or impossible; they only think and deliberate about things that are possible. When we refer to what is "possible," we mean that which is not impossible, and the postulation of whose existence entails no absurdity. 90.6

This is the aspect of acts that is connected to choice and to which human action especially pertains, and it requires the conditions we have enumerated in order for an act to be fully realized. However, a person who considers this aspect is liable to lose his way and get tangled up in those other aspects that are not connected to human beings and do not have their origin in them. He might consider things based on one particular aspect of acts and fail to consider the other aspects, so that his judgment on human action would be based on that one aspect alone. That would be akin to a person's considering an act from the aspect of the matter that specifically pertains to it and is necessary for its realization, while abandoning the other aspects also necessary for its realization. One might illustrate this with the example of paper used by a writer. Should one consider the writer's action from this aspect—in circumstances when he is unable to get hold of paper, that is—one might suppose that he is incapable of writing from this aspect and that he is barred from acting on its account. Yet this aspect does not connect to him insofar as he is a writer and chooses to write. The same applies if he lacks a reed pen and a sound limb or any of those elements that are conditions for any human act to be realized. Someone who considers matters this way will then rush to the conclusion that the person is under compulsion and will deny his having a choice. 90.7

وكذلك تكون حال من ينظر في فعله من حيث هو مختار فإنّه إذا نظر في هذه الجهة وتخلّى عن الجهات الأخر التي هي أيضاً ضروريّة في وجوده فإنّه أيضاً سيبادر إلى الحكم عليه بأنّه فاعل متمكّن ويُمنع من الجبر وهكذا حال كلّ شيء مركّب عن بسيط فإنّ الناظر في ذلك المركّب إذا نظر فيه بحسب جزء من أجزائه الذي تركّب منه وترك أجزاءه الباقية تعرض له الشكوك الكثيرة من أجزائه الباقية التي ترك النظر فيها والفعل الإنسانيّ وإن كان اسمه واحداً فوجوده معلّق بأشياء كثيرة لا يتمّ إلّا بها فمتى لحظ الناظر فيه شيئاً واحداً منها وترك ملاحظة الباقيات عرضت له الشكوك من تلك الأشياء التي أغفلها. ٨،٩٠

والمذهب الصحيح هو مذهب من نظر في واحد واحد منها فنسب الفعل إلى الجميع وخصّ كلّ جهة بقسط من الفعل ولم يجعل الفعل الإنسانيّ اختياراً كلّه ولا جبراً[١] كلّه ولهذا قيل دين الله بين الغلوّ والتقصير. فإنّ من زعم أنّ الفعل الإنسانيّ يكفي في وجوده أن يكون صاحبه متمكّناً من القوّة الفاعلة بالاختيار فهو غال من حيث أهمل الأشياء الهيولانيّة والأسباب القهريّة والعوائق التي عدّدتها قبل وهذا يؤدّيه إلى التفويض. وكذلك حال من زعم أنّ فعله يكفي في وجوده أن ترتفع هذه العوائق عنه وتحصل له الأشياء الهيولانيّة فهو مقصّر من حيث أهمل القوّة الفاعلة بالاختيار وهذا يؤدّيه إلى الجبر. وإذا كان هذا على ما بيّنّاه ولخّصناه فقد ظهر المذهب الحقّ وفيه جواب مسألتك عن الجبر والاختيار. ٩،٩٠

ويُعلم علماً واضحاً أنّ الإنسان إذا امتنع عليه فعله لنقصان بعض هذه الأشياء التي هي ضروريّة في ظهور فعله أو عرضيّة فيه أو قهريّة أو اتّفاقيّة فهو منسوب إلى تلك الجهة مثال ذلك أنّه إن كان امتنع من الفعل لنقصان الهيولى أو أحد الأربعة الأشياء الضروريّة فهو عاجز وإن امتنع لعائق قهريّ أو اتّفاقيّ فهو معذور من تلك الجهة وبحسبها وعلى مقدارها. فأمّا من حضرته القوّة الفاعلة بالاختيار وارتفعت ١٠،٩٠

[١] الأصل وط: تفويضا.

The same thing will happen if someone considers his action insofar as he is endowed with choice. For if one considers this aspect and relinquishes the other aspects also necessary for his act to be realized, one will also rush to the conclusion that he is a capable agent and deny his being under compulsion. This is how it is with all things that are compounds formed out of simpler elements. For if a person considers that compound on the basis of only one of the parts that compose it and leaves out the other parts, he is assailed by numerous doubts concerning the parts he left out. Even though human action is designated by a single term, its realization is contingent on many things indispensable for its completion. So, when the person considering it only has regard for one of these elements and omits the others, he is assailed by doubts concerning the elements he has neglected. 90.8

The right approach is that taken by those who give separate consideration to each of these elements and refer action to all of them, who assign every aspect a share in the act, and who do not consider human acts to be entirely a matter of choice or entirely a matter of compulsion. That is why it has been said: God's religion lies between excess and deficiency. For those who assert that all that is required for human action to be realized is that the agent possess the power to act through choice go too far and neglect the material elements, coercive causes, and impediments we enumerated earlier. This leads them to affirm the position of delegation. Likewise, those who assert that, for their acts to be realized, it suffices that these impediments be removed and that the material elements be vouchsafed them fall short to the extent that they neglect the power to act through choice. This leads them to affirm the position of compulsion. If our explanation and concise account of the matter stands, the correct view has emerged, and it provides a response to your question about compulsion and choice. 90.9

It is plain knowledge that if a person is unable to act because of the absence of some of the elements necessary for his act to be manifested, accidental to it, coercive, or a matter of chance, this is referred to the relevant aspect. For example, if he fails to act because the matter or one of the other necessary four elements is lacking, he is judged to be powerless. If he fails to act because of a coercive or chance impediment, he is exempt from blame from that aspect and in accordance and proportion to it. By contrast, when a person possesses the power to act through choice; when those hindrances have been lifted from him and all relevant impediments removed from him; when, additionally, 90.10

تلك الموانع عنه وأزيحت علله فيها كلّها ثمّ كان ذلك الفعل ممّا ينظر فيه على طريق الإضافة أن يكون طاعة لمن تجب طاعته أو معونة لمن تجب معونته أو غير ذلك من وجوه الإضافات الواجبة ثمّ امتنع من الفعل فهو ملوم غير معذور لأنّه قادر متمكّن ولأجل ذلك تلحقه الندامة من نفسه والعقوبة من غيره أو العيب والذمّ. وهذه الجهة التي تختصّ الإنسان من جهات الفعل المتعلّقة بالفكر وإجالة الرأي المسمّى بالاختيار هي ثمرة العقل ونتيجته ولولا هذه الجهة لما كان لوجود العقل فائدة بل يصير وجوده عبثاً ولغواً. ونحن نتيقّن أنّ العقل أجلّ الموجودات وأشرف ما منّ الله تعالى به ووهبه للإنسان ونتيقّن أيضاً أنّ أخسّ الموجودات ما لا ثمرة له ولا فائدة في وجوده وهو بمنزلة[١] اللغو والعبث فإذن أجلّ الموجودات على هذا الحكم هو أخسّ الموجودات هذا خلف لا يمكن أن يكون فليس هذا الحكم بصادق فنقيضه هو الصادق.

مسـألة

لم حنّ بعض الناس إلى السفر من لدن طفولته إلى كهولته ومنذ صغره إلى كبره حتّى ١،٩١
إنّه يعقّ الوالدين ويشقّ الخافقين صابرًا على وعثاء السفر وذلّ الغربة ومهانة الخمول ومذلّة المجهول وهو يسمع قول الشاعر [مجزوء الكامل]

إِنَّ ٱلْغَرِيبَ بِحَيْثُ مَا   حَطَّتْ رِكَائِبُهُ ذَلِيلُ
وَيَدُ ٱلْغَرِيبِ قَصِيرَةٌ   وَلِسَانُهُ أَبَدًا كَلِيلُ
وَٱلنَّاسُ يَنْصُرُ بَعْضُهُمْ   بَعْضًا وَنَاصِرُهُ قَلِيلُ

وآخر ينشأ في حضن أمّه وعلى عاتق ظئره ولا ينزع به حنين إلى بلد ولا يغلبه شوق إلى أحد كأنّه حجر جبله أو حصاة جدوله؟ لعلّك تقول مواضع الكواكب ودرجة

١ الأصل: وجوده بمنزلة.

the action at stake is of a kind that, considered from a relational perspective, represents an act of obedience to a person one is obligated to obey, an act of assistance to a person one is obligated to assist, or some other type of obligatory relational act; then if this person fails to act, he is subject to reproach and not given exemption, for he has the capacity and ability to act. That is why he experiences regret and receives punishment or is rebuked and blamed by others. This aspect, which, among the various aspects of action, pertains to human beings in particular and is connected to the kind of thinking and deliberation that is termed "choice," constitutes the benefit and product of reason. But for this, there would be no profit in the existence of reason, and its existence would be pointless and senseless. We know for certain that reason is the most exalted entity and the noblest thing that God bestowed on human beings. We also know for certain that the lowliest entities are those whose existence brings no benefit and no profit and that have the status of pointless and senseless things. So, if we followed this proposition, the most glorious entity would be the lowliest. Yet that is an impossible contradiction. Thus, this proposition cannot be true, and its contrary is true.

On the reason for the wanderlust experienced by certain people

Why do some people experience a hankering after travel from when they are children till they are fully grown men, from youth to old age, so much so that they disobey their parents and roam from one end of the world to the other, enduring the hardships of travel, the mortifications of living away from home, and the humiliations of being a nobody? After all, they know the words of the poet: 91.1

> The stranger is ill-regarded
> wherever his mounts set down.
> The stranger's reach is short,
> his tongue ever dull.
> People give aid to each other,
> but he has few to aid him.

Others grow up in their mothers' arms and on their wet nurses' shoulders, undisturbed by hankerings for other lands and unoppressed by a longing for

الطالع وشكل الفلك اقتضت له هذه الأحوال وقصرته على هذه الأمور فحينئذ تكون المسألة عليك في آثار هذه النجوم وتوزيعها هذه الأسباب على ما هي عليه من ظاهر التسخير أشدّ وتكلّف الجواب عنها آكد وأنكد.

الجواب

قال أبو عليّ مسكويه رحمه الله إنّ قوّة النزاع إلى المحسوسات تنقسم بانقسام الحواسّ ٢،٩١
وكما أنّ بعض المزاج تقوى فيه حاسّة البصر وبعضه تقوى فيه حاسّة السمع فكذلك الحال في القوّة النزاعيّة التي في تلك الحاسّة لأنّها هي التي تشتاق إلى تكمّل الحاسّة وتصييرها بالفعل بعد أن كانت بالقوّة. ومعنى هذا الكلام أنّ الحواسّ كلّها هي حواسّ بالقوّة إلى أن تدرك محسوساتها فإذا أدركتها صارت حواسّ بالفعل وإذا كان الأمر على ما وصفنا فليس بعجب أن يكون هذا المعنى في بعض الحواسّ قويًّا ويضعف في بعض فيكون بعض الناس يشتاق إلى السماع وبعضهم إلى النظر وبعضهم إلى المذوقات من المأكول والمشروب وبعضهم إلى المشمومات وألوان الروائح وبعضهم إلى الملبوسات من الثياب وغيرها وربّما اجتمع لواحد أن يشتاق إلى اثنين منها أو ثلاثة أو إليها كلّها.

ولكلّ واحد من هذه المحسوسات أنواع كثيرة لا تحصى ولأنواعها أشخاص بلا ٣،٩١
نهاية وهي على كثرتها وعددها الجمّ وخروجها إلى حدّ ما لا نهاية له ليست كمالات للإنسان من حيث هو إنسان وإنّما كماله الذي يتمّم إنسانيّته هو فيما يدركه بعقله أعني العلوم وأشرفها ما أدّى إلى أشرف المعلومات وإنّما صار البصر والسمع أشرف الحواسّ لأنّهما أخصّ بالمعارف وأقرب إلى الفهم والتمييز وبهما تُدرك أوائل المعارف ومنها يرتقى إلى العلوم الخاصّة بالنطق. وإذا كانت الحالة على هذه الصورة في الشوق إلى ما يتمّم وجود الحواسّ ويخرجها إلى الفعل وكان من الظاهر المتعارف أنّ بعض الناس

anything, as though they were a stone ever fixed on its slope or a pebble immobile in the stream. Perhaps you will say: It is the positions of the astral bodies, the degree of the ascendant, and the configuration of the celestial sphere that imposed these conditions on them and wedded them to these characteristics. You will then be confronted with a more exacting question concerning the influence of these stars and their ability to dispose these causes despite their ostensible state of subjugation, and with the more pressing and vexing task of responding to it.

Miskawayh's response

The power of desiring sensible objects divides into as many categories as there are senses. Just as the sense of sight may be stronger in one humoral mixture and the sense of hearing stronger in another, so it is with the desiderative power that is present in that sense: It is this that longs for the sense to attain its perfection and to emerge from actuality into potentiality. This means that all senses are senses in potentia until they perceive their objects; once they perceive them they become senses in actuality. If matters stand as we have described, it is hardly surprising that this element should be stronger in some senses and weaker in others, so that some people long to hear things, others to see things; some long for the tastes of food and drink, others for smells and different scents, and yet others for things like clothes and such that can be worn. Sometimes a single person will long for two or three things or for all of them together. 91.2

Each sensible object has countless species, and each species includes an infinite number of individuals. Despite their volume, vast quantity, and tendency toward an infinite number, they do not constitute perfections for human beings insofar as they are human beings; their perfection, that is, the perfection that completes their humanity, lies in what they perceive through reason—which is to say, in the various types of knowledge. The noblest are those that conduce to the noblest objects of knowledge. Their close association with learning and proximity to understanding and discernment is the reason why sight and hearing are the noblest senses. One grasps the first principles of the various forms of learning by means of them, and progress toward the forms of knowledge proper to rationality is made from them. Since this is how things stand concerning the longing for what completes the existence of 91.3

يشتاق إلى نوع منها فيحتمل فيه كلّ مشقّة وأذى حتّى يبلغ أربه فيه لم يكن بديعاً ولا عجباً أن يشتاق آخر إلى نوع آخر فيحتمل مثل ذلك فيه.

٤،٩١ إلّا أنّا وجدنا اللغة في بعض هذه عنيت فوضعت له اسماً وفي بعضها لم تعن فأهملته وذلك أنّا قد وجدنا لمن يشتاق إلى المأكول والمشروب إذا أفرطت قوّته النزاعيّة إليهما حتّى يعرض له ما ذكرت من الحرص عليهما والتوصّل إليهما وما[1] يحتمل معه ضروب الكلف والمشاقّ اسماً وهو الشره والنهم. ولم نجد لمن يعرض له ذلك في المشموم والمسموع اسماً وأظنّ ذلك لأجل كثرة ما يوجد من ذلك الضرب ولأنّ عيبه أفحش وما يجلبه من الآثام والقبائح أكثر. فقد ظهر السبب في تشوّق بعض الناس إلى الغربة وجولان الأرض وهو أنّ قوّته النزاعيّة التي تختصّ بالبصر تحبّ الاستكثار من المبصرات وتجديدها[2] ويظنّ أن أشخاص المبصرات تستغرق فهو يحتمل كثيراً من المشاقّ في الوصول إلى أربه من إدراك هذا النوع. وقد نجد من يحتمل أكثر من ذلك إذا تحرّك بقوّته النزاعيّة إلى سائر المحسوسات الأخر والاستكثار منها فتأمّل الجميع وأعد نظرك وتصفّح جزئيّاتها تجد الأمر فيها واحداً.

مسألة

١،٩٢ ما سبب رغبة الإنسان في العلم؟ ثمّ ما فائدة العلم؟ ما غائلة الجهل؟ ثمّ ما عائدة الجهل الذي قد شمل الخلق؟ وما سرّ العلم الذي قد طُبع عليه الخلق؟ فإنّ استشفاف هذه الفصول واستكشاف هذه الأصول يثيران علماً وحكماً جمّاً وإن كان فيها في البحث عنها وبعض أوائلها وأواخرها مشقّة على النفس وثقل على الكاهل. ولولا معونة الخالق من كان يقطع هذه التنائف[3] الملس؟ ومن كان يسلك هذه المهامه الخرس؟ ولكنّ الله تعالى وليّ المخلصين وناصر المطيعين ومغيث المستصرخين.

١ الأصل: ما. ٢ ط: وتحديدها. ٣ الأصل: النفايف؛ وصوابه من الهامش.

the senses and actualizes them, and since it is manifest and familiar that some people long for a certain species, enduring every hardship and trouble to fulfill their desire, then it is neither remarkable nor surprising that others should long for a different species and show a similar endurance.

Yet we find that some of these cases have been considered in the Arabic lexicon and assigned a name, whereas others have been neglected. So "greed" and "gluttony" are the words used when the power of desire in those who long for food and drink runs to such an excess that they experience the eagerness to obtain them that I described, one that entails all manner of strains and hardships. Yet there are no words for those who experience the same thing with respect to objects of smell or hearing. I believe that this is due to the prevalence of the former, the opprobrium that attaches to it, and the number of sins and wrongs it entails. It is now clear why some people long to leave their homes and roam the earth. For the desiderative power that specifically concerns sight loves to multiply and renew the objects of sight, and they think that individual objects of sight can be fully encompassed, so they endure many hardships in order to perceive that species. We may come across people of even greater endurance whose desiderative power drives them toward other kinds of sensible objects and the effort to multiply them. So ponder all of these together, review them afresh, and examine their particulars, and you will find that all conform to one and the same principle. 91.4

On why people desire knowledge, and on the benefits of knowledge

Why do people desire knowledge? What is the benefit of knowledge? What is the danger of ignorance? What is the advantage of the kind of ignorance that all people share? And what is the secret behind the kind of knowledge people possess by nature? For to strive to uncover these principles and penetrate into these specifics is to evoke a wealth of knowledge and sound judgment, even if the inquiry into them and their antecedents and consequents is arduous to the soul and onerous on the shoulder. But for the Creator's aid, who could cross these barren wastes and voiceless deserts? God protects the purehearted, supports the obedient, and helps those who cry out. 92.1

الجواب

٢،٩٢ قال أبو عليّ مسكويه رحمه الله مرّ لنا في عرض كلامنا على هذه المسائل ما ينبّه على جواب هذه المسألة ولكنّه لا بدّ من إعادة شيء منه يزيد في كشف الشبهة وإزالة الشكّ وهو أنّ العلم كمال الإنسان من حيث هو إنسان لأنّه إنّما صار إنسانًا بصورته التي ميّزته عن[1] غيره أعني النبات والجماد والبهائم وهذه الصورة التي ميّزته ليست في تخاطيطه وشكله ولونه والدليل على ذلك أنّك تقول فلان أكثر إنسانيّة من فلان فلا تعني به أنّه أتمّ صورة بدن ولا أكمل في الخلق التخطيطيّ ولا في اللون ولا في شيء آخر غير قوّته الناطقة التي يميّز بها بين الخير والشرّ في الأمور وبين الحسن والقبيح في الأفعال وبين الحقّ والباطل في الاعتقادات ولذلك قيل في حدّ الإنسان إنّه حيّ ناطق مائت فميّز بالنطق أعني بالتمييز بينه وبين غيره دون تخطيطه وشكله وسائر أغراضه ولواحقه.

٣،٩٢ وإذا كان هذا المعنى من الإنسان هو ما به صار إنسانًا فكلّما كثرت إنسانيّته كان أفضل في نوعه كما أنّ كلّ موجود في العالم إذا كان فعله الصادر عنه بحسب صورته التي تخصّه كان فعله أجود فإنّه[2] إذا كان فعله أجود كان أفضل وأشرف مثل ذلك الفرس والبازي من الحيوان والقلم والفأس من الآلات فإنّ كلّ واحد من هذه إذا صدر عنه فعله الخاصّ بصورته كاملاً كان أشرف في نوعه ممّن قصّر عنه وكذلك الحال في النبات والجماد فإنّ لكلّ واحد من أشخاص الموجودات خاصّ صورة يصدر عنه فعله وبحسبه يشرف أو يخسّ إذا كان تامًّا أو ناقصًا فأيّ فائدة أعظم ممّا يكمّل وجودك ويتمّم نوعك ويعطيك ذاتك حتّى يميّزك عن الجماد والنبات والحيوانات التي ليست بناطقة ويقرّبك من الملائكة والإله عزّ وجلّ وتقدّس وتعالى وأيّ غائلة أدهى وأمرّ وأكلم وأطمّ ممّا ينكّسك في الخلق ويردّك إلى أرذل وجودك ويحطّك عن شرف مقامك إلى خساسة مقامات ما هو دونك؟

---

١ الأصل: من. ٢ الأصل: تخصّه فإنّه.

Miskawayh's response

In the course of discussing these questions we have already pointed to the response to this one, but, in order to dispel the present uncertainty and remove the present doubt even more fully, it is necessary to go over some of the discussion again. Knowledge represents the perfection of human beings qua human beings, for it is the form that renders them human beings and distinguishes them from other beings—that is, plants, inanimate objects, and beasts. The form that distinguishes them does not consist in their external lineaments, their shape, or their color. This is proved by the fact that when we say "So-and-so has a greater degree of humanity than so-and-so," we do not mean that the person in question has a more complete bodily form or is more perfect with regard to his physical lineaments, his color, or anything else besides his rational power, through which he distinguishes between good and evil things, right and wrong actions, and true and false beliefs. This is why human beings have been defined as rational mortal animals. So it is not their lineaments, their shape, and all their other ends and adjuncts, but their rationality that distinguishes them—that is to say, distinguishes them from other beings. 92.2

As this is the element of human beings that renders them human beings, the greater the degree of their humanity, the more excellent they are in their species. This also applies to every existent in the world: When its act issues in accordance with the form proper to it, its act is better, and the better its act, the more excellent and noble it is. For animals, we can take the goshawk and the horse as examples, and for tools, the reed pen and the axe. For when the act proper to its form issues perfectly from each, it is nobler in its species than those that fall short. Similarly with plants and inanimate objects. For every individual existent has a proper form from which its act issues and that renders it noble or base, depending on whether that act is complete or deficient. So is there anything that can yield greater benefit than that which perfects your existence, completes your species, and delivers your being, distinguishing you from inanimate objects, plants, and nonrational animals and bringing you close to the angels and God? Is there anything that can brook a danger more calamitous and vexatious, more injurious and disastrous, than that which pulls you lower down in creation, casts you back to the vilest level of your existence, and demotes you from your noble station to the base station of inferior entities? 92.3

٤،٩٢ أظنك تذهب إلى أنّ العلم يجب أن يفيدك لا محالة جاهاً أو سلطاناً أو مالاً تمكّن به من شهوات ولذّات فلعمري إنّ العلم قد يفعل ذلك ولكن بالعرض لا بالذات لأنّ غاية العلم والذي يسوق إليه ويكمل به الإنسان ليس هو غايات الحواسّ ولا كمال البدن وإن كان قد يتمّ به ذلك في كثير من الأحوال ومتى استعملته في هذا النوع فإنّه يكمّل صورتك البهيميّة والنباتيّة وكأنّه استُعمل في أرذل الأشياء وهو معدّ لأن يُستعمل في أشرفها.

مسألة

١،٩٣ ما سبب تصاغي البهائم والطير إلى اللحن الشجيّ والجرم النديّ؟ وما الواصل منه إلى الإنسان العاقل المحصّل حتّى يأتي على نفسه؟ وهذا جار في العادة ومعروف عند المتعرّفين للأمور.

الجواب

٢،٩٣ قال أبو عليّ مسكويه رحمه الله قد مرّ لنا في المسألة الثالثة من هذه المسائل كلام كثير في سبب قبول الإنسان بعض الأسماء وكراهية بعضها وثقل بعض الحروف وخفّة بعضها وما يلحق النفس من الأصوات المختلفة بالحدّة والجهارة وغير ذلك. ونحن نزيد في هذا الموضع ما يليق بزيادتك في المسألة فنقول إنّ النفس وإن كانت صورة فاعلة من حيث هي كمال لجسم طبيعيّ[١] فإنّها هيولانيّة منفعلة من حيث هي قابلة رسوم الأشياء وصورها ولذلك صار لها سببان أحدهما[٢] ما تفعل به والآخر[٣] ما كانت[٤] تنفعل به. فالنفس تقبل نسب الاقتراعات بعضها إلى بعض كما تقبل نفس الاقتراعات مفردة مركّبة وذاك أنّ أفراد الأصوات ومجموعها غير نسب بعضها إلى

١ الأصل وط: طبيعيّ إلى ذي حياة بالقوّة. ٢ الأصل وط: أحدهما إلى. ٣ الأصل: أخرى إلى؛ ط: والأخر إلى.
٤ الأصل وط: كان.

I believe you take the view that knowledge ought necessarily to yield benefits such as honor, power, or money, through which one might then obtain the objects of one's appetites and different kinds of pleasures. Upon my life, knowledge may produce that result, but contingently and not essentially. For the end of knowledge, to which it drives and through which human beings are perfected, does not consist in the ends of the senses or the perfection of the body, even though it might achieve these in many circumstances. Used for that type of purpose, it serves to perfect one's beastly and vegetative form, so that it is used for the vilest things when designed to be used for the noblest. 92.4

On why people and other animals respond so powerfully to certain kinds of sounds and musical effects

Why do beasts and birds listen so intently to a heartrending melody and a resonant voice? What element of this so impinges on people of intelligence and learning that it can even cause them to pass away? This occurrence is familiar and well-known to those with wide experience of the world. 93.1

Miskawayh's response

We already had much to say on the topic, in our response to the third question you posed in this book, about why human beings like some names and hate others, why they find some letters heavy and others light, and how the soul is affected by sounds that vary in sharpness, loudness, and other qualities. Here we will extend these points to the degree that your extension of the question requires. We respond as follows. Even though the soul is an active form insofar as it constitutes the perfection of a natural body, it is material and passive insofar as it receives the impressions and forms of things. That is why two kinds of causes pertain to it: those through which it acts, and those through which it is passively affected. The soul receives the proportional relations of the different impactions to one another, just as it receives the impactions themselves in single or compound forms. For both the individual sounds and their ensemble are not the same as their proportional relations to one another. Proportional relations are a form of relation, and the relational mode of consideration is not 93.2

بعض لأنّ النسبة هي إضافة ما والنظر الإضافيّ غير النظر في ذوات الأمور وكذلك تأثير هذا غير تأثير ذاك.

٣،٩٣ ولمّا كانت هذه النسب كثيرة مختلفة وجب فيها ضرورة ما يجب في الأشياء المتكثّرة أعني أنّ لها طرفين[١] أحدهما الزيادة والآخر النقصان ولها من هذين الطرفين[٢] اعتدال فإن كانت الأطراف كثيرة فالاعتدالات أيضاً كثيرة والنفس تأبى الزيادة والنقصان وتميل إلى الاعتدال ولأنّ لها قوى تظهر بحسب الأمزجة فلتلك القوى المختلفة إضافات مختلفة إلى نسب مختلفة واعتدالات مختلفة وقد اجتهد أصحاب الموسيقى في تمثيل هذه النسب وتحصيل هذه الاعتدالات بأن جعلوا لها أمثلة في مقولة الكمّ من العدد وإن كان بعضها بمقولة الكيف أحقّ لأنّ الصناعة مؤلّفة من هاتين المقولتين أعني الكمّ والكيف ولكن الكمّ الذي هو العدد أقرب إلى الأفهام ومثّلوا ما كان من الكيفيّة بالكمّيّة ثمّ لخّصوا كلّ واحدة منهما تلخيصاً تجده مبيّناً في كتبهم.

٤،٩٣ وإذا قد قلنا ما الذي يصل إلى النفس من آثار الأصوات وما المحبوب منه وما المكروه على طريق الإجمال من القول فقد تبيّن أنّ الإفراط منه والخروج إلى إحدى الجهتين يؤثّر بحسب ذلك وقد كان تبيّن في مواضع كثيرة أنّ النفس والبدن كلّ واحد منهما مشتبك بالآخر وكثيراً ما يظهر أثر أحدهما في الآخر فإنّ الأحوال النفسيّة[٣] تغيّر مزاج البدن[٤] ومزاج البدن أيضاً يغيّر أحوال النفس فإذا قوي أثر ما في النفس حتّى يتفاوت به المزاج ويخرج عن اعتداله لم يقبل أثر النفس وعرض منه الموت لأنّ الموت ليس بأكثر من ترك النفس استعمال الآلات البدنيّة وقد علمنا أنّ دم القلب الذي له اعتدال ما إذا انتشر في البدن ورقّ بالسرور أكثر ممّا ينبغي أو عاد واجتمع إلى القلب بالغمّ أكثر ممّا ينبغي عرض من كلّ واحدة من الحالتين الموت أو ما يقارب الموت بحسب قوّة الأثر وما أكثر ما تؤثّر الأجسام في الأجسام تأثيراً طبيعيّاً فيتأدّى ذلك الأثر إلى النفس فيعرض لها حركة ما وتصير تلك الحركة سبباً لتأثير آخر

١ الأصل: طريقتين. ٢ الأصل: الطريقتين. ٣ الأصل: النفيسة. ٤ ط: البدان.

the same as the consideration of things themselves, just as the influence of the one is not the same as the influence of the other.

As these proportional relations are many and varied, what necessarily 93.3
applies to them is what applies to all things characterized by multiplicity. That is to say, they have two extremes, one a state of excess and the other a state of deficiency, and they have a balanced state relative to these extremes. If the extremes are many, the balanced states are also many. The soul rejects deficiency and excess, and inclines to the balanced state. As it possesses powers whose manifestation depends on the various mixtures, those powers have different relationships to different proportional relations and different balanced states. The masters of music strove to represent these proportional relations and to study these balances by assigning to them representations from the category of quantity using numbers, even though the category of quality would seem more appropriate for some. For the craft is formed out of these two categories, that is, quantity and quality; but quantity—which consists in numbers—is easier to grasp, so they represented the aspects of quality by means of quantity, and then presented each of these summarily, as you will find expounded in their books.

We have outlined in a general way what the effects of the different sounds 93.4
that reach the soul are, and which are enjoyable and which odious, so it will be clear that any excess in this regard and deviation toward one of the two sides must affect people accordingly. It has been shown at many junctures that the soul and the body are closely intertwined, and that the one often manifests its effect on the other, for the states of the soul alter the humoral mixture of the body, and the humoral mixture of the body also alters the states of the soul. So, if a certain effect grows so strong in the soul that the humoral mixture is impaired and departs from its balanced state, it ceases to receive the effect of the soul and death ensues, for death consists in nothing more than the soul's ceasing to use the bodily instruments. We know that if the blood of the heart, which possesses a particular balance, spreads through the body and becomes finer than it ought to be because of joy, or returns to concentrate in the heart more than it should because of grief, both situations result in death, or something just short of death, depending on the strength of the effect. It is very common for bodies to exercise a natural effect on bodies and for that effect to be conveyed to the soul, provoking a movement in the latter that becomes the cause of another effect in the body, which leaves it shaken and makes it

في الجسم يكون به انتفاضه[1] وخروجه عن الاعتدال وإذا تأمّلت ذلك في الأشياء المغضبة والمحزنة إذا كانت قويّة تبيّن لك ذلك فهذا كاف في هذا الموضع وإن أحببت الاتّساع فيه فعليك بكتب الموسيقى فإنّها تشفيك إن شاء الله.

مسألة

لم كلّما شاب البدن شبّ الأمل؟ قال أبو عثمان النهديّ قد أتت عليّ مائة وثلاثون[2] سنة وأنكرت كلّ شيء إلّا الأمل فإنّه أحدّ ما كان. ما سبب هذه الحال؟ وعلى ماذا يدلّ الرمز فيها؟ وما الأمل أوّلاً؟ وما الأمنيّة ثانياً؟ وما الرجاء ثالثاً؟ وهل تشتمل هذه على مصالح العالم؟ فإن كانت مشتملة فلم تواصى الناس بقصر الأمل وقطع الأماني وبصرف الرجاء إلّا في الله تبارك وتعالى وإلى الله؟ فإنّه ساتر العورة وراحم العبرة وقابل التوبة وغافر الخطيئة وكلّ أمل في غيره باطل وكلّ رجاء في سواه زائل؟ ١،٩٤

الجواب

قال أبو عليّ مسكويه رحمه الله هذه المسألة قد أخذ فيها فعل من أفعال النفس فقرن بفعل من أفعال الطبيعة التي بحسب البدن[3] والمزاج البدنيّ ثمّ وقعت المقايسة بينهما وهما يتباينان لا يتشابهان فلذلك عرض التعجّب منها وذلك أنّ الأمل والرجاء والمنى من خصائص القوّة الناطقة فأمّا الشيب والنقصانات التي تعرض للبدن وعجز القوى التابعة للمزاج فهي أمور طبيعيّة في آلات تكلّ بالاستعمال وتضعف على مرّ الزمان وأمّا أفعال النفس فإنّها كلّما تكرّرت وأديمت فإنّها تقوى ويشتدّ أثرها فهي بالضدّ من حال البدن. مثال ذلك أنّ النظر العقليّ كلّما استُعمل قوي واحتدّ وأدرك[4] في الزمان ٢،٩٤

١ ط: انتقاصه. ٢ ط: وثمانون. ٣ الأصل وط: البدن إلى الطبيعة. ٤ الأصل: وأدركت.

depart from the balanced state. If you ponder this phenomenon in connection with the things that occasion anger or sadness in strong degrees, it will become plain to you. This suffices for this context; if you wish to explore the topic more fully, then turn to the books of music, for they will meet your need, God willing.

On why older people are more liable to hope; on the meaning of "hope" and related terms

Why is it that the grayer one's hair becomes, the brighter one's hopes grow? 94.1
Abū ʿUthmān al-Nahdī said: I reached 130, and I abjured everything but hope, for that is keener than ever. What is the cause of this condition? And what hidden message does it contain? First, what is "hope"? Second, what is "wishing"? And third, what is "anticipation"? Do these phenomena promote worldly welfare? If they do, then why do people exhort each other to limit their hopes, to abandon their wishes, and to make God the sole object of their hope and anticipation? For He conceals sources of shame, takes pity on the shedding of tears, accepts repentance and forgives transgression, and all hope pinned elsewhere is vain, all anticipation ephemeral.

Miskawayh's response

This question took an act of the soul and connected it with an act of nature, of 94.2
the sort that depends on the body and the bodily mixture, and then a comparison was struck between the two, though they are distinct and do not resemble each other. This is why it provoked a sense of astonishment, for hope, anticipation, and wishes are qualities proper to the rational power; gray hair, the deficiencies that affect the body, and the failure of the powers subject to the humoral mixture are natural features arising in instruments that tire through exercise and weaken with the passage of time. By contrast, the acts of the soul grow stronger and their effect intensifies through repetition and continuous performance; this is the opposite of what applies to the body. For example, intellectual reflection becomes stronger and keener the more it is exercised, achieving in a short time what it had previously taken a long time to achieve and swiftly apprehending things that had previously seemed obscure. Sensory

القصير ما يدركه في الزمان الطويل ولحق الأمر الذي كان خفياً عنه بسرعة والنظر الحسّيّ كلّما استُعمل كلّ وضعف ونقص أثره إلى أن يضمحلّ.

٣،٩٤ فأمّا الفرق بين الأمل والرجاء وبين الأمنيّة فظاهر وذاك أنّ الأمل والرجاء يعلقان بالأمور الاختياريّة وبالأشياء التي لها هذا المعنى فأمّا الأمنيّة فقد تتعلّق بما لا اختيار له ولا رويّة فإنّه ليس يمنع مانع من تمنّي المحال والأشياء التي لا تمييز فيها ولا لها والأمل أخصّ بالمختار والرجاء كأنّه مشترك وقد يرجو الإنسان المطر والخصب وليس يأمل إلّا من له قدرة ورويّة وأمّا المنى فهو كما علمت شائع في الكلّ ذاهب كلّ مذهب فقد يتمنّى الإنسان أن يطير أو يصير كوكباً أو يصعد إلى الفلك فيشاهد أحواله وليس يرجو هذا ولا يأمله ثمّ قد يرجو[1] المطر وليس يأمل إلّا منزل القطر ومنشئ الغيث فهذه فروق واضحة.

٤،٩٤ فأمّا قولك لم تواصى الناس بقصر الأمل وقطع الأماني وصرف الرجاء إلّا في الله تعالى؟ فأقول لأنّ سائر الأشياء المأمولة والمرجوّة والمتمنّاة منقطعة المدد متناهية العدد ثمّ هي متلاشية في أنفسها مضمحلّة بائدة فاسدة لا يثبت شيء منها على حال واحدة لحظة واحدة فلو وصل الواصل إليها وبلغ نهمته منها لأوشك ان يتلاشى ويضمحلّ ذلك الشيء في نفسه أو يتلاشى ويضمحلّ الأمل فيه أو رجاؤه وتمنّيه فأمّا ما اتّصل من هذه بالله تعالى ذكره فهو أبديّ غير منقطع ولا مضمحلّ بل الله تعالى دائم الفيض به أبديّ الجود منه تعالى اسمه وتقدّس ولا قوّة إلّا به وهو حسبنا ومعيننا وناصرنا وهادينا إلى صراط مستقيم.

مسألة

١،٩٥ لم صارت[2] غيرة المرأة على الرجل أشدّ من غيرة الرجل على المرأة؟ هذا في الأكثر والأقلّ وكيفما كان ففيه خبأ وهو المشدّد على أحدهما والمخفّف عن الآخر. وقد أدّت

١ الأصل: يرجوا. ٢ الأصل: صار.

vision tires and grows weaker when exercised, and its effect decreases until it disappears.

The distinction between the terms “hope,” “anticipation,” and “wishing” is obvious. For hope and anticipation attach to voluntary matters, and to things that bear this aspect. Wishing, by contrast, may attach to things that are not the subject of voluntary choice or deliberation; for there is nothing to prevent us from wishing for the impossible and for things that involve no discrimination. Hope pertains more narrowly to subjects that have voluntary choice, whereas anticipation seems to carry both meanings. A person may anticipate rain and fertility, whereas hope can only attach to a person endowed with the capacity to act and deliberate. Wishes, as you know, are diffuse and tend in every direction. A person may wish he could fly, become a star, or ascend to the heavens and view his life from there, but he cannot anticipate it or hope for it. Furthermore, we might anticipate rain, but we can only put our hope in the one who brings down the rain and creates the downpour. These are clear distinctions. 94.3

To your question “Why do people exhort each other to limit their hopes, to abandon their wishes, and to make God the sole object of their hope and anticipation?” my response is as follows. All objects of hope, anticipation, and wishing are limited in duration and finite in number. They are evanescent in themselves and bound to succumb to corruption, fade away, and perish; none of them abides in the same state for a single moment. So, were someone to gratify his desire for them by attaining them, they would soon evanesce and fade away in themselves, or the hope, anticipation, and wish attached to them would soon evanesce and fade away. By contrast, the things that relate to God are everlasting and neither come to an end nor fade away; rather, God diffuses them eternally and is everlastingly generous with them. There is no strength but through Him; He is our sufficiency, our helper, our supporter, and our guide to the straight path. 94.4

On why women are more jealous than men; on the nature and moral status of jealousy

Why are women more jealous over men than men are over women? The phenomenon is encountered in varying degrees, yet however that may be, there is a hidden force here that explains why its grip on one group is tighter and on the 95.1

الغيرة جماعة إلى تلف النفوس وإلى زوال النعم وإلى الجلاء عن الأوطان. ثمّ قلت في المسألة التالية لهذه ما الغيرة أوّلاً؟ وما حقيقتها؟ وكيف أصلها وفصلها؟ وعلى ماذا يدلّ اشتقاقها؟ وهل هي محمودة أو مذمومة؟ وهل صاحبها ممدوح أم ملوم؟ فإنّ إثارة هذا أبلغ بك إلى الفوائد وأجرى معك إلى الأمد وبوقوفك عليها تعرف غيرها وتتخطّى إلى ما عداها.

الجواب

٢،٩٥ قال أبو عليّ مسكويه رحمه الله أمّا الغيرة فهي خلق طبيعيّ عامّ للإنسان والبهائم وهو ممدوح إذا كان على شرائط سائر الأخلاق أعني إذا وُضع في خاصّ موضعه ولم يُتجاوز به المقدار الذي يجب ولم ينقص عنه على مثال ما ذكرناه فيما مضى من سائر الأخلاق كالغضب والشهوة فإنّ هذه أخلاق طبيعيّة وإنّما يُحمد منها ما لم يخرج عن الاعتدال أو أصيب به موضعه الخاصّ به. وحقيقة الغيرة هي منع الحريم وحماية الحوزة لأجل حفظ النسل والنسب فكلّ من كانت غيرته لأجل ذلك ثمّ لم يتجاوز ما ينبغي حتّى يحكم بالتهمة الباطلة فيصدّق بالظنون الكاذبة ويبادر إلى العقوبة على ذلك ولم ينقص عمّا ينبغي حتّى يتغافل عن الدلائل الواضحة ويترك الامتعاض من الرؤية والسماع إذا كان حقّاً وكان معتدل الخلق بين هذين الطرفين يغضب كما ينبغي وعلى ما ينبغي فهو محمود غير ملوم.

٣،٩٥ فأمّا من فرط أو أفرط في الغيرة فسبيله سبيل من تجاوز الاعتدال في سائر الأخلاق إلى الزيادة أو النقصان فقد بيّنّا أنّ الزيادة والنقصان في كلّ خلق يهجم بصاحبه على ضروب من الشرّ وأنواع من البلايا والمكاره ويكون هلاكه على مقدار زيادته أو نقصانه منها ومن شرائطها المذكورة في الأخلاق. فأمّا زيادة حظّ الأنثى على الذكر من الغيرة أو الذكر على الأنثى فليس بلازم طريقة واحدة ولا جار على وتيرة واحدة. بل ربّما زاد ذكر على أنثاه في هذا المعنى وربّما زادت أنثى على ذكرها فيه

other is slacker. With some people, jealousy has led to the destruction of life, the loss of blessings, and the abandonment of their home. Then in the subsequent question you asked: What is jealousy in the first place? What is its basic reality? What is one to say about its principles and its specifics? What does its etymological derivation reveal? Is it commendable or is it blameworthy? Is the person who experiences it deserving of praise or censure? By bringing up these topics, you are more certain to arrive at instructive insights and reach the goal you desire, and by uncovering them you will also gain knowledge of other topics and pass on to topics beyond them.

Miskawayh's response

Jealousy is a natural ethical trait that is present among both human beings and beasts. 95.2 It is praiseworthy if it conforms to the conditions that apply to all traits, that is, if it is put in its proper place and neither oversteps nor falls short of the requisite measure, after the pattern of all the ethical traits we mentioned earlier, such as anger and appetite. For these are natural ethical traits; the ones praised are those that do not depart from the balanced state and attain the place proper to them. The basic reality of jealousy consists in guarding one's womenfolk and the protection of their chastity for the sake of preserving progeny and lineage. So the person who deserves to be commended and not censured is the one whose jealousy is directed to that end, and who neither oversteps what is right by ruling on the basis of groundless accusations and by giving credence to false suppositions and, on their basis, hastening to mete out punishment, nor falls short of what is right by overlooking clear indications and by failing to be roused to rancor by things seen and heard if these are true. He is the one who, with his ethical trait balanced between these extremes, feels anger in the right manner and for the right reasons.

Those who are remiss or immoderate in jealousy are like those who, in all 95.3 ethical traits, overstep the balance, be it to excess or deficiency. We have shown clearly that excess and deficiency in every ethical trait expose the person to many kinds of evils and all manner of adversities and woes; and one's ruin is proportionate to the degree of excess or deficiency exhibited and to the conditions mentioned earlier in our discussion of ethics. There is no single pattern or principle for whether the female has a greater share of jealousy than the male, or the male a greater share than the female. Sometimes the male may

كما يعرض لهما ذلك في قوّة الغضب وغيره من الأخلاق على أنّ الذكر أولى بالمحاماة وأخصّ بهذا الخلق لأنّه تُستعمل فيه قوّة الغضب والشجاعة وهذا أولى بالذكر منه بالأنثى وإن كانت الأنثى تشارك فيه الذكر.

٤،٩٥ وههنا خلّة لا بأس بذكرها والتنبيه عليها فإنّ كثيرًا من الناس يضلّ عن وجه الصواب فيها وهي أنّ الغيرة إذا هاجت قوّتها وكان سببها الشهوة وحبّ الاستئثار وأن يختصّ الإنسان بحال لا يشاركه فيها غيره وكان هذا العارض له في غير حرمته ولا من أجل حفظ نسبه وزرعه فهو أمر قبيح وإن كانت على شرائطها التي ذكرت فهو أمر حسن جميل وأمّا سقوط هذه القوّة دفعة فهجنة قبيحة فقد نجد في بعض الحيوان من لا تعرض له الغيرة كالكلب والتيس والخنزير[١] ويُسبّ به الإنسان إذا ذُكر به وسمّي باسمه ونجد أيضاً بعضها غيوراً محامياً كالكبش وغيره من فحول الحيوان فيُمدح بذكره الإنسان إذا شُبّه به وسُمّي باسمه فلست أعرف وجه السبّ بالتيس والمدح بالكبش إلّا لما يظهر من هذا الخلق في أحدهما دون الآخر. فهذه حال الغيرة وحقيقتها وما يجب أن يُمدح منها أو يُذمّ.

مسـألة

١،٩٦ ما السبب في أنّ الذين[٢] يموتون وهم شبّان أكثر من الذين يموتون وهم شيوخ؟ الشاهد على ذلك أنّك تجد الشيوخ أقلّ ولولا ذلك لكانوا يكثرون لأنّهم كانوا يتجاوزون الشبيبة إلى الكهولة والكهولة إلى الشيخوخة فلمّا دبّ الحمام في ذوي الشباب أفناهم وتخطّى القليل منهم فبلغوا التشيّخ وهو قليل.

١ الأصل: والخنزير، زيادة من الهامش. ٢ الأصل: في الذين.

exceed his female partner in his response, while sometimes the female may exceed her male partner, as happens with the power of anger and other ethical traits. Yet protective action is more appropriate for males, and this trait is more specific to them, as it involves the exercise of the power of anger and courage; this is more appropriate to males than to females, though females also have a share.

There is no harm in mentioning and highlighting a particular aspect here, 95.4
as many people err on this point. It is repugnant if the power of jealousy is excited and this is caused by appetite, by the desire for sole possession and for exclusive enjoyment of a condition shared by nobody else, and if this response concerns women who are not one's own and is not directed to the preservation of one's lineage and seed. It is a good and fine thing if it conforms to the conditions I have mentioned. The sudden onslaught of this power, however, is a repugnant defect. We find certain animals unaffected by jealousy, such as dogs, billy goats, and swine. The names of these animals serve as terms of abuse when used to describe human beings. We also find some that are prone to jealousy and protective behavior, such as rams and other stud animals, and these names serve as terms of praise when human beings are likened to them. I know of no other reason why "male goat" serves as a term of abuse and "ram" as a term of praise apart from the manifestation of this particular trait in one and not the other. These are the facts concerning jealousy, its basic reality, and which expressions of it are to be praised and which blamed.

On why more people die young than die old

What is the reason there are more people who die young than die old? This is 96.1
attested by the fact that we see fewer old people around us; otherwise there would be more of them, for they would pass from youth to middle age, and from middle age to old age. Death, prevalent among the young, depletes their ranks, and only a fraction pass from that stage to old age, so they are few and far between.

الجواب

قال أبو عليّ مسكويه رحمه الله الحياة تابعة لمزاج ما خاصّ بإنسان إنسان وذلك ٢،٩٦
المزاج له بمنزلة النقطة من الدائرة أعني أنّه شيء واحد والخروج عنه إلى النقط التي حواليه ممّا يقرب منه أو يبعد عنه بلا نهاية وذلك أنّ لكلّ إنسان وبالجملة لكلّ حيوان اعتدالاً خاصّاً به بين الحرارة والرطوبة والبرودة واليبوسة فإذا انحرف عن ذلك الاعتدال إلى أحد الأطراف كان مرضه أو هلاكه. ثمّ إنّ الأمور التي تخرجه إلى الأطراف كثيرة من الأغذية والأشربة والهواء الواصل إليه بالاستنشاق وغيره وحركاته الطبيعيّة وغير الطبيعيّة ممّا يخرجه عن هذا الاعتدال كثيرة والآفات الأخرى التي تطرأ من خارج ممّا لا تُحتسب كثيرة. وإذا كانت الأسباب التي يخرج الإنسان بها عن الاعتدال كثيرة بلا نهاية والأسباب التي يثبت بها على الاعتدال الخاصّ[1] به قليلة ويسيرة لم يكن ما ذكرته عجباً بل العجب لو اتّفق ضدّه.

ولولا أنّ العناية الموكلة بحفظ الحيوان كلّه والإنسان من بينها شديدة والوقاية ٣،٩٦
له تامّة بالغة لكان لا يكون بين وجوده وعدمه كبير زمان فتأمّل جميع ما ذكرته من الآفات الداخلة والخارجة عن بدن الإنسان وحركاتها المختلفة أعني منازعة الناريّة فيه إلى حركة العلوّ ومنازعة المائيّة منه إلى حركة السفل ثمّ حرص كلّ واحد منهما بطبيعته على إفناء الآخر وإحالته ثمّ المجاهدة الواقعة في حفظ الاعتدال بينهما حتّى لا تزيد قوّة أحدهما على الآخر مع كثرة الشهوات والمنازعات إلى ما هو لا محالة زائد في أحدهما ناقص من الآخر تجد الأمر محفوظاً بعناية شديدة إلى أكثر ممّا يمكن في مثله من الحفظ حتّى يأتي شيء طبيعيّ لا سبيل إلى مقاومته.

ومثل ذلك سراج يُحفظ بالفتيلة والدهن والموادّ تجيئه من خارج أعني الدهن ٤،٩٦
الكثير الذي هو سبب إطفائه والنار العظيمة التي هي كذلك والرياح العاصفة التي لا طاقة له بها ولا سبيل إلى حفظه معها فإذا سلم من جميع ذلك مدّة طويلة فلا بدّ من

---

١ الأصل: خاصّ.

Miskawayh's response

Life is contingent on the humoral mixture peculiar to each person. This mixture is like a point within a circle; that is, it is a single thing and any departure from it toward the points that surround it, whether near or far, can extend ad infinitum. All people, and all animals generally, have a balance between heat, moisture, coldness, and dryness peculiar to them, and if they deviate from the balance to one of the extremes, they succumb to illness or death. Moreover, there are many things that displace them to the extremes, including, among other things, foods, drinks, and the air that reaches them through breathing. Many of their natural and nonnatural movements displace them from this balance, and many other unforeseeable impairments befall them from external sources. Given the plethora of innumerable causes that displace people from the balanced state, and given the paucity and sparsity of causes that keep them in that state, there is little to wonder at in the situation you described—but it would indeed be worthy of wonder if the opposite obtained. 96.2

But for the enormous care directed to the preservation of all animals and human beings in particular, and the consummate and extensive protection afforded to them, there would not be a great length of time between their existence and nonexistence. So let your thoughts dwell on all I have mentioned: on the impairments internal and external to the human body and their different movements, that is, the way the element of fire it incorporates inclines to an upward movement and the element of water it incorporates inclines to a downward movement; on the ardent desire to annihilate and transmute the other natural to each; on the struggle required to preserve the balance, so that the power of the one does not exceed that of the other, set against the existence of numerous appetites and inclinations toward things that are calculated to increase the one and decrease the other. You will then find that everything is preserved with enormous care to the greatest extent possible in such circumstances, until finally some natural element that cannot be withstood presents itself. 96.3

One might compare this to a lamp preserved through a wick and oil while different material elements come to it from the outside—large quantities of oil and strong flames that cause it to be extinguished, and strong winds that it cannot resist and in the face of which it cannot possibly be preserved. If it survives all this for a long period of time, it unavoidably succumbs to natural exhaustion. That is, across the passage of time the heat inevitably depletes 96.4

الفناء الطبيعيّ أعني أنّ الحرارة تستغرق لا محالة ما يغتذي به على طول الزمان فيكون الفناء به ومن أجله فإنّ هذا مثل صحيح مطابق للممثّل به وإذا تفقّدت الحرارة الغريزيّة وحاجتها إلى ما يحفظ قواها بلا زيادة ولا نقصان وإفنائها الرطوبة الأصليّة مع الموادّ التي تأتيها من خارج وقوّتها على الإحالة وضعفها اطّلعت على ما سألت عنه وتبيّن لك ما ضربت به المثل.

مسـألة

ما السبب في طلب الإنسان فيما يسمعه ويقوله ويفعله ويروّي فيه الأمثال؟ وما فائدة المثل؟ وما غناؤه من[1] مأتاه؟ وعلى ماذا قراره؟ فإنّ في المَثل والمِثل والمماثلة والتمثيل كلاماً رائقاً وغاية شريفة. ١،٩٧

الجواب

قال أبو عليّ مسكويه رحمه الله إنّ الأمثال إنّما تُضرب فيما لا تدركه الحواسّ ممّا تدركه والسبب في ذلك أنسنا بالحواسّ وإلفنا لها منذ أوّل كونها ولأنّها مبادئ علومنا ومنها نرتقي إلى غيرها. وإذا أُخبر الإنسان بما لم يدركه أو حُدّث بما لم يشاهده وكان غريباً عنده طلب له مثالاً من الحسّ فإذا أُعطي ذلك أنس به وسكن إليه لإلفه له. وقد يعرض في المحسوسات أيضاً هذا العارض أعني أنّ إنساناً لو حُدّث عن النعامة أو الزرافة والفيل والتمساح لطلب أن يُصوّر له ليقع بصره عليه ويحصل تحت حسّه البصريّ ولا يقنع فيما طريقه حسّ البصر بحسّ السمع حتّى يردّه إليه بعينه. ٢،٩٧

وهكذا الأمر في الموهوبات فإنّ إنساناً لو كُلّف أن يتوهّم حيواناً لم يشاهد مثله لسأل عن مثله وكلّف مُخبِره أن يصوّر له مثل عنقاء مغرب فإنّ هذا الحيوان ٣،٩٧

---

[1] الأصل: وهو من.

what nourishes it, and exhaustion ensues accordingly. This is a sound comparison adequate to its target. If you examine the innate heat and its need for what preserves its powers without excess or deficiency, its complete consumption of the original moisture along with the different material elements that come to it from the outside, and its power or lack of power to exercise a transmuting effect, you will grasp the object of your inquiry and the basis of my comparison will become clear.

On why people seek likenesses

Why do people seek likenesses in all they hear, say, do, and ponder? What is the benefit of likenesses? How are they independent of their source, and where do they find their purchase? Likenesses and similitudes, the fact of being alike and the act of likening, are noble objects of concern, a subject for limpid words. 97.1

Miskawayh's response

Likenesses are struck for objects not perceived by the senses drawing on objects perceived by the senses, because of the familiarity and intimate relationship we have with the senses from the beginning of their development, and because they form the foundations of our knowledge, from which we progress to other kinds of knowledge. So if we inform a person about something he has never perceived or speak to him about something foreign to him, something he has never personally witnessed before, he asks for a model derived from the senses. Once furnished with this, he feels a sense of ease and familiarity because of his intimate acquaintance with the object of comparison. This phenomenon may also arise among sensible objects. Thus, were we to speak to someone about ostriches, giraffes, elephants, and crocodiles, he would ask for visual representations so that he could see them with his own eyes and subsume them under his sense of sight. He would not be content to use the sense of hearing for something that is to be grasped through the sense of sight, and he would finally refer the object to that specific sense. 97.2

The same applies to objects of imagination, for were a person tasked with imagining an animal the like of which he had never set eyes on, he would ask 97.3

وإن لم يكن له وجود فلا بدّ لمتوهّمه أن يتوهّمه بصورة مركّبة من حيوانات قد شاهدها. فأمّا المعقولات فلمّا كانت صورها ألطف من أن تقع تحت الحسّ وأبعد من أن تُمثّل بمثال الحسّ إلّا على جهة التقريب صارت أحرى أن تكون غريبة غير مألوفة والنفس[1] تسكن إلى مثل وإن لم يكن مثلاً لتأنس به من وحشة الغربة فإذا ألفتها وقويت على تأمّلها بعين عقلها من غير مثال سهل حينئذ عليها تأمّل أمثالها والله الموفّق لجميع الخيرات.

مسـألة

كيف قوي الوهم على أن ينقش في نفس الإنسان أوحش صورة وأمقت شكل وأقبح تخطيط ولم يقو على أن يصوّر أحسن صورة وألطف شكل وأملح تخطيط؟ ألا ترى أنّ الإنسان كلّما اعترض في وهمه أوحش شيء عرته شمأزيزة وعلته قشعريرة ولحقه صدوف ورهقه نفور؟ فلو قوي الوهم على تصوير أحسن الحسن تعلّل به الإنسان عند فراغ باله وخلوته. فما هذا وكيف هذا؟ ولا عجب فلهذا الإنسان من هذه النفس والعقل والطبيعة أمور تستنفد العجب وتحيّر القلب. جلّ من أودع هذا الوعاء هذه الطرائف وعرّضه لهذه الغايات وزيّن ظاهره وحسّن باطنه وصرّفه بين أمن وخوف وعدل وحيف وحجبه في أكثر ذلك عن لِمَ وكيف. ١،٩٨

[1] الأصل: النفس.

what it is like, and would demand that his informant represent it for him. Take the phoenix as an example; even though this animal does not exist, any attempt to imagine it must be based on a visual image composed out of animals that have actually been seen. It is all the more natural that the forms of intelligible things should be foreign and unfamiliar, for they are too subtle to become objects of sense perception and too remote to be provided with a sensible model except by way of approximation. The soul finds comfort in a likeness, even if it is not a true likeness, as it helps it alleviate the strangeness of the foreign. It becomes easier for it to contemplate their likes upon a more intimate acquaintance with intelligible things and an acquisition of the ability to contemplate them without a model through the eye of reason. Every good is attained through the grace of God.

On why we find it easier to represent extreme ugliness in our imagination than exquisite beauty

How it is that the imagination has the power to depict the most repulsive images, the most odious forms, and the ugliest limnings in the human soul, yet it lacks the power to depict the most beauteous images, the finest forms, and the most pleasing limnings? Don't you see that when a person's imagination is exposed to the most repulsive things, he is filled with disgust, overcome by shuddering, gripped by aversion, and overtaken by revulsion? Indeed, if the imagination were capable of representing the highest beauty, a person would make that his occupation whenever he was on his own and free from care. So what is the meaning of this? And what is the reason for it? No wonder! For there are things about human beings and their relation to the soul, the intellect, and nature that carry us to the ends of wonder and plunge our hearts into perplexity. Glory be to Him who deposited these rarities into these vessels and made the attainment of these ends possible, who adorned their exterior and beautified their interior, who disposed them between security and fear, between justice and wrongdoing, and withheld from them the knowledge of the "why" and the "how" in most of those matters. 98.1

الجواب

٢،٩٨ قال أبو عليّ مسكويه رحمه الله إنّ الحسن هو صورة تابعة لاعتدال مزاج[١] وصحّة مناسبات من الأعضاء بعضها إلى بعض في الشكل واللون وسائر الهيئات وهذه حال لا يتّفق اجتماع جميع أجزائها على الصحّة ولذلك لا تقوى الطبيعة نفسها على إيجادها في الهيولى على الكمال لأنّ الأسباب لا تساعد عليها أعني أنه لا يتّفق في الهيولى والأشكال والصورة والمزاج أن تقبل الصورة الأخيرة على غاية الصحّة. فإذا كانت الطبيعة تعجز عن إيجاد هذا الاعتدال وهذه المناسبة الصحيحة التي يتبعها الحسن التامّ فكم بالحريّ يكون الوهم أعجز عنه؟ وإنّما الوهم تابع للحسّ والحسّ تابع للمزاج والمزاج تابع أثر من آثار الطبيعة ومثال ذلك أنّ الأوتار الكثيرة إنّما يُطلب بها وبكثرة الدساتين عليها أن تخرج من بينها كلّها نغمة مقبولة وتلك النغمة إنّما يُتوصّل إليها بجميع الآلة وأجزائها من الأوتار والدساتين بالقرعات المختلفة فالنغمة وإن كانت واحدة فإنّها تتمّ بمساعدة جميع تلك الأجزاء فإذا خان واحد منها خرجت النغمة كريهة إمّا بعيدة من القبول وإمّا قريبة على قدر عجز الأسباب وقصور بعضها.

٣،٩٨ فكذلك الهيولى في حاجتها إلى مزاج ما بين اسطقصات وصور أخر[٢] كثيرة تصير بجميعها مستعدّة لقبول صور الحسن الذي هو اعتدال ما ومناسبة ما صحيحة بين أمزجة وأعضاء في الهيئة والشكل واللون وغيرها من الأحوال التي مجموعها كلّها هو الحسن. والحسن وإن كان أمرًا واحدًا وصورة واحدة فهو مثل النغمة الواحدة المقبولة التي تحتاج إلى هيئات كثيرة وصور مختلفة جمّة ليحصل من بينها هذا الاعتدال المقبول. والوهم في خروجه عن الاعتدال سهل الحركة فأمّا في حفظه إيّاه[٣] وتوصّله إليه فإنّه يحتاج إلى تعب شديد وأخذ مقدّمات كثيرة واستخراج اعتدال بينها وهكذا الحال في كلّ اعتدال فإنّ حفظه والثبات عليه صعب فأمّا الخروج عنه

١ ط: المزاج. ٢ ط: أخرى. ٣ الأصل: إيّاها.

Miskawayh's response

Beauty is a form contingent on a balanced humoral mixture and on the existence of sound relations between the different parts of the body as regards shape, color, and other external features. It is rarely the case that all components of this state are brought together in a sound manner. That is why nature itself is not capable of producing it in matter in a perfect way, for the operative causes do not provide assistance; that is, it does not often come about that the matter, the shapes, the form, and the humoral mixture are such that the last form is received in the soundest possible manner. If nature is incapable of generating the balanced state and the sound relation that results in complete beauty, is it a surprise that the imagination should be incapable of it? For the imagination depends on the senses, the senses depend on the humoral mixture, and the humoral mixture depends on an effect of nature. For example, what one desires from many strings set on many frets is that a pleasing note should issue therefrom; and that note is achieved through the whole of the instrument and its parts—the strings, the frets, and the different strokes applied to them. So the note, even though it is a single thing, is produced through the cooperation of all parts. If one part falters, the note that issues is repulsive, its relative distance from a sound that is pleasing being commensurate with the extent of the powerlessness of the causes and the inadequacy of some of them. 98.2

So it is with matter in its need for a particular mixture of elements and many other forms. All of these in combination prepare it to receive the forms of beauty, which consists in a particular balance and a particular sound relation between mixtures and bodily parts with regard to external aspect, shape, color, and other features that, taken jointly, constitute beauty. Even though beauty is a single thing and a single form, it resembles that single pleasing note which requires a large number of external features and an abundance of different forms in order for that pleasing balance to emerge. The imagination moves with facility when it is a matter of departing from the balanced state, whereas in order to attain and preserve that state, it must expend great effort and rely on many prerequisites that it must bring into balance. The same applies to every kind of balance; it is difficult to preserve and persist in, but it only takes 98.3

فهو بأدنى حركة فإن اتّفق أن يكون لذلك الاعتدال تمامات من خارج ومعاونات من أمور مختلفة كانت الصعوبة في تحصيله أشدّ.

مسـألة

لم صار السرور إذا هجم كان تأثيره أشدّ وربّما قتل؟ وقد حكى الثقة من تأثيره أمورًا. ١،٩٩
ولقد خُبّرت والدة بعض الناس أنّ ابنها وُلّي إمرة فبرقت وانحرفت وما زالت تنتفض حتّى ماتت. وقال لي ابن الخليل الحيرة التي تلحق واجد الكنز هي من إفراط فرحه وغلبة سروره ولذلك ما يبين على شمائله وتنمّ به حركاته[١] ويضيق عطنه عن كتمانه ما به وسياسته. ولا تكاد تجد هذا العارض في الغمّ والهمّ النازل الملمّ وقلّ ما وُجد من انشقّت مرارته وانتقضت بنيته وانحلّت معاقده ومآسره بخبر ساءه وناءه ومكروه غشيه وناله فإن كان فهو أيضاً قليل وإن ساوى عارض السرور فذاك أعجب والسرّ فيه أغرب.

الجواب

قال أبو عليّ مسكويه رحمه الله قد مرّ جواب هذه المسألة في عرض ما تكلّمنا عليه ٢،٩٩
في المسائل المتقدّمة وقلنا إنّ النفس تؤثّر في المزاج المعتدل عن البدن كما أنّ المزاج يؤثّر في النفس وبيّنّا جميع ذلك وضربنا له الأمثال. ولسنا نشكّ أنّ السرور يحمرّ منه الوجه وأنّ الخوف يصفرّ منه وما ذاك إلّا لانبساط الدم من ذاك في ظاهر البدن وغوره من الآخر إلى قعر البدن والحرارة التي في القلب هي التي تفعل هذا أعني أنها تنبسط فترُقّ الدم تارة وتنقبض فتغلّظه أخرى ويتبع ذلك الحال السرور ويتبع هذه

١ الأصل: يتم بحركاته؛ ط: وينمّ بحركاته.

the merest movement to depart from it. The difficulty of realizing it becomes even greater, should this balance require external elements to complete it and a variety of things to assist it.

On why sudden joy affects people so violently

Why does joy have such a violent effect when it assails one suddenly, so that it can even kill? A variety of stories about its effects have been recounted on good authority. When the mother of a certain man was notified that her son had assumed the office of governor, her vision blurred, she keeled over, and she went into convulsions until she died. Ibn al-Khalīl said to me: The bewilderment that comes over a person who discovers a hidden treasure is due to the extreme happiness and overpowering joy he experiences. This is the reason for his public behavior and his movements, and the reason why he finds it difficult to keep what is happening to him a secret and maintain it under control. Yet we hardly encounter this phenomenon when grief and sorrow descend upon us and overwhelm us. We rarely find that someone's gallbladder has ruptured, his physical constitution has become infirm, and his limbs have gone limp and sinews weakened because of a piece of news that vexed and oppressed him, or some evil that befell and overtook him. Though this does happen, it is rare. And when it has the same effect as joy, that is all the more astonishing and the secret behind it all the more remarkable. 99.1

Miskawayh's response

We have already answered this question in the course of discussing the earlier ones.[18] We said that the soul has an effect on the mixtural balance of the body, just as the humoral mixture has an effect on the soul, and we clarified all of that and provided examples. We know for a fact that joy causes the face to redden and that fear causes it to blanche—one causes the blood to expand over the exterior of the body, and the other to sink into the recesses of the body. The heat in the heart is responsible for this; at one time it expands and causes the blood to become fine, and at another time it contracts and causes it to thicken. Joy is attended by the former condition, grief by the latter. If it runs to excess in either direction, it results in a departure from the balanced state, and 99.2

الغمّ فإذا كان زائد المقدار في أيّ الطرفين كان تبعه الخروج عن الاعتدال وبحسب الخروج عن الاعتدال يكون الموت الوحيّ أو المرض الشديد.

مسألة

١،١٠٠ ما السبب في أنّ إحساس[١] الإنسان بألم يعتريه أشدّ من إحساسه بعافية تكون فيه[٢] حتّى لو شكا[٣] يوماً كان[٤] أيّاماً وهو يمرّ في لباس العافية فلا يجد لها وقعاً وإنّما يتبيّنه إذا مسّه وجع أو دهمه فزع ولهذا قال الشاعر [كامل]

وَٱلْحَادِثَاتُ وَإِنْ أَصَابَكَ بُؤْسُهَا ... فَهُوَ ٱلَّذِي أَنْبَاكَ كَيْفَ نَعِيمُهَا

وممّا يحقّق هذا أنّك تجد شكوى المبتلى أكثر من شكر المعافى وإنّما ذلك لوجدان أحدهما ما لا يجده الآخر.

الجواب

٢،١٠٠ قال أبو عليّ مسكويه رحمه الله السبب في ذلك أنّ العافية إنّما هي حال ملائمة موافقة للحال الطبيعيّ من المزاج المعتدل الموضوع لذلك البدن والملاءمة والموافقة لا يُحسّ بهما وإنّما الحسّ يكون للشيء الطارئ الذي لا موافقة فيه والسبب في ذلك أنّ الحسّ إنّما أعطي الحيوان ليتحرّز به من الآفات الطارئة عليه وليكون ألمه بما يرِد عليه ممّا لا يوافقه سبباً لتلافيه وتداركه قبل أن يتفاوت مزاجه ويسرع هلاكه فأنشئت[٥] لذلك أعصاب من الدماغ وفُرّقت[٦] في جميع البدن ونُسجت[٧] بها الأعضاء التي[٨] تحتاج إلى إحساس كما بُيّن ذلك في التشريح وفي منافع الأعضاء فكلّ موضع من البدن فيه عصب فهناك حسّ وكلّ موضع خلا منه فلا حسّ فيه ولم يخل منه إلّا ما لا حاجة به إلى حسّ.

١ الأصل: في إحساس. ٢ الأصل: فيها. ٣ الأصل: شاك. ٤ الأصل: لأنّ. ٥ الأصل: وأنشئ. ٦ الأصل: وفرق.
٧ الأصل: ونسج. ٨ الأصل: الذي.

death or severe illness supervenes, depending on the extent of the departure from the balanced state.

On why we experience states of suffering more intensely than states of well-being

Why do people feel the pain that befalls them more acutely than they feel the state of well-being they are in? A single day's suffering leads to a dozen days' moaning, whereas going about cosseted in well-being makes no impression on them, and they only notice it when visited by some hurt or affected by some fear. This is why the poet said: 100.1

> Though the wheel of fate brings its miseries,
> the suffering teaches you the meaning of joy.[19]

This is corroborated by how we find the complaints of the afflicted outstripping the gratitude of the healthy; this must be because the former experience something the latter do not.

Miskawayh's response

This is because well-being is a state congruent with and in agreement with the natural state that results from the balanced mixture set for that body. Congruence and agreement are not things that can be sensed; things that supervene and do not involve agreement are what is sensed. Sensation was granted to animals to use as protection against injuries that befall them, and so that the pain produced in them by things that happen but that do not agree with them should cause them to remedy and redress these things before their mixture becomes impaired and they quickly succumb to destruction. The science of anatomy and discussions of the benefits of the parts of the body have explained why nerves were generated from the brain, dispersed throughout the whole body, and woven into those parts of the body that require sensation.[20] So wherever in the body there are nerves there is sensation, and those parts of the body that do not have them lack sensation; the only parts of the body that do not have them are those that have no need for sensation. 100.2

٣،١٠٠ وإنّما وفّرت الأعصاب على الأعضاء الشريفة لتصير أذكى حسّاً ولتكون بما يرد عليها من الآفات أسرع إحساساً وكلّ ذلك ليبادر إلى إزالة ما يجده من الألم بالعلاج ولا يغفل عنه بتوانٍ ولا غيره ولو خلا الإنسان من الحسّ ومن الألم ومكانه لكان هلاكه وشيكاً من الآفات الكثيرة وأمّا الحال الملائمة فلا يحتاج إلى إحساس بها[1] وهذه حال جميع الحواسّ الخمس في أحوالها الطبيعيّة وأنّها لا تحسّ بما يلائمها وإنّما تحسّ بما لا يوافقها.

٤،١٠٠ أقول إنّ حسّ اللمس الذي هو مشترك بجميع البدن إنّما يدرك ما زاد أو نقص عن اعتداله الموضوع له فإنّ البدن له اعتدال من الحرارة مثلاً فإذا لاقاه من حرارة الهواء ما يلائمه ويوافقه لم يحسّ به أصلاً فإن خرج الهواء عن ذلك الاعتدال الذي للبدن إمّا إلى برد أو حرّ أحسّ به فبادر إلى تلافيه وإصلاحه وكذلك الحال في البرد والرطوبة واليبوسة فأمّا سائر الحواسّ فلكلّ واحد منها اعتدال خاصّ به لا يحسّ بما يلائمه وإنّما يحسّ بما يضادّه ويزيله عن اعتداله كالعين فإنّها لا تحسّ بالهواء وبكلّ ما لا لون له ولا كيفيّة تزيلها عن اعتدالها وكذلك السمع وباقي الحواسّ وهذا باب مستقصى في مواضعه من كتب الحكمة فليُرجع إليها.

مسألة

١،١٠١ قد نرى من يضحك من عجب يراه ويسمعه أو يخطر على قلبه ثمّ ينظر إليه ناظر من بُعد فيضحك لضحكه من غير أن يكون شريكه فيما يضحك من أجله وربّما أربى ضحك الناظر على ضحك الأوّل فما الذي سرى من الضاحك المتعجّب إلى الضاحك الثاني؟

[1] الأصل: به.

The noble parts of the body were provided with nerves in order for them to be able to sense things more acutely and to sense the injuries that come upon them more quickly. The purpose of this is to make us hasten to eliminate the pain we experience through treatment, and not neglect it through indolence or other factors. Were a person to be free from sensation and from pain and its locus, it would not be long before he succumbed to destruction through a multiplicity of injuries. Congruent states, by contrast, do not need to be sensed. This is how things stand with all of the five senses in their natural states; they do not sense the things that are congruent with them, but rather, sense the things that do not agree with them. 100.3

The sense of touch, shared across the entire body, perceives that which exceeds or falls short of the balance set for it. For example, the body has a particular balance with respect to heat, and it does not sense the temperature of the air that it encounters if it is congruent with it or agrees with it. By contrast, the body senses the air if it departs from the particular balance of the body, whether in the direction of cold or heat, and rushes to remedy or rectify it. The same applies to cold, moisture, and dryness. Each of the other senses has a balanced state proper to it; it does not sense that which is congruent with it, but rather only senses that which opposes it and displaces it from its balanced state. Take the eye: It does not sense the air or any of the objects that lack color and a modality that would displace it from its balanced state. The same applies to hearing and to the other senses. This topic is discussed thoroughly in the appropriate sections of the books of philosophy, so let these be consulted. 100.4

On why seeing someone laughing causes others to laugh

We sometimes see a person laughing at some remarkable thing he sees or hears or thinks of, and then another person sees him and begins to laugh at his laughter without sharing in the object of his laughter. And sometimes the second person's laughter makes the first person laugh even harder. What is it that passes from the person who's laughing out of amazement to the second person laughing? 101.1

الجواب

قال أبو علي مسكويه رحمه الله إنّ النفس الشخصيّة تتأثّر من النفس الشخصيّة ضروباً من التأثيرات بعضها سريعة وبعضها بطيئة وقد مرّ لنا كلام كثير في هذا المعنى. فمن تأثيراتها السريعة بعضها في بعض النوم والتثاؤب وكثير من الراحات فإنّه قد اشتهر في الناس أنّ من نعس أو تناعس عند المستيقظ الذي لا فتور به أنعسه ونوّمه وكذلك المتثائب والمتكاسل عن عمل. وقد يعرض قريب من ذلك في النشيط للعمل أن ينشط أوّلاً ثمّ يعدي الثاني[1] ولكنّ الأوّل أنشط وأبين والسبب في ذلك أنّ النفس وإن كانت كثيرة بالأشخاص فهي واحدة في ذاتها فليس بعجب أن يتأدّى من بعض الأشخاص إلى بعض آثار نفسيّة سريعة بلا زمان بتّة. وليس يحتاج هذا المعنى إلى شيء يسري على طريق النقلة والحركة الجسميّة التي تقطع في زمان بل يكفي في ذلك أن تتلاحظ النفسان فإنّ التأثير من أحدهما في الآخر يقع بلا زمان. وينبغي أن يُتذكّر في هذا المعنى اللطيف الأثر الذي يقبله الناظر من المنظور إليه فإنّ هذا وإن كان بوساطة الجسم فإنّه يكون بلا زمان بتّة فلست تقدر أن تقول إنّ الناظر إلى كوكب من الكواكب الثابتة يكون بين فتحة عينه وبين رؤيته إيّاه زمان. ٢،١٠١

مسـألة

لم اشتدّ عشق الإنسان لهذا العالم حتّى لصق به وآثره وكدح فيه مع ما يرى من صروفه وحوادثه ونكباته وغيره وزواله بأهله؟ ومن أين استفاد الإنسان هذا العرض؟ ١،١٠٢

١ الأصل: أوّلا فلكن.

Miskawayh's response

One individual soul can have many kinds of effects on another individual soul, some rapid and others tardy. We have already said much about this. The rapid effects they have on one another include sleeping, yawning, and other forms of relaxation. It is a well-known fact that when a person grows drowsy or feigns drowsiness in the presence of a person who is wide awake and feels no tiredness, he causes the latter to grow drowsy and sends him off to sleep. The same applies to people who yawn and shirk work. Something similar may happen with someone who sets to work energetically, so that his energy passes over to another person, though the first person remains more energetic and this quality is more evident in him. The reason for this is that the soul is one in its essence, even though it is characterized by multiplicity through the multiplicity of individuals. So it is hardly surprising that certain rapid effects of the soul should be conveyed from some individuals to others without any time lag. This process does not require that anything should "pass" through any physical transfer and motion that unfolds in time. It is enough for the two souls to see each other, for the effect the one exercises on the other occurs without any lapse of time. On this subtle point, one should recall the effect on the observer of the object of observation; for though accomplished by means of the body, it requires no lapse of time whatsoever. Thus we cannot say that, when a person observes a fixed star, there is a lapse of time between the moment he opens his eyes and the moment he sees it. 101.2

On why human beings are so attached to the world despite the misfortunes and suffering they experience in it

Why are human beings so passionately attached to this world—clinging to it, cherishing it, and laboring after it—despite the vicissitudes, accidents, calamities, and other woes they see it contains, and despite the extinction to which its inhabitants are exposed? Whence did human beings acquire this attribute? 102.1

الجواب

قال أبو عليّ مسكويه رحمه الله وكيف لا يشتدّ عشقه للعالم وهو طبيعيّ وجزء له؟ إنّما مبدؤه منه ومنشؤه فيه وتولّده عنه ألا تراه يبتدئ وهو نطفة فينشأ نشوء النبات أعني أنّه يستمدّ غذاءه بعروق موصولة برحم أمّه فيستقي المادّة التي تقيمه كما تستقي عروق الشجر فإذا تمّ وصار ﴿خَلْقًا ءَاخَرَ﴾ وأنشأه الله تعالى حيوانًا أخرجه من هناك فحينئذ يغتذي بفمه ويتنفّس ويصير في مرتبة الحيوان غير الناطق ولا يزال كذلك إلى أن يقبل صورة النطق أوّلاً فيصير إنسانًا ثمّ يتدرّج في إنسانيّته حتّى ينتهي إلى غاية ما يؤهّل له من المراتب فيها وليس ينتهي إلى الرتبة الأخيرة التي هي غاية الإنسانيّة إلّا الأفراد من الناس والواحد بعد الواحد في الأزمنة الطوال والفترات الكثيرة. ٢،١٠٢

وعامّة الخلق وجمهور الناس واقفون في منزلة قريبة من البهيميّة وغاية نطقهم وتمييزهم أن يرتّبوا تلك البهيميّة ترتيبًا ما فيه نظام عقليّ وأمّا أن يفارقوها ويصيروا إلى الحدّ الذي طالبت به فلا وإنّما يصير إلى هناك الحكيم التامّ الحكمة الذي يستوفي جميع أجزائها علمًا وعملاً أو نبيّ له تلك المنزلة بالإلهام والتوفيق ثمّ لا بدّ من المادّة البشريّة التي يأخذها من هذا العالم وإن كان بلا عشق ولا لصوق شديد ولا إيثار. وهذا المعنى واسع البحر طويل الميدان قد أكثر فيه الناس وفيما أومأت إليه وصرّحت به كفاية والسلام. ٣،١٠٢

مسألة

لم قيل لولا الحمق لخربت الدنيا؟ وما في حياة الحمق من الفائدة على الدين والدنيا؟ وهل الذي قالوه حقّ؟ ١،١٠٣

Miskawayh's response

How could they not be passionately attached to the world when they are natural beings and form part of it? For they originate in it, develop in it, and are born out of it. Don't you see how they begin as a drop of sperm and develop like plants, deriving their nourishment by means of roots connected to their mothers' wombs, and drawing their sustenance the way a tree does? God transfers them from that location when they are completed and become «another creature»,[21] and He molds them into animals; then they take nourishment through the mouth and breathe, and reach the rank of nonrational animals. They remain thus until they receive the form of rationality for the first time and become human beings. Then they progress in their humanity until they reach the ultimate ranks they are intended to attain—and only a few isolated individuals across many eons arrive at the final rank that constitutes the ultimate end of humanity. 102.2

The vast majority of people occupy a station close to the beastly one, and their rationality and discrimination do not go beyond imparting a certain order with a rational structure to this beastly nature. For them to abandon this nature and reach the point you demanded is out of the question. This is only attained by philosophers who achieve the fullness of philosophical wisdom and exhaust all of its parts through both knowledge and action, or by prophets, who occupy that station by means of divine inspiration and guidance. Even so, they need the material substance of human existence, which they derive from this world, though they do so without passionate attachment and without clinging to it greatly or cherishing it. This topic is inexhaustible and wide-ranging, and people have discussed it at length. What I have indicated and stated suffices. I have no more to say. 102.3

On why people say the world would fall to ruin if it weren't for fools

Why was it said: But for fools, the world would fall to ruin? What worldly or religious benefit do the lives of fools bring? Is what was said true? 103.1

الجواب

قال أبو عليّ مسكويه رحمه الله قد تبيّن أنّ الإنسان مدنيّ بالطبع وأنّه لا يعيش متوحّدًا كما يعيش الطير والوحش لأنّ تلك مكتفية بما خُلق لها من الرياش والهداية إلى مصالحها وأقواتها والإنسان عار لا طاقة له ولا هداية إلى قوته ومصلحته إلّا بالاجتماع والتعاون وهذا الاجتماع والتعاون هو المدنيّة. ثمّ إنّ المدنيّة لها حال تسمّى عمارة ولها حال تسمّى بالإضافة للأولى خرابًا[1] فأمّا حال عمارتها فإنّما يتمّ بكثرة الأعوان وانتشار العدل بينهم بقوّة سلطانهم[2] الذي ينظّم أحوالهم ويحفظ مراتبهم ويرفع الغوائل عنهم وأعني بكثرة الأعوان تعاون الأيدي والنيّات بالأعمال الكثيرة التي بعضها ضروريّة في قوام العيش وبعضها نافعة في حسن الحال في العيش وبعضها نافعة في تزيين العيش فإنّ اجتماع هذه هي العمارة. فأمّا إن فات المدنيّة واحدة من هذه الثلاث فإنّها خراب وإن فاتها اثنتان أعني حسن الحال والزينة جميعًا فهي غاية في الخراب. وذلك أنّ الأشياء الضروريّة في قوام العيش إنّما يتبلّغ بها الزهّاد الذين لا يعمرون الدنيا وليسوا في عدد العمّار. ٢،١٠٣

وعمارة الدنيا التامّة وقوامها بثلاثة أشياء هي كالأجناس العالية ثمّ تنقسم إلى أنواع كثيرة. وأحد الأشياء الثلاثة إثارة الأرض وفلاحتها بالزرع والغرس والقيام عليها بما يصلحها ويستعدّ لما يراد منها أعني الآلات المستخرجة من المعادن كالحجارة والحديد المستعملة في إثارة الحرث والطحن وإساحة الماء على وجه الأرض من العيون والأنهار[3] والقُنِيّ والدوالي وغير ذلك. والثاني آلات الجند والأسلحة المستعملة لهم في ذبّ الأعداء عن أولئك الذين وصفناهم ليتمّ لجماعتهم العيش ويُقام غرضهم فيما اجتمعوا له بالمعاونة. وللجند أيضًا صنّاع وأصحاب فهم يعدّون لهم الخيل بالرياضة ٣،١٠٣

١ الأصل: تسمّى عمارة والأولى بالإضافة إلى الأولى خرابا. ٢ ط: السلطان. ٣ الأصل: بالأنهار.

Miskawayh's response

It has been established that human beings are political by nature and that they do not live in isolation as the birds and wild beasts do. For the latter can satisfy their own needs, having been provided with plumage and with the ability to attain the things they need for their welfare and nourishment. Human beings, by contrast, are naked and powerless and lack the ability to attain the things they need for their welfare and nourishment without cooperating and forming communities; and this constitutes political association. Furthermore, political association can be characterized by a state designated as "flourishing," and by another state designated, relative to the first, as "ruin." This state of flourishing is realized when helpers abound and justice reigns through their power of political authority, which orders their affairs, preserves their stations, and relieves them from adversities. By an "abundance of helpers" I mean that people's physical powers and intentions should work together to effect a plethora of actions, some of which are necessary for life to be sustained, others of which are conducive to living in a good condition, and yet others are conducive to the embellishment of life. Flourishing is the conjunction of all these aspects. If political association lacks any one of these three, it is in a state of ruin. If it lacks two—specifically, both the good condition and embellishment of life—then it is in an advanced state of ruin. For it is only ascetics who content themselves with just the things that are absolutely necessary to sustain life, and they do not cause the world to flourish, nor are they to be counted among those who can do so. 103.2

The subsistence of the world, its complete flourishing, is accomplished through three things, which are like high-level genera that then subdivide into numerous species. The first consists in working and cultivating the land through planting and sowing, and tending to it with means that put it in good order and prepare it for the use desired of it. I refer here to using tools derived from mined materials such as stones and iron for tilling, grinding, and irrigating the land with water that comes from springs, rivers, canals, waterwheels, and the like. The second consists in the implements of soldiers and the weapons they use to protect the people we have described from enemies, so that the people can live as a group and fulfill the purpose they have come together to achieve through cooperation. Additionally, soldiers have craftsmen and attendants who train horses for them, and who fashion shields that serve for protection, as well as other weapons that serve for repelling and driving off the enemy. The third 103.3

والجنن للوقاية وسائر الأسلحة للدفع والذبّ. والثالث الجلب والتجهيز الذي يتمّ بنقل[1] ما يعزّ في أرض إلى أرض وما يكون في بحر إلى برّ. وهذه الأحوال الثلاث زين وجمال يزيد في حسن أحوالها ولها أصحاب يختصّون بجزء جزء من أقسام الأحوال الثلاثة التي ذكرناها.

٤،١٠٣ وينبغي أن تعلم أنّ العيش غير جودة العيش وحسن الحال في العيش لتعلم أنّ العمارة متعلّقة بجودة العيش وحسن حاله وقد عرفنا أنّ هذه الأمور لا تتمّ إلّا بالمخاطرات الكثيرة وركوب الأهوال واحتمال المشاقّ والتعرّض للمخاوف ولو تبلّغ الناس بضروراتهم وطرحوا فضول العيش وعملوا بما يقتضيه مجرّد العقل لصاروا كلّهم زهّاداً ولو كانوا كذلك لبطل هذا النظام الحسن والزين الذي[2] في العالم وعاشوا عيشة قشفة كعيشة أهل القرى الضعيفة القليلة العدد أو كعيشة سكّان الخيم وبيوت الشعر وأظلال القصب وهذه هي الحال التي تسمّى خراب المدن.

٥،١٠٣ فأمّا قولك هل يسمّى القوّام بعمارة الدنيا حمقى؟ فأقول إنّه لا يجوز أن يسمّيهم بذلك كلّ أحد وذلك أنّ الذين وصفنا أحوالهم من سكّان القرى وأطراف الأرض والذين لا يكلمون لتحسين معايشهم هم أولى بهذا النبز من الذين استخرجوا بعقولهم وصفاء أذهانهم ودقّة نظرهم هذه الصناعات الكثيرة الجميلة العائدة بمنافع الناس وإنّما يسوغ ذلك لمن اطّلع على جميع العلوم والمعارف وميّزها ونزّلها منازلها فترك ما ترك منها عن خبر وعلم وآثر ما آثر منها على رويّة وبعد يقين. فإنّ الحكماء إنّما تركوا النظر في عمارة الدنيا لأنّها عائدة بعمارة الأبدان ولمّا اطّلعوا على شرف النفس على البدن ورأوا لها عالماً آخر وجمالاً يليق بذلك العالم وصناعات وعلوماً ومسالك ركوبها أشقّ وأعسر من ركوب مخاطرات الدنيا ولزوم مجّتها والدؤوب فيها بالنظر والعمل أصعب وأكثر

---

١ الأصل: ينقلون. ٢ الأصل: التي.

consists in procuring and supplying, which is accomplished by transporting to another place things rare in one place, and to the land things that are found in the sea. These three elements constitute an adornment and beautification that further ameliorate the condition of the world, and there are people specifically devoted to each of the subdivisions of the three elements we have mentioned.

You must understand that to live is not the same as to live excellently or in a 103.4
good condition; you will then understand that flourishing is connected to how excellent life is. We know for a fact that these things can only be achieved by incurring many risks, exposing oneself to fear, enduring hardships, and confronting terror. People would all become ascetics were they to content themselves with necessities, cast aside the superfluities of life, and act purely on the basis of what reason demands. And were that to happen, the good and beautiful order present in the world would disappear, and they would lead the abstemious lives led by people who dwell in sparsely populated, defenseless villages, or led by people who live in tents, yurts, or reed huts. This is the state of polities designated as ruin.

To your question "Are the people who cause the world to flourish to be 103.5
called fools?" I respond: It is not permissible for everyone to call them that. For this derogatory appellation is more fittingly applied to the people we have described—those who dwell in villages and remote parts of the earth and who show themselves unequal to improving their living conditions—than to those who have used their intelligence, perspicacity, and acumen to develop this plethora of fine crafts that work to the advantage of people. That is only admissible for those who have acquainted themselves with, and distinguished between, all forms of knowledge and learning, assigning them to their proper stations, abstaining from those they abstain from out of experience and knowledge, and choosing those they choose based on reflection and secure conviction. The reason why philosophers have abstained from inquiring into the flourishing of the world is that it conduces to the flourishing of the body. They ascertained that the soul is superior to the body, and perceived that there is another world that belongs to it, with a beauty that befits it, and with its own crafts, forms of knowledge, and pathways. It is more taxing and arduous to venture on these paths than to venture on the hazards of the mundane world, and more demanding and toilsome to persist and persevere in these crafts and forms of knowledge through inquiry and action than to persevere and act in the mundane world. Therefore they chose contentment, and contented

تعباً من الدؤوب والعمل في الدنيا آثروا التبلّغ[1] وتبلّغوا بالقوت الضروريّ من الدنيا على أنّهم هم الذين عملوا لهؤلاء أصول الصناعات والمهن وتركوهم وإيّاها لمّا لم يكملوا لغيرها ثمّ اشتغلوا وشغلوا من جالسهم بالأمر الأعلى الأفضل.

مسألة

١،١٠٤ ما السبب في قلق من تأبّط سوأة واحتضن ريبة واستسرّ فاحشة؟ حتّى قيل من أجل ما يبدو على وجهه وشمائله كاد المريب يقول خذوني. وما هذا العارض؟ ومن أين مثاره؟ وبأيّ شيء زواله؟

الجواب

٢،١٠٤ قال أبو عليّ مسكويه رحمه الله هذه المسألة إنّما تعترض الحيرة فيها لمن لا يعترف بالنفس وأنّ حركات البدن الاختياريّة كلّها إنّما تكون بها ومنها. فأمّا من علم أنّ النفس هي المدبّرة لبدن الحيّ ولا سيّما الإنسان المختار الذي مدبّره النفس المميّزة العاقلة فلا أعرف لحيرته وجهاً. وذاك أنّ النفس إذا عرفت شيئاً واستعملت ضدّ ما يليق بتلك المعرفة لحقها من الاضطراب ما يلحق الطبيعة إذا كانت حركتها يمنة فحُرّكت يسرة بقوّة دون قوّتها أو مساوية لها فإنّ الاضطراب يظهر هناك مثل ما يظهر ههنا.

مسألة

١،١٠٥ لم إذا كان الواعظ صادقاً نجع كلامه ونفع وعظه وسهل الاقتداء به وخفّت الطاعة له والأخذ بما قاله؟ ولم إذا كان بخلاف ذلك لم يؤثّر كلامه وإن راق ولا ينفع وعظه

[1] الأصل: آثروا بلغ.

themselves with as much nourishment in the mundane world as is necessary. Yet it is they who created the foundations of the different crafts and trades for that other people, and who left them to that other people when they showed themselves unequal to any other tasks. Then the philosophers occupied themselves and their disciples with the loftier and more excellent matters.

On the anxiety experienced by people who have something to hide

What is the reason for the anxiety experienced by the person who hides something shameful, harbors something dubious, and conceals some wicked deed? His face and behavior give him away such that people remark: The guilty person might as well declare, "Here I am, take me in." What is this phenomenon all about? How is it provoked? And through what means can it cease? 104.1

Miskawayh's response

This question only provokes perplexity in people who do not acknowledge the reality of the soul and the fact that all the voluntary movements of the body have their origin in it and are accomplished through it. I cannot see how anyone who knows that the soul governs the body of living beings, and particularly of human beings who are vested with voluntary choice and governed by the rational discriminating soul, could find any cause for perplexity. For when the soul is aware of something and it produces acts that are contrary to what befits that awareness, it experiences the kind of disturbance that nature experiences when its movement is to the right but it is moved to the left by a force inferior to or equal to its own force. Disturbance appears in the former, just as it appears in the latter. 104.2

On why we are more likely to heed a preacher who practices what he preaches

Why is it that when a preacher is honest, his words have an effect, his preaching achieves results, and it is easy to follow his example, to obey him and adhere to what he has said? And why is it that if the opposite holds true of him, his words 105.1

وإن بلغ؟ وما في انسلاخه من حقيقة ما يقول مع حقيقة القول وصحّة الدلالة وسطوع الحجّة؟ وكيف صار فعله مشيّداً لقوله وخلافه موهناً لدلالته؟ أليس الحكمة قائمة في نفسها مستقلّة بصحّتها؟ ولهذا قيل الموعظة إذا خرجت من القلب وقعت في القلب وإذا خرجت من اللسان لم تجاوز الآذان.

الجواب

قال أبو عليّ مسكويه رحمه الله لأنّ الواعظ إنّما يأمر بما عنده أنّه الأصوب فإذا ٢،١٠٥
خالف نفسه أوهم غيره أنّه كذب وغشّ وإنّما نهى عن الدنيا لتُترك له وتوفّر عليه وظنّ من عجز عن رتبته وسقط عن بلوغ درجته في النظر أنّه إنّما يقتدر على الوعظ بحسن اقتداره على التلبيس وإظهار المموّه في صورة الحقّ ولو اعتقد ما يظهر بلسانه لعمل بحسبه فهذا وأشباهه تعرض في قلب المستمع لوعظ من لا يعمل بوعظه هذا. وربّما كان أكثر من تراه من الواعظين هو بالحقيقة غير معتقد لما يظهره وإنّما غايته أن يشغل الناس عمّا في أيديهم أو لتتمّ له رئاسة باجتماع الناس إليه أو لأرب له من الدنيا. فأيّ موقع لكلام مثل هذا إذا عرف الموعوظ غايته وأشرف على نيّته ومذهبه. والأمر بالضدّ فيمن عمل واجتهد وأخلص سرّه ووافق عمله علمه وقوله نيّته فإنّه يصير إماماً يقتدى به ويُوثق بكلامه ويكثر أتباعه والناظرون فيما ينظر فيه والمصدّقون بحكمه.

have no influence, be they ever so pure, and his preaching does no good, be it ever so eloquent? Why does it matter if he dissociates himself from the truth of his words when the words are true, the evidence sound, and the proof incontestable? How can his action fortify his words while its contrary can enervate his evidence? Doesn't wisdom subsist in itself, and isn't it the guarantor of its own soundness? That is why it has been said: When sermons come from the heart they enter the heart, and when they come from the tongue they go no further than the ears.

Miskawayh's response

Preachers command people to do what they consider the most proper course of action. So, if they go against their own word, they give others the impression that they have lied and been deceitful, and that the reason why they exhort people against enjoying the mundane world is for it to be left to them and be available for their enjoyment. Observers who fall short of that rank and are unable to reach the same level of reflective examination form the notion that preachers derive their ability to preach from their heightened ability to fool people and to disguise falsehoods as truths, for if they believed the words they spoke, they would act on their basis. These are the kinds of things that occur to people's minds when they hear a preacher who does not behave as he preaches. It may be that the majority of preachers one sees do not in fact subscribe to what they publicly express, and their goal is rather to distract people's attention from what they possess, to gain a position of eminence by having people flock to them, or to satisfy some other worldly desire. So what impact can the words of such people have once the people they are preaching to have become cognizant of their designs and have discovered where they are tending? It is the opposite with those who do good works and strive for righteous behavior, whose heart is sincere, and whose deeds are in accord with their knowledge, their words, and their intentions. They become models whose example is emulated and whose words are trusted. They attract a great number of adherents, and many pursue the same reflective inquiry that they do and place credence in their judgment. 105.2

مسألة

لمِ عظم ندم الإنسان على ما قصّر فيه من إكرام الفاضل وتعظيمه واقتباس الحكمة منه بعد فقده؟ ولِمَ كان يعرض له الزهد فيه مع التمكّن منه والانقطاع إليه وقد كان في الوقت الأوّل أفرغ قلباً وأوسع مذهباً وأبين قوّة؟[1] ١،١٠٦

الجواب

قال أبو عليّ مسكويه رحمه الله هذه مسألة قد أجيب عنها فيما تقدّم ولا معنى لتكرير الكلام فيها. ٢،١٠٦

مسألة

لمِ اعتزت العرب والعجم في مواقف الحرب وأيّام الهياج والاعتزاء هو الانتساب إلى الآباء والأجداد وإلى أيّام مشهورة وأفعال مذكورة؟ وما الذي حرّك أحدهم من هذه الأشياء حتّى ثار وتقدّم وبارز وأقدم وأخطر نفسه واقتحم وربّما سمع في ذلك الوقت بيتاً أو تذكّر مثلاً أو رأى من دونه في البيت والمنصب والعرق والمركب دون ما يقدّر يفعل فوق ما يفعل فتأتيه الأنفة فتقوده بأنفه إلى مباشرة حتفه؟ ما هذه الغرائب المبثوثة والعجائب المدفونة في هذا الخلق عن هذا الخلق؟ جلّ من هذا بعلمه وبأمره ومن فعله وهو الإله الذي انقادت له الأشياء طوعاً وكرهاً وأشارت إليه تعريضاً وتصريحاً. ١،١٠٧

الجواب

قال أبو عليّ مسكويه رحمه الله الغضب في الإنسان يكون بالقوّة إلى أن يخرجه إلى الفعل أمر مغضب وكذلك سائر قوى النفس وما تُخرجه إلى الفعل ينقسم قسمين ٢،١٠٧

---

١ ط: مذهبا.

On why people regret their failure to honor and benefit from great men during their lifetime

Why do people feel great regret at their failure to honor and acclaim men of excellence and to acquire wisdom from them once they are gone? Why did they shun them when they had the chance to consult them and the opportunity to devote time to them, when they had fewer cares, were more open in their views, and clearly had more power? 106.1

Miskawayh's response

This question has already been answered, and there is no point in repeating the discussion.[22] 106.2

On why Arabs and non-Arabs declare their pedigrees in times of war

Why do Arabs and non-Arabs declare their pedigrees during times of war and unrest? To declare one's pedigree is to state who one's fathers and forefathers are and to state one's relation to famous events and notable deeds of the past. What is it that rouses them and makes them bristle and advance, enter the fray and boldly venture forth, risking their lives as they storm ahead? At that moment they may hear some verse, remember some proverb, or see someone of inferior family, station, stock, and origin conducting himself in a way that is superior to the way they are conducting themselves, and a sense of pride seizes them and drags them by the bit to their death. What are these curiosities and these wonders pertaining to this ethical constitution that lie widely dispersed and deeply buried in this physical constitution? Glory be to the One through whose knowledge, command, and action this is accomplished. He is God, to whom all things submit themselves, whether freely or grudgingly, and to whom all things point, whether covertly or overtly. 107.1

Miskawayh's response

Anger exists as a potentiality in human beings until it is actualized by something that causes anger. The same principle applies to all powers of the soul. 107.2

إمّا من خارج وإمّا من داخل فالذي يكون من خارج فهو مثل انتهاك الحرمة وشتم العرض وما أشبه ذلك والذي يكون من داخل فهو مثل تذكّر الذنوب والأحقاد وجميع الأحوال التي من شأنها قدح هذه القوّة. ومن شأن النفس إذا كانت ساكنة والتمس الإنسان فعلاً قويًّا منها لم تستجب له الأعضاء عمّا يلتمس فحينئذ يضطرّ إلى تحريك النفس وإثارتها وبحسب تلك الحركة من النفس تكون قوّة ذلك الفعل وأنت تتبيّن ذلك من المسرور إذا أراد أن يظهر غضباً أو يفعل فعل الغضوب كيف تتخاذل أعضاؤه ويظهر عليه أثر التكلّف فربّما أضحك من نفسه وضحك هو أيضاً في أحوج ما كان إلى قوّة الغضب فيحتاج في تلك الحال إلى إثارة القوّة الغضبيّة بتذكّر أمر يهيّج تلك القوّة حتّى يصدر فعله على ما ينبغي.

٣،١٠٧ وهذه الحال تعرض في الحرب إذا لم يخصّ المحارب أمرها وأعني بذلك أنّ المحارب ربّما حضر الحرب التي لا يخصّه أمرها بل لمساعدة غيره أو لأجرة يأخذها فإذا شهد الحرب لم تأخذه الحميّة والأنفة فيحتاج حينئذ إلى الاعتزاء وهو تذكّر لأحوال شجاعات ظهرت لأوّليه[1] ليكون ذلك قدحاً له وإثارة لشجاعته وسبباً لحركة قويّة من نفسه. فإذا ثارت هذه القوّة كان مثلها مثل النار التي تبتدئ ضعيفة وتقوى بمباشرة الأفعال وبالإمعان فيها حتّى تصير تلك الأفعال لها بمنزلة المادّة للنار تتزيّد بها إلى أن تلتهب وتستشيط ويصير بمنزلة السكران في قلّة الضبط والتمييز وهي الحال التي يلتمسها المحارب من نفسه.

مسألة

١،١٠٨ ما السبب في أنّ الناس يقولون هذا الهواء أطيب من ذلك الهواء وذلك الماء أعذب من ذلك الماء وتربة بلد كذا وكذا أصلب من تربة كذا وطين مكان كذا أنعم من

١ ط: لأوّلين.

The things that actualize it are of two kinds: those that arise externally, and those that arise internally. Examples of things that arise externally include violations of honor, insults, and the like. Examples of things that arise internally include the remembrance of wrongs and grudges and all those states that tend to fuel this power. It is characteristic of the soul that, when it is at rest and a person seeks to elicit a powerful action from it, his bodily members do not comply with his desire. He is then forced to move and rouse the soul, and that movement of the soul determines the degree of powerfulness of that action. We perceive this clearly in people who are feeling happy: When they try to display anger or to behave in the way angry people do, their bodily members abandon them, and they exhibit signs of forced behavior. Sometimes they provoke others to laughter, and also laugh themselves, though they are in the most pressing need of the power of anger. In that situation, it is necessary for them to rouse their irascible power by remembering something that stirs up that power so their action can issue in the right manner.

This situation arises in times of war if the war does not specifically concern 107.3
the person fighting in it—I mean that the fighter might be participating in a war that does not specifically concern him with the aim of helping others or of obtaining some financial reward. Confronted by the sight of war, he fails to be seized by a sense of zeal and pride, and then needs to declare his pedigree, which involves remembering acts of courage performed by his forbears, in the hope that this will stoke his passions, rouse his courage, and elicit a powerful movement from his soul. If roused, this power becomes like a fire, which begins feebly and then grows stronger as it engages in actions and applies itself to them with dedication. Those acts become like the material fed into a fire, which kindles it until it flares up and blazes fiercely, and he becomes like someone in a state of intoxication, so diminished is his self-control and his capacity for discrimination. This is the state the fighter seeks to produce in himself.

On why people distinguish between different kinds of air, water, and earth, but not different kinds of fire

Why do people say, "This air is more agreeable than that," "This water is fresher 108.1
than that," "The ground of such and such a region is firmer than that one," and "The soil of such and such a place is softer, more putrid, or more briny than

طين مكان كذا وأعفن وأسبخ؟ ثمّ لا يقولون في قياس هذا بلد كذا ناره أجود وأحسن وأصفى أو أشدّ حرًّا وإحراقًا وأعظم لهيبًا بل يصرفون هذه الصفات على اختلاف الموادّ كأنّها في الحطب اليابس أبين سلطانًا وفي القطن المنفوش أسرع نفوذًا؟

الجواب

قال أبو عليّ مسكويه رحمه الله إنّ الأركان الأربعة وإن اشتركت في أنّ بعضها يأخذ قوّة بعض بالأقلّ والأكثر حتّى يكون بعضها أخلص في صورته ونوعه من بعض فإنّ النار من بينها خاصّة أقلّ قبولًا لقوّة غيرها وأعسر ممازجة وذلك أنّ صورة النار غالبة على مادّتها. وبيان هذا أنّ الأرض تقبل من ممازجة الماء والهواء ما تستحيل به عن صورتها الخاصّة بها حتّى تصير منها الحمأة والملح وضروب الأشياء التي تختلف بها الترب وكذلك الماء يقبل من الأرض التي تجاوره والهواء الذي يليه ضروب الطعوم والأرايح والصفاء والكدر حتّى يخرج من صورته الخاصّة به خروجًا بيّنًا وهذه حال الهواء في قبول الآثار من الأرض والماء حتّى يصير بعضه غليظًا وبعضه رطبًا ويابسًا ومعتدلًا. فتظهر في هذه الثلاثة آثار بعضها في بعض حتّى تتبيّن للحسّ بيانًا ظاهرًا وتنقص آثار بعضها عن بعض حتّى يحكم كلّ إنسان بخروجه عن اعتداله وخروجه عن اعتداله سبب الاستضرار البيّن في الأبدان. ٢،١٠٨

فأمّا النار فإنّ صورتها الخاصّة بها غالبة على مادّتها[1] حتّى لا تقبل من المزاج ما يظهر للحسّ منه نقصان أثر من الإحراق الذي هو فعلها أو الضوء الذي هو خاصّتها وعلى أنّ النار أيضًا قد تقبل من المزاج ومجاورة ما تليه أثرًا ما ولكنّه بالإضافة إلى الآثار التي تقبلها أخواتها يسير[2] جدًّا. مثال ذلك أنّ النار التي مادّتها النفط الأسود والكبريت الصرف لونها بخلاف لون النار التي مادّتها الزيت الصافي ودهن البنفسج الخالص لأنّ تلك حمراء وهذه بيضاء ولكنّ الفعل المطلوب من النار للجمهور غير ٣،١٠٨

١ الأصل وط: مائيّتها. ٢ الأصل: يسيرة.

the soil of that place," yet they do not then say in analogy: "The fire of such and such a region is superior, better, and purer, or emits stronger heat, burns more strongly, and has a fiercer flame," but instead they attribute these qualities to the differences between materials, saying for example that its power is plainer to see in dry timber and is faster to take hold in combed cotton?

Miskawayh's response

The four elements have in common the fact that each admits the power of the other in smaller or larger degrees, so that some are purer in their form and species than others; yet fire in particular is less receptive to the power of the others and more resistant to entering into mixtures. That is because the form of fire dominates over its matter. To explain the point: Earth is receptive to forming mixtures with water and air that displace it from its proper form, resulting in the mud, salt, and the various aspects that account for the differences between soils. Similarly, water receives from the earth contiguous to it and the air surrounding it many kinds of tastes and smells, purities and impurities, such that it undergoes an evident departure from its proper form. The same holds true of air, insofar as it accepts different effects from the earth and water, with some of it becoming thick and some moist, dry, and balanced. So the effects of these three elements on one another are manifested in such a way that they are plainly perceived by the senses, and the effects of some relative to others become deficient in a such a way that every person can judge that they have departed from their balanced state. Their departure from their balanced state causes evident harm to bodies. 108.2

With fire, by contrast, its proper form dominates over its matter, so that it is not receptive to forming mixtures that result in one of its effects—be it the effect of burning, which constitutes its act, or the effect of light, which constitutes its specific property—becoming deficient in a way that is plain to the senses. Fire may indeed also receive a certain effect through mixture and through contiguity with nearby objects, but it is extremely meager in comparison with the effects received by its counterparts. For example, the fire whose material consists in black naphtha and unmixed sulfur has a different color when compared with the fire whose material consists in clear oil and pure violet ointment; for the former is red, whereas the latter is white. But the act one wishes the fire to effect on this ensemble—that is, to burn and 108.3

ناقص أعني الإحراق والضوء وإن نقص بحسب الموادّ فإنّ تلك الحال منها مشتركة في البلدان كلّها لا تخصّ بعضها دون بعض وإذا حصل للناس أغراضهم من أفعال النار تبلّغوا به إلى حاجاتهم ولم ينظروا في الموادّ التي تخصّ البلدان لا سيّما والموادّ متّفقة فيها وليس هكذا[1] أخوات النار.

مسألة

لم فرح الإنسان بنيل مال وإصابة خير من غير احتساب له وتوقّع أكثر من فرحه ١،١٠٩
بدرك ما طلب ولحوق ما زاول؟ ألأنّه في أحد الطرفين ينبغي طلب شيء متأخّر[2] أم لغير ذلك؟

الجواب

قال أبو عليّ مسكويه رحمه الله إنّ جميع ما يصيب الإنسان ممّا يخصّ نفسه أو جسمه ٢،١٠٩
إذا وصل إليه بتدريج قلّ إحساسه به وضعف ظهور أثره عليه وإذا وصل إليه بغتة وضربة كثر إحساسه به. أمّا مثال ذلك في الجسم فإنّ الأمراض التي يخرج بها عن الاعتدال على تدريج فليس يشعر بها[3] إلّا شعورًا يسيرًا وربّما لم يشعر بها[4] البتّة فإن خرج بها على غير تدريج تألّم منها[5] جدًّا كالحال في الدوى[6] وأشباهه من الأمراض فإنّ الإنسان يخرج عن الاعتدال بها إلى الطرف الأقصى الذي يليه الموت فلا يحسّ بألمه لأنّه على تدريج ولو خرج دون ذلك الخروج ضربة للحقه من الألم ما لا قوام له به. وكذلك الحال في اللذّات لأنّ اللذّة إنّما هي عود الإنسان إلى اعتداله ضربة فاللذّة والألم حالان يستويان في أنّهما يردان دفعة بلا تدريج

---

١ الأصل: هذه. ٢ الأصل وط: متخيّر. ٣ الأصل: به. ٤ الأصل: به. ٥ الأصل: منه. ٦ الأصل: الدق.

emit light—does not suffer deficiency. Suffering deficiency as a result of the specific materials characterizes it in all geographical regions alike and is not exclusive to one as opposed to another. If people obtain what they want from the action of fire, they content themselves with meeting their needs, and give no consideration to the materials specific to given countries, particularly since the materials are common among them. This is not how things stand with the counterparts of fire.

On why people feel happier when they unexpectedly obtain something they weren't seeking than when they obtain what they were seeking

Why do people experience a greater sense of happiness when they come into some money or realize some good when they're not expecting or anticipating it than they do when they attain what they were seeking and achieve what they were pursuing? Is it because in the one case they must seek something deferred, or is there some other reason? 109.1

Miskawayh's response

Every occurrence that concerns a person's soul and body and that reaches him in a gradual manner is felt without much acuteness and manifests a weak effect on him. When it reaches him suddenly and in one fell swoop, it is felt acutely. In the case of the body, this is exemplified by the fact that we take little notice of the illnesses that make us depart from the balanced state in a gradual manner, and sometimes we take no notice of them at all. By contrast, if they bring about this departure in a non-gradual manner, we experience a great amount of pain. This is how it is with consumption and similar illnesses; for they make us depart from the balanced state toward the farthermost extreme, right to death's door, but we do not feel the pain because it occurs gradually. Were this to happen differently, all at once, we would be exposed to an amount of pain that would be difficult to bear. The same thing applies to pleasures, for pleasure in fact consists in a person's return in one fell swoop to his balanced state. Pleasure and pain are similar conditions in that they appear all at once, in a non-gradual manner, and they are thus alike in the intensity with 109.2

فيستويان في باب شدّة الإحساس. وهذه المسألة أحد الآثار التي ترد على الإنسان مرّة بتدريج ومرّة بغير تدريج فتصير حال الإنسان بما لم يحتسبه ولم يتدرّج إليه بالمزاولة حال ما يصيبه ضربة واحدة ممّا ضربنا مثاله فيكثر إحساسه به وظهور أثره عليه.

مسـألة

لم صار البنيان الكريم[1] والقصر المشيّد إذا لم يسكنه الناس تداعى عن قرب وما هكذا هو إذا سُكن واختُلف إليه؟ لعلّك تظنّ أنّ ذلك لأنّ السكّان[2] يرمّون منه ما استرمّ ويتلافون ما تداعى وتهدّم ويتعهّدونه بالتطرية والكنس فاعلم أنّ هذا ليس لذاك لأنّك تعلم أنّهم يؤثّرون في المسكن بالمشي والاستناد وأخذ القلاعة وسائر الحركات المختلفة ما إن لم يضعفه على رمّهم ولمّهم كان بإزائه ومقابله فقد بقيت العلّة على هذا وستسمعها في عرض الجواب عن جميع مسائل هذا الكتاب. ١،١١٠

الجواب

قال أبو عليّ مسكويه رحمه الله إنّ معظم آفات البنيان يكون من تشعيث الأمطار وانسداد مجاري المياه بما تحصّله الرياح في وجه المآزيب ومسالك المياه التي تردّ المياه إلى أصول الحيطان من خارج البناء وداخله وبما يتثلّم من وجوه البنيان الكريمة بالآفات التي تعرّضها لحركات الهواء والأمطار والبرد والثلوج وربّما كان سبب ذلك قصبة أو هشيم من تبن الطين الذي تطيّره الأرواح إلى مسلك الماء فتعطف الماء إلى غير جهته فيكون به خراب البنيان كلّه فأمّا ظهور الهوامّ[3] في أصول الحيطان والعناكب في سقوفه وأخذها من الجميع ما يتبيّن أثره على الأيّام فشيء ظاهر وذلك أنّ هذا الضرب من الخراب قبيح الأثر جدّاً ينبو الطرف عنه ويسمج به البناء الشريف ٢،١١٠

١ الأصل: الكريمة. ٢ الأصل: الإنسان. ٣ الأصل: الهواء.

which they are felt. This question concerns an effect that sometimes comes to people in a gradual manner and sometimes in a non-gradual manner. The way a person responds to things he has not anticipated and has not arrived at gradually by pursuing them is similar to the way he responds to the examples we gave, which happen in one fell swoop; he thus feels them acutely, and their effect on him is strongly manifested.

On why fine edifices fall to ruin when left uninhabited

Why is it that fine buildings and imposing mansions quickly become dilapidated when uninhabited, but not when they are inhabited and frequented? 110.1 You might suppose that this is because the inhabitants undertake repairs when necessary, restore them when they're dilapidated and fallen to ruin, and care for them by replastering them and sweeping them clean. Yet rest assured that this is not the reason. For you know that they have an impact on the dwelling by walking on it, by causing it to support their weight, by wearing down layers of plaster and daub, and by all those other movements that have a similar tendency and effect, even if they do not weaken it in view of the repairs and restorations they undertake. So the question about the cause of this persists, and you will hear it in the course of responding to my questions in this book.[23]

Miskawayh's response

Most types of damage to buildings are either due to decay caused by rain and 110.2 water, when the drains are blocked by objects swept by the wind into the pipes and watercourses, for this causes the water to back up and flood the foundations of the walls from outside and inside the building; or result from defective cracks that appear in the exterior of fine buildings, exposing them to the air, rain, cold, and snow. Sometimes the damage may be caused when the wind blows reeds or chaff from the chopped straw of the bricks into the watercourse, for this diverts the water in the wrong direction and causes the entire building to become dilapidated. The damage done by vermin springing up at the foundations and by spiders on the ceilings, effectively wearing away at all of the building's features over time, is plain. Dilapidation of this type produces a very ugly effect that is repulsive to behold and renders a distinguished building unseemly. Sometimes the inhabitants of a building might neglect a room, be it

وربّما أغفل السكّان بيتاً من عرض البناء إمّا بقصد وإمّا بغير قصد فإذا فُتح عنه يوجد فيه[1] من آثار الدبيب من الفأر والحيّات وضروب الحشرات التي تتّخذ لنفسها أكنّة بالنقب والبناء كالأرضة والنمل وما تجمعه من أقواتها ومن نسج العنكبوت وتراكم الغبرة على النقوش ما يمنع من دخوله هذا إن سلم من الوكف وتطرّق المياه وهدمها[2] لما تسيل عليه من حائط وسقف ورضّه بما يثقله من طين السطوح وتقصف منها جميع الخشب والسنادات والعمد وإذا كان فيها السكّان منعوا هذه الأسباب العظيمة في الخراب وكان ما يشعّثونه بعد هذه الأشياء يسيرًا بالإضافة إليها فكان البناء إلى العمران أقرب ومن الخراب أبعد.

مسألة

لم صار الكريم الماجد النجد يلد اللئيم الساقط الوغد؟ وهذا يلد ذاك على تباين ما ١،١١١ بينهما في أغراض النفس وأخلاقها مع قرب ما بينهما في أصولها وأعراقها.

الجواب

قال أبو عليّ مسكويه رحمه الله إنّ أخلاق النفس وإن كانت تابعاً لمزاج البدن فإنّ ٢،١١١ التأديب والسياسة يصلح منها إصلاحاً كثيرًا وربّما كان مزاج الابن بعيداً من مزاج الأب وانضاف إلى ذلك سوء تأديب ورداءة سياسة ويكفي أحدهما في الفساد فتختلف الشيمتان والمذهبان.

مسألة

لم إذا كان الإنسان بعيداً عن وطنه ومسقط رأسه وملهى عينه ومضطجع جنبه ١،١١٢ ومطرب نفسه ومعدن أنسه يكون أخمد شوقاً وأقلّ قلقاً وأطفأ نائرة وأسلى نفساً

١ الأصل: من فيه. ٢ الأصل: وهدمه.

intentionally or unintentionally, so when it is opened up it cannot be entered because of the activity of animals that creep along the ground (rats, snakes, and insects that build nests by boring holes, such as woodworms and ants), the food they collect, spiderwebs, and dust covering the ornaments. This assumes that it has been spared from seepage, and from water that destroys the walls and the ceilings over which it flows, causing them to crumble from the clay the water sweeps down from the roof and breaking all of the timber, supports, and stays. If the building is occupied, the inhabitants prevent these great causes of dilapidation from taking effect. The decay produced by inhabitants is negligible in comparison with these things, so the building is more likely to flourish and less likely to become dilapidated.

On why men of sublime character beget knaves

Why do men of a noble, honorable, valiant nature beget ignoble, disreputable scoundrels? The former beget the latter with all the disparity between their souls' aims and traits and for all the propinquity between their origins and roots. 111.1

Miskawayh's response

Discipline and governance have a large hand in reforming the character traits of the soul, though they are contingent upon the humoral mixture of the body. Sometimes the humoral mixture of the son may be distant from the humoral mixture of the father, and this may be compounded by faulty discipline and bad governance, though even one of these is enough to produce corruption; so the two dispositions and comportments become different. 111.2

On why our longing for home grows more intense the nearer we come to it

Why is it that when a person is far from his homeland and birthplace—where his eye takes its delight, his head finds its rest, his soul tastes its joy, and his spirit derives its warmth—his sense of longing is less fierce, his sense of disquiet 112.1

وألهى فؤادًا حتّى إِذَا دَنَتِ ٱلدِّيَارُ مِنَ ٱلدِّيَارِ وقوي الطمع في الجوار نفد الصبر وذهب القرار وحتّى قال الشاعر [وافر]

وَأَعْظَمُ مَا يَكُونُ ٱلشَّوْقُ يَوْمًا   إِذَا دَنَتِ ٱلدِّيَارُ مِنَ ٱلدِّيَارِ

وهل هذا معنى يعمّ أو يخصّ؟ وما علّته؟ وهل له علّة؟

الجواب

٢،١١٢ قال أبو عليّ مسكويه رحمه الله هذا المعنى موجود في الأشياء الطبيعيّة أيضًا مستمرّ فيها وذاك أنّك لو أرسلت حجرًا من موضع عال إلى مركزه لكان يبتدئ بحركته وكلّما قرب من مركزه احتدّت الحركة وصارت أسرع إلى أن تصير عند قربه من الأرض على أحدّ ما تكون وأسرعه وكلّما كان الموضع الذي يُرسل منه الحجر أعلى كان هذا المعنى فيه أبين وأظهر وكذلك حكم النار والعناصر الباقية إذا أُرسلت من غير أمكنتها الخاصّة بها فإنّها كلّما قربت من مراكزها اشتدّت حركتها ونزاعها ومثل هذه المواضع لا يُسأل عنها بِلِمَ لأنّها أوائل طبيعيّة وغايتنا فيها أن نعرفها ونعلم أنّها كذلك وكذلك حال النفس في أنّها إذا كانت بعيدة من مألفها كان نزاعها أيسر فكلّما دنت منه اشتدّ نزاعها وحركتها التي تسمّى شوقًا.

٣،١١٢ وإنّما قلت إنّ هذه المواضع لا يُبحث عنها بلم لأنّ لم إنّما يُبحث بها عن طلب علّة ومبدأ وهذه مبادئ في أنفسها وليس لها علّة أكثر من أنّ الأمور أنفسها كذلك أي مبادئها هي أنفسها ولم تكن كذلك لعلّة أخرى مثال ذلك أنّ لو أنّ[١] قائلًا قال لم صارت العين تبصر بهذه الطبقات من العين؟ ولم صارت ترى الشيء بحسب الزاوية التي بينها وبين المبصر إن كانت كبيرة فكبيرة وإن كانت صغيرة فصغيرة أو

١ ط: لوأن.

more abated, his feelings less inflamed, his soul filled with greater cheer, and his heart filled with greater delight, yet as he approaches his home and his eagerness to set foot there increases, his patience gives out and his equanimity deserts him? The poet thus said:[24]

> Longing burns fiercest on the day when the native returns

Is this a phenomenon that has a general or a particular application? What is its cause? Does it have a cause?

Miskawayh's response

This phenomenon is encountered and attested among natural things as well, for if you cast a stone from a height down to its resting position on the ground where it belongs, from the time it begins to move, the closer it gets to its resting position, the more vigorous the movement grows and the faster it becomes, and it attains its greatest velocity when close to the ground. The higher the point from which the stone is thrown, the starker and more manifest this phenomenon is. The same holds true of fire and the other elements when cast from a place that is not proper to them. The closer they get to their resting positions, the more intense their movement and inclination become. We do not ask "why" regarding such topics, for they form first principles of nature, and our only aim can be to become cognizant of them and to know that this is how they stand. The same applies to the soul, insofar as its inclination is weaker when it is far from the place it is accustomed to; the closer the soul draws to that place, the more intense both its inclination and the movement called "longing" become. 112.2

The reason I have said that one does not inquire into these topics by asking "why" is that "why" is used in inquiry when one is searching for a cause or foundation. Yet these constitute foundations in themselves, and they have no other cause beyond the fact that this is how things stand in themselves. That is, they themselves constitute their own foundations, and they do not stand that way because of some other cause. For example, should a person inquire, "Why does the eye see by means of these specific ocular layers? And why does it see things according to the angle between itself and the object of vision—large if the object is large, and small if it is small?" or should he ask, 112.3

سأل لم صارت الأذن تحسّ باقتراع الهواء على هذا الشكل لم يلزم الجواب عنه لأنّ الأشياء الواضحة التي هي أوائل أنّيّاتها هي لميّاتها.

مسـألة

١،١١٣ لم قيل الرأي نائم والهوى يقظان ولذلك غلب الهوى الرأي؟ يروى هذا عن حكيم العرب عامر بن الظرب. أليس الرأي من حزب العقل وأوليائه؟ فكيف غُلب مع علوّ مكانه وشرف موضعه؟ وما معنى قول الآخر من الأوائل العقل صديق مقطوع والهوى عدوّ متبوع؟ ما سبب هذه الصداقة مع هذا العقوق؟ وما سبب تلك العداوة مع تلك المتابعة؟ وهل يري هذا حقائق الأمور معكوسة منكوسة فإنّ الظاهر خارج عن حكم الواجب جار على غير النظام الراتب.

الجواب

٢،١١٣ قال أبو عليّ مسكويه رحمه الله هذا كلام خرج في معرض فصاحة وخطابة فأمّا معناه فهو أنّ الهوى فينا قويّ جدّاً والرأي ضعيف وسبب ذلك أنّا معشر الناس طبيعيّون وجزء الطبيعة فينا أغلب من جزء العقل لأنّا في عالم الطبيعة والعقل غريب عندنا ضعيف الأثر فينا ولذلك نكلّ عند النظر في المعقولات ولا نكلّ عند النظر في الطبيعيّات ذلك الكلال والعقل وإن كان في نفسه شريفاً عالي الرتبة فإنّ أثره عندنا يسير والطبيعة وإن كانت ضعيفة بالإضافة إلى العقل منحطّة الرتبة فإنّها قويّة فينا لأنّا في عالمها ونحن أجزاء منها ومركّبون من عناصرها وفينا قواها أجمع وهذا واضح غير محتاج إلى الإطناب في الشرح.

"Why does the ear perceive things by means of an impaction of the air in this specific fashion?" it would not be necessary to respond, for with evident things that constitute first principles, the *that* is identical to the *why*.

On the meaning of the dictum that judgement sleeps while passion keeps watch

Why was it said: Judgment sleeps while passion keeps watch—this is why passion defeats judgment? This is a remark ascribed to the sage of the Arabs, ʿĀmir ibn al-Ẓarib. Doesn't judgment belong to the party of the intellect and its supporters? So how could it be defeated given its lofty status and noble position? And what is the meaning of the remark made by another early thinker: "The intellect is the friend we disavow; passion the enemy to whom we bow"? What is the cause of such friendship joined to such disobedience? And what is the cause of such enmity joined to such subordination? Does this show the reality of things to be reversed and subverted? For what is manifested deviates from what is mandated and conforms to an order that is infirm. 113.1

Miskawayh's response

This point was framed for literary effect and in a rhetorical manner. In terms of content, the point is that passion is very strong in us, whereas judgment is weak; the reason is that we humans are natural beings and within us the element of nature dominates over the element of the intellect. For we live in the world of nature, and the intellect is foreign and has a weak effect upon us. That is why it fatigues us to inquire into intellectual matters, but it does not fatigue us as much to inquire into natural matters. The effect of the intellect on us is very limited, though it is noble in itself and occupies an exalted rank. And even though in comparison with the intellect nature is weak and occupies a lowly rank, it is strong in us because we live in its world, form part of it, are composed from its elements, and all of its powers are present within us. This is evident and needs no lengthy explanation. 113.2

مسـألة

حضر أبو بشر متّى صاحب شرح المنطق مجلساً فقال له أبو هاشم المتكلّم عائباً للمنطق هل المنطق إلّا في وزن مفعل من النطق؟ فحدّثني أأنصف أبو هاشم وحزّ الحقّ أم تشيّع وقال ما لا يجوز أن يُسمع منه؟ هذا مع محلّه وشدّة توقّيه في مقالته فإنّ البيان عن هذا القدر يأتي على كنائن العلم ويوضح طرق الحكمة. ١،١١٤

الجواب

قال أبو عليّ مسكويه رحمه الله أمّا من طريق الوزن فقد صدق فيه أبو هاشم وأمّا من طريق الازدراء والعيب إن كان قصد ذلك فقد ظلم لأنّه لا عيب على العلم إلّا من جهة خطأ المخطئ فيه لا من جهة اسمه ولو كايله أبو بشر مكايلة فقال له وهل المتكلّم إلّا في وزن متفعّل من الكلام وتصفّح سائر العلوم فقال فيها[١] مثل هذا وقال هل التفقّه إلّا تفعّل من قولك فقهت الشيء وهل النحو إلّا مصدر قولك نحوت الشيء أي قصدته لكان هذا مستمرًّا. وما أكثر ما يسمّى الشيء من العلم بما لا تستحقّه رتبته وما أكثر ما يسمّى بما يحطّ من رتبته فلا ذاك ينفع في ذلك العلم ولا هذا يضرّ في هذا العلم. وقد عرفت قوماً سمّوا أنفسهم المدركين وسمّوا علومهم الإدراك الحقيقيّ وهو في غاية البعد من حقائق الأمر وقد سمّى قوم أنفسهم المستحقّين وأهل الحقّ وما أشبه ذلك فكانوا فيه مدّعين باطلاً وهذا لا يستحقّ أكثر من هذا القول. ٢،١١٤

١ الأصل: فيه.

On a remark concerning logic made by the dialectical theologian Abū Hāshim to the philosopher Abū Bishr Mattā

Abū Bishr Mattā, the commentator on logic, once attended a learned gathering and, as a reproach of logic, the dialectical theologian Abū Hāshim asked him:[25] Isn't "logic" simply a derivation from the term "speech"? So tell me: Was Abū Hāshim being fair? Did he hit upon the truth, or was he guilty of partisanship in saying something that he never should have, despite his status and extreme caution in how he expressed his doctrines? An exposition of this point would yield hidden caches of knowledge and illuminate the ways of wisdom. 114.1

Miskawayh's response

Abū Hāshim was right about the morphological pattern, but was wrong in expressing disdain and reproach—if that was indeed his aim. For the only reason why some form of knowledge could be reproached is if someone has made a mistake, not because of its name. The same point would have applied had Abū Bishr responded in kind by asking, "Isn't 'dialectical theologian' (*mutakallim*) simply derived morphologically from the term 'talking' (*kalām*)?" He could also have considered all other forms of knowledge and posed similar questions. "Doesn't 'legal knowledge' simply derive from the expression 'I understood something,' adopting the morphological pattern?" and "Doesn't 'grammar' simply derive from the expression 'I headed toward something,' that is, 'I directed myself toward it'"? It often happens that a name is applied to a particular form of knowledge that is not merited by its station, and that a name is applied to it that demeans its station; the former does not benefit the knowledge in question, nor does the latter harm it. I know some people who called themselves the "discerners" and called their forms of knowledge "true discernment," when this was a far cry from how things actually stood. Others called themselves "the deserving," "the people of truth," and suchlike, and in doing so made false claims. That is as much discussion as the topic deserves. 114.2

مسألة

رأيت رجلاً يسأل شيخاً من أهل الحكمة فقال له العرب تؤنّث الشمس وتذكّر القمر فما العلّة في ذلك؟ وأيّ معنى عنوا بهذا الإطباق؟ فإنّه إن خلا من العلّة جرى مجرى الاصطلاح على غير غرض مقصود فلم يورد ذلك الشيخ شيئاً ولهذا لم أسمّه فإنّ في ذكره مع إظهار عجزه تعريضاً به وتحقيراً لشأنه وما يستحقّ بهذا اليسير أن يجحد ما يصيب فيه من الصواب الكثير. فقال السائل فإنّ المنجّمين يذكّرون الشمس ويؤنّثون القمر وهذا أيضاً من المنجّمين اتّفاق فأجاب ههنا وقال ما قالوه ولم يجز عن المسألة الأخرى لقصر باعه في الأدب ولكن لم يحفظ فيها جواباً عن أهل العربيّة. والمعنى فيه خاف ليس من شأن المتمسّحين[1] في العلم بل من شأن المتبحّرين فيه الخائضين في غماره البالغين إلى قراره وهيهات ذلك العلم عميق البحر عالي الفلك وليس كلّ قلب وعاء لكلّ سانح ولا كلّ لسان ناطقاً بكلّ لفظ ولا كلّ فاعل آتياً بكلّ عمل. ١،١١٥

الجواب

قال أبو عليّ مسكويه رحمه الله أمّا النحويّون فلا يعلّلون هذه الأمور ويذكرون أنّ الشيء المذكّر بالحقيقة ربّما أنّثته العرب والمؤنّث بالحقيقة ربّما ذكّرته العرب. فمن ذلك أنّ الآلة من المرأة بعينها التي هي سبب تأنيث كلّ ما يؤنّث هي مذكّر عند العرب وأمّا آلة الرجل فلها أسماء مؤنّثة فأمّا العقاب والنار وكثير من الأسماء التي هي أولى الأشياء بالتذكير وهي مؤنّثة وأمثالها فكثير ولكنّ الشمس التي قصد السائل قصدها بعينها فإنّي أظنّ السبب في تأنيث العرب إيّاها أنّهم كانوا يعتقدون في الكواكب الشريفة أنّها بنات الله تعالى الله عن ذلك علوّاً كبيراً وكلّ ما كان منها أشرف عندهم عبدوه وقد سمّوا الشمس ٢،١١٥

[1] الأصل: المسنمجين.

On why some Arabic words are feminine and others masculine

I once saw a man asking an established philosopher: The Arabs treat the noun "sun" as feminine noun and the noun "moon" as masculine. What is the cause of that? And what was their object in agreeing on this practice? For if it lacks a cause, it is akin to a convention established to serve no particular aim. This scholar offered no response, and so I have not named him, for to mention his name while revealing the limits of his abilities is to expose him and impugn his dignity, and he does not deserve that his many successes in reaching the truth should be denied on account of this minor failure. The questioner then said: The astronomers treat the sun as masculine and treat the moon as feminine, and this also constitutes an agreement among astronomers. Here, the philosopher responded, providing an account of their views. The reason he was unable to deal with the other question was not inadequate erudition, but he could not recall any response given on the topic by the authorities on the Arabic language. The issue at stake is hidden from view, not merely of those who have skimmed the surface of knowledge, but indeed of experienced navigators, who have sailed its open seas, braved its waves, and plumbed its depths. Alas, the waters of this knowledge run deep, and the ship that sails on it floats high. It is not every heart that can compass every thought, not every person that can utter every word, and not every agent that can bring forth every deed. 115.1

Miskawayh's response

The grammarians, on their part, do not assign causes to these things, and they point out that the Arabs may treat something that is in reality masculine as a feminine noun and treat something that is in reality feminine as a masculine noun. An example is the fact that women's reproductive organs themselves, which are the ground for the feminineness of everything feminine, are treated as a masculine noun by the Arabs, and there are feminine terms used to refer to the reproductive organs of men. Examples abound of nouns like "eagle," "fire," and such, which really ought to be treated as masculine but are treated as feminine. Yet the question asked specifically about the sun, and I think the reason why the Arabs treat it as feminine is that they believed that the lofty stars were the daughters of God—may He be exalted far above such notions—and they worshipped whichever they deemed noblest. They referred to the 115.2

خاصّة باسم الآلهة فإنّ اللات اسم من أسمائها فيجوز أن يكونوا أنّثوها لهذا الاسم ولاعتقادهم أنّها بنت من البنات بل هي أعظمهنّ عندهم.

مسـألة

هل يجوز لإنسان أن يعي العلوم كلّها على افتنانها وطرقها واختلاف اللغات ١١٦،١
والعبارات عنها؟ فإن كان يجوز فهل يجب؟ وإن وجب فهل يوجد؟ وإن كان وُجد فهل عُرف؟ وإن كان جائزًا فما وجه جوازه وإن كان يستحيل فما وجه استحالته؟ فإنّ في الجواب بيانًا عن خفيّات العالم.

الجواب

قال أبو عليّ مسكويه رحمه الله أحد الحدود التي حُدّت بها الفلسفة أنّها علم الموجودات ١١٦،٢
كلّها بما هي موجودات ولكن ليس على الشرائط التي ذكرتها في مسألتك أعني قولك على افتنانها وطرقها واختلاف اللغات بها والعبارات عنها فإنّ علمًا واحدًا من بين العلوم لا يجوز أن يحتوي على جميع هذه الشرائط فيه لأنّ جزئيّات العلوم بلا نهاية وما لا نهاية له لا يخرج إلى الوجود ولكنّ المطلوب من كلّ علم هو الوقوف على كلّيّاته التي تشتمل على جميع أجزائه بالقوّة مثال ذلك أنّ الطبّ إذا تعلّمت أصوله وقوانينه التي بها يُستخرج نوع المرض ونوع العلاج فقد كفى فيه ذلك فأمّا أن يُعرف منه جميع أجزاء الأمراض فذلك محال. وكذلك تجد كتب جالينوس وغيره من الأطبّاء فإنّها تعلّمك أصول الأمراض والعلاجات فإذا باشرت الصناعة ورد عليك من أجزاء مرض واحد ما لا يمكنك إحصاؤه ويبقى من أجزائه ما لا يمكن إحصاؤه أحدًا بعدك. وإذا كان الأمر على ذلك فالجواب عن مسألتك يكون مقيّدًا على ما ذكرته فأمّا اختلاف الطرق

sun in particular by the name of a goddess, for one of its names is "al-Lāt." So it is possible that the reason they treat it as feminine is because of this name and because of their belief that it is one of God's daughters—indeed, the greatest one in their view.

On whether a human being could know everything

Is it possible for one human being to grasp all forms of knowledge, in all their varieties and paths and in all their different languages and locutions? If it is possible, is it also obligatory? If it is obligatory, is it encountered in reality? And if it is encountered, is it known? If it is possible, what is the ground of its possibility? And if it is impossible, what is the ground of its impossibility? A response to this question would shed light on the hidden recesses of the world. 116.1

Miskawayh's response

One of the ways in which philosophy has been defined is that it is the knowledge of all existents qua existents, but not according to the terms you set out in your question—that is, when you referred to "their varieties and paths and their different languages and locutions." For it is not possible for a single form of knowledge to encompass the entirety of these terms, since its particulars are infinite in number, and what is infinite in number cannot enter existence. But the objective with every form of knowledge is to arrive at its universals, which contain all of its particulars *in potentia*. In medicine, for example, it is enough to learn the principles and ordinances through which the type of illness and type of treatment can be determined; to seek to know all the particular elements of the different illnesses would be impossible. This is how the books by Galen and other physicians are written: They instruct a person in the principles and treatments of the different illnesses. Once a physician begins practicing the craft, he comes across innumerable particular elements relating to a single illness, and the illness continues to harbor particular elements that no one who comes after him could ever enumerate. If this is how things stand, the response to your question is subject to the qualification I have mentioned. There is no point in seeking to learn the different paths and locutions, for one's objective in pursuing the different kinds of knowledge is the knowledge itself, 116.2

والعبارات فلا معنى لتعاطي معرفتها فإنّ المقصود من العلوم هي ذواتها ومن أيّ طريق وُصل إليها وبأيّ لغة عُبّر عنها كان كافياً.

٣،١١٦ وأمّا قولك هل يجب فأقول إنّه واجب لأنّ التفلسف واجب من أجل أنّه كمال الإنسانيّة وبلوغ أقصى درجتها وكلّ شيء كان له كمال فإنّ غايته البلوغ إلى ذلك الكمال ومن قصّر من الناس عن بلوغ كماله مع حصول الأسباب وارتفاع الموانع عنه فهو غير معذور فيه.

٤،١١٦ وأمّا قولك هل يوجد فإنّه موجود لأنّ الفلسفة موجودة وهي صناعة الصناعات وما رُتّب شيء من أجزائها كما رتّبت هي نفسها فإنّه قد بُدئ من أدنى درجة يبتدئ بها المتعلّم إلى أقصى مرتبة يجوز أن يبلغها ولهذا[1] جميعه أصول وشروح على غاية الإحكام وهي معروفة موجودة غير ممنوع منها ولا مضنون بها على من يطلبها وفيه منّة لتعلّمها.

مسألة

١،١١٧ ما غضب الصارف على المصروف؟ هكذا تنشأ هذه المسألة وصورتها أنّك تُولّى إمرة بلد أو قضاء مدينة فترد البلد وبه أمير قبلك صُرف بك فتعنّف به وتغضب عليه وتكلح وجهك في وجهه وهو ما[2] أغضبك ولا آذاك وليس بينكما لقاء ولا إساءة ولا إحسان ومن جنس هذا الغضب غضب الجلّاد والسيّاف.

الجواب

٢،١١٧ قال أبو عليّ مسكويه رحمه الله لمّا[3] كان الصارف يستشعر من المصروف أنّه يبغضه ويكرهه لا محالة وفي الطباع أن يكره الإنسان من يكرهه ويبغض من يبغضه عرض

١ الأصل: وهذا. ٢ الأصل: فما. ٣ الأصل: قال لمّا.

and whatever the path used to reach it and whatever the language used to express it, knowledge would meet the purpose.

To your question "Is this obligatory?" I respond: It is indeed obligatory, because philosophical inquiry is obligatory inasmuch as it constitutes the perfection of humanity and the attainment of its ultimate degree. When an entity has a specific perfection, its end is to attain that perfection. People who fall short of attaining their perfection, even though they possess the means and the obstacles before it have been removed, are held to account. 116.3

Regarding your question "Is it encountered in reality?" it is indeed so, because philosophy is encountered, and it is the craft of all crafts, and none of its parts have been ordered as it has been ordered itself. For it starts from the lowest level at which the learner begins and reaches the highest grade possible for him to reach. All of this involves principles and explanations that enjoy the utmost firmness, and they are known and available. There is nothing to prevent us from reaching them, nor are they begrudged to those who seek them, and they are a grace to those who learn them. 116.4

On why new incumbents are harsh toward the officials they replace

What is the meaning of the anger felt by the new incumbent of an office toward the official he has replaced? This is how this question is articulated. For example, you are appointed governor of a particular province, or judge in a particular city. You arrive in the province and find the former governor whom you are to replace. You treat him harshly, get angry, and scowl openly at him. Yet he has done nothing to anger you, nor has he ever done you any harm. You have never met, and there has been no exchange of any kind, good or bad, between you. The anger experienced by public floggers and executioners belongs to the same class. 117.1

Miskawayh's response

The new official intuits that the official he is replacing must hate and loathe him, and human beings are naturally disposed to loathe those who loathe them and to hate those who hate them. As a result, every newly appointed official experiences this reaction vis-à-vis the incumbent. Sometimes other elements may 117.2

هذا العارض لكلّ صارف على كلّ مصروف وربّما انضاف إلى ذلك أشياء أخر منها أنّ المصروف ربّما صُرف عن خيانة أو جناية كثيرة يعرض في مثلها الغضب بالواجب وربّما انضاف إلى ذلك أن يُؤمر الصارف بالقبض على المصروف ومواقفته على جناياته واستصفاء ماله وهذه أشياء تثير الغضب وتزيد في مادّته لا سيّما والمصروف يحتجّ لنفسه ويدفع عنها كلّ ما نُسب إليه من القبيح ويدافع عن ماله بما أمكنه فأين يذهب الغضب عن هذا المكان؟ وهل هو إلّا في حقيقة موضعه الخاصّ به؟ فأمّا الجلّاد والسيّاف فلهما وجه آخر من العذر وهو أنّهما إنّما يأخذان أجرة على صناعتهما وإن لم يوفّياها حقّها خشيا اللائمة والاستخفاف وليس يمكنهما توفية صناعتهما حقوقها[١] إلّا بإثارة الغضب هذا مع العلّة الأولى التي ذكرتها في الصارف والمصروف.

مسـألة

١،١١٨ لم كان اليتم في الناس من قبل الأب وفي سائر الحيوان من قبل الأمّ؟ فإن قلت لأنّ الأمّ ههنا كافلة فإنّ الأمر في الناس كذلك وفيه سرّ غير هذا ونظر فوقه.

الجواب

٢،١١٨ قال أبو عليّ مسكويه رحمه الله إنّ الإنسان من حيث هو حيوان مشارك للبهائم في هذا المعنى محتاج إلى ما يقيمه من الأقوات التي تحفظ عليه حيوانيّته ومن حيث هو إنسان مشارك للفلك في هذا المعنى يحتاج إلى ما يبلّغه هذه الدرجة بالتعليم والتأديب لأنّ الأدب يجري من النفس مجرى القوت من البدن والذي يقوم بالحال الأولى هي الأمّ والذي يقوم له بالحال الثانية هو الأب. ولمّا كانت الحالة الثانية أشرف أحواله وهي التي بها[٢] يصير هو ما هو أعني أن يصير إنسانًا وجب أن يكون يتمه

١ الأصل: حقوقهما. ٢ الأصل: به.

be added; for example, the official being replaced might have been deposed because of an act of great treachery or a great felony, such as rightly provoke anger. In addition to that, often the new appointee has been ordered to detain his predecessor, to take him to task for embezzlement of funds, and to liquidate his assets. These are things that provoke anger and enhance its material basis, particularly as the official being replaced will defend himself, deny every evil ascribed to him, and try to protect his assets to the best of his ability. So how could anger be excluded from this context? Doesn't this in fact constitute its true and proper occasion? The behavior of floggers and executioners admits a different kind of justification, for they are recompensed for practicing their trade, and if they fail to execute it properly they will be exposed to censure and derision, and the only way for them to execute their trade properly is by rousing themselves to anger. This is supplementary to the first reason I mentioned regarding the new official and the incumbent being replaced.

On why human beings are considered to be orphans after losing their father rather than their mother

Why is it that with human beings someone is deemed an orphan when he loses 118.1
his father, whereas among other animals this is based on the loss of the mother? If you say: The reason is that among the latter the mother is the provider, the same holds true of human beings. There must be another secret behind this, and the matter must admit further consideration.

Miskawayh's response

Insofar as human beings are animals and via this aspect share kinship with 118.2
the beasts, they need nourishment to sustain them and preserve their animal nature. Insofar as they are human beings and via this aspect share kinship with the celestial sphere, they need the things that enable them to attain this station through instruction and discipline, for discipline is to the soul what nourishment is to the body. The person who attends to the first condition is the mother, and the person who attends to the second is the father. As the second is their noblest condition and that through which they become what they are—human beings—it follows that their status as orphans must be based on the loss of their father. As the perfection of the animal nature of other animals consists

من قبل أبيه ولمّا كان سائر الحيوانات كما حيوانيّتها في القوت[1] البدنيّ وجب أن يكون يتمها من قبل الأمّ ولعلّ الإنسان قبل أن يبلغ حدّ التعلّم من الأب وفي حال حاجته إلى الرضاع إذا فقد أمّه سُمّي يتيماً من قبل الأمّ ولم يمتنع إطلاق ذلك عليه.

مسألة

قال المأمون إنّي لأعجب من أمري أدبّر آفاق الأرض وأعجز عن رقعة يعني الشطرنج ١،١١٩
وهذا معنى شائع في الناس فما السبب فيه؟ فإنّه إنّما عجب من خفاء السبب.

الجواب

قال أبو عليّ مسكويه رحمه الله إنّ الصناعات لا يُكتفى فيها بالعلم المتقدّم والمعرفة ٢،١١٩
السابقة بها حتّى يُضاف إلى ذلك العمل الدائم والارتياض الكثير وإلّا لم يكن الإنسان ماهراً والصانع هو الماهر بصناعته مثال ذلك الكتابة فإنّ العالم بأصولها وإن كان سابق العلم غزير المعرفة إذا أخذ العلم فلم تكن له دربة انقطع فيها ولم ينفعه جميع ما تقدّم من علمه بها وكذلك حال الخياطة والبناء وبالجملة كلّ صناعة مهنيّة كقيادة الجيش ولقاء الأقران في الحروب ليس تكفي فيها الشجاعة ولا العلم بكيفيّتها حتّى يحصل فيها الارتياض والتدرّب فحينئذ تصير صناعة. ولمّا كان الشطرنج أحد الأشياء الجارية هذا المجرى من الصناعات لم يُكتف فيه بالتدبير ولا حسن التخيّل ولا جودة الرأي حتّى تنضاف إلى ذلك مباشرة الأمر والدربة فيه فإنّ لكلّ ضربة يتغيّر بها شكل الشطرنج ضربة من الرسيل مقابلة لها[2] إمّا على غاية الصواب وإمّا بخلافه ويُحتاج إلى ضبط جميع ذلك وتخيّل تلك الأشكال كلّها ضربة بعد ضربة على وجوه تصاريفها وليس يمكن ذلك إلّا مع دربة ورياضة.

---

١ الأصل: في القلوب. ٢ الأصل: له.

in bodily nourishment, it follows that their orphanhood must be based on the loss of the mother. A person might lose his mother before he reaches the point of receiving instruction from the father and while in need of suckling. He is then called an orphan on account of the loss of his mother, and there is no objection to designating him as such.

On why chess is so hard to master

Al-Ma'mūn said: "I wonder at myself. I have the ends of the earth under my power, yet I cannot master a small square"—he was referring to chess. This is something commonly reported among people, so what is its cause? For his wonder was aroused by the obscurity of the cause. 119.1

Miskawayh's response

Without the addition of constant application and regular training, acquired knowledge and prior learning do not suffice in crafts, for otherwise a person cannot become skillful. The craftsman is the person who is skilled in his craft. Take the scribal craft as an example; if the person who knows its principles acquires knowledge but lacks practice, then, despite any prior knowledge and assiduous learning, he comes to a standstill, and none of the knowledge he has previously acquired regarding it avails him. The same applies to sewing or building, and in general to every professional craft, such as leading an army and military combat. Neither courage nor knowledge of its modalities suffices without the acquisition of training and practice; this is when it becomes a craft. Since chess is a craft that conforms to this pattern, neither deliberative power nor good imagination nor excellent judgment suffices without the addition of active engagement and practice. For every move that changes the shape of the game is met by an opponent's countermove, be it apt or inept. All this needs to be determined, and all potential patterns need to be represented in the imagination, move by move, in all their different configurations, and this can only be achieved through practice and training. 119.2

مسـألة

ما السبب في استيحاش الإنسان من نقل كنيته أو اسمه؟ فقد رأيت رجلاً غيّر كنيته لضرورة لحقته وحال دعته فكان يتنكّد[1] ويقلق وكان يكنى أبا حفص فاكتنى أبا جعفر وكان سببه في ذلك أنّه قصد رجلاً يتشيّع فكَرِهَ أن يعرفه بأبي حفص. وكيف صار بعض الناس يمقت الشيء لاسمه دون عينه أو للقبه دون جوهره؟ وما النفور الذي يسرع إلى النفس من النبز واللقب؟ وما السكون الذي يرد على النفس من النعت؟ وما هما إلّا متقاربان في الظاهر متدانيان في الوهم. ١،١٢٠

الجواب

قال أبو عليّ مسكويه رحمه الله إنّ المعاني تلزمها الأسماء ويعتادها أهل اللغات على مرّ الأيّام حتّى تصير كأنّها هي وحتّى يشكّ قوم فيزعمون أنّ الاسم هو المسمّى وحتّى زعم قوم أفاضل أنّ الأسامي بالطباع تصير إلى مطابقة المعاني كأنّهم يقولون إنّ الحروف التي تؤلّف لمعنى القيام أو الجلوس أو الكوكب أو الأرض لا يصلح لغيرها من الحروف أن تسمّى به لأنّ تلك بالطبع صارت له. واضطرّ لأجل هذه الدعوى أن يشتغل كبار الفلاسفة بمناقضتهم ووضع الكتب في ذلك فليس بعجب أن يألف إنسان اسم نفسه حتّى إذا غُيّر ظنّ أنّه إنّما يغيّر هو وإذا دعي بغير اسمه فإنّما دعي غيره بل يرى كأنّما بُدّل به نفسه. ٢،١٢٠

ولقد سمعت بعض المحصّلين يستشير طبيباً ويخاف فيما يشكوه أنّه قد أصابه الماليخوليا فقلت له وما الذي أنكرت من نفسك؟ قال يخيّل لي أنّ يميني قد تحوّل شمالاً وشمالي يميناً لست أشكّ في ذلك فلمّا امتدّ بي النظر في مسألته وجدته كان قد تختّم في يمينه ٣،١٢٠

[1] الأصل وط: ينكّر.

On why people dislike changing their name or patronymic, and why they have a sense of aversion toward certain names and titles

Why are people averse to changing their patronymic or their name? I once knew a man who, on account of a contingency that prompted him to do so, changed his patronymic, and he felt unhappy and ill at ease. His patronymic was "Abū Ḥafṣ" and he adopted the patronymic "Abū Jaʿfar." His reason for doing so was that he asked a Shiʿi for a favor and did not wish to be known as Abū Ḥafṣ.[26] Why is it that some people hate certain things because of their name rather than their intrinsic nature, or their title rather than their inner substance? What is the meaning of the revulsion the soul is quick to feel when confronted with particular sobriquets and titles? What is the meaning of the tranquility that comes over the soul when it encounters particular appellations? And yet the two are similar in appearance and close in imagination. 120.1

Miskawayh's response

Names bind themselves to meanings, and with the passage of time speakers of a language grow so used to them that the two come to be virtually identified. This is what led a group of scholars to the controversial assertion that the name is identical with the thing it names, and what led a group of eminent learned men to assert that names correspond to particular meanings by nature.[27] This seems to involve saying that only the letters that in fact combine to designate the meaning "standing" or "sitting," "star" or "earth," are fit to be used for referring to those meanings and no others, for those letters have come to belong to them by nature. This claim imposed upon the greatest philosophers the task of refutation and composing books on the topic. Therefore, it is little wonder that a person should grow so accustomed to his own name that he should think that he himself has undergone a change if it is changed, and if he is addressed with another name, he should think that someone else has been addressed, and that, indeed, it should seem to him as though his very self has thereby been altered. 120.2

I heard an accomplished scholar consulting a doctor and expressing concern that his symptoms might mean that he had been stricken by melancholy. I asked him: What is it you find unusual in yourself? He replied: It seems to me as though my right side has become my left side, and my left side has become 120.3

مدّة للتقرّب إلى بعض الرؤساء من أصدقائه ثمّ لمّا فارقه لسفره اتّفقت له إعادة إلى التختّم في اليسار فعرض له من الإلف والعادة هذا العارض فاعتبر بذلك يسهل جواب مسألتك وتعلم ما في العادة من المشاكلة لما في الطبع.

٤،١٢٠ فأمّا كراهة الناس الشيء لاسمه أو للقبه ونبزه فالجواب عنه قريب من الجواب عن هذه المسألة وذلك أنّ الأسماء والألقاب أيضاً تُكره لكراهة[1] ما تدلّ عليه للعادة الأولى فلو أنّك نقلت اسم الفحم إلى الكافور فيما بينك وبين آخر لكان متى ذُكر الفحم تصوّر السواد ولم يمنعه ما انتقل فيما بينه وبينك إلى مسمّى آخر أبيض طيّب الرائحة وذلك لأجل العادة اللّٰهمّ إلّا أن يكون تركيب الحروف تركيباً قبيحاً والحروف أنفسها مستهجنة فإنّ الجواب عن ذلك قد مرّ في صدر هذه المسائل مستقصى.

مسألة

١،١٢١ قال أبو حيّان لم صار صاحب الهمّ ومن غلب عليه الفكر في ملمّ يولع بمسّ لحيته وربّما نكت الأرض بإصبعه وعبث بالحصى؟ وقد يختلف الحال في ذلك حتّى إنّك لتجد واحداً يحبّ عند صدمة الهمّ ولوعة الحزن جمعاً وناساً ومجلساً مزدحماً يريغ بذلك تفريحاً ويجد عنده خفّاً وآخر يفزع إلى الخلوة ثمّ لا يقنع إلّا بمكان موحش وبصر[2] ضيّق وطريق غامض وآخر يؤثر الخلوة ولكن يحنّ إلى بستان حالٍ وروض مزهر ونهر جارٍ ثمّ تختلف الحال بين هؤلاء حتّى إنّك لتجد واحداً عند غاشية ذلك

١ الأصل: وذلك أنّ الأسماء أيضا تُكره والألقاب لكراهة. ٢ ط: ونشز.

my right—I have no doubt about that. After questioning him extensively, I discovered that he had worn his ring on his right hand for a certain period of time in order to ingratiate himself with a powerful friend of his; when he left him, he happened to return his ring to his left hand, and he experienced this reaction as a result of custom and habit. If you consider this example, your question will become easy to answer, and you will grasp the similarity that joins habit and nature.

The answer to your question about the revulsion people experience toward something on account of its name, title, or sobriquet is closely related to the answer to this question. For names and titles also provoke revulsion on account of what they designate, because of prior habit. So, were a person to agree with another to reassign the name "coal" so that it designated camphor, whenever the word "coal" was mentioned, the image of something black would come to mind, and the fact that this had been reassigned to another object that is white and sweet-smelling would do nothing to prevent it. This is due to habit, unless of course the combination of the letters is repugnant and the letters themselves provoke distaste. The explanation of the latter phenomenon was discussed exhaustively in the earlier section of these questions.[28] 120.4

On the mannerisms of people whose mind is preoccupied, and on why people have so many different ways of behaving when they feel anxious or unhappy

Al-Tawḥīdi asked: Why do people who feel anxious or who are preoccupied with ruminating about some contretemps love to touch their beard, tap the ground with their finger, or fidget with pebbles? People may vary in that respect, so that we find one person who, when anxiety attacks and grief bites, loves to be among large crowds, around people, and in packed social gatherings, endeavoring thereby to raise his spirits and experience a cheering effect. Another person, by contrast, seeks refuge in solitude and is only to be found in deserted places, confined spaces, or dark roads. Yet another likes solitude but longs for leafy gardens, blooming meadows, and flowing rivers. Furthermore, things vary among these people, so that we find one person who, faced with the adversity that overshadows his thought, exhibits a purer nature, a quicker heart, and a greater presence of mind, reciting rare poems and composing 121.1

الفكر أصفى طبعاً وأذكى قلباً وأحضر ذهناً وحتّى يقول القافية النادرة ويصنّف الرسالة الفاخرة وحتّى يحفظ علماً جمّاً ويستقبل أيّامه نصحاً وآخر يذهل ويعله ويزول عنه الرأي ويتحيّر حتّى لو هدي ما اهتدى ولو أُمر لما فقه ولو نهي لما وَبِه.

الجواب

قال أبو عليّ مسكويه رحمه الله إنّ النفس لا تعطّل الجوارح إلّا عند النوم لأسباب ليس هذا موضع ذكرها. والعقل يستهجن البطالة ولا بدّ من تحريك الأعضاء في اليقظة إمّا بقصد وإدارة وبصناعة ولأغراض مقصودة وإمّا بعبث ولهو وعند غفلة وسهو ولأجل ذلك نهت الشريعة عن الغفلة ونهى الأدب عن الكسل وأُمر الناس وسوّاس المدن بترك العطلة واشتغال الناس بضروب الأعمال ولقباحة العطلة ونفور العقل عنها اشتغل الفرّاغ بلعب الشطرنج والنرد على سخافتهما وأخذهما من العمر وذهابهما بالزمان في غير طائل فإنّ الجلوس بلا شغل ولا حركة بغير ضرورة أمر يأباه الناس كافّة لما ذكرناه. ٢،١٢١

فصاحب الفكر والهمّ لا تتعطّل جوارحه وإنّما ينبغي أن يتعوّد الإنسان بالتأديب حركات جميلة مثل القضيب الذي وُضع للملوك وقد كُره ذلك أيضاً ونُسب إلى النزق وجُعل في جنس الولع بالخاتم فأمّا مسّ اللحية وقلع الزئبر من الثوب فمعدود من المرض لأنّه حركة غير منتظمة ولا جارية على سنّة الأدب بل هو عبث يدلّ على أنّ صاحبه قد احتمل حتّى عزب عقله وذهب تمييزه دفعة ولا ينبغي ذلك لمن له تمييز وبه مسكة أن يفعله بل ينبّه عليه من نفسه ويتركه إن كانت عادته. فأمّا اختلاف الحال في الناس فيمن يحبّ الاجتماع مع الناس أو يحبّ الخلوة وغير ذلك ممّا حكيته وذكرت أقسامه فإنّ ذلك تابع للمزاج وذاك أنّ صاحب السوداء والفكر السوداويّ يحبّ الخلوة ٣،١٢١

magnificent epistles, acquiring large bodies of knowledge and turning the experience he confronts into sound counsel, whereas another person is stunned and stupefied, his judgment takes flight and his mind is plunged in confusion, so that he would fail to accept guidance were he to be given it, he would fail to comprehend any order, and he would fail to take heed of any prohibition.

Miskawayh's response

The only time the soul puts the limbs out of operation is during sleep, though this is not the right occasion to go into the reasons. Reason disapproves of inertia, and during wakefulness the bodily members must necessarily move, whether intentionally and voluntarily, in a skilled manner and for specific purposes, or by way of idle play and diversion and in a state of inattentiveness and distraction. This is why the religious Law prohibits inattentiveness, why the principles of good breeding forbid laziness, and why citizens and their rulers have been commanded to avoid inactivity and to occupy themselves with different kinds of work. Because inactivity is repugnant and reason is averse to it, people in their leisure time busy themselves with games of chess and backgammon despite their foolishness and despite the fact that they consume part of one's life and fritter away time to no profit, for nobody wants to sit about without occupation and without moving unless it is an unavoidable necessity, for the reasons we mentioned above. 121.2

The limbs of the person lost in thought or feeling anxious do not become inactive, but through discipline a person must habituate himself to performing seemly movements, the way staffs were appointed for the use of kings, which is also deemed reprehensible and viewed as a kind of frivolousness, being considered to belong to the same category as infatuation with rings. Touching the beard and plucking the fibers off a new garment are considered symptoms of illness, for they are a disordered type of movement that does not conform to the standards of good breeding; in fact, they are an idle type of movement which indicates that the person soldiered on until, in one fell swoop, he lost his reason and his discrimination. A person possessed of discrimination and intelligence will not engage in this; he must be made conscious of what he is doing and must desist from it if it is his wont. The variations between different people—such as those who like to associate with people and those who like solitude, and all the other things you recounted and whose subdivisions you listed—are contingent 121.3

والتفرّد ويأنس بذلك وأمّا صاحب الفكر والفكر الدمويّ فإنّه يحبّ الاجتماع والناس وربّما آثر النزهة والفرجة.

وأمّا ما حكيت عمّن يصنع الشعر ويصنّف الرسالة ويشغل نفسه بالعلوم فجميع ذلك إنّما يكون بحسب عادة من يطرقه الفكر فإن كان قبل ذلك ممّن يرتاض ببعض هذه الأشياء أو يكثر الفكر فيها فإنّه بعد ورود العارض يلجأ إلى ما كان عليه ويعود إلى عادته بنفس ثائرة مضطرّة إلى الفكر فينفذ فيما كان فيه ولا بدّ أن يصير ذلك الفكر من جنس ما دهمه أعني أنّه يقول القافية ويصنّف الرسالة في ذلك المعنى الذي طرأ عليه لكن يستعين عليه بفكر كأن يتصرّف في شعر آخر فيردّه إلى الهمّ[1] الذي يقلقه ويحفّزه فيجيء كلامه وشعره أحدّ وأصفى ممّا كان وأمّا الذي يذهل ويعلّه ويتحيّر فهو الذي لم يكن قبل ورود ذلك الشغل عليه ممّن لا يرتاض الشعر[2] ولا ترسّل ولا عادته أن يلجأ إلى فكره ويستعمله في استخراج الخبايا واللطائف فإذا طرقه عارض يحتاج فيه إلى فكر لم يجده وأصابه من الوله والدهش ما ذكرت. ٤،١٢١

مسـألة

رأيت سـائلاً سـأل فقال ما بال أصحاب التوحيد لا يخبرون عن البارئ إلّا بنفي الصفات؟ فقيل له بيّن قولك وابسط فيه إرادتك قال إنّ الناس في ذكر صفات الله تعالى على طريقتين فطائفة تقول لا صفات له كالسمع والعلم والبصر والحياة والقدرة لكنّه مع نفي هذه الصفات موصوف بأنّه سميع بصير حيّ قادر عالم وطائفة قالت هذه أسماء الموصوف بصفات هي العلم[3] والقدرة والحياة ولا بدّ من إطلاقها وتحقيقها. ١،١٢٢

١ الأصل وط: الأهمّ. ٢ ط: بشعر. ٣ الأصل: العالم.

on the humoral mixture. People affected by black bile and by melancholy thought like to be solitary and apart, and find it congenial, whereas people affected by sanguine thought like to associate with and be around people, and are sometimes fond of excursions and entertaining spectacles.

Let's take the points you made about those who turn out poetry, compose 121.4
epistles, and busy themselves with different forms of knowledge—all of this depends on the habits of the people beset by thought and worry. If previously they had been the type of people who occupied themselves with them or devoted much thought to them, after the supervening incident, they resort to their former state and return to their habitual activity with a soul that has been roused and compelled to think, acquitting themselves with skill in their familiar activity. It is unavoidable that their thoughts be directed to the kind of thing that befell them—that is, that they compose poems and epistles relating to the matter that affected them, but with the assistance of thought—for example, by applying themselves to some other poetry and referring it back to the worries troubling and galvanizing them; then their words and their poetry come out keener and purer than before. People who are stunned and stupefied and whose mind is plunged into confusion, by contrast, are those who did not practice poetry or compose epistles before they were visited by the matter that preoccupies them, and who did not have a habit of resorting to thought and of using it to unearth hidden subtleties. So, when they are beset by an incident that requires them to think, they cannot find the means, and are struck by the kind of bewilderment and dazed condition you have described.

On different ways of approaching God's attributes

I saw someone pose the following question: Why is it that the only way the 122.1
adherents of God's unity describe the Creator is by denying Him any attributes?[29] He was told: Explain your point and clarify your intention. He said: People follow two approaches in discussing the attributes of God. One faction says: He possesses no attributes—such as hearing, knowledge, sight, life, and power—yet even though these attributes are to be denied, He is qualified as hearing, seeing, living, powerful, and knowing. Another faction says: These are names that belong to a subject qualified by attributes that consist in knowledge, power, and life, and these must be applied and affirmed. Both factions

ثمّ إنّ هاتين الطائفتين تطابقتا على أنّه عالم لا كالعالمين وقادر لا كالقادرين وسميع لا كالسامعين ومتكلّم لا كالمتكلّمين. ثمّ عادت القائلة بالصفات على أنّ له علماً لا كالعلوم واتّكأت على النفي في جميع ذلك. وكانت الطائفتان في ظاهر الرأي مثبتة نافية معطية آخذة إلّا أن يبيّن ما يزيد على هذا. هذا آخر المسألة والجواب عنها حرفان مع الإيجاز إن ساعد فهم وتبسيط مع البيان إن احتيج إليه في موضعه إن شاء الله[1].

الجواب

قال أبو عليّ مسكويه رحمه الله أمّا قولك الجواب عنه حرفان مع الإيجاز فهو قريب ممّا قلت وذاك أنّ كلّ صفة وموصوف يقع عليه وهم وينطلق به لسان فهو جود من الله تعالى وإبداع له ومنّ مِنه أمتن به على خلقه وليس يجوز أن يوصف الله تعالى بما هو مبدع ومخلوق له فهذا مع الإيجاز كاف. ولا بدّ من أدنى بسط وبيان فنقول إنّ البرهان قد قام على أنّ البارئ الأوّل الواحد هو عزّ اسمه متقدّم الوجود على كلّ معقول ومحسوس وأنّه أوّل بالحقيقة أي ليس له شيء يتقدّمه على سبيل علّة ولا سبب ولا غيرهما وما ليس له علّة تتقدّمه[2] فوجوده أبداً وما وجوده أبداً فهو واجب الوجود وما كان كذلك فهو لم يزل وما لم يزل فليس له علّة فليس بمتركّب ولا متكثّر لأنّه لو كان مركّباً أو كان متركّباً لكان قد تقدّمه شيء أعني بسائطه أو آحاده. وقد قلنا إنّه أوّل لم يتقدّمه شيء فإذن ليس بمركّب ولا متكثّر والأوصاف التي يثبتها له من يثبتها ليس تخلو من أن تكون قديمة معه أو محدثة بعده ولو كانت قديمة معه موجودة بوجوده لكان هناك كثرة ولو كانت كثرة لكانت لا محالة متركّبة من آحاد ٢،١٢٢

---

١ الأصل: إن شاء. ٢ الأصل: تهدمه.

agree on the view that God is qualified as "knowing" in a way unlike the way other beings are qualified as "knowing," qualified as "powerful" in a way unlike the way other beings are qualified as "powerful," qualified as "hearing" in a way unlike the way other beings are qualified as "hearing," and qualified as "speaking" in a way unlike the way other beings are qualified as "speaking." Furthermore, the faction that affirms God's attributes has resorted to the view that He has knowledge that is unlike the knowledge of other beings, and they have adopted a stance of negation with regard to all of it. Pending further clarification, it seems, on the face of it, that both factions affirm and deny, give and take. That is the end of the question. The response can be given in a few lines and, with the assistance of understanding, in brief, and by way of an expansive exposition if required in the relevant context, God willing.

Miskawayh's response

Your remark, "The response to it can be given in a few lines and . . . in brief . . ." **122.2** is close to what I have said. For every attribute and every subject of attributes that one's imagination alights on and that one's tongue pronounces is given by God's generosity, originates with Him, and is a bounty He bestows on His creation; it is impermissible that God be qualified by means of things He has originated and created. That suffices as a brief response, but it is necessary to provide minimal clarification and exposition. We therefore say as follows. It has been demonstrated that the One, the First Creator, is prior in existence to all intelligible and sensible things and that He is first in reality, that is, there is nothing that precedes Him as a cause or ground or in any other way. A being that is not preceded by a cause exists eternally, and a being that exists eternally exists necessarily. A being that is such has always been, and a being that has always been has no cause, and is neither composite nor characterized by multiplicity. For were it composed or a composite, there would be something that preceded it—namely, its elements or parts. Yet we have said that He is first and has not been preceded by anything, so He cannot be composed or characterized by multiplicity. The attributes affirmed of Him by those who affirm them might either be eternal alongside Him or originated after Him. If they were eternal alongside Him and their existence were conjoined with His existence, there would be multiplicity, and if there were multiplicity, it would inevitably be a composite of parts. If the parts were prior, or if the unity—particularly the

ولو كانت الآحاد متقدّمة أو الوحدة سيّما التي منها تركّبت[1] الآحاد والكثرة متقدّمة لم يكن أوّلاً[2] وقد قلنا إنّه أوّل ولو كانت أوصافه بعده لكان خالياً منها فيما لم يزل وخلصت له الوحدة وإنّما حدث له ما حدث عن سبب وعلّة تعالى الله وجلّ عمّا يقول[3] المبطلون وقد قلنا إنّه لا سبب له ولا علّة.

٣،١٢٢ وأمّا إطلاقنا ما نطلقه عليه من الجود والقدرة وسائر الصفات فلأنّ العقل إذا قسم الشيء إلى الإيجاب والسلب أو إلى الحسن والقبيح أو إلى الوجود والعدم وجب أن ينظر في كلّ طرفين فينسب الأفضل منهما إليه إن كنّا لا محالة مشيرين إليه بوصف مثلاً كأنّا سمعنا بالقدرة والعجز وهما طرفان فوجدنا أحدهما مدحاً والآخر ذمّاً فوجب أن ننسب إليه ما هو مدح عندنا وكذلك نفعل في الجود وضدّه والعلم وخلافه ومع ذلك فينبغي ألّا نقيس على هذا القدر أيضاً إلّا إذا كان معنا رخصة في شريعة أو إطلاق في كتاب منزل لئلّا نبتدع له من عندنا ما لم تجر به سنّة أو فريضة ونحذر كلّ الحذر من الإقدام على هذه الأمور. ولأنّا ضمنّا ترك الإطالة في جميع أجوبة هذه المسائل فلنقتصر على هذا النبذ ومن أحبّ الإطالة والتوسّع فيه فليقرأه من موضعه الخاصّ به من كتابنا الذي سمّيناه الفوز أو من كتب غيرنا المصنّفة في هذا المعنى إن شاء الله.

مسألة

١،١٢٣ لم صار الإنسان في حفظ الصواب أنفذ منه في حفظ الخطأ؟ شاهد هذا أنّك لو سُمت الغُفل أن يتعلّم الأدب ويعتاد الصواب في اللفظ كان أحرى بذلك وأجرأ عليه من قاض أو عدل أو أديب عالم تسوم واحداً منهم أن يتخلّق بخلق بعض العامّة

[1] ط: تركّبت منها. [2] الأصل: أوّل. [3] الأصل: يقولون.

one from which the parts were composed—and the multiplicity were prior,[30] He would not have been first, yet we have said that He is first. Were His attributes posterior to Him, He would be free from them in the beginning of time and He would be truly characterized by unity, but what accrued to Him would have accrued to Him on account of a ground and a cause—may He be exalted and glorified far above what the purveyors of falsehoods claim—yet we have said that He has no ground or cause.

The reason for our application of generosity, power, and all other attributes 122.3
to Him is that when reason divides something into affirmation and negation, right and wrong, existence and nonexistence, it is necessary that each of the opposing extremes be considered and that the best of the two be ascribed to Him, insofar as it is unavoidable that we refer to Him using an attribute at all. For example, having learned about power and impotence, which form opposing extremes, we find that one of these is praiseworthy, while the other is blameworthy, so it is necessary that we ascribe to Him what is praiseworthy for us. We do the same with regard to generosity and its contrary, and knowledge and its reverse. Nevertheless, we must not proceed analogically on this basis unless we have been given license by a religious Law and granted permission by a divinely revealed book, so that we do not ascribe to Him figments of our own devising unsanctioned by norm or ordinance, and we should be on the strongest possible guard against doing such a thing. But we have pledged to avoid going on at length in our answers to these questions, so let us confine ourselves to this modest amount. Those who wish to dwell on the topic at length and to expand on it may read about it in the relevant part of our book, which we have entitled *The Book of Triumph*, or in the books composed by others on this topic, God willing.[31]

On why we find it easier to remember what is correct than what is defective

Why are people more successful at remembering what is correct than what is 123.1
erroneous? This is attested by the fact that if we were to task a simpleminded person with acquiring literary culture and developing the habit of correct speech, he would be more adequate to that task and bolder in pursuing it than a learned judge, a trustworthy witness, or a man of letters whom we tasked

أو يقتدي بلفظه في خطائه[1] وفساده ولهذا تجد مائة ينشدونك لأبي تمّام والبحتريّ ولا تجد ثلاثة ينشدونك للطرميّ وأبي العبر.

الجواب

قال أبو عليّ مسكويه رحمه الله إنّ الصواب شيء واحد وله سمت يشير إليه العقل وتقتضيه الفطرة السليمة من كلّ أحد فأمّا الانحراف عن ذلك السمت والخطأ فيه وعنه فأمر لا نهاية له فلذلك لا يمكن ضبطه. وإن انحرف عنه منحرف فإنّما يكون ذلك منه كما جاء واتّفق لا بإشارة من فهم ولا دليل من عقل. وحفظ مثل هذا عسير جدّاً إذ كان الحفظ إنّما هو تذكّر لصورة قيّدها العقل وتلك الصورة هي مقتضى العقل أو رسم من رسوم قوى العقل فالإنسان مُعان على هذا الرسم بالفطرة ومعان على تذكّره أيضاً بالفطرة. فأمّا العدول عنه فهو كالعدول عن نقطة الدائرة التي تسمّى مركزاً فإنّ النقطة في الدائرة التي ليست مركزاً هي كثيرة بلا نهاية وإنّما المحدودة منها هي نقطة واحدة أعني التي بعدها من جميع محيط الدائرة بالسواء. ٢،١٢٣

مسـألة

لم صار العروضيّ رديء الشعر قليل الماء والمطبوع على خلافه؟ ألم تُبن العروض على الطبع؟ أليست هي ميزان الطبع فما بالها تخون؟ قد رأينا بعض من يتذوّق وله طبع يخطئ ويخرج من وزن إلى وزن وما رأينا عروضيّاً له ذلك فلم كان هذا مع هذا الفضل أنقص ممّن هو أفضل منه؟ ١،١٢٤

[1] ط: خطابه.

with acquiring the disposition of a commoner or emulating his erroneous and corrupt speech. That is why we find a hundred people who can recite to us Abū Tammām and al-Buḥturī, yet we cannot find three who can recite to us al-Ṭarmī and Abū l-ʿIbar.

Miskawayh's response

What is correct is a single thing and follows a course indicated by reason and demanded from everyone by our sound natural constitution. By contrast, deviations from the course, errors committed in it and against it, are infinite in number, hence their insusceptibility to precise determination. If a person deviates from it, he does so in a haphazard and contingent way, not on the basis of an indication provided by the understanding or a proof on the part of reason. The retention of something of this kind is extremely difficult, for retention consists in the recollection of a form bound by reason, and that form represents a demand of reason or a prescription on the part of one of the powers of reason. Human beings are assisted by their natural constitution in responding to this prescription, and they are also assisted by their natural constitution in recollecting it. Veering from it, by contrast, is like veering from the central point of a circle. For there are an infinite number of points of a circle that do not constitute the center but there is only a single point that is uniquely determined, which is the one equidistant from the entire circumference of the circle. 123.2

On why prosodists tend to produce flat poetry

Why do versifiers and prosodists produce bad poetry and their works lack luster and élan, whereas the reverse is true for naturally gifted poets? Isn't prosody founded on nature? Doesn't it constitute the measure of nature? Why then does it betray one's expectations? We have seen people possessed of taste and a natural gift for poetry committing mistakes by slipping from one meter to another, and we have not seen this happen to any versifiers or prosodists. So why are they, despite such excellence, more deficient than those they excel over? 124.1

الجواب

قال أبو عليّ مسكويه رحمه الله إنّ المطبوع من المولّدين يلزم الوزن الواحد ولا يخرج ٢،١٢٤
عنه ما دام طبعه يطيع ذلك ولكن ربّما سمعنا للشعراء الجاهليّين المتقدّمين أوزاناً لا تقبلها طباعنا ولا تحسن في ذوقنا وهي عندهم مقبولة موزونة يستمرّون عليها كما يستمرّون في غيرها كقول المرقّش [مجزوء البسيط]

لِابْنَةِ عَجْلَانَ بِالطَّفِّ رُسُومْ   لَمْ يَتَعَفَّيْنَ وَالْعَهْدُ قَدِيمْ

وهي قصيدة مختارة في المفضّليات ولها أخوات لا أحبّ تطويل الجواب بإيرادها كانت مقبولة الوزن في طباع أولئك القوم وهي نافرة عن طباعنا نظنّها مكسورة وكذلك قد يستعملون من الزحاف في الأوزان التي تستطيبها ما يكون عند المطبوعين منّا مكسوراً وهي صحيحة. والسبب في جميع ذلك أنّ القوم كانوا يجبرون بنغمات يستعملونها مواضع من الشعر يستوي بها الوزن ولأنّا نحن لا نعرف تلك النغمات إذا أنشدنا الشعر على السلامة لم يحسن في طباعنا والدليل على ذلك أنّا إذا عرفنا في بعض الشعر تلك النغمة حسن عندنا وطاب في ذوقنا كقول الشاعر [مديد]

إِنَّ بِالشِّعْبِ الَّذِي دُونَ سَلْعٍ   لَقَتِيلاً دَمُهُ مَا يُطَلُّ

فإنّ هذا الوزن إذا أُنشد مفكّك الأجزاء بالنغمة التي تخصّه طاب في الذوق وإذا أُنشد كما يُنشد سائر الشعر لم يطب[١] في كلّ ذوق. وهذه سبيل الزحاف الذي يقع في الشعر ممّا يطيب في ذوق العرب وينكسر في ذوقنا ولولا أنّ الموسيقى مركوزة في الطباع ووزن النغم ومقابلة بعضها بعضاً على الإيقاع مجبول[٢] عليه النفس لما تساعدت النفوس كلّها على قبول حركات[٣] بعينها وتلك الحركات المقبولة هي النسب التي يطلبها الموسيقيّ ويبني[٤] عليها رأيه وأصله.

١ الأصل: ممّا يطيب. ٢ ط: بعضه بعضا مجبولة. ٣ ط: حركات أخر. ٤ الأصل: ويبنئ.

Miskawayh's response

Naturally gifted poets who are not of pure Arab descent[32] stick to a single meter, and do not abandon it so long as their nature acquiesces to it. But we sometimes hear the early poets of pre-Islamic times using meters disagreeable to our nature and displeasing to our taste, which find them agreeable and well-measured and use them as regularly as they use others. An example is the line by al-Muraqqish: 124.2

> Traces of Bint ʿAjlān in al-Ṭaff not yet effaced,
> though a long time has passed.[33]

This is a poem included in al-Mufaḍḍal's *Anthology*—and there are others like it that I do not wish to prolong this response by citing—whose meter was agreeable to the nature of those people, yet it is repugnant to our own nature, and we regard it as rhythmically unacceptable. Similarly, they might sometimes employ variations[34] in the meters they approve of that the naturally gifted poets of our own time consider rhythmically unacceptable, though they are correct. The reason is that those people would redress things by voicing particular sounds at various points in the poem that would make the meter come out right. We have no knowledge of those sounds, so when we recite the poetry properly it is not pleasing to our nature. This is proved by the fact that when we do know these sounds in certain pieces of poetry, we find them pleasing and to our taste. An example is the line of the poet:[35]

> In the mountain pass with no cleft
> lies a slain hero whose blood will be avenged.

If this meter is recited in a segmented fashion using the sounds proper to it, it is to our taste, whereas if it is recited the way other poetry is recited, it is not to everyone's taste. This is how things stand with those metrical variations in poetry that the taste of the Arabs approves of but our own taste regards as rhythmically unacceptable. Were music not embedded in people's natures and were the measures of different sounds and their relationships to one another in rhythmic patterns not naturally ingrained in the soul, different souls would diverge about which specific open syllables they found agreeable; agreeable open syllables are the proportional relations musicians seek and on which they ground their judgment and principles.

والعروضيّ[1] إنّما يتبع هذه الحركات والسكنات التي في كلّ بيت فيحصّلها بالعدد وبالأجزاء المتقابلة المتوازنة فإن نقص جزء من الأجزاء أساكن[2] أو متحرّك فإنّما يجبره المنشد بالنغمة حتّى يتلافاه فمتى ذهب عنه ذلك لم يستقم في ذوقه ولم يساعد عليه طبعه. فأمّا من نقص ذوقه في العروض فإنّما ذلك للغلط الذي يقع له في بعض الزحافات التي يجيزها العروض وله مذهب عند العرب فيقع لصاحب الذوق الذي لا يعرف تلك النغمة التي تقوم بذلك الزحاف أنّه جائز في كلّ موضع فيغلط من ههنا ويتّهم أيضاً طبعه حتّى يظنّ أنّ المنكسر من الشعر أيضاً هو في معنى المزاحف وأنّه كما لم يمتنع المزحوف من الجواز كذلك لا يمتنع هذا الآخر الذي يجري عنده مجراه وهذا غلط قد عُرف وجهه ومذهب صاحبه فيه. وأمّا واضع العروض فقد كان ذا علم بالوزن وصاحب ذوق وطبع فاستخرج صناعة من الطباع الجيّدة تستمرّ لمن ليست له طبيعة جيّدة في الذوق ليتمّم بالصناعة تلك النقيصة. وكذلك الحال في صناعة النحو والخطابة وما يجري مجراها من الصنائع العلميّة وليس يجري صاحب الصناعة وإن كان ماهراً في صناعته مجرى الطبع الجيّد الفائق. ٣،١٢٤

مسألة

ما معنى قول بعض القدماء العالم أطول عمراً من الجاهل بكثير وإن كان أقصر عمراً عنه؟ ما هذه الإشارة والدفينة فإنّ ظاهرها مناقضة؟ ١،١٢٥

الجواب

قال أبو عليّ مسكويه رحمه الله قد تبيّن من مباحث الفلسفة أنّ الحياة على نوعين أحدهما حياة بدنيّة وهي البهيميّة التي تشاركنا فيها الحيوانات كلّها وحياة نفسيّة وهي ٢،١٢٥

---

١ الأصل: والعروض. ٢ ط: ساكن.

Prosodists and versifiers track the open and closed syllables found in every verse, and study them in terms of their number and in comparison with the elements that are facing and parallel to them. If one element is lacking, whether an open or closed syllable, the reciter redresses this by voicing a certain sound so as to remedy the problem. Whenever that is not possible, his taste finds it awry and his nature does not go along with it. People's taste falls short in prosody because they are mistaken about some of the metrical variations permitted by prosody. The Arabs have a specific approach to this. People guided by taste but unaware of the sound through which that metrical variation is accomplished form the notion that it is permissible in every context, and accordingly fall into error. They also impugn their nature, so that they come to believe that poetry with metrical defects is of the same order as poetry that contains metrical variations, and that just as poetry that contains metrical variation is allowable, the former—which they think belongs to the same class—is also allowable. The basis of this error and the way people are led to commit it have been identified. For his part, the person who invented prosody understood meter and possessed taste and natural gifts, and he developed a craft based on his outstanding natural disposition that can also serve those who lack an outstanding natural disposition with regard to taste, allowing them to use the craft to make up for their deficiency. This also applies to the crafts of grammar, rhetoric, and other scientific crafts of the same class. However skilled practitioners of a craft may be, they are not in the same class as people of superlative, outstanding natural dispositions. 124.3

On the meaning of the dictum that the learned live longer than the ignorant

What did an ancient thinker mean when he said, "Even if they live shorter lives, the learned live longer than the ignorant"? What does this indicate, and what is the secret it harbors? For on the surface it implies a contradiction. 125.1

Miskawayh's response

Philosophical inquiries have established that life is of two kinds: the life of the body, which is the beastly life that all animals share with us, and the life of the soul, which is the human life realized through the attainment of various 125.2

الحياة الإنسانيّة التي تكون بتحصيل العلوم والمعارف وهذه هي الحياة التي يجتهد الأفاضل من الناس في تحصيلها فالواجب أن يُظنّ بالجاهل الذي يحيا حياة بدنيّة أنّه ليس بحيّ بتّة أعني أنّه ليس بإنسان ولا حَيِيَ حياته فأمّا العالم فالواجب أن يُقال فيه إنّه هو الحيّ بالحقيقة كما أنّ غيره هو الميّت.

مسـألة

١،١٢٦ لم صارت[١] بلاغة اللسان أعسر من بلاغة القلم؟ وما القلم واللسان إلّا آلتان وما مستقاهما إلّا واحد فلِمَ ترى عشرة يكتبون ويجيدون ويبلغون وثلاثة منهم إذا نطقوا لا يجيدون ولا يبلغون؟ والذي يدلّك على قلّة بلاغة اللسان إكبار الناس البليغ باللسان أكثر من إكبارهم البليغ بالقلم.

الجواب

٢،١٢٦ قال أبو عليّ مسكويه رحمه الله ذلك لأنّ البلاغة التي تكون بالقلم تكون مع رويّة وفكرة وزمان متّسع للانتقاد والتخيّر والضرب والإلحاق وإجالة الرويّة لإبدال الكلمة بالكلمة ومن تباده بالكلام متى لم يكن لفظه ومعناه متوافيين عرض له التتعتع والتلجلج وتمضّغ الكلام وهذا هو العيّ المكروه المستعاذ منه. فأمّا البليغ فهو حاضر الذهن سريع حركة اللسان بالألفاظ التي لا يقتصر منها أن يبلّغ ما في نفسه من المعنى حتّى تتفرّغ له قطعة من ذلك الزمان السريع إلى توشيح عبارته وترتيبها باختيار الأعذب فالأعذب وطلب المشاكلة والموازنة والسجع وكثير ممّا يُحتاج في مثله إلى الزمان الكثير والفكر الطويل.

١ الأصل: صار.

kinds of knowledge and learning. This is the life that excellent people strive to attain. So, ignorant people who live a bodily life must be viewed as not living at all, meaning that they are not human beings and do not live human lives. The learned must be said to be those who are really alive, whereas the others are dead.

On why it is harder to speak eloquently than to write eloquently

Why is eloquence with the tongue harder than eloquence with the pen? The **126.1** tongue and the pen are only tools, and draw from a single source, so why is it that for every ten people who write excellently and express themselves eloquently, there are three who, when speaking, fail to acquit themselves well and express themselves eloquently? One of the indications of how rare eloquence with the tongue is is the greater esteem shown by people for those who are eloquent with the tongue than for those who are eloquent with the pen.

Miskawayh's response

The reason for this is that the eloquence achieved through the pen is achieved **126.2** with reflection and thought, and with enough time for critical judgment, choices, erasing and adding things, and deliberation about replacing one word with another. If people extemporize when their words and meanings are incompletely formed they succumb to stammering, stuttering, and slurred speech—precisely the repugnant inarticulacy we seek to guard against. Eloquent people, for their part, are endowed with presence of mind, and words flow from their tongue so rapidly that they do not confine themselves just to expressing the ideas inside their mind but have some time left over to embellish their phrases, to arrange them by deploying the most agreeable ones in turn, to look for affinities, balance, and rhyme—in short, to achieve things that ordinarily require much time and prolonged thought.

مسألة

على ماذا يدلّ انتصاب قامة الإنسان من بين هذا الحيوان؟ فقد قال أبو زيد البلخيّ الفلسفيّ كلاماً سأحكيه. ١،١٢٧

الجواب

قال أبو عليّ مسكويه رحمه الله هذا الرجل الفاضل الذي ذكرته إذا كان يوجد له كلام في هذا المعنى فالأولى بنا أن نستعفيك الكلام فيه وإذا كنت غير معفينا فالأولى أن نكتفي بالإيماء إلى المعنى دون الإطالة. فنقول إنّ الحرارة إذا كانت مادّتها لطيفة مؤاتية في الرطوبة والاستجابة إلى الامتداد فهي تمدّ الجسم الذي تعلّقت به إلى جهتها أعني العلوّ مدّاً مستقيماً. وإنّما يعرض الانكباب والميل إلى جهة الأرض لشيئين إمّا لضعف الحرارة وإمّا لقلّة استجابة المادّة التي تعلّقت بها. وأنت تتبيّن ذلك وتتأمّله في الأشجار التي بعضها يتشعّب بشعب مرجحنّة نحو الأرض وبعضها ممتدّة على جهة الاستقامة إلى فوق وبعضها مركّبة الحركة بحسب مقاومة المادّة لأنّ حركة الشيء المركّب تكون أيضاً مركّبة[1] وما كان من الشجر والنبات ممتدّاً على وجه الأرض غير منتصب فهو لكثرة الأجزاء الأرضيّة فيه ولضعف الحرارة عن مدّه نحو العلوّ وما كان من الشجر منتصباً وقد تشعّبت منه شعبٌ نحو الأرض ويميناً وشمالاً فلأنّ حركتي النار والأرض قد تركّبتا فحدث منهما هذا الشكل المركّب بين الانتصاب والارجحنان وما كان الشجر ممتدّاً كالقضيب إلى فوق كالسرو وما أشبهه فلأنّ أجزاءه الأرضيّة والرطوبة المائيّة فيه لطيفة والحرارة قويّة فلم يمتنع من الحركة المستقيمة التي تحرّكها النار وإذا تأمّلت حقّ التأمّل هذه الأمثلة لم يعسر عليك نقلها إلى الحيوان إن شاء الله. ٢،١٢٧

١ ط: المركّب.

On the significance of the fact that human beings are the only animals to stand upright

What is the significance of the fact that among all animals, human beings are the only ones that stand upright? Abū Zayd al-Balkhī the philosopher has pronounced some remarks on the topic that I will recount. 127.1

Miskawayh's response

If that excellent man you mention has pronounced some remarks on this topic, it is appropriate for us to ask you to exempt us from delivering any of our own. If you do not grant us this exemption, it is appropriate that we content ourselves with an allusive rather than an elaborate discussion of the point. We therefore reply: When the material substrate of heat is soft and well-disposed in terms of moisture and susceptibility to extension, heat causes the body to which it attaches to extend in its direction—that is, upward—in a straight manner. Things bend and incline toward the earth for two reasons: either because the heat is weak, or because the material substrate to which it attaches has limited susceptibility. One can perceive and contemplate that phenomenon in relation to trees, some of which grow branches that dangle toward the earth, while others extend upward in a straight manner, and yet others grow in a composite way, depending on the resistance of their matter, for the movement of composite entities is also composite. Trees and plants that grow on the ground and do not stand erect do so because of the large number of earthly parts they contain and because the heat is too weak to make them extend upward. Trees that stand erect and sprout branches that spread right and left and incline toward the earth do so because the movements of the fire and the earth have formed a composite, producing a composite shape that combines standing erect and downward inclination. Trees that, like rods, extend upward, such as cypresses and the like, do so because the earthly parts and aqueous moisture they contain are soft, and the heat is strong, so there is nothing to hinder the straight movement that fire produces. If you ponder these examples with due attention, it will not be difficult for you to transfer the principle to animals, God willing. 127.2

مسـألة

لم صار اليقين إذا حدث وطرأ لا يثبت ولا يستقرّ والشكّ إذا عرض أرسى ١٫١٢٨
وربض؟ يدلّك على هذا أنّ الموقن بالشيء متى شككته نزا فؤاده وقلق به والشاكّ متى وُفّقت به وأرشدته وأهديت الحكمة إليه لا يزداد إلّا جموحاً ولا ترى منه إلّا عتوًّا ونفوراً.

الجواب

قال أبو عليّ مسكويه رحمه الله أظنّ السائل عن اليقين لم يعرف حقيقته وظنّ أنّ لفظة ٢٫١٢٨
اليقين تدلّ على المعرفة المرسلة أو على الإقناع اليسير وليس الأمر كذلك فإنّ مرتبة اليقين أعلى مرتبة تكون في العلم وليس يجوز أن يطرأ عليه شكّ بعد أن صار يقيناً ومثال ذلك أنّ من علم أنّ خمسة في خمسة خمسة وعشرون ليس يجوز أن يشكّ فيه في وقت وكذلك من علم أنّ زوايا المثلّث مساوية لقائمتين ليس يجوز أن يشكّ فيه وهذه سبيل العلوم المتيقّنة بالبراهين وبالأوائل التي بها تُعلم البراهين فأمّا ما دون اليقين فمراتبه كثيرة على ما بُيّن في كتاب المنطق والشكوك تعترض كلّ مرتبة بحسب منزلتها من الإقناع وإذا كان الأمر كذلك فليس يرد قلب[1] المتيقّن أبداً شكّ ينزو منه فؤاده بل هو قارّ وادع لا تحرّك منه الشكوك[2] بتّة.

فأمّا ما ذكرته من أنّ الشاكّ إذا أُرشد وأهديت له الحكمة لا يزداد إلّا جموحاً فإنّ ٣٫١٢٨
ذلك يعترض لأحد شيئين إمّا لأنّ المرشد لم يتأتّ للشاكّ ولم يدرّجه إلى الحكمة فحمّله ما لا يضطلع به وإمّا لأنّ الحكيم ربّما نهى عن أشياء يميل إليها الطبع بالهوى وقد علمت بما بيّنّاه فيما تقدّم أنّ قوى الهوى أغلب وأقوى فينا من قوى العقل فيصير حاله حال من يجذبه حبلان أحدهما ضعيف والآخر قويّ لا محالة يستجيب للأقوى

١ ط: على قلب. ٢ الأصل: منه الشكوك منه.

On why certainty is less enduring than doubt

Why is it that when certainty obtains, it does not last long enough to take root, whereas when doubt assails, it drops anchor and stays put? This is demonstrated by the fact that when a person who is certain of something is given reasons to doubt it, his spirit is jolted and he is filled with unease, whereas when you take a person who harbors doubt by the hand, give him guidance, and offer wise insight, you only make him more recalcitrant, and all you get is insolence and repugnance. 128.1

Miskawayh's response

I believe that the person who posed this question about certainty was unaware of its real meaning, and fancied that the term "certainty" refers to some loose notion of learning or light conviction. This is not how things stand; for certainty constitutes the highest possible rank that knowledge can reach, and doubt cannot possibly assail a person after certainty has been formed. For example, once someone has come to know that five times five makes twenty-five, doubt is not possible at any point in time. Similarly, once someone has come to know that the sum of the angles of a triangle is equal to the sum of two right angles, doubt is not possible. This is how it is with the kinds of knowledge that are established with certainty by means of demonstrative proofs and by means of the first principles through which demonstrative proofs are known. The kinds of belief that fall below certainty admit of many ranks, as explained in the *Book on Logic*,[36] and each rank is vulnerable to doubt depending on the degree of conviction it involves. Given this, the heart of the person who has attained certainty never succumbs to a doubt that "jolts" his spirit; he is tranquil and at ease and utterly immune to being moved by doubt. 128.2

You mentioned that if one offers guidance and wise insight to the doubter, this only makes him more recalcitrant. This happens for one of two reasons: either because the person offering guidance does not approach the doubter gently and does not introduce him to wise insight in a gradual way, instead burdening him with more than he can bear; or because the wise person might sometimes forbid things that nature inclines to through blind desire. Through our earlier exposition, you know that the forces of blind desire are dominant, and stronger than the forces of reason. The doubter thus becomes like a 128.3

إلى أن تقوى عزيمته على الأيّام فيضعف القويّ ويقوى الضعيف كما أشار به الحكماء وشرعه الأنبياء.

مسـألة

لم صار الناس يضحكون من السخرة[1] والمضحك إذا لم يضحك أكثر من ضحكهم منه إذا ضحك؟ وهذا عارض موجود في كلّ من ألهاك ولم يضحك. ١،١٢٩

الجواب

قال أبو عليّ مسكويه رحمه الله إنّ من شأن المضحك أن يتطلّب أمورًا معدولة عن جهاتها ليستدعي بذلك تعجّب السامع وضحكه وإذا لم يضحك هو إنّما يدلّ من نفسه أنّه متماسك غير مكترث للسبب الذي من شأنه أن يعجب منه ويضحك فيتضادّ الحال بالسامع حتّى يقترن إلى السبب الأوّل السبب الثاني. ٢،١٢٩

مسـألة

ما معنى قول العلماء على طبقاتهم النادر لا حكم له هكذا تجد الفقيه والمتكلّم والنحويّ والفلسفيّ فما سرّ هذا؟ وما علمه وعلّته؟ ولم إذا ندر خلا من الحكم وإذا شذّ عري من التعليل؟ ١،١٣٠

الجواب

قال أبو عليّ مسكويه رحمه الله ليس الأمر على ما ظننته من أنّ جميع الطبقات من العلماء يستعملون هذه اللفظة وإنّما يستعملها منهم من كان طبقته في العلوم المأخوذة ٢،١٣٠

١ الأصل: المسخرة.

person pulled in different directions by two ropes, one weak, the other strong. He inevitably submits to the stronger one, until with the passage of time his resolve is strengthened and the strong part grows weak and the weak strong, in accordance with what the philosophers have indicated and the prophets have legislated.

On why we laugh harder when a person keeps a straight face

Why do people laugh harder at a ridiculous person who makes them laugh when he does not laugh himself than they do when he laughs? This phenomenon arises whenever someone amuses you but does not laugh. 129.1

Miskawayh's response

The person who provokes laughter typically goes after things distorted from their proper place in order to amaze his listener and make him laugh. By not laughing, he shows himself to be composed and indifferent to the cause that should naturally induce amazement and laughter; this conflicts with the state of the listener, so a second cause is joined to the first. 129.2

On the meaning of the scholars' proposition that a rare instance attracts no ruling

What is the meaning of the statement we hear from scholars of all persuasions: "The rare instance attracts no ruling"? We hear jurists, dialectical theologians, grammarians, and philosophers saying this. So what is its secret? What is the truth behind it, and what is its cause? Why is it that a rarity carries no ruling, and an anomaly admits no explanation? 130.1

Miskawayh's response

It is not the case, as you suppose, that scholars of all persuasions use this expression. It is used by those who belong to the kind whose knowledge derives from incidental observation and from widespread views, for according to some people these constitute first principles of the sciences they cultivate. By "first 130.2

من التصفّح والآراء المشهورة فإنّ هذه أوائل عند قوم في علومهم. وأعني بقولي أوائل أي أنّهم يجعلونها مبادئ مسلّمة بمنزلة الأشياء الضروريّة من مبادئ الحسّ والعقل فإذا فعلوا ذلك لم يخل من أن يرد عليهم ما يخالف أصولهم فيجعلونه نادرًا وشاذًّا مثال ذلك أنّه تصفّح رجل منهم يومًا في السنة كيوم السبت من كانون أنّه يجيء فيه مطر وبقي[1] إلى ذلك سنين حُكم بأنّ هذا واجب لا بدّ منه فإن انتُقض عليه ذلك زُعم أنّه شاذّ نادر. وكذلك من يتبرّك بيوم في الشهر ويتشاءم بآخر كما تفعله الفرس بأوّل يوم من شهرهم المسمّى هرمز وبآخر يوم المسمّى بانيران فإنّه لا يزال يُحكم بأنّ هذا على هذه الوتيرة[2] فإن انتقض قالوا هذا شاذّ ونادر.

٣،١٣٠ وكذلك حال كلّ من[3] حكم بحكم مأخوذ من أوائل غير طبيعيّة وغير ضروريّة فإنّه غير مستمرّ له استمرار العلوم المبرهنة المأخوذة الأوائل من الأمور الضروريّة وأنت ترى ذلك عيانًا ممّن لا يعرف علل الأشياء ولا أسبابها من جمهور الناس فإنّ أحدهم إذا رأى أمرًا حدث عند حضور أمر آخر نسبه إليه من غير أن يبحث هل هو علّته أم لا وذلك أنّه إذا رأى حالاً تسرّه عند حضور زيد زعم أنّ سبب ذلك الحال زيد فإن اتّفق حضور زيد مرّة أخرى واتّفقت له حال أخرى سارّة قوي ظنّه وزادت بصيرته فإن اتّفق ثالثة قطع الحكم. وكذلك تكون الحال في أكثر أمور هذا الصنف من الناس لا جرم أنّه متى انتقض الأمر زعموا أنّه شاذّ ولهذه الحال عرض كثير وذلك أنّه ربّما مازج أسبابًا صحيحة كما يُحكم في الشتاء أنّه يجيء مطر يوم كذا لأنّه كذلك اتّفق في العام الماضي فلأنّ الوقت شتاء ربّما اتّفق ذلك مرارًا كثيرة ولكن ليس سبب المطر ذلك اليوم بل له أسباب أخر وإن اتّفق فيه.

٤،١٣٠ فأمّا الرجل الفلسفيّ فإنّه إذا تشبّه بغيره أو أخذ مقدّماته من مثل تلك المواضع عرض له لا محالة ما عرض لغيره ولذلك وجب أن تنزل الأمور منازلها فما كان منها ذا برهان لم يتغيّر ولم ينتظر ورود ضدّ عليه ولا شكّ فيه وإذا كان غير ذي برهان[4]

---

١ الأصل: ولق. ٢ الأصل: على الوتيرة. ٣ ط: حال من. ٤ الأصل: وإذا كان ذو البرهان.

principles" I mean that they assign them the status of accepted foundations on a par with necessary foundations such as those provided by the senses and by reason. Having done so, they inevitably come across things that conflict with their assumptions, so they classify them as "rare" or "anomalous." For example, a person of this type happens to observe that it rains on a particular day of the year—on a Saturday in December,[37] say—and continues to do so for years. He therefore rules that this forms an ineluctable necessity; any event that contravenes this rule is declared anomalous and rare. The same applies to people who consider a particular day of the month blessed and another ill-starred, as the Persians do with the first day of the month, which they call "Hurmuz," and the last day of the month, which they call "Anīrān." Thus there persists the ruling that things follow this specific pattern, and any contravention of the pattern is said to be anomalous and rare.

The same applies to all of those who base their rulings on principles that are 130.3
not natural or necessary, for they are not as consistent as forms of knowledge established through demonstration, whose principles are based on necessary matters. We see this firsthand among the ordinary people who do not know the causes or grounds of things. For if one of them sees one thing take place upon the appearance of some other thing, he attributes the former to the latter without inquiring into whether or not it was its cause. Thus, if he sees some delightful circumstance the moment Zayd appears, he asserts that Zayd was its cause. If Zayd happens to appear at some other time and another delightful circumstance happens, his opinion is reinforced, and his sense of insight increases. If it happens a third time, he pronounces his ruling with categorical certainty. This applies to most things that concern this category of people. It is little wonder then that they claim it is an anomaly when the pattern is contravened. There are many instances of this phenomenon; the reason is that sometimes true causes may be involved, as when one rules in wintertime that rain will fall on such and such a day because that is what happened in the previous year. Since it is winter, this may happen a great number of times, but the cause of the rain is not that specific day; there are other causes, even if rain happens to fall on that day.

If people who engage in philosophical inquiry follow others' examples or 130.4
draw their premises from such sources, they will inevitably fall prey to the same thing others do. This is why it is imperative to assign things to their proper places. Things that rest on demonstrative proof do not undergo change,

إلّا أنّ له دليلاً مستمرّاً صحيحاً سُكن إليه ووُثق[1] به فأمّا ما ينحطّ إلى الإقناعات الضعيفة فينبغي ألا يُسكن إليه ولا يُوثق به وانتظر أن ينقضه شيء طارئ عليه ولم يمتنع من الشكوك والاعتراضات عليه.

مسألة

١،١٣١ قال بعض المتكلّمين قد علمنا يقيناً أنّه لا يجوز أن يتّفق أن يمسّ أهل محلّة لحاهم في ساعة واحدة وفصل واحد وحال واحدة وإن جاز هذا فهل يجوز أن يتّفق في أهل بلدة؟ وإن جاز فهل يجوز في جميع من في العالم؟ وإن كان لا يجوز أن يتّفق هذا فما علّته؟ فإنّ المتكلّم سكت عند الأولى حين ذكر اليقين والضرورة ولعمري إنّ الغشاء[2] حقّ ولكنّ العلّة باقية. وسيمرّ بيان ذلك على حقيقته[3] في الشوامل إن شاء الله.

الجواب

٢،١٣١ قال أبو عليّ مسكويه رحمه الله إنّ الكلام على الواجب والممتنع والممكن قد استقصاه أصحاب المنطق وبلغ صاحب المنطق فيه الغاية. والذي يليق بهذا الموضع هو أن يقال إنّ الواجب من الأمور هو الذي يصدق فيه الإيجاب ويكذب فيه السلب أبداً والممتنع ما يكذب فيه الإيجاب ويصدق فيه السلب أبداً والممكن ما يصدق فيه الإيجاب أحياناً ويكذب فيه أحياناً ويكذب فيه السلب أحياناً ويصدق فيه أحياناً. فإذا كانت طبائع هذه الأمور مختلفة فمسألتك هذه من طبيعة الممكن فإن جُوّز فيه أن يكون جميع الناس يفعلونه في حال واحدة صُيّر من طبيعة الواجب وهذا محال. وأيضاً فإن أرسطوطاليس قد بيّن[4] أنّ المقدّمات الشخصيّة في المادّة الممكنة والزمان المستقبل لا تصدق معاً ولا تكذب معاً ولا تقتسم الصدق والكذب مثال ذلك زيد

١ ط: وثق. ٢ كذا في الأصل. ٣ الأصل: على حقيقة. ٤ ط: تبيّن.

and one should not anticipate that anything will arise that opposes them or casts them in doubt. If they do not rest on demonstrative proof but involve a proof that is consistent and sound, one may place one's assurance and trust in them. The ones that do not rise above the level of weak convictions must not command assurance or trust; one should anticipate that something will arise to overturn them, and they are not immune to doubt or objection.

On the possibility of certain kinds of coincidences obtaining

A certain dialectical theologian said: We know for certain that it is impossible that all the inhabitants of a particular quarter should, by coincidence, touch their beards at a particular hour, in a particular season, and in a particular situation. If this is possible, is it possible that all the people living in a town should happen by coincidence to do so? If this is possible, is it possible that everyone in the world should happen by coincidence to do so? And if it is not possible that this should happen by coincidence, what is the cause? The theologian mentioned certainty and necessity, then did not go beyond the first question. Upon my life, the fact stands but the question of the cause remains. The truth of the matter will be fully expounded in your book of responses, God willing.[38] 131.1

Miskawayh's response

The logicians have probed the notions of the necessary, the impossible, and the possible in depth, and Aristotle, the author of the books on logic, has provided a consummate discussion of the topic. The appropriate position to take in this context is the following: The "necessary" is that whose affirmation is always true and whose negation always false. The "impossible" is that whose affirmation is always false and whose negation always true. The "possible" is that whose affirmation is sometimes true and sometimes false, and whose negation is sometimes false and sometimes true. These things have different natures, and your question concerns the nature of the possible. If it were allowed that all people should do that at one particular moment, it would be assigned the nature of the necessary, and that is incoherent. Moreover, Aristotle has explained that individual propositions which concern what is possible and are in the future tense cannot both be true or both be false, and cannot distribute truth and falsehood.[39] An example is the proposition "Zayd will 131.2

يستحمّ غداً وليس[1] يستحمّ غداً زيد. فإنّ هاتين المقدّمتين ليس يجوز أن تصدقا معاً لئلاّ يكون شيء واحد بعينه موجوداً وغير موجود ولا يجوز أن تكذبا[2] معاً لئلاّ يكون شيء واحد موجوداً وغير موجود ولا يمكننا أن نقول إنّهما تقتسمان[3] الصدق والكذب لئلاّ يُرفع بذلك الممكن. وهذا قول محيّر فلذلك ألطف أرسطوطالس فيه النظر فقال إنّ الشيء الممكن إنّما يصدق عليه الإيجاب أو السلب على غير تحصيل. والشيء الواجب والممتنع يصدق عليهما الإيجاب والسلب على تحصيل أعني أنّه إنّما يقتسم الصدق والكذب المقدّمات الممكنة بأن توجد على طبيعتها الإمكانيّة. فأمّا الضروريّة فإنّها تقتسم الصدق والكذب على أنّها ضروريّة وهذا كلام بيّن واضح لمن ارتاض بالمنطق أدنى رياضة ومن أحبّ أن يستقصيه فليعد إليه في مواضعه يجده شافياً.

مسألة

١،١٣٢ سُئل بعض العلماء بالنحو واللغة فقيل له أيستمرّ القياس في جميع ما يُذهب إليه في الألفاظ؟ فقال لا. فقال السائل فينكسر القياس في جميع ذلك؟ فقال لا. فقيل له فما السبب؟ فقال لا أدري ولكنّ القياس يُفزع إليه في موضع ويُفزع منه في موضع. وعرضت هذه المسألة على فيلسوف فأفاد جواباً سيطلع عليك مع إشكاله إن شاء الله.

الجواب

٢،١٣٢ قال أبو عليّ مسكويه رحمه الله أمّا قياس النحويّين فليس مبنيّاً على أوائل ضروريّة فلذلك لا يستمرّ وإنّما أجاب هذا الرجل العالم بالنحو عن القياس الذي يخصّ صناعته ولم يلزمه إلّا ذلك فأمّا الفيلسوف فقياساته كلّها مستمرّة لا ينكسر منها شيء لا سيّما

١ الأصل: ليس. ٢ الأصل: أن يكونا. ٣ الأصل: إنّها يقتسم.

bathe tomorrow" and "Zayd will not bathe tomorrow." These propositions cannot both be true. Otherwise, the very same thing would both exist and not exist. Nor can they both be false; otherwise, the same thing would both exist and not exist. And we cannot say that they distribute truth and falsehood, as this would nullify possibility. This view is liable to provoke perplexity, so Aristotle nuanced his account further, with the following explanation. With regard to possible things, affirmation and negation are true indefinitely. With regard to necessary and impossible things, affirmation and negation are true definitely. That is to say, possible propositions distribute truth and falsehood by virtue of their nature qua possible. Necessary propositions distribute truth and falsehood on the basis that they are necessary. These remarks are clear and plain to those with the slightest training in logic. Those who wish to probe them in depth may consult the proper sources, where they will find satisfaction.

On the role of analogical reasoning in the linguistic sciences

A scholar of grammar and lexicography was asked: Is analogical reasoning consistently maintained across all phenomena that relate to words? He replied: No. The questioner asked: Is analogical reasoning violated across all of them? He replied: No. He was then asked: What is the reason? He replied: I don't know, but one has recourse to analogical reasoning in one context and one avoids it in another. I posed this question to a philosopher and he offered an answer that, despite its difficulties, will be presented before you, God willing. 132.1

Miskawayh's response

The analogical reasoning of the grammarians is not grounded in necessary first principles, and this is why it is not consistently maintained. The reply given by this grammarian concerned the analogical reasoning that pertains to his craft, and that was what was required of him. By contrast, all the forms of reasoning used by philosophers are consistently maintained, especially the kind of syllogistic reasoning termed a "demonstration," and none are subject to violation. 132.2

ضرب من القياس وهو المسمّى برهانًا وقد تقدّم في المسألة المتقدّمة أنّ النادر لا حكم له كلام يصلح أن يجاب به ههنا فلتعد إليه إن شاء الله.

مسألة

١،١٣٣ سأل سائل هل خلق الله تعالى العالم لعلّة أو لغير علّة؟ فإن كان لعلّة فما هي؟ وإن كان لغير علّة فما الحجّة؟ وهذه مسألة فيها شعب كثيرة ولها أهداب طويلة وليس الكلام فيها بالهيّن السهل.

الجواب

٢،١٣٣ قال أبو عليّ مسكويه رحمه الله ليس يجوز أن يُقال إنّ الله خلق العالم لعلّة لما تقدّم من قولنا إنّ العلّة سابقة للمعلول بالطبع فإن كانت العلّة أيضًا معلولة لزم أن تكون لها علّة تتقدّمها وهذا مارّ بغير نهاية وما لا نهاية له لا يصحّ وجوده فإذن لا بدّ من أن يقال أحد شيئين إمّا إنّ العلّة لا علّة لها وإمّا إنّ العالم لا علّة له غير ذات البارئ تعالى ذكره. فإن قيل إنّ للعالم علّة غير ذات البارئ تعالى فإنّ تلك العلّة لا علّة لها فيجب من ذلك أن تكون العلّة أزليّة لأنّها واجبة الوجود وإذا كانت كذلك لزم فيها جميع ما سلم في ذات البارئ تعالى ولو كان كذلك أوّلاً لم يزل. وقد قلنا في البارئ تعالى ذلك بالبراهين التي تأدّت إلى القول به وليس يجوز أن يكون شيئان لهما هذا الوصف أعني أنّ كلّ واحد منهما أوّل لم يزل وذلك أنّه لا بدّ أن يتّفقا في شيء به صار كلّ واحد منهما أوّل لم يزل[١] وأن[٢] يختلفا في شيء به صار كلّ واحد منهما غيرًا لصاحبه وذلك الشيء الذي اشتركا فيه والذي تباينا به لا بدّ أن يكون فصلاً مقوّمًا أو مقسّمًا فيصير لهما جنس ونوع لأنّ هذه حقيقة الجنس والنوع فالجنس متقدّم على النوع بالطبع والنوع الذي يلزمه فصل مقوّم ليس بأوّل لأنّه مركّب من ذات وفصل

١ ط: أوّل. ٢ الأصل: فإن.

Some of my remarks to the previous query—regarding the claim that the rare instance attracts no ruling—could serve as a response to this, so you can refer back to it, God willing.

On whether God created the world for a cause

A person asked: Did God create the world for a cause or for no cause? If for a cause, what was that cause? If for no cause, what is the argument for that? This is a complex question with many ins and outs, and it is no easy task to discuss it. 133.1

Miskawayh's response

It is not possible to say that God created the world for a cause because of the point we made before—namely, that a cause naturally precedes its effect. If the cause is also caused, it must have a cause that precedes it. This would continue ad infinitum, and that which is infinite cannot exist. Thus, it is only possible to say one of two things: Either the cause has no cause, or the world has no cause other than the Creator's essence. If we said that the world has a cause other than the Creator's essence, that cause would have no cause and would have to exist from eternity, as it would exist necessarily. If that were the case, everything conceded regarding the Creator's essence would have to apply to it. And if that were the case, it would have to be first and to have always existed. This is something we predicated of the Creator based on demonstrative proofs that concluded in its predication. Yet it is impossible that there should be two entities to which this qualification applies, that is, that both of them should be first and have always existed. For these two entities must agree in one feature—one that renders both of them first and such that they have always existed—and must differ in another feature—one that renders each distinct from the other. The feature they have in common and the feature that distinguishes them must be a constitutive or divisive difference, so that they acquire a genus and a species, for this is the basic reality of "genus" and "species." The genus is naturally prior to the species. The species, which requires a constitutive difference, is not first, for it is composed of an essence and a constitutive difference, and 133.2

مقوّم والمركّب متأخّرعن بسيطه الذي تركّب منه فهذه أحوال يناقض بعضها بعضاً ولا يصحّ معها أن يدّعى في شيئين أنّ كلّ واحد منها أوّل لم يزل. وشرح هذا المعنى وإن طال فهوعائد إلى هذا النبذ الذي يكتفي به ذو القريحة الجيّدة والذكاء التامّ.

مسألة

لم يضيق الإنسان في الراحة إذا توالت عليه وفي النعمة إذا حالفته؟ وبهذا الضيق يخرج إلى المرح والنزوان وإلى البطر والطغيان وإلى التحكّك بالشرّ والتمرّس به حتّى يقع في كلّ مهوى بعيد وفي كلّ أمر شديد ثمّ يعضّ على أنامله غيظاً على نفسه بسوء اختياره وأسفاً على تركه محمود الرأي ومجانبته نصيحة الناصحين مع ما يجد من الألم في صدره من شماتة الشامتين. فما السرّ المنزي والمعنى الموثب؟ ولذلك قالت العرب في نوادر كلامها نزت به البطنة أي أطغاه الشبع وأبطرته الكفاية وأترفته النعمة حتّى بطر وأشر واضطرب وانتشر. ومن أجل ذلك قال بعض السلف الصالح العافية ملك خفيّ لا يصبر عليها إلّا وليّ ملهم أو نبيّ مرسل. هذا والناس مع اختلافهم يحبّون العافية ويميلون إلى الراحة ويعوذون من الشرّ وممّا يورث منه ويستعقب عنه. ١،١٣٤

الجواب

قال أبو عليّ مسكويه رحمه الله السبب في ذلك أنّ الراحة إنّما تكون عن تعب تقدّمها لا محالة وجميع اللذّات يظهر فيها أنّها راحات من آلام. وإذا كانت الراحة إنّما تكون عن تعب فهي إنّما تُستلذّ وتستطاب ساعة يُتخلّص من الشيء المتعب. فإذا اتّصلت الراحة وذهب ألم التعب لم تكن الراحة موجودة بل بطلت وبطل معناها ومع بطلانها بطلان اللذّة ومع بطلان اللذّة غلط الإنسان في الشوق إلى اللذّة التي يجهل ٢،١٣٤

a composite entity is posterior to the element from which it was composed. These are mutually contradictory facts, and they make it inadmissible to claim that the two entities are both first and have always been. Even the lengthiest explanations of this issue come down to this core point, which is sufficient for people endowed with an excellent mind and developed intelligence.

On why a life of comfort makes people feel oppressed and leads them to behave wantonly

Why do people feel oppressed when surrounded by constant comforts and attendant blessings? This sense of oppression encourages exuberant and impetuous, wanton and unrestrained behavior, and gets them mixed up in evil, so that they end up in awful situations and get into ghastly scrapes. Then they grind their teeth in anger at their bad choices and in regret at abandoning sound judgment and at turning their back on those who offered them well-intentioned counsel, in addition to the pain caused by the malicious pleasure of the ill-intentioned. What is the secret reason for the impetuosity and the element that makes one act fitfully? This is why we have one of the exceptional sayings of the Arabs: "Repletion gave him impetus"; that is, a full belly made him unrestrained, abundance made him wanton, and luxury provoked him, agitated and swollen with lust, to willful arrogance. That is why one of our pious forefathers said, "Well-being is a secret possession that only inspired saints and prophets sent by God can endure." This is so even though everyone without exception loves well-being and inclines to comfort, and seeks protection against evil and its corollaries and consequences. 134.1

Miskawayh's response

Comfort must follow prior discomfort. Pleasure clearly constitutes a relief from pain. Since comfort follows discomfort, it is experienced as pleasant and delightful when we are delivered from the cause of discomfort. If comfort continues uninterrupted and the pain of discomfort departs, then comfort is not realized but is rather nullified, as is its meaning; and with its nullification comes the nullification of pleasure. As pleasure is nullified, people err in longing for pleasure, whose true reality they are ignorant of. That is to say, they long for pleasure, but are ignorant of the fact that it is simply relief from pain. 134.2

حقيقتها أعني أنّه يشتاق إلى معنى اللذّة ويجهل أنّها راحة من ألم فصار الإنسان كأنّه يشتاق إلى تعب ليستريح بعقبه. وهذا المعنى إذا لاح للعالم به وتبيّنه لم يشتق إلى اللذّة بتّة وصار قصاراه إذا آلمه الجوع أن يداويه بالدواء الذي يسمّى الشبع لا أنّه[1] يقصد اللذّة نفسها بل يرى اللذّة شيئاً تابعاً لغرضه لا[2] أنّها مقصوده الأوّل ولذلك يزهد العالم في الأشياء البدنيّة أعني الدنيويّة وهي ما تتّصل بالحواسّ وتسمّى لذيذة. فأمّا الجاهل فلأنّه يعترض له ما ذكرناه بالضرورة صار يقع فيه دائماً فيحصل في هموم وآلام وأمراض لا نهاية له وعاقبة جميع ذلك الندم والأسف.

مسألة

لم صار بعض الأشياء تمامه أن يكون غضّاً طريّاً ولا يُستحسن ولا يستطاب إلّا كذلك؟ وبعض الأشياء لا يختار ولا يُستحسن إلّا إذا كان عتيقاً قديماً قد مرّ عليه الزمان؟ ولم[3] لم تكن الأشياء كلّها على وجه واحد عند الناس؟ وما السبب في انقسامها على هذين الوجهين ففيه سرّ سيظهر؟[4] ١،١٣٥

الجواب

قال أبو عليّ مسكويه رحمه الله لمّا كانت كمالات الأشياء مختلفة أعني أنّ بعضها تتمّ صورته التي هي كماله في زمان قصير وبعضها تتمّ صورته في زمان طويل كان انتظار الإنسان للكمال منها وتفضيله[5] إيّاها بحسبه. ولمّا كان الشيء يبتدئ وينتهي إلى الكمال ثمّ ينحطّ حتّى يتلاشى ويعود إلى ما منه بدأ كان أفضل أحواله وقت انتهائه إلى الكمال فأمّا حين صعوده إليه أو انحطاطه عنه فحالان ناقصان وإن كانت الأولى أفضل من الثانية. ولمّا كانت هذه[6] القضيّة مستمرّة فيما كان في عالمنا هذا أعني عالم ٢،١٣٥

١ الأصل: إلا أنّه. ٢ الأصل: إلّا. ٣ الأصل: ولو. ٤ ط: سرّ. ٥ الأصل: وتفضيلهم. ٦ الأصل: وهذه.

So people essentially long for discomfort in order to experience subsequent comfort. Once a person grasps this and perceives it clearly, he stops longing for pleasure, and when he feels the pain of hunger he attends to its treatment through the remedy called satiation, without aiming at pleasure itself, instead seeing pleasure as a concomitant of his purpose rather than as his primary end. That is why people who are cognizant of this fact limit their desire for corporeal things, that is to say worldly things, those which are connected to the senses and are termed "pleasurable." Ignorant people, however, cannot avoid being affected by what we have described, so they perpetually succumb to it, and become embroiled in innumerable troubles, pains, and maladies. The outcome is remorse and regret.

On why some things are best when they're new and others are best when old

Why is it that some things achieve their consummate form when they are fresh and tender, and are only commended and judged to be good when in that state, whereas other things are only chosen and commended when aged and old, marked by the passage of time? Why don't people regard everything from a single perspective? Why are things divided according to these two perspectives? Is there a secret behind this that can be revealed? 135.1

Miskawayh's response

The perfection of things varies; for some the form that constitutes their perfection is completed in a short period of time, while for others the form is completed over a long period of time. Therefore, the length of time people must wait for their perfection, and the preference they show toward them, vary accordingly. Every entity begins, reaches perfection, and then enters decline, until it is eventually annihilated and returns to the point from which it began, so its optimal state is when it has attained perfection. Its progression to that point and its decline are deficient states, though the former is better than the latter. As this rule applies consistently to things that form part of this world of ours—that is, the world of generation and corruption—it follows that people's 135.2

الكون والفساد وجب من ذلك أن تكون استطابة الناس واستحسانهم لصورة الكمال في واحد واحد من الأشياء المختلفة أيضاً مختلفاً لأجل ما ذكرناه.

مسألة

لم صار الإنسان إذا صام أو صلّى زائداً على الفرض المشترك فيه حقّر غيره واشتطّ ١،١٣٦
عليه وارتفع على مجلسه ووجد الخنزوانة في نفسه وطارت النعرة في أنفه حتّى كأنّه صاحب الوحي أو الواثق بالمغفرة والمنفرد بالجنّة؟ وهو مع ذلك يعلم أنّ العمل معرّض للآفات وبها يحبط ثواب صاحبه ولهذا قال الله تعالى ﴿وَقَدِمْنَا إِلَى مَا عَمِلُوا مِنْ عَمَلٍ فَجَعَلْنَاهُ هَبَاءً مَنْثُورًا﴾ ولما يعرض له من هذا العارض علّة ستنكشف في جواب المسألة. وكان بعض أصحابنا يضحك بنادرة في هذا الفصل قال أسلم يهوديّ غداة يوم فما أمسى حتّى ضرب مؤذّناً وشتم آخر وغضب على آخر فقيل له ما هذا أيّها الرجل؟ فقال نحن معاشر القرّاء فينا حدّة.

الجواب

قال أبو عليّ مسكويه رحمه الله كلّ من استشعر في نفسه فضيلة وكان هناك نقصان ٢،١٣٦
من وجه آخر وخشي أن تنكتم تلك الفضيلة أو لا يعرفها غيره منه عرض له عارض الكبر لأنّ معنى الكبر هو هذا أي أنّ صاحبه يلتمس من غيره أن يذعن له بتلك الفضيلة ويعرفها له فإذا لم يعرفها تحرّك ضروب الحركة المضطربة ولهذا صدق القائل ما تكبّر أحد إلّا عن ذلّة يجدها في نفسه. وإنّما السلامة من هذا العارض هو أن يلتمس الإنسان الفضيلة لنفسه لا لشيء آخر أكثر من أن يصير هو بنفسه فاضلاً لا لأن يُعرف ذلك منه أو يُكرم لأجله فإن اتّفق له أن يُعرف فشيء موضوع في موضعه وإن لم يُعرف له ذلك لم يلتمسه من غيره ولم يكترث لجهل غيره به فقد علمنا أنّ التماس الكرامة ومحبّتها رذيلة. ولأجل محبّة الكرامة تعرّض قوم للمتالف وعرض لقوم الصلف

judgments regarding the form of perfection that is good and commendable in each of these various things must also vary for the reasons we mentioned.

On why people who display great piety are prone to arrogance

Why is it that if a person fasts or prays beyond the stipulated amount common 136.1
to all, he conceives a scorn for others, treats them peremptorily, and puffs himself up in social gatherings, swollen with pride and stung by some gadfly as though he were the recipient of divine afflatus, was assured of forgiveness, and had exclusive rights to Paradise? Yet he knows that action is susceptible to different kinds of impairment, through which the reward of the agent may be undone. This is why God said: «We shall advance upon what work they have done, and make it a scattered dust.»[40] The phenomenon that affects him must have a cause, which will be revealed in the response to the question. One of our companions used to laugh at an anecdote on this topic. He said: One day a Jew converted to Islam in the early morning, and before evening he had struck a muezzin, cursed a second, and unleashed his anger on yet a third. "What kind of behavior is this?" people asked him. "We religious devotees are a sharp-tempered lot!" he rejoined.

Miskawayh's response

Arrogance affects everyone who knows that he possesses a certain virtue but 136.2
who also suffers a deficiency from another perspective, and who fears that that virtue might remain hidden or that nobody else might know he possesses it. For this is the meaning of arrogance; that is, the person affected tries to get another to concede and acknowledge that he possesses that virtue; if the other fails to acknowledge it, he succumbs to all manner of disturbed movements. That person spoke truly who said that the reason for the display of arrogance is some baseness discerned in the self. The way to avoid being affected by this phenomenon is for a person to seek to possess virtue for no other reason than that he should become virtuous in himself, and not in order that this should receive acknowledgment or honor for it. It is right and proper if it happens to be acknowledged, but if it is not, he should not seek this from others and should be unconcerned about the fact that others do not know about it, for we

ولآخرين الهرب من الناس إلى غير ذلك من المكاره. والذي يجب على العاقل هو أن يلتمس الفضائل في نفسه ليصير بها على هيئة كريمة ممدوحة في ذاتها[1] أُكرم أم لم يُكرم وعُرف ذلك له أم لم يُعرف. ويجعل مثاله في ذلك الصحّة فإنّ الصحّة تُطلب[2] لذاتها ويحرص المرء عليها ليصير صحيحاً حسب لا ليُعتقد فيه ذلك ولا ليُكرم عليها. وكذلك إذا جُعلت له صحّة النفس بحصول الفضائل لا ينبغي أن يطلب من الناس أن يكرموه لها ولا أن يعتقدوا فيه ذلك ومتى خالف هذه الوصيّة وقع في ضروب من الجهالات التي أحدها الكبر والحالة التي وصفت.

مسألة

١،١٣٧ حكى بعض أصحابنا أنّ الرشيد قال لإسحاق الموصليّ كيف حالك مع الفضل بن يحيى وجعفر بن يحيى؟ فقال يا أمير المؤمنين أمّا جعفر فإنّي لا أصل إليه إلّا على عسر فإذا وصلت إليه قبّلت يده فلا يلتفت إليّ بطرف ولا ينعم لي بحرف ثمّ إنّي أصير إلى منزلي فأجد صلته وبرّه وهداياه وتحفه قد سبقتني فأبقى حيران من شأنه وأمّا الفضل فإنّي ما أغشى بابه إلّا ويتلقّاني ويهشّ لي ويخصّني ويسألني عن دقيق أمري وجليله ويصحبني من بشره وطلاقة وجهه وتهلّله ورقّة نغمته ما يغمرني ويعجزني عن الشكر وأبقى خجلاً في أمره وليس غير ذلك. فقال الرشيد عند هذا الحديث يا أبا إسحاق فأيّهما عندك آثر وفعل[3] أيّهما من نفسك أوقع؟ فقال فعل الفضل هذا آخر الحكاية.

٢،١٣٧ وموضع المسألة منها ما السبب في تشريف إسحاق فعل الفضل دون فعل جعفر؟ والفضل مبذوله عرض لا بقاء له ولا منفعة به ومبذول جعفر جوهر له بقاء والحاجة إليه ماسّة والرغبات به منوطة والآمال إليه مصروفة. الدليل على ذلك أنّك لا تجد

١ الأصل وط: ذاته. ٢ الأصل: لا تُطلب. ٣ الأصل: في فعل.

know that it is a defect to love and seek honor. Some people have been ruined by the love of honor, some have been affected by pomposity, and others have fled human society, and other such odious things. What the person endowed with reason should do is to seek to possess the virtues so as to acquire a disposition honorable and praiseworthy in itself, regardless of whether he is honored or not, and whether it is acknowledged or not. In this it resembles health, for health is desired for its own sake, and the reason a person is keen to possess it is simply in order to be healthy, not in order that he should be thought to be so, nor in order to be honored for it. Similarly, if it is given to one to achieve the health of the soul by realizing the virtues, one must not demand honor for it or acknowledgment of one's achievement. Whenever this guiding principle is contravened, one falls prey to all sorts of ignorant behavior, among them arrogance and the condition described.

On why a warm manner is more pleasing than a cold benefaction

One of our companions reported that Hārūn al-Rashīd asked Isḥāq al-Mawṣilī, 137.1
"How are your relations with al-Faḍl ibn Yaḥyā and Jaʿfar ibn Yaḥyā?"[41] He said, "Sire, I only gain an audience with Jaʿfar with difficulty, and when I reach him I kiss his hand, but he doesn't glance at me or grace me with a single word. Then I go home and I find his tokens of kindness and charity and his gifts and presents waiting for me, and I am at a loss what to make of him. No sooner is my hand on the door knocker than al-Faḍl has received me, and he treats me amiably and gives me special attention, asking about all of my affairs high and low and vivifying me with his cheerful mien, beaming countenance, joyful air, and gentle tone. This overwhelms me and makes me feel I could never thank him enough, and I am left nursing a sense of bashfulness toward him. This is how things stand." When he heard this, al-Rashīd said, "Abū Isḥāq, which of the two are you fonder of, and whose actions have the strongest effect on you?" "Al-Faḍl's," he replied. This is the end of the report.

My question is: Why did Isḥāq esteem al-Faḍl's action more highly than 137.2
Jaʿfar's? What al-Faḍl expends is contingent: It does not endure and yields no profit, whereas what Jaʿfar expends is a substance that endures and is an object of pressing need on which desires are fastened and hopes pinned. The proof of this is that no one on the face of the earth sets out to obtain a man's cheerful

طالباً في الدنيا لبشر رجل ولا ضارباً في الأرض لهشاشة إنسان وأنت ترى البرّ والبحر مترعين بمنتجعي المال وأبناء السؤال وخدم الآمال عند الرجال.

الجواب

٣،١٣٧ قال أبو عليّ مسكويه رحمه الله أمّا الحكاية فأظنّها مقلوبة وذلك أنّ الموصوف بالكبر هو الفضل وهو صاحب الشرف في العطاء وأمّا جعفر فهو الموصوف بالطلاقة والبشر إلّا أنّ المتّفق عليه أنّ إسحاق فضّل صاحب الطلاقة وإن كان في الأكثر خالياً من برّه على صاحب البرّ والعطاء الجزيل لمّا قرنه بالكبر والتيه والناس على تفاوت عظيم في الموضع الذي سألت عنه وتعجّبت منه. وذلك أنّ منهم المحبّ للثروة واليسار ومنهم المحبّ للكرامة والجاه. فأمّا محبّ الثروة فقد يحبّ الجاه والكرامة ولكن ليكتسب بهما مالاً وأمّا محبّ الجاه والكرامة فقد يحبّ المال والثروة ولكن ليكتسب جاهاً وينال كرامة. وكلّ طائفة من هاتين الطائفتين تزعم أنّه هو الكيّس وأنّ صاحبه هو الغافل الأبله.[1] والصحيح من ذلك أنّ كلّ واحد منهما ينازع إلى أمرطبيعيّ وإن[2] كان قد مال السرف بهما جميعاً إلى الإفراط وذاك أنّ المال ينبغي أن يُعتدل في طلبه ويُكتسب من وجهه ثمّ يُنفق في موضعه فمتى قصّر في أحد هذه الوجوه صار شرهاً وأورث ذلّة وكسب بخلاً وإثماً. وأمّا الكرامة فينبغي أن تكون في الإنسان فضيلة يستحقّ بها أن يُكرم لا أن تُطلب الكرامة بالعسف أو بالكبر الذي ذممناه فيما تقدّم من المسائل آنفاً. فإذا كان الأمر على ما ذكرناه وكانت الكرامة تابعة للفضيلة فالكرامة أشرف من المال تتبعها[3] اللذّة.

٤،١٣٧ وبالجملة فإنّ المال ليس بمطلوب لذاته بل هو آلة يوصل به إلى المآرب والأشجان الكثيرة وإنّما يُحبّ لأنّه بإزاء جميع المطلوبات أي به يُتوصّل إلى المحبوبات فأمّا في نفسه فهو حجر لا فرق بينه وبين غيره إذا نُزعت عنه هذه الخصلة الواحدة. فأمّا الكرامة

١ ط: أنّها هي الكيّسة وأنّ صاحبتها هي الغافلة البلهاء. ٢ الأصل: فإن. ٣ الأصل وط: تتبعه.

mien or wanders the earth in search of a friendly face. Yet both land and sea are replete with people seeking wealth, begging, and servicing hopes at others' doorsteps.

Miskawayh's response

I believe the story has been reported the wrong way around. It was al-Faḍl who was described as being arrogant, and he was the one who showed honor by bestowing gifts, and it was Jaʿfar who was described as having a bright, cheerful manner. What is undisputed is that Isḥāq preferred the person with the beaming countenance, even if he rarely received tokens of generosity from him, to the person who was lavish and acted kindly, because of the pride and hauteur the latter conjoined to these acts. There are enormous variations between people with regard to the point you are asking about and find surprising. For there are those who love riches and material comfort, and there are those who love honor and high standing. Those who love riches might love high standing and honor, but only as a means for acquiring wealth. Those who love high standing and honor may love wealth and riches, but only as a means for acquiring high standing and honor. Each of these factions alleges that it is truly astute and that the other faction is ignorant and foolish. The truth of the matter is that each is driven toward something natural, but extravagance has led both to excess. For wealth must be sought in moderation and acquired in the proper way, and then spent under the appropriate circumstances. When a person falls short in any of these respects, he becomes greedy, is gripped by baseness, and falls into avarice and wrongdoing. A person must possess a form of excellence that makes him deserving of honor, and honor should not be sought out without a just claim or in the arrogant manner censured in one of the previous questions. Honor is nobler than wealth, and is attended by pleasure, if things are as we described and honor attends excellence. 137.3

In general, money is not desired for its own sake, but rather serves as an instrument for attaining a plethora of wishes and wants. The reason it is loved is because it is equivalent to all objects of desire, that is, because lovely objects may be obtained by its means. Taken on its own, and abstracted from this one characteristic, it is simply a stone with nothing to distinguish it from other objects. Honor, however, may be desired for its own sake if a person desires it 137.4

فقد تُطلب لذاتها إذا كان الطالب لها من جهة الاستحقاق بالفضيلة وذلك لما تحصل عليه النفس من الالتذاذ الروحانيّ والسرور النفسانيّ. وإن كانت من جهة النفس الغضبيّة فإنّ هذه النفس وإن كانت دون الناطقة فإنّها فوق النفس البهيميّة التي تلتذّ اللذّات البدنيّة التي تشارك فيها النبات والخسيس[1] من الحيوانات.

٥،١٣٧ فأمّا قولك إنّك تجد محبّي المال أكثر من محبّي الكرامة فكذا يجب أن يكون لأنّ أكثر الناس هم الذين يشبهون البهائم وإنّما[2] يتميّز القليل منهم بالفضائل. فكما أنّ المتميّزين بفضائل النفس الناطقة أقلّ من القليل فكذلك المتميّزون بفضائل النفس الغضبيّة أقلّ من الجمهور.

مسألة

١،١٣٨ ما بال خاصّة الملك والدانين منه والمقرّبين إليه لا يجري من ذكر[3] الملك على ألسنتهم مثل ما يجري على ألسنة الأباعد منه مثل البوّابين والشاكريّة والساسة فإنّك تجد هؤلاء على غاية التشيّع بذكره ونهاية الدعوى في الإشارة إليه والتكذّب عليه.

الجواب

٢،١٣٨ قال أبو عليّ مسكويه رحمه الله لسببين أحدهما أنّ الأقربين إلى الملوك هم المؤدّبون المستصلحون لخدمتهم وفي جملة الآداب التي أُخذوا بها ترك ذكر الملك فإنّ في ذكرهم إيّاه ابتذالاً له وانتهاكاً لهيبته وهتكاً لحرمته. فأمّا أولئك الطبقة فلسوء آدابهم لا يميّزون ولا يأبهون لما ذكرته فهم يجرون على طباعهم العامّة اللائقة بهم في الافتخار بما لا أصل له وادّعاء ما لا حقيقة له ولظنّهم أنّهم ينالون بذلك كرامة ومحلاً عند أمثالهم. وأمّا السبب الآخر فخوف حاشية الملك من عقوبته فإنّ الملك يعاقب على

---

١ الأصل: الخسيسة. ٢ الأصل: فإنّما. ٣ الأصل: من ذلك.

on account of merit grounded in virtue, and this is due to the spiritual pleasure and psychological joy he derives, for even though it arises from the irascible soul and this soul is inferior to the rational one, it is superior to the beastly soul, which delights in bodily pleasures that it shares with plants and lowly animals.

You remark that one sees more people who love wealth than people who 137.5
love honor—this is as it should be. For the people who resemble the beasts represent the majority, while only a small number distinguish themselves through the virtues. Just as those who distinguish themselves through the virtues of the rational soul are few in number, those who distinguish themselves through the virtues of the irascible soul are fewer than the multitude.

On why those closest to a king are less inclined to prattle about his person than those at the farthest remove from him

Why is it that the elite members of the king's circle, those who are his close 138.1
intimates, do not speak about the king the way those who are distant from him—such as doormen, soldiers, and stablemen—do? For we find the latter displaying a lusty appetite for speaking about the king, taking their claims about him to an extreme and spinning yarns about him.

Miskawayh's response

There are two reasons for this. One is that those close to the king have refined 138.2
manners and have been judged fit to serve him, and among the manners they have been held to is that they refrain from speaking about the king. For speaking about him involves demeaning him, violating his dignity, and impugning his venerability. By contrast, the latter class of people, because of their bad manners, fail to discern and pay heed to any of the things I mentioned, and, as is natural and befitting to commoners, they make groundless boasts and untrue claims, out of a belief that by doing so they may gain honor and standing among their peers. The other reason is the fear of punishment among members of the king's entourage, for the king metes out punishment for this

هذا الذنب ويراه سياسة له لئلا يتعدّى ذاكروه إلى إفشاء سرّ وإخراج حديث لا ينبغي إخراجه.

مسـألة

١،١٣٩ ما الشبهة التي عرضت لابن سالم البصريّ فيما تفرّد به من مقالته حين زعم أنّ الله تعالى لم يزل ناظرًا إلى الدنيا رائيًا لها مدركًا لها وهي معدومة فإنّ شغبه وشغب ناصريه وأصحابه قد كثر بين العلماء فما وجه باطله إن كان قد أبطل؟ وما وجه الحقّ إن كان قد حقّق؟

الجواب

٢،١٣٩ قال أبو عليّ مسكويه رحمه الله أمّا شبهة صاحب هذه المقالة فمركّبة وذلك أنّه لحظ إدراك الحيّ منّا فوجده بنوعين أحدهما عقليّ والآخر حسّيّ والحسّيّ منه وهميّ ومنه بصريّ. فأمّا الحسّيّ البصريّ فإنّما يدرك المبصر بآلة ذات طبقات ورطوبات وعصبة[1] مجوّفة آتية[2] من بطن الدماغ ويحتاج إلى جرم مستشفّ يكون بينه وبين البصر وإلى ضوء معتدل ومسافة معتدلة وألّا يكون بينهما حاجز ولا مانع. وأمّا الوهم فقد ذكرنا من أمره أنّه يتبع الحسّ فلا يجوز أن يُتوهّم ما لا يُدرك الحسّ أو يُدرك له نظير. وأمّا الإدراك العقليّ فليس يحتاج إلى شيء من الحواسّ بل للعقل نفسه قوّة ذاتيّة بها يدرك الأشياء المعقولة والكلام على هذا الإدراك ألطف وأغمض من الكلام في الإدراك الحسّيّ.

٣،١٣٩ ولمّا اختلطت على صاحب المسألة هذه الإدراكات وعلم أن البارئ جلّت عظمته عالم بالأمور الكائنة سمّي هذا العلم إدراكًا وظنّه من جنس إدراكنا وعلومنا الوهميّة

---

١ ط: وقصبة. ٢ الأصل وط:ذاتيّة.

offense and views this as a principle of good government, lest those who speak about him end up divulging a secret or making public words that should not be made public.

On Ibn Sālim al-Baṣrī's claim that God perceived the world while it was nonexistent

What was the confusion that Ibn Sālim al-Baṣrī[42] succumbed to when he voiced his unique position, claiming that from pre-eternity God looked at the world, viewed it, and perceived it, during the entire time it was nonexistent? For he and his supporters have created a widespread ruckus among the learned. If his claim is false, in what respect is it false? If it is true, in what respect is it true? 139.1

Miskawayh's response

The confusion the author of this position succumbed to is compound. For he considered the way in which living beings like us perceive things, and he found that there are two types of perception, one intellectual and the other sensory, with the sensory subdividing into the imaginary and the visual. In the visual sensory type, the visual object is perceived through an organ possessed of layers, moistures, and a hollowed nerve leading out from the ventricle of the brain. It requires a transparent medium that lies between it and the visual object, as well as balanced, moderate light; moderate distance; and the absence of any intervening barrier or obstacle. We have said that the imagination is contingent on sense perception, so it is not possible to imagine something that cannot be perceived, or something the like of which cannot be perceived. Intellectual perception, by contrast, does not require any of the senses; rather, reason itself has an intrinsic power through which it perceives intelligible things. The discussion of the latter type of perception harbors a greater amount of subtlety and obscurity than the discussion of sensory perception. 139.2

The person addressing the point at issue mixed up these types of perception, and knowing that the Creator knows everything that is, he called this knowledge "perception" and assumed that it is of the same kind as our perception and our imaginary knowledge. So his confusion was a compound formed 139.3

فتركّبت الشبهة له من هذه[1] الظنون الكاذبة وتحقيق هذه الإدراكات وتمييزها حتّى يُعلم ما يختصّ به الحيّ منّا ذو العقل والحسّ وكيف تكون إدراكاته للأمور الموجودة وتنزيه البارئ جلّ اسمه عن جميعها إذ كانت هذه كلّها منّا انفعالات أعني العلوم والمعارف كلّها وأنّه لا يجوز أن نعلم شيئاً محسوساً ولا معقولاً بغير انفعال وأنّ الله تقدّس وتعالى ذكره ليس بمنفعل وإنّما يعلم الأشياء بنوع أعلى وأرفع ممّا نعلمه أمر صعب يحتاج فيه إلى تقدمة علوم كثيرة وفيما ذكرناه كفاية في إيضاح وجه شبهة لهذا الرجل فيما ذهب إليه.

مسـألة

حـدّثني عن ولوع الشاعر بالطيف وتشبيبه به واستهتاره بذكره وهكذا تجد أصناف ١،١٤٠
الناس وهذا معروف عند من عبثت به الصبابة ولحقته الرقّة وألفت عينه حلية شخص ومحاسنه وعلق فؤاده هواه وحبّه.

الجواب

قال أبو عليّ مسكويه رحمه الله الطيف هو اسم لصورة المحبوب إذا حصّلته النفس ٢،١٤٠
في قوّتها المتخيّلة[2] حتّى تكون تلك الصورة نصب عينه وتجاه وهمه كلّما خلا بنفسه وهذه حال تلحق كلّ من لهج بشيء فإنّ صورته ترتسم في قوّته هذه التي تسمّى المتخيّلة وتكون ببطن الدماغ المقدّم. فإذا تكرّرت هذه الصورة على المحبوب على هذه القوّة انتقشت فيها ولزمتها فإذا نام الإنسان أو استيقظ لم تخل من قيام تلك الصورة فيها ويجد المشتاق في النوم خاصّة إنسانه لأنّ النوم يُتخيّل فيه أشياء ممّا في نفسه فربّما

---

١ ط: من. ٢ الأصل: المختلّة.

out of these false assumptions. It is an arduous task, and one that presupposes many kinds of knowledge, to investigate and distinguish these types of perception so as to determine what pertains to living beings possessed of reason and sense perception like ourselves and how such beings perceive existent things, and then to establish that the Creator transcends them all. For in our case, all of these—that is to say, all kinds of knowledge and learning—are forms of passive affection, as it is impossible for us to know anything of a sensible or intelligible kind without being passively affected. Yet God cannot be passively affected. Rather, He knows things in a higher and loftier manner than we do. What we have said provides sufficient clarification of the reason for the confusion this man suffered in assuming his particular position.

On why the poets love to dwell on the apparitions that come to them in their sleep

Tell me about the infatuation of poets with apparitions that visit them while they are sleeping, about their passion for evoking them, and their presence in erotic verse. We encounter this among all stripes of people, and it is a familiar phenomenon among those who, overcome by tender feeling, have become the plaything of ardent love, whose eyes have grown fond of the form and beauties of a particular individual, and whose heart has become attached to this person in desire and love. 140.1

Miskawayh's response

The term "apparition" refers to the form of the beloved when acquired within the imaginative power of the soul, so that this form stands before one's eyes and in front of one's fancy whenever one is alone. This is a condition that affects everyone who has a passion for a particular thing, for its form imprints itself on this power called the imagination, located in the anterior ventricle of the brain. If this power is repeatedly exposed to the form of the beloved, the latter engraves itself in it and remains there; so whenever a person goes to sleep or wakes up, that form invariably arises within it. It is especially in sleep that we find the person we long for, for in sleep we see images based on things contained in our soul. Thus, we might see in our sleep that we have gained access to the other in accordance with our desire. This results in 140.2

رأى في النوم أنّه قد وصل إليه الوصول الذي يهواه فيكون من ذلك الاحتلام واستفراغ المادّة التي تحرّكه إلى الشوق والاجتماع مع المحبوب فيزول عنه أكثر ذلك العارض ويصير سبباً لبرء تامّ فيما بعد.

مسـألة

١٬١٤١ مـا السبب في ترفّع الإنسان عن التنبيه على نفسه بنشرفضله وعرض حاله وإثبات اسمه وإشاعة نعته؟ وليس بعد هذا إلّا إثبات الخمول والخمول عدم ما وهو إلى النقص ما هو لأنّ الخامل مجهول والمجهول نقيض المعدوم ولا تبارئ في المعدوم ولا تماري في الموجود. وكان منشأ هذه المسألة عن حال هذا وصفها عرض بعض مشايخنا كتاباً له صنّفه علينا فلم نجده ذكرعلى ظهره تأليف فلان ولا تصنيفه ولا ذكر اسمه من وجه الملك فقلنا له ما هذا الرأي؟ فقال هو شيء يعجبني لسرّ فيه ثمّ أخرج لنا كتباً قد كتبها في الحداثة فيها اسمه وقال هذا أثر أيّام النقص.

الجواب

٢٬١٤١ قال أبو عليّ مسكويه رحمه الله إنّ الفضل ينبّه على نفسه وليست حاجة إلى تنبيه الإنسان عليه من نفسه. وذاك أنّ الفضائل التي هي بالحقيقة فضائل تشرق إشراق الشمس ولا سبيل إلى إخفائها لو رام صاحبها ذلك وأمّا الشيء الذي يُظنّ أنّه فضيلة وليس كذلك فهو الذي يخفى. فإذا تعاطى الإنسان مدح نفسه وإظهار فضيلته بالدعوى تصفّحت العقول دعواه فبان عواره وظهر الموضع الذي يغلط فيه من نفسه فإن اتّفق أن يكون صادقاً وكانت فيه تلك الفضيلة فإنّما يدلّ بتكلّف إظهارها على أنّه غير واثق بآراء الناس وتصفّحهم أو هو واثق ولكنّه يتبجّح عليهم ويفخر والناس لا يرضون شيئاً من هذه الأخلاق لدناءتها. فأمّا الإنسان الكبير الهمّة فإنّه

dreams about sexual intercourse, and in the discharge of the substance that prompts our longing and drives us to be united with our beloved. The greater part of that effect passes away, and this subsequently leads to a complete recovery.

On why people are reluctant to advertise their merits

What makes people reluctant to call attention to themselves by advertising their merits, displaying their qualities, establishing their name, and publicizing their attributes? This simply results in obscurity, and obscurity is a form of nonexistence and has a familiar relationship to deficiency. For what is obscure is unknown, and the unknown is the contrary of the nonexistent;[43] and there is no debating the nonexistent and no disputing the existent. This question originated in the following circumstances. One of our masters showed us a book he had composed, and we discovered that he had not noted on the outside "Written or composed by so-and-so," nor had he even noted that he was the owner of the book. We asked him, "What is your reasoning?" He answered, "There are secret reasons that make it attractive to me." Then he brought out several books written during his youth and containing his name, and he said, "These are the relics of my days of deficiency." 141.1

Miskawayh's response

Merit calls attention to itself, and does not need people to call attention to it themselves. For the virtues that are truly virtues shine out like the sun, and cannot be hidden, even if their possessor wished it. Those that can be hidden are deemed virtues but are not. People employ reason to scrutinize the claims of anyone who sets about praising himself and making claims in order to draw attention to his virtue, so his imperfections become apparent and the points on which he is deceived about himself become manifest. If he happens to be speaking truthfully, and he indeed possesses the virtue in question, he reveals, by taking such pains to manifest it, that he is not confident in people's judgments and their powers of scrutiny; or he may be confident, but is boastful and proud. People do not like any of these character traits because they are base. The great-spirited person, by contrast, belittles the virtues he possesses 141.2

يستقلّ لنفسه ما يكون فيه من الفضائل لسموّه إلى ما هو أكثر منه ولأنّ المرتبة التي تحصل للإنسان من الفضل وإن كانت عالية فهي نزر يسير بالإضافة إلى ما هو أكثر منه وهو متعرّض لطباع الإنسان مبذول له وإنّما يمنعه العجز الموكل بطبيعة البشر عن استيعابه وبلوغ أقصاه أو يشغله عنه[1] بنقائص تعوقه عن التماس الغاية القصوى من الفضائل البشريّة.

مسألة

سأل سائل عن النظم والنثر وعن مرتبة كلّ واحد منهما ومزيّة أحدهما ونسبة هذا ١،١٤٢
إلى هذا وعن طبقات الناس فيهما[2] فقد قدّم الأكثرون النظم على النثر ولم يحتجّوا فيه بظاهر القول وأفادوا مع ذلك به وجانبوا خفيّات الحقيقة فيه وقدّم الأقلّون النثر وحاولوا الحجاج فيه.

الجواب

قال أبو عليّ مسكويه رحمه الله إنّ النظم والنثر نوعان قسيمان تحت الكلام والكلام ٢،١٤٢
جنس لهما وإنّما تصحّ القسمة هكذا الكلام ينقسم إلى المنظوم وغير المنظوم وغير المنظوم ينقسم إلى المسجوع وغير المسجوع ولا يزال ينقسم كذلك حتّى ينتهي إلى آخر أنواعه. ومثال ذلك ممّا جرت به عادتك أن تقول الكلام بما هو جنس يجري مجرى قولك الحيّ فكما أنّ الحيّ ينقسم إلى الناطق وغير الناطق ثمّ إنّ غير الناطق ينقسم إلى الطائر وغير الطائر ولا تزال تقسّمه حتّى تنتهي إلى آخر أنواعه. ولمّا كان الناطق والطائر يشتركان في الحيّ الذي هو جنس لهما ثمّ ينفصل الناطق عن الطائر بفضل النطق فكذلك النظم والنثر يشتركان في الكلام الذي هو جنس لهما ثمّ ينفصل النظم عن النثر بفضل الوزن الذي به صار المنظوم منظوماً. ولمّا كان الوزن حلية زائدة

[1] الأصل: عن. [2] الأصل: فيها.

because he aspires to more; for however high the degree of merit a person acquires, it is nugatory compared with that which surpasses it. He is subject to the natural disposition of human beings and under its control, and the limitations vested in human nature prevent him from acquiring it fully and attaining its utmost degree, or he is distracted by deficiencies that hinder him from seeking the highest level of human virtue.

On the relative merits of verse as against prose

Someone posed a question about the ranks of verse and prose, their respective **142.1** merits, the relation of one to the other, and the classes people occupy with regard to them. Most people place verse higher than prose, without offering a clear argument in support of their view; even so, they make that claim and avoid delving into the hidden aspects of the truth involved. A small minority place prose higher, and attempt to argue their case.

Miskawayh's response

Verse and prose are species that form subdivisions of speech; speech consti- **142.2** tutes their genus. The correct mode of division is as follows: Speech divides into that which is arranged in verse and that which is not arranged in verse. That which is not arranged in verse divides into that which employs rhyme and that which does not employ rhyme. The process of division continues until the final species is reached. Let us illustrate this with an example familiar to you: Insofar as it is a genus, speech follows the same principle as the term "living being." For living beings divide into the rational and the nonrational, nonrational beings divide into those that can fly and those that cannot fly, and one continues the process of division until one reaches the final species. Rational beings and beings that can fly have in common the fact that they are living beings, which is their genus, and rational beings and beings that can fly are then differentiated by virtue of rationality. Similarly, verse and prose have in common the fact that they are forms of speech, which is their genus, and verse is then differentiated from prose by virtue of meter, through which verse

وصورة فاضلة على النثر صار الشعر أفضل من النثر من جهة الوزن. فإن اعتُبرت المعاني كانت المعاني مشتركة بين النظم والنثر وليس من هذه الجهة تميّز أحدهما من الآخر بل يكون كلّ واحد منهما صدقاً مرّة وكذباً مرّة وصحيحاً مرّة وسقيماً أخرى. ومثال النظم من الكلام مثال اللحن من النظم فكما أنّ اللحن يكتسي منه النظم[1] صورة زائدة على ما كان له كذلك صفة النظم الذي يكتسي منه الكلام صورة زائدة على ما كان له وقد أفصح أبو تمّام عن هذا حين قال [كامل]

هُوَ جَوْهَـرٌ نَثْرٌ فَإِنْ أَلَّفْتَـهُ   بِٱلنَّظْمِ صَارَ قَلَائِدًا وَعُقُودَا

مسـألة

١٬١٤٣ لم صار الحظر يثقل على الإنسان؟ وكذا الأمر إذا ورد أخذ بالمخنق وسدّ الكظم وقد علمت أنّ نظام العالم يقتضي الأمر والنهي ولا يتمّان إلّا بآمر وناه ومأمور ومنهيّ وهذه أركان ودعائم ولكنّها هنا[2] مكتومة بالإشراف عليها يكمل الإنسان فيعرف الملتبس من المتخلّص.

الجواب

٢٬١٤٣ قال أبو عليّ مسكويه رحمه الله إنّ الأمر الذي أومأت إليه والحظر إنّما يقعان في جنس الشهوات التي بجح بالإنسان إلى القبائح وبلزوم الأعمال التي فيها مشقّة وتؤدّي إلى المصالح. ولمّا كان الإنسان ميله بالطبع إلى تعجّل الشهوات غير ناظر في أعقاب يومه وإلى الهوينى والراحة في عاجل اليوم دون ما يكسب الراحة طول الدهر ثقل عليه حظر شهواته والأمر الذي يرد عليه بالأعمال التي فيها مشقّة. وهذه حال لازمة

١ الأصل: منه المنطق النظم. ٢ الأصل وط: ولكن هاهنا.

is constituted as verse. Since meter is an additional quality and a surplus form relative to prose, poetry excels over prose on account of its meter. Verse and prose have meanings in common, so it is not through this aspect that the one is distinguished from the other; rather, each of them may be sometimes true and sometimes false, sometimes sound and sometimes defective. The relation of verse to speech is like the relation of melody to verse. Just as melody imparts to verse a form that is additional to the one it had previously possessed, similarly, the quality of versified arrangement imparts to speech a form additional to the one it had previously possessed. Abū Tammām put the point eloquently when he said:

> They are jewels strewn about, but if you unite them in verse
> they become necklaces and strings of pearls.

On why people feel oppressed when things are prohibited to them

Why do human beings find interdiction oppressive? Similarly, when a command is issued, it seizes us by the throat and stifles our very breath. And yet we know that the order of the world requires commands and prohibitions, and this can only be achieved through someone who commands and prohibits, and through something that is commanded and prohibited. These are basic elements and principles, but their meaning is withheld from us here, and by gaining an overview human beings may be perfected and distinguish what is obscure from what is clearly distilled. 143.1

Miskawayh's response

The commands and prohibitions you refer to arise in connection with those appetites that wantonly drive human beings to evil actions, and concern the necessitation of actions that involve hardship but lead to our good. Human beings naturally incline to immediate gratification of their appetites without regard for consequence, and to a preference for ease and repose here and now over what will bring repose throughout the time to come. Thus they find it oppressive when their appetites are forbidden and when commanded to perform acts involving hardship. This is a condition that cleaves to human beings 143.2

للإنسان منذ الطفولة فإنّ أثقل الأشياء عليه منع والديه[1] مأربه وأخذهما إيّاه بكلف الأعمال النافعة ثمّ إذا كمل صار أثقل الناس عليه طبيبه ومعالجه ونصيحه في المشورة وسلطانه الذي يأخذه بمنافعه ومصالحه. وهذه حال أكثر الناس المنقادين لشهواتهم المتّبعين لأهوائهم. وقد يقع فيهم الجيّد الطبع الصحيح الرويّة القويّ العزيمة فلا يأتي من الأمور إلّا أجملها قامعاً لهواه متحمّلاً ثقل مؤونة ذلك لما ينتظره من حسن العاقبة وإحمادها. ومثل هذا قليل بل أقلّ من القليل وليس إلى أمثاله يوجّه الخطاب بالأمر والنهي ولا إيّاه خُوّف بالوعد والوعيد وأُنذر العذاب الأليم.

مسألة

١،١٤٤ ما سبب[2] الخطيب على المنبر وبين السماطين وفي يوم المحفل فيما يعتريه من الحصر والتتعتع والخجل في شيء قد حفظه وأتقنه ووثق بحسنه ونقائه؟ أتراه ما الذي يستشعر حتّى يضلّ ذهنه ويعصيه لسانه ويتحيّر باله ويملك عليه أمره.

الجواب

٢،١٤٤ قال أبو عليّ مسكويه رحمه الله إنّ انصراف النفس بالفكر إلى جهة من الجهات يعوقه عن التصرّف في غيرها من الجهات ولذلك لا يقدر أحد أن يجمع بين الفكر في مسألة هندسيّة وأخرى نحويّة أو شعريّة بل لا يتمكّن أحد من تدبير أمر دنيويّ وآخر أخرويّ في حال واحدة ومن تعاطى ذلك فإنّما يقطع لكلّ واحد جزءاً من الزمان وإن

[1] الأصل: ولادته. [2] ط: سبب في أنّ.

from childhood. For what they find most onerous is their parents' denial of their wishes and admonitions to do things that are difficult yet beneficial. When they grow to adulthood, the people they find most oppressive are their physicians and healers, those who dispense counsel to them in deliberative matters, and those who rule over them and impose upon them what benefits them and serves their welfare. This is the condition of most people, who are governed by their appetites and follow their blind desires. Yet one may also encounter among them people of outstanding natural disposition, sound judgment, and firm resolve, who only do what is finest and suppress their blind desires, enduring the toilsome burden of doing so on account of the excellent and meritorious outcome they anticipate. Such people are few and far between, indeed a rare exception; commands and prohibitions are not addressed to people such as these—they have no need of being galvanized by promises and threats, or warnings of painful retribution in the life to come.

On why preachers are affected by stage fright when addressing large audiences

Why are preachers overcome by inarticulacy, stuttering, and embarrassment when they stand in the pulpit among large numbers of people on days of assembly, even though they have memorized and mastered what they want to say and are confident of its excellent quality? What is it that they experience, one wonders, that makes their minds stray from the track, makes their tongues defy their orders, plunges their thoughts into confusion, and takes complete possession of them? 144.1

Miskawayh's response

When the soul applies thought in one particular direction, its application in other directions is hindered. This is why no one is able to think simultaneously about a question of geometry and a question of grammar or poetry. In fact, we are incapable of attending at the same time to a mundane and otherworldly matter. People who do so apportion a separate segment of time, however small, to each matter, but there is no way for the time occupied by the one and by the other to coincide exactly. This happens to us because we human beings are enmeshed with matter, and because the soul employs material 144.2

قلّ فأمّا أن يكون زمانه[1] هو بعينه زمان هذا فلا وإنّما عرض لنا هذا معاشر الناس لأجل التباسنا بالهيولى واستعمال النفس للمادّة والآلة والأمر في ذلك واضح بيّن مشاهد بالضرورة. ولمّا كان الفكر يوم الحفل منصرفاً إلى ما ينصرف إليه الناس من عيب إن وجدوا وتقصير إن حفظوا اشتغل الإنسان بتخوّف هذه الحال وأخذ الحذر منه فكان هذا عائقاً عن الأفعال التي تخصّ ذلك[2] المكان وهذا الاضطراب من النفس هو الذي يجعل الآلات مضطربة حتّى تحدث فيها حركات مختلفة على غير نظام أعني التتعتع وما أشبهه وذلك أنّ مستعمل الآلة إذا اضطرب تبعه اضطراب آلته لا محالة.

مسألة

١،١٤٥ وما السبب في خجل الناظر إليه وحياء الواقف عليه خاصّة إذا[3] كان منه بسبب وضمّهما نسب ورجعا إلى حال جامعة ومذهب مشترك وما الفاصل[4] من المنظور إليه إلى الناظر؟ وما الواصل[5] من المتكلّم إلى السامع حتّى يغضي طرفه حياله ويسدّ أذنه؟ هذا شيء قد شاهدته بل قد دُفعت إليه. وإنّما التأمت المسألة بالحادثة لأنّ التعجّب تمكّن والاستطراف ثبت إلى أن وُقف على السبب الجالب والأمر الغالب وعند ظهور العلّة يثبت الحكم وبانكشاف الغطاء ينقطع ولوع المستكشف فسبحان من له هذه اللطائف المطويّة وهذه الخبيئات الملويّة عن العقول الزكيّة والأذهان الذكيّة.

الجواب

٢،١٤٥ قال أبو عليّ مسكويه رحمه الله ينبغي أن نعيد ذكر السبب في الحياء والخجل ذكراً مجملاً فنقول إنّ الحياء هو انحصار يلحق النفس[6] خوفاً من قبيح فإذا كان هذا هو الحياء فإنّ الإنسان إذا كان[7] بسبب من المتكلّم لحق نفسه من العارض قريب ممّا يلحق المتكلّم لأنّه

١ الأصل: هذا زمان هو؛ ط: زمانه هذا. ٢ ط: هذا. ٣ الأصل: وقلت إذا. ٤ الأصل: وما الفاضل وما الفاضل.
٥ الأصل: وما الوصل. ٦ الأصل وط: الناس. ٧ الأصل: فإن النفس إذا كانت.

substance and instruments. This is clear and plain and immediately evident to all. On days of congregation, our thoughts become absorbed by the things that absorb people's attention—the faults they might find or the deficiencies they might be mindful of—so we consume ourselves with fearful anticipations of the prospect and with the need to guard against it; and this impedes the acts proper to the occasion. This disorder within the soul is what brings its instruments into disorder, producing in them a variety of disjointed movements, such as stuttering and the like. For when the user of an instrument is in disarray, his instrument inevitably follows suit.

On the anxiety that affects onlookers when they see preachers affected by stage fright

Why does someone who looks at and attends to someone else feel embarrassed and ashamed, particularly if there is a relation between them, if they are joined by a bond of kinship or are united by a common characteristic or shared doctrine? What is it that separates the one who is looking from the one who is being looked at? And what is it that connects the speaker to the listener and makes him shut his eyes and seal his ears as he faces him? This is something I have seen with my own eyes—indeed, something I have been driven to myself. This second question annexes itself to the first because wonder takes hold of us and curiosity stands firm until such time as the underlying cause and the prevailing facts have been brought to light. When the cause becomes evident, the ruling is established, and once the veil is cast aside, the ardor of those who try to peer through it abates. Praise be to God, who controls those well-guarded subtleties and secrets withheld from pure intellects and sharp minds. 145.1

Miskawayh's response

It is necessary to rehearse here in summary form our account of the causes of shame and embarrassment. Shame is a contraction that affects the soul as a result of a fear of doing wrong. Since this is what shame is, the soul of a person, when he is related to the speaker, is beset by a disturbance similar to the one that besets the speaker because he fears he will do something wrong or say something he will be criticized for, just as the speaker is afraid. We had 145.2

يخشى من وقوع أمر قبيح منه أو كلام يُعاب عليه مثل ما يخشاه المتكلّم. وقد كنّا أومأنا فيما سبق إلى أنّ[1] النفس واحدة وإنّما تتكثّر بالموادّ ولولا ذلك لما كان لأحد سبيل إلى أن ينقل ما في نفسه إلى نفس غيره بالإفهام وفيما مرّ من ذلك فيما مضى كفاية لأنّ ما يُحتاج إليه ههنا هو أن يظهر أنّ القبيح الذي يختصّ بزيد يعمّ عمراً أيضاً من جهة وإن كان عمرو غريباً من زيد فكيف إذا ضمّه وإيّاه سبب أو نسب؟

٣،١٤٥ وليس يحتاج أن ينفصل من المنظور إلى الناظر شيء لأنّ أفعال النفس وآثارها لا تكون على هذه الطريقة الحسّيّة والجسميّة لا سيّما واستشعار كلّ واحد من المتكلّم والسامع استشعار واحد في تخوّف القبيح والحذر من الزلل والخطأ فإنّ هذا الاستشعار يعرض منه الحياء والخجل كما قلنا ومتى غلب على ظنّ السامع أنّ المتكلّم يسيء ويزيغ صار خوفه وحذره يقيناً أو شبيهاً باليقين فعظم العارض له من الحياء حتّى يلحقه ما ذكرت من الحركة المضطربة وكذلك حال المتكلّم إذا لم يثق بنفسه أو لم تكن له عادة بالوقوف في ذلك المقام والكلام فيه فإنّ حذره يشتدّ وحياءه يكثر وبزيادة الحياء يزداد الاضطراب ويمتنع القدر من الكلام الذي تسمح به النفس عند توفّر قوّتها واجتماع بالها وسكون جأشها وهدوء حركاتها.

مسألة

١،١٤٦ ما علّة كراهية النفس الحديث المعاد؟ وما سبب ثقل إعادة الحديث على المستعاد؟ وليس فيه في الحال الثانية إلّا ما فيه في الحالة الأولى فإن كان فارق بينهما فما هو؟

الجواب

٢،١٤٦ قال أبو عليّ مسكويه رحمه الله إنّ النفس تأخذ من الأخبار المستطرفة والأحاديث الغريبة عندها شبيهاً بما يأخذه الجسم من أقواته وما حصّلته النفس من المعارف

[1] الأصل: سبق أن.

occasion to point out earlier that the soul is one, and multiplicity only enters it through the multiplicity of material substrates.[44] Otherwise, it would be impossible for anyone to convey what is in his soul to the soul of another and make himself understood. What has already been said about this topic suffices for the purpose, for what is required at this juncture is to bring out that what Zayd does badly also concerns ʿAmr from another perspective, even if ʿAmr is a stranger. How much more so when the two are united by some relation or a bond of kinship?

It is not necessary for something to separate the one looking from the one 145.3
being looked at, for the acts and effects of the soul are not of this sensible, bodily order, especially given that both the speaker and the listener are experiencing one and the same thing—a fear of doing wrong, and an apprehensiveness about slipping up and making mistakes. For this is the state of mind, as we said, from which shame and embarrassment stem. When the listener is convinced that the speaker will perform badly and miss the mark, his fear and apprehension turn into certainty or into something not far removed from that, so the shame that affects him intensifies and he succumbs to the disordered kind of movements you spoke of. The same thing happens to the speaker if he lacks self-confidence or if he isn't used to standing up and speaking in such a context. His apprehension mounts and his shame increases, and with the increase of shame comes an increase of disorder, and it becomes impossible to speak as freely as the soul permits when its power is full, it is in a state of composure and equanimity, and its movements are calm.

On why we hate hearing the same thing twice

Why do we hate hearing the same thing twice? Why does the person who hears 146.1
the same thing twice find it oppressive, even though the second time is no different from the first? If there is a difference between the two, then what is it?

Miskawayh's response

From uncommon reports and unfamiliar discourses the soul derives a nourish- 146.2
ment similar to that which the body derives from its aliments. To offer to the soul for a second time information and knowledge it has already assimilated is like offering to the body for a second time food it has already eaten its fill

والعلوم فإعادته عليها بمنزلة الغذاء من الجسم الذي اكتفى منه فإذا أعيد عليه غذاء هو الأوّل ثقل عليه واستعفى منه فكذلك حال النفس في المعارف. وينبغي أن تؤخذ هذه الأمثلة التي أورِدُها من الأجسام على ما ليس بالجسم أخذاً لطيفاً لا يحصل منه ظلّ في تلك الأمور الشريفة فيفسد على الإنسان تخيّله ويذهب وهمه منه مذهباً غير لائق بالمعنى المقصود. وأرجو أن يكفي الناظر في المسائل ما حدّدته فإنّي إنّما أجبت من له[1] قدم في هذه العلوم وتحرّم بها. وينبغي لمن لم تكن له هذه الرتبة أن يرتاض أوّلاً بهذه العلوم ارتياضاً جيّدا ثمّ ينظر في هذه الأجوبة إن شاء الله.

مسألة

١،١٤٧ سألني سائل فقال هل يجوز أن ترد الشريعة من قبل الله تعالى بما يأباه العقل ويخالفه ويكرهه ولا يجيزه كذبح الحيوانات وكإيجاب الدية على العاقلة؟ وقد جهّزت المسألة إليك ووجّهت أملي في الجواب عنها نحوك وأنت المدّخر لغريب العلم ومكنون الحكمة. فإن تفضّلت بالجواب وإلّا عرضت عليك ما قلت للسائل ورويت ما دار بيني وبين المجادل فإن كان سديداً عرّفتنيه وإن كان ضعيفاً نصحتني فيه فالعلم بعيد الساحل عميق الغور شديد الموج ولولا فضل الله العظيم على هذا الخلق الضعيف لما وُقف على شيء ولا نُظر في شيء لكنّه لطيف بعباده رؤوف يبتدئ بالنعمة قبل المسألة وبالخير قبل التعرّض.

الجواب

٢،١٤٧ قال أبو عليّ مسكويه رحمه الله ليس يجوز أن ترد الشريعة من قبل الله تعالى بما يأباه العقل ويخالفه ولكنّ الشاكّ في هذه المواضع لا يعرف شرائط العقل وما يأباه فهو أبداً يخلطه بالعادات ويظنّ أنّ تأبّي الطباع من شيء هو مخالفة العقل وقد سمعت كثيراً من

[1] الأصل: أجبت له.

of. Given the same food twice, the body finds it oppressive and turns away from it. It is likewise with the soul's relationship to knowledge. The analogies I have drawn here between bodies and non-bodily things have to be taken with discrimination, so as not to tarnish these exalted matters in ways that corrupt one's imagination and lead one's fancy down roads that comport ill with the intended meaning. I pray that the statements to which I have confined myself will suffice for those perusing the present questions; for I have been addressing my answers to a reader who already has a purchase on these subjects and so commands respect. Whoever is not at this level must school himself well in these subjects first, and only then, God willing, peruse these answers.

On whether the religious Law can conflict with human reason

Someone put the following question to me: Is it possible that the Law handed down by God should contain things that reason rejects—that it opposes, declares repugnant, and rules impermissible—such as the sacrifice of animals or the imposition of blood money on the clan of an offender? I earmarked this question for you and have fixed my hopes on seeing it answered by you, for you are a storehouse of arcane learning and recondite wisdom. Kindly answer it; otherwise, I will convey to you the answer I gave to this question, and give you an account of what took place between me and this disputant; if you find it sound, you can tell me so, whereas if you find it weak, you can give me the benefit of your judicious counsel. For the shores of knowledge lie distant, its depths are unfathomed, and its waves tower and crash. But for God's great bounty toward creatures as infirm as us, we would be unable to inquire into anything or to reach any conclusion. Yet God is kind and gracious toward His servants, providing beneficence before it has been solicited, and good before it has been sought. 147.1

Miskawayh's response

It is not possible that the Law handed down by God should contain things that reason rejects and opposes—those who raise such doubts are ignorant of the provisions of reason and of what it rejects. For they always confound it with acquired customs, and they suppose that if people's natural disposition recoils from something, this amounts to an opposition on the part of reason. I have 147.2

الناس يتشكّكون بهذه الشكوك وحضرت خصوماتهم وجدالهم فلم يتعدّوا ما ذكرته وينبغي أن نوطّئ للجواب توطئة من كلام نبيّن فيه الفرق بين ما يأباه العقل وبين ما يأباه الطبع ويتكرّهه الإنسان بالعادة فنقول إنّ العقل إذا أبى شيئاً فهو أبديّ الإباء له لا يجوز أن يتغيّر في وقت ولا يصير بغير تلك الحال وهكذا جميع ما يستحسنه العقل أو يستقبحه وبالجملة فإنّ جميع قضايا العقل هي أبديّة واجبة على حال واحدة أزليّة لا يجوز أن يتغيّر عن حاله وهذا أمر مسلّم غير مدفوع ولا مشكوك فيه. فأمّا أمر الطبع والعادة فقد يتغيّر بتغيّر الأحوال والأسباب والزمان والعادات وأعني بقولي الطبع طبع الحيوان والإنسان لا الطبيعة المطلقة الأولى وذاك أنّ اسم الطبيعة مشترك فقد بيّنّا ما أردنا بالطبع.

وإذا كان ذلك بيّناً من الأمثلة والأحوال المقرّ بها فإنّا نعود فنقول إنّ ذبح الحيوان ٣،١٤٧
ليس من الأشياء التي يأباها العقل وينكرها[١] بل هو من القبيل الآخر أعني من الأشياء التي يأباها بعض الطباع بالعادة ولو كان ممّا يأباه العقل لكان أبديّاً لا يرضاه في وقت ولا يأمر به ولا يأنس له. ونحن نشاهد من يأبى قتل الحيوان لأنّ عادته لم تجر به ومتى جرت به عادته هان عليه وسهل فعله وجرى مجرى سائر الأفعال عند أصحابه وأنت ترى القصّاب والجزّار بل مشاهدي الحروب يهون عليهم ما يصعب على غيرهم. وأيضاً فإنّ الحيوان الذي يألم بمرض لا يُعرف علاجه إذا أشفق عليه العاقل وكره مقاساته لما لا علاج له يأمر بذبحه ليكون خلاصه في الموت الوحيّ. أفترى العقل الذي أمر بذبحه يستحسن ما كان مستقبحاً له؟ أم تغيّر فعله الأبديّ بطارئ طرأ وحادث حدث؟ مع اعترافنا بأنّ العقل ليس من شأنه ذلك لأنّه جوهر أبديّ وجوهره هو حكمه ولذلك هو أبديّ الحكم.

---

١ الأصل: ولا ينكرها.

heard many people giving voice to these misgivings, and I have attended their verbal jousts and disputations, but they never go beyond what I have said. We must preface our response with a few remarks that help clarify the distinction between what is rejected by reason and what is rejected by the natural disposition and found repugnant by human beings as a result of acquired custom. So we respond as follows: When reason rejects something, its rejection holds forever; it can never change at any point in time, and its position can never be other than what it is. The same thing applies to everything reason judges to be good or bad. In general, all of the judgments of reason are valid forever. They have held necessarily from the beginning of time, and there can be no change in this status. This is something that is widely accepted as true and that cannot be gainsaid or doubted. Matters of natural disposition and custom, on the other hand, may change with shifting circumstances, causes, times, and customs. In talking about what is "natural," I am referring to the natural disposition of animals and human beings, not to primary nature in the absolute sense. For "nature" is an equivocal term; but we have clarified what we mean by "natural disposition."

If that is clear from examples and facts that muster general assent, then we 147.3
can return to our question and say: The sacrifice of animals is not something reason rejects and denounces, but rather belongs to the second category, that is, to those things which some people's natural dispositions reject because of acquired custom. For were it one of the things that reason rejects, it would always be so, and reason would never approve of it, dictate it, or feel at ease with it. Yet we see people who reject the sacrifice of animals because it has not been part of their custom; and then, once they become accustomed to it, they find it easy and have no trouble performing it, and it becomes just like any other act they perform. And we observe how butchers and slaughterers—indeed, even those who have taken part in wars—find it easy to countenance things that others find hard. Similarly, when an animal is in agony because of an incurable illness, any rational person who takes pity on it and is loath to watch it suffer from something incurable would order that it be slaughtered so that it might find reprieve in a speedy death. So one must ask: Is reason, in ordering it to be slaughtered, now declaring good something it had formerly judged to be evil? Or has its eternally enduring act undergone a change due to a sudden contingency or newly arisen factor? Yet we acknowledge that it is not in the nature of reason for this to happen, and that is because it is an eternal substance, and its substance consists in its rulings. Thus, its rulings have eternal duration.

فإنّنا لا نظنّ بأن حكم العقل على العدد والهندسة وسائر البراهين الطبيعيّة تغيّر عمّا كان عليه منذ عشرة آلاف سنة أو يتغيّر إلى مثل هذا الزمان أو أكثر أو أقلّ بل نثق بأنّه أبداً كان ويكون على وتيرة واحدة. فأمّا الأمور التي تُستقبح مرّة وتُستحسن أخرى وتتأبّى تارة وتُتقبّل ثانية فإنّما لها أسباب أخر غير العقل المجرّد فإنّ السياسات أبداً يعترض فيها ذلك وأمراض الأبدان والأمور غير الأبديّة[1] كلّها أبداً معرّضة للتغيّر ويتغيّر الحكم بتغيّرها بل لا يجوز أن تبقى لازمة بحال واحدة لأنّها أبداً في السيلان والدثور للزوم الحركة إيّاها والحركة نفسها هي تغيّر الأشياء المتحرّكة إذ[2] كلّها متغيّرة. وكذلك الزمان وما تعلّق به هو تغيّر بتغيّره. وما يعرض للإنسان من كراهية ذبح الحيوان[3] إنّما هو لمشاركته إيّاه في الحيوانيّة ويخطر بباله عند مكروه ينال البهيمة أنّ مثل ذلك المكروه سيناله لمشاركته إيّاه في الحيوانيّة فيحدث له من النفور عند هذا الخاطر[4] ما يحدث لكلّ حيوان إذا تصوّر مكروهاً حتّى إذا أنس بذلك الفعل زال عنه ذلك النفور وصار الذبح والسلخ والتقصيب يجري عنده مجرى بري القلم ونحت الخشب وكذلك حال من شاهد الحروب وأنس بها عند العراء المستوحش منها. ٤،١٤٧

وههنا حال أخرى أبين ممّا ذكرته وهو أنّ العقل قد حسّن عند الإنسان إذا حصل في مكروه غليظ من الأعداء كمن يرى في أهله وولده ما لا يطيق مشاهدته أن يبذل نفسه للقتل ويختار الموت الجميل على الحياة القبيحة وهذه[5] الرخصة من العقل مستمرّة في كلّ حال يقبح بالإنسان أن يعيش فيها أعني أن يختار الموت عليها. فالجواب إذاً عن أمثال هذه المسائل أن يقال إنّ العقل لا يستحسن ولا يستقبح شيئاً منها إلّا بقرائن وشرائط فأمّا هذا الفعل بعينه وحده فلا يتأبّاه ولا يتقبّله أعني لا يحكم فيه[6] بحكم أبديّ أوّليّ كأحكامه التي عرفناها وأحطنا بها. ٥،١٤٧

١ الأصل: والأمور الأبديّة. ٢ الأصل: إذا. ٣ ط: الحيون. ٤ الأصل: الحاضر. ٥ الأصل: وهذا. ٦ الأصل: فيها.

We do not suppose that the rulings of reason on questions of arithmetic or geometry or other types of natural proof have changed in the last ten thousand years, or will change over the next ten thousand years, or over shorter or longer spans. We are confident that they have always been and always will be the same. Those things, by contrast, which are disapproved of at one time and approved of at another, that are rejected on one occasion and accepted the next, have their origins elsewhere than pure reason. Matters relating to political governance always involve such things. Likewise, bodily illnesses[45] and impermanent things on the whole are always exposed to change, and the relevant rulings change as they do. Indeed, it is impossible for them to adhere to a single state, for insofar as motion necessarily adheres to them, they are always passing from one state to another or passing into nothing. Motion itself consists in the change of moving things, for they are all changing. Similarly with time and what it attaches to; it changes as it changes. But the sense of repugnance people feel about slaughtering animals is due to the fact that they share in their animal nature. For when something bad happens to a beast, it crosses their mind that something similar will happen to them because they share animality with it. This thought produces in them the kind of revulsion that is produced in all animals whenever they envisage the occurrence of something bad. Yet once they grow familiar with this act, their sense of revulsion falls away, and slaughter and butchery come to seem no different to them than sharpening a pencil or carving wood. It is the same with those who take part in wars, and come to see them as normal even in the midst of fearsome carnage. 147.4

There is another case in this context that is even clearer than those I have mentioned. When a person is confronted with an abominable evil at the hands of enemies—as when one sees one's wife and children undergoing things one cannot bear to witness—reason deems it permissible for one to give up one's life and opt for a noble death instead of an ignominious life. The license granted herein by reason—the license to choose death, that is—extends to all cases in which it is ignoble for a person to continue living. Questions of this kind should therefore be addressed as follows: When reason judges any of these things to be good or bad, it does so on the basis of contextual factors and conditions. It neither rejects nor accepts a given act taken by itself and in isolation; that is, it does not pronounce a timelessly valid, primary ruling like those we know and are well acquainted with. 147.5

وهكذا الحال في الأشياء التي تُعرف بالخير والشرّ فإنّ كثيرًا من الجهّال يعتقد أنّ[1] الأشياء كلّها منقسمة إلى هذين وليس الأمر كذلك. فإنّ اليسار والتمكّن من الدنيا ليس بخير ولا شرّ حتّى يُنظر في ماذا يستعمله صاحبه فإن استعمل يساره وماله في الأشياء التي هي خير فإنّ يساره خير وإن استعمله في الشرّ فهو شرّ وكذلك كلّ شيء كان صالحًا للشيء ولضدّه فليس يُطلق عليه أنّه واحد منهما بل الأولى أن يقال إنّه يصلح لهما جميعًا كالآلات التي يُصلح بها ويُفسد فإنّ الآلات لا توصف بأنّها مصلحة ولا مفسدة ولا أيضًا تسمّى بالصلاح والفساد إلّا بعد أن تستعمل. فهكذا يجب أن يقال في الأمور التي تُستحسن أو تُستقبح في أحوال وبحسب عادات إنّها ليست حسنة عند العقل ولا قبيحة على الإطلاق حتّى يُتبيّن واضعها ومستعملها وزمانها وأحوالها فإنّ القصاص إذا وقع[2] عليه هذا الاسم حسن لما فيه من حياة الناس وإذا وقع عليه اسم القتل بغير هذا الاعتبار صار قبيحًا لما فيه من تلف الحيوان. ٦،١٤٧

وقد خرجت في هذه المسألة عن عادتي في هذا الكتاب من الاختصار والإيماء إلى النكت لكثرة ما أسمعه من جهّال المانويّة ومن اغترّ بأمثلتهم وجنح إلى أقاويلهم مصدّقًا بالخديعة التي خلصوا بها إلى قلوب الأغمار من الناس حتّى عدلوا بهم عن الشرائع الصحيحة ولو أنّ واحدًا منهم سئل عن القبيح والحسن مطلقًا أو مقيّدًا لما عرفه إلّا على سبيل الاختلاط على أنّه لا يمتنع كلّ عاقل منهم إذا رأى حيوانًا يضطرب ويطول ذماؤه في قروح خارجة به أو قولنج قد يئس من برئه أو مهواة تردّى فيها فتكسّر منها أن يشير بذبحه وإن لم يتولّ ذلك بنفسه ولعلّ ضروبًا من المكاره تلحق الحيوان إذا طال عمره ليست بدون ما ذكرناه خلاصه منها بالموت الوحيّ لو فطن له وإنّما لا يتولّى الذبح بنفسه ويشير على غيره به لأجل العادة والاستشعار الذي لزمه. ٧،١٤٧

---
١ الأصل يفعل. ٢ الأصل: أحد وقع.

This is how matters stand with regard to things known as good and evil. Many ignorant people believe that everything falls into either of these categories. Yet this is not the case. For material prosperity and worldly power are neither good nor evil, and one must first consider the uses to which their owners put them. If they put their prosperity and wealth to good use, then their prosperity is good; if they use it for evil, it is evil. Similarly, anything that can serve two contrary ends should not be identified with one or the other; it is more appropriate to say that it can serve for both without distinction, like tools that can be put to a good or a bad use. For tools are not described as beneficial or harmful, nor can the notions of "benefit" or "harm" be applied to them until they have been put to use. Thus, one must say that things judged good or bad under particular circumstances and on the basis of particular customs are, from the viewpoint of reason, neither good nor bad absolutely, and one must first examine those who produce them and put them to service, as well as the time and circumstances in which they occur. For if an act is called "retaliation," it is good because it involves the preservation of human life, while if, on the basis of a different consideration, it is called "murder," it is bad because of the destruction of life it involves. 147.6

In this question, I deviated from the practice adopted throughout this book, of writing concisely and restricting myself to the key points. This is because of the sheer amount of verbiage I hear from ignorant Manichaeans and those who, duped into following their example, have gone over to their views, falling for the deceit through which they have gained access to the hearts of simple people and turned them away from the true laws. Yet were you to ask any of them about the distinction between taking "bad" and "good" in an absolute as against a restricted sense, they would only be able to give you a confused account. For all that, it is not impossible that any rational person among them who saw an animal covered in open ulcers, suffering from a colic recognized as untreatable, or lying with its limbs broken after falling into a ditch, tossing and turning in the throes of a prolonged death—that such a person would give the signal for it to be killed, even if he did not take on the task himself. Other kinds of evils may afflict an animal that lives a long life, commensurate with those we mentioned, from which the only redemption, if one is judicious enough to discern it, lies in a speedy death. Yet such a person would not take on the task of killing it himself, and would ask another to do it, on account of custom and of the way his feelings are fixed. And were a rational person such as this to have the 147.7

ولو أنّ هذا العاقل منهم بُلي بسلطان يعذّبه عذاباً يريد به أن يأتي على نفسه في زمان طويل ليذيقه العذاب لبادر إلى الحكم بما يأباه قبل وتناول سمّ ساعة أو سأل أن يُراح من الحياة. وكذلك لو فُعل بولده أو عترته[1] ما يكرهه لاختار الموت على رؤيته فكيف يكون المكروه مختاراً محبوباً والمستقبح مستحسناً من جهة العقل لولا ما ذكرناه؟

٨،١٤٧ فقد ظهر الجواب عن هذه المسألة وتبيّن[2] أنّ كلّ ما كان قبيحاً في وقت دون وقت لا يجوز أن يُنسب إلى العقل المجرّد وإلى أحكامه الأوّليّة الأزليّة بل لا يقال فيه إنّه قبيح ولا حسن على الإطلاق وإنّما يُنسب إلى الطباع والعادات ثمّ يقال قبيح بحسب كيت وكيت وحسن لكذا وكذا مقيّداً غير مطلق ولا منسوب إلى العقل المجرّد. فأمّا الدية التي على العاقلة فقد تكلّم الناس في وجه السياسة بها ووجه حسنها بيّن لا سيّما والمسألة المتقدّمة قد أوضحتها وبيّنت وجه الصواب في أمثالها من الشبه.

مسألة

١،١٤٨ قال أحمد بن عبد الوهّاب في جواب أبي عثمان الجاحظ عن التربيع والتدوير لا يقدر أحد أن يكذب كذباً لا صدق فيه من جهة من الجهات وهو[3] يقدر أن يصدق صدقاً لا كذب فيه من جهة من الجهات.

الجواب

٢،١٤٨ قال أبو عليّ مسكويه رحمه الله إن[4] كان الصدق والكذب إنّما يقعان في الخبر خاصّة من بين[5] أقسام الكلام والخبر هو الذي يسمّيه المنطقيّون القول الجازم وهو الذي تقع

١ الأصل: عزّته. ٢ الأصل: ويتبيّن. ٣ الأصل: فيه وهو. ٤ الأصل: الجواب إن. ٥ الأصل: من بين دون.

misfortune of being subjected to torture by a ruler who wished to bring about a slow death, in order to make him suffer woefully from the torture, he would be quick to rule that he should do that which he had previously rejected, and take a fast-acting poison or ask to be relieved of his life. Similarly, if his children and family were subjected to something he found abhorrent, he would prefer to die rather than to see it happen. So how else could something loathsome come to be readily chosen as desirable, and something deemed bad be deemed good from the perspective of reason, unless things are as we have described?

The answer to this question has thus emerged clearly, and it has been made 147.8
plain that all those things that are bad at one time but not at another cannot be attributed to pure reason and to its timelessly valid primary judgments, and indeed that the terms "bad" or "good" cannot be predicated of them absolutely. Rather, they must be ascribed to natural dispositions and acquired customs, and one may then say: x is bad under such-and-such conditions, or good given such-and-such factors, in a restricted, not in an absolute, manner, and without attributing this to pure reason. People have discussed the reason why communities should be governed by the principle of levying blood money on the clan of an offender. The reasons why it is good are evident, particularly as the foregoing question has elucidated them and has clarified the right view to take on similar points of confusion.

On a remark made by Aḥmad ibn ʿAbd al-Wahhāb concerning the possibility of uttering something that is completely false versus something completely true

Aḥmad ibn ʿAbd al-Wahhāb said in response to Abū ʿUthmān al-Jāḥiẓ's work, 148.1
The Square and the Round: Nobody can say something false that contains no truth of any kind, whereas one can say something true that contains no falsehood of any kind.

Miskawayh's response

If truth and falsehood pertain to that specific type of the divisions of speech 148.2
designated "statements," and statements are what logicians call "declarative" utterances—that is, utterances that convey information—and if those divisions are as discussed by practitioners of that craft, statements can indeed be purely

فيه الفوائد وكانت أقسامه هي التي تكلّم عليها أهل هذه الصناعة فإنّ الخبر قد يكون كذباً محضاً كما يكون صدقاً محضاً. وإن كان ذهب أحمد بن عبد الوهّاب في الصدق والكذب إلى غير ما عرفه هؤلاء القوم وتكلّموا عليه فإنّي غير محصّل له ولا متكلّم عليه.

مسـألة

ذكرت في هذه المسألة مسألة ذكرها أبو زيد البلخيّ حاكياً ومرّ أيضاً بجوابها راوياً قال ١،١٤٩
أبو زيد الفلسفيّ البلخيّ قيل لبعض العلماء ما معنى سكون النفس الفاضلة إلى الصدق ونفورها عن الكذب؟ فقال العلّة في ذلك كيت وكيت.

الجواب

قال أبو عليّ مسكويه رحمه الله إنّما تسكن النفس الفاضلة إلى ما كان من الخبر مقبولاً ٢،١٤٩
إمّا بوجوب ممّا اقتضاه دليل من برهان أو إقناع قويّ[١] وما لم يكن كذلك فإنّ النفس لا محالة تردّه وتأباه وأظنّ صاحب المسألة إنّما أراد من هذه المسألة كيف صارت النفس تسكن إلى الحقّ بالقول المرسل. فالجواب إنّ النفس إنّما تحرّك حركتها الخاصّة بها أعني إجالة الرويّة طلباً للحقّ لتصيبه ولولا طلبها لما تحرّكت ولولا حركتها هذه لما كانت حيّة تفيد الجسم أيضاً الحياة. فالنفس بهذه الحركة الدائمة الذاتيّة حيّة بل الحياة هي هذه الحركة من النفس وهي ذاتيّة لها كما قلنا. وأنت تعرف ذلك قريباً من أنّك لا تقدر أن تعطّلها من الرويّة والفكر لحظة واحدة لأنّها أبداً إمّا مرويّة جائلة في المحسوس[٢] أو مرويّة جائلة في المعقول بلا فتور أبداً. وكذلك هي دائمة الحركة وهذه الحركة إنّما هي تلقاء أمر ما أعني به إصابة الحقّ فإذا أصابته سكنت من ذلك الوجه ولا تزال تتحرّك حتّى تصيب الحقّ من الوجوه التي تمكن إصابته منها فإذا أصابته

١ كذا في الأصل. ٢ الأصل: جالية في للحواسّ.

false just as they can be purely true. If Aḥmad ibn ʿAbd al-Wahhāb takes a view of truth and falsehood that is different from what these people are familiar with and have spoken about, then I know nothing of the matter and cannot speak about it.

On why excellent souls find repose in the truth and find falsehood repugnant

In this question you mentioned a question quoted by Abū Zayd al-Balkhī, the answer to which he also reported. Abū Zayd al-Balkhī the philosopher said: A philosopher was asked, Why do excellent souls find rest in the truth and find falsehood repugnant? He said: The reason for that is as follows . . . 149.1

Miskawayh's response

Excellent souls find rest in statements that are acceptable, either as a result of a powerful conviction or necessarily as entailed by a demonstrative proof. Anything that does not fall into this class inevitably meets with rejection and refusal in the soul. I believe that the person who posed this question meant to ask the unqualified question: How does the soul find rest in the truth? The answer is as follows. The soul carries out its proper motion—that is, the roving of reflection—so as to attain the truth it pursues. But for its pursuit, it would not move, and but for the motion it carries out, it would not be alive and impart life to the body. The soul is alive through this perpetual, essential motion. We are immediately made aware of this by the fact that we are incapable of making it halt reflection and thought for a single moment. For it is always either reflecting on and roving over sensory things, or reflecting on and roving over intelligible things, without ever ceasing. It is thus perpetually in motion, and this motion is directed toward a certain object, that is, the attainment of the truth. Once it attains it, it finds rest from that aspect. It never ceases moving until it has attained the truth from all the aspects from which it is possible to attain it. Once it attains it, it finds rest; for the end of every moving thing is to come to rest once it has reached the end it was 149.2

سكنت لأنّ غاية كلّ متحرّك أن يسكن عند بلوغه الغاية التي تحرّك إليها. ولعلّك تقف من هذا الإيماء على غور بعيداً جدّاً أعانك الله تعالى عليه بلطفه.

مسألة

١،١٥٠ قال أحمد بن عبد الوهّاب في معاياة الجاحظ لم صار الحيوان يتولّد في النبات ولا يتولّد النبات في الحيوان؟ أي قد تتولّد الدودة في الشجرة ولا تنبت شجرة في حيوان فلم لم يجب؟

الجواب

٢،١٥٠ قال أبو عليّ مسكويه رحمه الله إنّ الحيوان يحتاج في وجوده إلى وجود النبات والنبات لا يحتاج في وجوده إلى وجود الحيوان. والسبب في ذلك أنّ الحيوان أكثر تركيباً من النبات لأنّه مركّب منه ومن جواهر[١] أخر أعني النفس الحيوانيّة ولذلك يكون الحيوان في أوّل تكوّنه نباتاً ثمّ تحصل من بعد حركة الحيوان. وحصول أثر النفس في الإنسان إنّما يكون بعد أن تستتمّ في الرحم صورة النبات ويكون استمداده الغذاء به هناك بعروق متّصلة برحم أمّه شبيهة بعروق النبات حتّى إذا استكمل أيضاً صورة الحيوان وحصلت له النفس الحيوانيّة تقطّعت تلك العروق وهو الطلق الذي يلحق الأمّ ويحرّك الولد للخروج. فإذا خرج وتنفّس في الهواء فتح فمه واغتذى به ولا يزال تكمل فيه صورة الحيوان إلى أن يقبل أثر النفس الناطقة ثمّ يكمل بها ويصير إنساناً بقدرة الله تعالى ولطف حكمته جلّ اسمه.

٣،١٥٠ فالنبات كما ذكرنا أبسط وأقدم وجوداً من الحيوان أعني أنّه لا يحتاج في وجوده إلى وجود الحيوان فهو يكتفي بمادّته من الأرض والهواء والماء والحرارة التي تأتيه من

١ الأصل: جوهر.

moving toward. These allusive remarks may open up a very wide vista to you. May God help you in this through His grace.

On a question put by Aḥmad ibn ʿAbd al-Wahhāb concerning why animals are generated inside plants but plants are not generated inside animals

Aḥmad ibn ʿAbd al-Wahhāb confronted al-Jāḥiẓ with the following abstruse question:[46] Why are animals generated inside plants, whereas plants are not generated inside animals? That is, a worm might be generated inside a tree, whereas no tree grows inside an animal. Why did he not reply? 150.1

Miskawayh's response

Animals need plants for their existence, whereas plants do not need animals for their existence. The reason is that animals are more composite than plants, because they are composed from the latter and from other substances, that is, the animal soul. This is why at the first stage of their formation animals are plants, the movement of animals emerging at a subsequent stage. The effect of the soul emerges in human beings after the vegetative form has been completed within the womb. While they are there, they draw their nourishment by means of roots that are connected to the womb of their mother and that resemble the roots of plants. Once the animal form is perfected as well and the animal soul emerges in them, those roots are sundered, which is what produces the labor pains that the mother experiences and that move the child out of the womb. Once the child emerges from the womb and breathes in the open air, he opens his mouth and receives nourishment through it. The animal form continues to be perfected within him until he receives the effect of the rational soul, and then he is perfected through it and he becomes a human being through the power of God and through the grace of His wisdom. 150.2

As we have mentioned, plants are simpler than animals and prior to them in existence; that is, they do not need animals for their existence. The earth, the air, the water, and the heat they receive from the sun are all the material substance they need in order to be completed and to enter existence. For animals, 150.3

الشمس حتّى يتمّ ويحصل وجوده. فأمّا الحيوان فلا يكتفي بتلك الأشياء حتّى تنضاف إليها مادّة أخرى تغذوه إذ كان لا يكتفي بالبسائط من الماء والأرض والهواء ويحتاج إلى النبات حتّى يغذوه ويكمّل وجوده ويحفظ عليه قوامه فإذا كان وجوده وقوامه بالنبات جاز أن يتولّد فيه. ولمّا كان وجود النبات يتمّ بغيره ولا يحتاج إليه لم يتولّد فيه ولو تولّد فيه النبات في الحيوان.[1] مع أنّه لا يغذوه ولا يحتاج إليه والطبيعة لا تفعل شيئاً باطلاً ولا لغواً لأفسد الحيوان وفسد هو في ذاته. أمّا إفساده الحيوان فلحاجته إلى ما يصرّف فيه عروقه التي يمتصّ بها مادّته التي تحفظ عليه ذاته وتعوّضه ممّا يتحلّل منه ومتى ضرب عروقه في بدن الحيوان تفرّق اتّصاله وفي تفرّق اتّصال بدن الحيّ هلاكه. وأمّا هلاكه في نفسه وفساده فلأنّه لا يجد الماء البسيط والأرض البسيطة والهواء الذي منه قوامه ومادّته فإنّ الحيوان لا توجد فيه هذه البسائط بالفعل وهذا كاف في هذه المسألة.

مسـألة

ما سبب تساوي الناس[2] في طلب الكيمياء حتّى إنك لتجد الغنيّ في غناه والمتوسّط ١،١٥١
في توسّطه والفقير في فقره على شيمة واحدة؟ وما هو أوّلاً؟ وهل له حقيقة؟ فقد طال خوض الخائضين فيه وكثر كلام الناس عليه واصطرع الحقّ والباطل والخطأ والصواب والإحالة فيه. فكأنّ الذي يثبته غير متحقّق به والذي يدفعه غير ساكن إلى دفعه وإبطاله. هذا وقد تمّت من الناس به حيل على الناس. ومتى وقفت على هذه المسألة وقفت من الحقائق على غيب شريف ومعنى لطيف. وهل ما يعزى إلى جابر ابن حيّان حقّ ولما يسند[3] لخالد بن يزيد أصل؟ وهل يسلم مثل هذا في الموضوع

١ الأصل: في الحيوان لكان. ٢ الأصل: سبب الناس. ٣ الأصل: ولمّا ينشد.

by contrast, those elements are not enough unless they are supplemented by another type of material substance that serves to nourish them. For the simple elements—water, earth, and air—are not enough, and they need plants to nourish them, to perfect their existence, and to preserve them in their proper state. Since they depend on plants in order to exist and be sustained, it is possible for them to be generated inside them; and since plants achieve their existence through other means and do not need them, they are not generated inside them. Were plants to be generated inside animals—even though they are not nourished by the latter and do not need them, and even though nature does nothing in vain or in error—this would expose animals to destruction, and they themselves would be destroyed in their own being. It would expose animals to destruction because of the need plants have for a base in which they may distribute their roots, through which they absorb the material substance that preserves them in their being and that replaces those of their parts that dissolve. Were they to strike their roots inside the bodies of animals, the latter would disintegrate, and when the body of a living being disintegrates, it perishes. The plants themselves would also perish because they would not find the simple water, earth, and air that sustain them and provide them with their material substance. For these simple elements are not actually to be found within animals. This amount of discussion suffices for the present question.

On the nature of alchemy and why people are so enamoured of it

Why does everyone converge on the pursuit of alchemy? We that find the rich, 151.1
the poor, and those neither rich nor poor share the same disposition irrespective of their level of material comfort. What is alchemy in the first place? Does it have any real substance? Long have inquiries into the topic been pursued, and people have said much about it; it is a battleground for truth and falsehood, errors, sound views, and incoherencies. Those who affirm it seem to lack conviction, and those who reject it seem unassured of their dismissal. What's more, it has been used to deceive. To lay this question bare is to lay bare truths about a noble domain hidden from view and a topic subtle to grasp. Is there truth in what is ascribed to Jābir ibn Ḥayyān, and is there a basis for what is attributed to Khālid ibn Yazīd? Can such a thing be conceded with respect to something fabricated and contrived, concocted and wrought

المختلق والمفتعل المخترق؟ وإذا اشتبه الأمر هذا الاشتباه كيف نخلص إلى ما يرفع الريب ويوضح الحال ويؤيّد اليقين؟ فقد رأيت ورأينا ناساً اختلفت بهم أحوال وتقلّبت عليهم أمور بتصديق هذا الباب وتكذيبه. وأطرف ما أرى فيه حلاوة الحديث وخلابة المتحدّث بذكره وميل النفوس إليه حتّى إنّ المكذّب ليفرغ له[1] باله ويصغي أذنه ويخلي ذهنه من غير أن يحلى بطائل أو يحظى بنائل.

الجواب

٢،١٥١ قال أبو عليّ مسكويه رحمه الله أمّا سبب طلب الناس الكيمياء فظاهر بيّن وهو أنّهم حريصون على جميع المتع والشهوات المختلفة في المأكل والمشرب والمنكح والنزه التي تقتسم بين الحواسّ ومحبّة الاستكثار والاستبداد والنهم على الجمع والادّخار شيء في الطبيعة. وليس يوصل إلى جميع ذلك إلّا بالذهب والفضّة لأنّهما بإزاء جميع المآرب على اختلافها وكلّ إنسان يعلم أنّه متى حصّلهما أو واحداً منهما فقد حصّل جميع المآرب على كثرتها متى همّ بها وأرادها ومع ذلك فهو يعدّها ذخراً لولده ولأوقات شدّته التي تلحقه من فجائع الدنيا ومحنها. فبهذين الحجرين يتوصّل إلى جميع ما ذكرناه ويدفع جميع الشرّ والمحن أيضاً بهما فهذا سبب طلب الناس لهما وحرصهم عليهما وليس يوصل إليهما إلّا بالمخاطرات الكثيرة وركوب الأهوال وتجشّم الأعمال الصعبة وغير ذلك ثمّ هما معرّضان للآفات والمتسلّطين وأهل العيث وهما من هذه الجهة إن صحّت أسهل شيء وأهونه.

٣،١٥١ فأمّا قولك ما هو وهل له حقيقة فإنّ البحث المستقيم أن نبدأ أوّلاً بهل هو ثمّ بما هو وإذا بحثنا عن هل هو وجدنا الأمر فيه مشكلاً يحتاج فيه إلى أخذ مقدّمات كثيرة طبيعيّة وصناعيّة. وينبغي أن نورد شكوك الناس في تلك المقدّمات واحتجاج[2] من يروم حلّها من مثبتي الصناعة فقد أكثروا في ذلك ثمّ نروم نحن

[1] الأصل: به. [2] الأصل وط: احتياج.

by guile? And if matters are so ambiguous, how can we arrive at a position that removes doubt and guarantees certainty? I have known, as have we both, people who have changed and shifted their position as to whether they give or deny credence to this field. Its most curious aspect, it seems to me, is how sweet it is to speak about, how much it captivates speakers to touch upon, and how strongly people's souls incline to it, so that even those who deny its credibility give it their undivided attention, lend a listening ear, and devote their minds to it, with no hope of benefit or profit.

Miskawayh's response

The reason why people pursue alchemy is manifest and clear—namely, that they have a keen desire for all the various pleasures and appetites to do with food, drink, sexual relations, and other sensual amusements. The love of obtaining ever larger amounts and of having exclusive possession of things and the insatiable desire to amass and hoard are rooted in nature. Silver and gold are the only means to do this, for they are equivalent to any of the various objects of desire. Every person knows that when he acquires both, or one of them, he can acquire any of the countless possible objects of desire whenever he has a mind or will to do so. At the same time, he views them as provisions laid up for his children and for times of hardship when he is visited by the misfortunes and trials of the world. By means of these precious metals one gains access to all we have mentioned, and one repels every evil and tribulation. This is the reason why people seek and desire them keenly. One can only obtain them by facing many hazards, venturing on frightful undertakings, and braving arduous deeds, among other things—and even then, they are vulnerable to damage and to the brute force and depredations of others. By contrast, obtaining them in this way, through alchemy—supposing it stands up to scrutiny—would be the simplest and easiest thing in the world. 151.2

The proper way to inquire into your questions "What is it?" and "Does it have a real substance?" is, first, to begin by asking whether something exists, and only afterward to ask what it is. If we inquire into whether it exists, we find that the matter is riddled with obscurities and requires one to draw on a large number of premises related both to nature and to craft. Therefore, before we proceed to examine them ourselves, we must adduce the doubts directed by detractors against those premises and the arguments offered by 151.3

النظر فيها وقد اختلفت المتقدّمون من الفلاسفة في ذلك والمتأخّرون. وآخر من تكلّم على بطلان الكيمياء وإبطال دعاوي أصحابها يوسف بن إسحاق الكنديّ[1] وكتابه مشهور في ذلك وردّ عليه محمّد بن زكريّا الرازيّ وكتابه أيضاً[2] معروف. ثمّ قد شاهدنا في أهل عصرنا جماعة يثبتون هذه الصناعة والأكثرون[3] يبطلونها. فأمّا المتكلّمون وطبقاتهم من أصناف الناس فمجمعون على إبطالها لأنّهم يزعمون أنّ في ذلك إبطال معجزات الأنبياء صلوات الله عليهم إذ كان ما يدعونه قلب الأعيان وهو لا يصحّ عندهم إلّا على يد نبيّ حسب وإنّ الله عزّ وجلّ هو القادر على قلب الأعيان دون مخلوقيه.

ولكلٍّ حجج وسننظر فيها نظرًا شافيًا ونورد أقاويل الجميع ويكون بحثنا عن ذلك بحث من قصده تعرّف الحقّ دون الثمرة المرجوّة من الكيمياء فإنّ هذا هو غاية من يتفلسف في نظره وبحثه ولا نبالي بعد ذلك صحّ أم بطل لئلّا تدعونا محبّة صحّته ورجاؤنا إلى إثباته بخديعة النفس للهوى أو نفيه على طريق العصبيّة. وفي هذا النظر طول لا يحتمله هذا الكتاب مع ما شرطنا فيه من الإيجاز ولكن سنفرد له مقالة كما فعلنا ذلك في مسألة العدل لمّا طال الكلام فيها أدنى طول وإذا فعلنا هذا في المقالة التي وعدنا بها نظرنا فإن صحّت لنا هليّته أتبعناها بالنظر في المائيّة وإن بطل الأوّل بطل الثاني لا محالة. ٤،١٥١

١ كذا في الأصل. ٢ ط: وكتابه. ٣ الأصل: والأكثرين.

supporters of the craft who have sought to counter them—for they have had much to say on the subject. Ancient and modern philosophers have differed over this topic. Al-Kindī was the most recent scholar to have spoken against the validity of alchemy and refuted the claims of its practitioners; his book on the subject is familiar to all. Muḥammad ibn Zakariyyā al-Rāzī countered him, and his book is also well-known.[47] Among the people of our times, we have observed a number of people affirming the soundness of this craft, whereas the majority deny its validity. The dialectical theologians, for all the different types who belong to their classes, are unanimous in denying its validity, alleging that this would nullify the miracles of the prophets, given that what the alchemists claim to be doing is changing one specific object into another. This is something that they believe can only be accomplished by a prophet; and it is God and not His creatures who has the exclusive power to change one specific object into another.

Each party has arguments in support of its case, and we will provide a satisfactory examination of them and adduce the views of all parties. We will approach our inquiry into the topic with the aim to discover the truth rather than to reap the benefit one hopes alchemy will provide. That is the end pursued by those who philosophize when they examine and inquire; beyond that we care not whether it proves valid or invalid, so that we do not let the soul be deceived by blind desire and thus are led to affirm it by our wish and hope that it be valid or deny it for partisan reasons. This kind of examination would be lengthy, and, given the principle of concision we stipulated, the present book cannot accommodate it, but we shall devote a separate treatise to the topic as we did with the topic of justice when the discussion grew somewhat lengthy.[48] Once we have carried out this task in the treatise we have promised, we may then go on to consider the question further. If the question of whether it exists has been answered affirmatively, we will continue by examining the question of what its nature is. If the first question is declared null, the second will inevitably be declared null as well. 151.4

مسألة

قال أحمد بن عبد الوهّاب في جواب التربيع والتدوير لأبي عثمان الجاحظ ما الفرق بين المستبهم والمستغلق؟ وهذا بيّن الجواب ولكنّي سقته ههنا لكيت وكيت. ١،١٥٢

الجواب

قال أبو عليّ مسكويه رحمه الله المستبهم من الأمور مرتبة زائدة على المستغلق يدلّك على ذلك الاشتقاق فإنّ الاشتقاق ملائم للمعاني موافق لها لأنّ صاحبه إنّما يشتقّ لكلّ معنى من اسم موافق[1] له لا محالة وإلّا لم يكن لاشتقاقه معنى ولا لتكلّفه ذلك فائدة. وليس يُظنّ هذا بالمميّز منّا فكيف بواضع اللغة. ولمّا كان الغلق إنّما يكون للباب وما أُغلق منه يُرجى فتحه كذلك يكون حال ما شُبّه له واشتُقّ له اسم منه أو تصريف. وأمّا المستبهم فلا يقال في الباب أبهمته إلّا إذا تجاوزت حدّ الغلق إلى السدّ وما يجري مجراه فالطمع فيه أقلّ فهذه حال المسائل والأمور المستغلقة المستبهمة تشبيهاً بالأبواب التي ذكرنا أحوالها. ٢،١٥٢

مسألة

حضرت مجلساً لبعض الرؤساء فتدافع الحديث بأهله على جدّه وهزله فتحدّى بعضهم الحاضرين وقال والله ما أدري ما الذي سوّغ للفقهاء أن يقول بعضهم في فرج واحد هو حرام ويقول الآخر فيه بعينه هو حلال والفرج فرج وكذلك المال مال نعم وكذلك في النفس وما بعدها كلام هذا يوجب[2] قتل هذا وصاحبه يمنع من قتله. ويختلفون ١،١٥٣

١ الأصل: وافق. ٢ الأصل: ما يوجب.

On a question put by Aḥmad ibn ʿAbd al-Wahhāb concerning the difference between the words "indeterminable" and "impenetrable"

Aḥmad ibn ʿAbd al-Wahhāb said in response to Abū ʿUthmān al-Jāḥiẓ's book *The Square and the Round*: What is the difference between the term "indeterminable" and the term "impenetrable"? The answer to this is plain, but I have adduced it here for such and such a reason. 152.1

Miskawayh's response

Things that are termed "indeterminable" are one level above those that are termed "impenetrable."[49] This is shown by their etymological derivations. Etymological derivation occurs in a way conformable with meanings, for the one who performs it derives a word for every meaning from a term that necessarily agrees with it; otherwise, there would be no point in performing the derivation and no benefit in taking this trouble. We would not impute pointless activity like this to discerning adults, let alone to the institutor of language. Since the root term refers to the closing of a door, and since one may hope that a door that is closed can be opened, the same thing will apply to that which has been compared to it and has had its name or inflection derived from it. As for "indeterminable," the root verb is only used to say that one has closed the door if one has not merely closed it but blocked it and the like, so the prospects are dimmer. This is how things stand with regard to questions and matters referred to as "impenetrable" and "indeterminable" by comparison with doors. 152.2

On the disagreements between jurists

I once attended a social gathering of some eminent figures. The conversation raged back and forth over topics alternately grave and jovial, and then the attendees were challenged with the question: By God, it is beyond me how it is possible for one jurist to state that a particular pudendum is unlawful while another states that the selfsame pudendum is lawful. Yet a pudendum is a pudendum, just as money is money. Likewise with the taking of life and the topics that follow; one person says things that make it out to be obligatory to put a given person to death, whereas his colleague prohibits it. They 153.1

هذا الاختلاف الموحش ويتحكّمون التحكّم القبيح ويتّبعون الهوى والشهوة ويتّسعون في طريق التأويل وليس هذا من فعل الدين والورع ولا من أخلاق ذوي العقل والتحصيل. هذا وهم يزعمون أنّ الله تعالى قد بيّن الأحكام ونصب الأعلام وأفرد الخاصّ من العامّ ولم يترك رطباً ولا يابساً إلّا أودع كتابه وضمن خطابه.

٢،١٥٣ وهذه مسألة ليس يجب أن يكون مكانها في هذه الرسالة لأنّها ترد على الفقهاء أو على المتكلّمين الناصرين للدين لكنّي أحببت أن يكون في هذا الكتاب بعض ما يدلّ على أصول الشريعة وإن كان جلّ ما فيه منزوعاً من الطبيعة ومأخوذاً من علية الفلاسفة وأشياخ التجربة وذوي الفضل من كلّ جنس ونحلة وعلى الله تعالى بلوغ الإرادة والسلامة من طعن الحسدة.

الجواب

٣،١٥٣ قال أبو عليّ مسكويه رحمه الله أمّا قول الفقهاء إنّ الله تعالى بيّن الأحكام ونصب الأعلام ولم يترك رطباً ولا يابساً ﴿إِلَّا فِي كِتَابٍ مُبِينٍ﴾ فكلام في غاية الصدق ونهاية الصحّة. وكيف لا يكون كذلك وأنت لا تقدر أن تأتي بحكم لا أصل له من القرآن من تأويل يرجع إليه أو نصّ ظاهر يقطع عليه ثمّ لا يخلو مع ذلك من إنباء بغيب وإخبار عمّا سلف من القرون ومثل لما نوعد به وإشارة إلى ما ننقلب إليه وتنبيه على ما نعمل به من سياسة دنيا ومصلحة آخرة. فأمّا الذي سوّغ للفقهاء أن يقولوا في شيء واحد إنّه حلال وحرام فلأنّ ذلك الشيء تُرِك واجتهاد الناس فيه لمصلحة أخرى تتعلّق على هذا الوجه بالناس وذاك أنّ الاجتهاد لا يكون في الأحكام متساوياً أعني أنّه لا يؤدّي إلى أمر واحد كما يكون ذلك في غير الأحكام من الأمور الواجبة.

٤،١٥٣ وبيان هذا أنّ كلّ من اجتهد في إصابة الحقّ في أنّ الله تعالى واحد فطريقه واحد وهو لا محالة يجده إذا وفّى النظر حقّه فإن عدل عن النظر الصحيح ضلّ وتاه ولم يجد مطلوبه واستحقّ الإرشاد أو العقوبة إن عاند. وليس كذلك الاجتهاد في الأحكام

are divided by such troubling differences and pass rulings with odious willfulness, following their blind desires and appetites and wandering far and wide in their interpretations. This is not the way devout and God-fearing people should behave, nor is this the character one expects of people endowed with intelligence and learning. This is how they carry on, even as they assert that God made the rulings manifest, set up their indications, separated the particular from the general, and left "not a thing, fresh or withered"[50] that He failed to deposit in His book and incorporate into His address of mankind.

This epistle is not the proper place for this question, as it directs itself to the jurists or the dialectical theologians who defend our religion. But it was my wish that this book should contain something that points to the principles of the religious Law, even if the bulk of it is taken from nature and draws on philosophers of distinction, masters of empirical knowledge, and people of excellence of every type and creed. It is for God to bring what we will to fruition and to preserve us from envious backstabbing. 153.2

Miskawayh's response

The jurists speak with the utmost truth and the greatest soundness when they say that God made the rulings manifest, set up their indications, and left not a thing, fresh or withered, «but in a Book manifest». How could it be otherwise? For we are incapable of coming up with a single ruling that has no basis in the Qur'an, whether by recourse to interpretation or by the categorical affirmation of an evident text; the Qur'an also informs us about the transcendent realm, apprises us of events that took place centuries ago, offers us similitudes regarding the future life we have been promised, indicates the outcome awaiting us, and alerts us to the way we should act, whether in administering the present world or achieving our welfare in the next. It is possible for jurists to say that a single thing is both lawful and unlawful because this issue was left to the interpretive effort of human beings, in order to realize another advantage that accrues to human beings thereby, for interpretive efforts to determine the rulings are never alike, that is, they never lead to a single result, as is the case with other rulings that relate to necessary matters. 153.3

To explain the point: In the interpretive effort to arrive at the truth concerning God, there is only one route for the interpreter to follow, and he will inevitably find it if he gives rational inquiry its due. If he veers from sound inquiry, 153.4

لأنّ بعض الأحكام يتغيّر بحسب الزمان وبحسب العادة وعلى قدر مصالح الناس لأنّ الأحكام موضوعة على العدل الوضعيّ وربّما كانت المصلحة اليوم في شيء وغداً في شيء آخر وكانت لزيد مصلحة ولعمرو مفسدة. وعلى أنّ الاجتهاد الذي يجري مجرى التعبّد واختيار الطاعة أو لعموم المصلحة في النظر والاجتهاد نفسه لا في الأمر المطلوب ليس يضرّ فيه الخطأ بعد أن يقع فيه الاجتهاد موقعه. مثال ذلك أنّ المراد من ضرب الكرة بالصولجان إنّما هو الرياضة بالحركة فليس يضرّ أن يخطئ الكرة ولا ينفع أن يصيبها وإن كان الحَكَم قد أمر بالضرب والإصابة لأنّ غرضه كان في ذلك الأمر نفس الحركة والرياضة. وكذلك إن دفن حكيم في بريّة دفيناً وقال للناس اطلبوه فمن وجده فله كذا وكان غرضه في ذلك أن يجتهد الناس فيعرف مقادير اجتهادهم ليكون ذلك الطلب عائداً لهم بمنفعة أخرى غير وجود الدفين فإنّه لا يضرّ أيضاً في ذلك أن يخطئ الدفين ولا ينفع أن يصيبه وإنّما الفائدة في السعي والطلب وقد حصلت للطائفتين جميعاً أعني الذين وجدوه والذين لم يجدوه.

٥،١٥٣ وأصناف الاجتهادات والنظر الذي يجري هذا المجرى كثيرة فمن ذلك كثير من مسائل العدد والهندسة وسائر الموضوعات ليس غرض الحكماء فيها وجود الغرض الأقصى من استخراج ثمرتها وإنّما مرادهم أن ترتاض النفس بالنظر وتتعوّد الصبر على الرويّة والفكر إذا جريا على منهاج صحيح ولتصير النفس ذات ملكة وقنية للفكر الطويل ومفارقة الحواسّ والأمور الجسميّة فإذا حصلت هذه الفائدة فقد وُجد الغرض الأقصى من النظر فما كان من الشرع متروكاً غير مبيّن فهو ما جرى منه هذا المجرى وكان الغرض فيه والمصلحة منه حصول النظر والاجتهاد حسب ثمّ ما أدّى إليه الاختلاف كلّه صواب وكلّه حكمة.[1] وليس ينبغي أن يتعجّب الإنسان من الشيء الواحد أن يكون حلالاً بحسب نظر الشافعيّ وحراماً بحسب نظر مالك وأبي حنيفة فإنّ الحلال والحرام في الأحكام والأمور الشرعيّة ليس يجري مجرى الضدّين أو المتناقضين في الأمور الطبيعيّة وما جرى مجراها لأنّ تلك لا يستحيل

١ الأصل: كلّه صوابا وكلّه كلمة.

he goes astray and loses his way, failing to find what he is looking for, and, if he stubbornly clings to his error, he merits instruction or punishment. This is not how things stand with the interpretive effort that relates to rulings, because some rulings change depending on the time, the custom, or considerations of human welfare. For rulings are posited on the basis of conventional justice, and welfare may be vested in one thing one day and in another the next, or something may serve the welfare of Zayd but undermine the welfare of ʿAmr. Yet insofar as interpretive effort has the status of a devotional exercise and is an act of obedience, or insofar as general welfare is served by inquiry and interpretive effort itself as against the object of pursuit, there is no harm if mistakes are made once the interpretive effort has been properly carried out. By way of analogy, the aim in hitting a ball in polo is to exercise by moving, and there is no harm done if one misses the ball, and there is nothing gained if one hits it, even if the umpire's orders are to hit the ball, for the purpose in engaging in the activity is exercise through movement. Similarly, suppose a sage were to bury a treasure in the desert and say to people, "Search for it. He who finds it will get such and such a reward," the purpose being that people should make an effort and that he should observe how much effort they expend, in order that this search, and not the discovery of the treasure, should benefit them. In that case, likewise, no harm would be done if the treasure were not found, and no gain if found. The benefit lies in the effort of searching, and both parties would realize that—that is, both those who found it and those who did not.

Many kinds of interpretive efforts and inquiry follow this principle. This 153.5
includes questions of arithmetic, geometry, and many other subjects. The philosophers' purpose in pursuing these is not to achieve the utmost results. Their intention, rather, is that the soul should be trained through inquiry and should become accustomed to persevering in properly conducted deliberation and thought, so that it acquire a disposition and settled aptitude for prolonged thought and for separating itself from the senses and from corporeal things. The ultimate purpose of inquiry has been achieved if this benefit is realized. Those aspects of the Law left undetermined and not fully elucidated answer to the same principle; the purpose they achieve and the welfare they serve lie in the inquiry and interpretive effort alone. Beyond that, every conclusion that the disagreements of jurists lead to is correct and judicious. People should not be amazed that one and the same thing could be deemed lawful by al-Shāfiʿī and unlawful by Mālik and Abū Ḥanīfah. For "lawful" and "unlawful," as these

أن يكون الشيء الواحد منها حلالاً وحراماً بحسب حالين أو شخصين أو على ما ضربنا له المثل من ضرب الكرة بالصولجان ووجود دفين الحكيم على الوجه الذي اقتصصناه.

وإذا كان الأمر كذلك فينبغي للعاقل إذا نظر في شيء من أحكام الشرع وكان صاحب اجتهاد له أن ينظر أعني أنّه يكون عالماً بالقرآن وأحكامه وبالأخبار الصحيحة والسنن المرويّة والاجتماعات الصحيحة أن يجتهد في النظر ثمّ يعمل حسب اجتهاده ذلك. ولغيره إذا كان في مثل مرتبته من المعرفة أن يجتهد ويعمل بما يؤدّيه إليه اجتهاده وإن كان مخالفاً للأوّل واثقاً بأنّ اجتهاده هو المطلوب منه ولا ضرر في الخلاف اللّهمّ إلّا أن يكون ذلك الأمر المنظور فيه من غير هذا الضرب الذي حكيناه وضربنا له الأمثال مثل الأصول التي غاية النظر فيها هو إصابة الحقّ لا غير فإنّ هذا مطلب آخر وله نظر لا بدّ أن يؤدّي إليه. وكما أنّ الرياضة المطلوبة بضرب الصولجان وإصابة الكرة إنّما كانت لأجل الصحّة ثمّ لم يضرّ بعد حصول الرياضة التي حصلت بها الصحّة كيف جرى الأمر في الكرة أصبناها أم أخطأناها فكذلك[1] الحال في الوجه الآخر أعني الذي لا بدّ من إصابة الحقّ فيه بعينه فإنّ مثله مثل الفصد الذي لا بدّ في طلب الصحّة من إصابته بعينه وإخراج الدم دون غيره ولا ينفع منه شيء غيره. وإذا حصّلت هذين الطريقين من النظر وأعطيتهما قسطهما من التمييز لم يعرض لك العجب فيما حكيته من مسألتك وخرج لك الجواب عنها صحيحاً إن شاء الله. ٦،١٥٣

١ الأصل: وكذلك.

pertain to rulings and legal matters, do not have the status of contraries or contradictories as when they pertain to natural matters and the like. It is not impossible that one and the same thing belonging to the former class should be lawful or unlawful depending on the circumstances or the persons involved, or in the way we illustrated through the examples of hitting a ball with a stick or of discovering the sage's buried treasure.

If this is correct, then when an intelligent person examines any of the rul- 153.6
ings of the Law—assuming that he is capable of making an interpretive effort and has the competence to conduct such examination, which is to say that he has knowledge of the Qur'an and its rulings, and of sound hadith, of transmitted prophetic practices, and correct instances of scholarly consensus—he must make an effort to examine matters and then act on the basis of that interpretive effort. Other people with a similar level of learning can make an interpretive effort and act on the basis of whatever conclusion their interpretive effort leads them to, even if this conflicts with the conclusion of the first party, in the confident knowledge that interpretive effort is what is required of them and that there is no harm in disagreement. The only possible exception is if the matter under examination does not fall in the class we mentioned and illustrated through different examples—for instance, when it concerns principles with regard to which the end of examination is to arrive at the truth and nothing else, for that forms a different object and involves a kind of examination which must necessarily lead to it. Just as the exercise of swinging the stick and hitting the ball is done for the sake of our health, and, once health-inducing exercise has been carried out, it does not matter what happens to the ball—whether one hits it or whether one misses it—so it is with this second aspect, that is, the one in which it is necessary specifically to arrive at the truth itself. It resembles bloodletting, which one must specifically get right and let the blood, as opposed to any other treatment, if health is to be achieved, and bloodletting alone can help. Once you have grasped these two modes of examination and discriminated between them appropriately, you will no longer be amazed by what you reported in your question, and you will perceive the soundness of my response, God willing.

مســألة

لم إذا عرفت العامّة حال الملك في إيثار اللذّة وانهماكه على الشهوة واسترساله في هوى النفس استهانت به وإن كان سفّاكًا للدماء قتّالاً للنفوس ظلوماً للناس مزيلاً للنعم وإذا عرفت منه العقل والفضل والجدّ هابته وجمعت أطرافها منه؟ ما شهادة الحال في هذه المسألة فإنّ جوابها يشرح علماً فوق قدر المسألة؟ ١،١٥٤

الجواب

قال أبو عليّ مسكويه رحمه الله إنّ الملك هي صناعة مقوّمة للمدنيّة حاملة للناس على مصالحهم من شرائعهم وسياساتهم بالإيثار وبالإكراه وحافظة لمراتب الناس ومعايشهم لتجري على أفضل ما يمكن أن تجري عليه. وإذا كانت هذه الصناعة في هذه الرتبة من العلوّ فينبغي أن يكون صاحبها مقتنياً للفضائل كلّها في نفسه فإنّ من لم يقوّم نفسه لم يقوّم غيره وإذ تهذّب في نفسه بحصول الفضائل له أمكن أن يهذّب غيره. وحصول فضائل النفس يكون أوّلاً بالعفّة التي هي تقويم القوّة الشهويّة حتّى لا تنازع إلى ما لا ينبغي وتكون حركتها إلى ما يجب وكما يجب وعلى الحال التي تجب. وثانياً تقويم القوّة الغضبيّة حتّى تعتدل هذه القوّة أيضاً في حركتها فيستعملها كما ينبغي وعلى من ينبغي وفي الحال التي تنبغي ويعدّلها في طلب الكرامة واحتمال الأذى والصبر على الهوان بوجه وجه والنزاع إلى الكرامة على القدر الذي ينبغي وعلى الشرائط التي وُصفت في كتب الأخلاق. وإذا اعتدلت هاتان القوتان في الإنسان فكانت حركتهما على ما يجب معتدلة من غير إفراط ولا تقصير حصلت له العدالة التي هي ثمرة الفضائل كلّها. وبحصول هذه الفضائل تقوى النفس الناطقة وتستمرّ للإنسان الصورة الكماليّة التي يستحقّ بها أن يكون سائس مدينة أو مدبّر بلد ومتى لم تحصل هذه له فينبغي أن يكون مسوساً بغيره مدبّرًا بمن يقوّمه ويعدّله فأيّ شيء أقبح ٢،١٥٤

On why people despise kings who are governed by pleasure and fear kings governed by reason

Why is it that if the common people know the king to be fond of pleasures, engrossed in his appetites, and given over to the caprices of his soul, they make light of him, even if he is a murderer, a killer, a wrongdoer, and a ravager, whereas if they know him to be a man of reason, merit, and gravity, they stand in awe of him and take care not to cross him? What evidence do present circumstances give on this question? For to answer it is to elucidate a piece of knowledge that far exceeds the measure of the question. 154.1

Miskawayh's response

Kingship is a craft that effects political order; induces people, by choice or force, to conform to the religious laws and governing policies that serve their welfare; and preserves people's stations and livelihoods so that they might follow the best possible course. Since this craft occupies such a lofty rank, it is necessary that its practitioner have acquired all of the excellences within himself. For he who has not put himself in order cannot put others in order, but it is possible for him to refine others, if he himself has been refined through the realization of the excellences. The way the soul realizes the excellences is, first, by realizing temperance, which consists in putting the appetitive power in order so that it not incline to the wrong objects and that it move toward the things it ought, in the manner it ought, and under the circumstances it ought. Second, it does this by putting the irascible power in order, so that the movement of this power might also be balanced, and that it be exercised in the right manner, toward the right people, and under the right circumstances, and so that it be adjusted properly in seeking honor, tolerating harm, and enduring disdain as the case requires, and in desiring honor in the right measure and according to the conditions described in books of ethics. That person has realized the quality of justice, the fruit of all of the excellences, if these two powers come into balance within him, and their movement is balanced as it ought to be, neither running to excess nor falling short. Through the realization of these excellences, the rational soul is fortified and a person comes to stably possess the perfected form that makes him fit to be the governor of a city or the ruler of a region. A person who has not realized these excellences needs 154.2

من عكس هذه الحال وإجرائها على غير وجهها؟ وطباع الإنسانيّة تأبى الاعوجاج في الأمور فكيف الانتكاس وقلب الأشياء عن جهاتها؟

فأمّا قولك وإن كان الملك ذا بطش شديد وعسف كثير بسفك الدماء وانتهاك ٣،١٥٤
الحرم فهذه حال تنقصه من شروط الملك ولا تزيد فيه وهو بأن يسقط من عين رعيّته أقرب إذ كانت شريطة الملك أن يستعمل هذه الأشياء على ما ينبغي وعلى جميع الشرائط التي قدّمت. وهل هذا إلّا مثل طبيب يدّعي أنّه يبرئ من جميع الأعلال ويتضمّن بسلامة الأبدان على اختلاف أمزجتها وحفظها على اعتدالاتها ثمّ إذا نظر يوجد مسقاماً مختلف المزاج بسوء التدبير. ولمّا سئل وتُصفّحت حاله وجد من سوء البصيرة وفساد التدبير لنفسه بحيث لا ينتظر منه إصلاح مزاج بدنه فكيف لا يعرض من مثل هذا الضحك والاستهزاء وكيف لا يستهين به من ليس بطبيب ولا يدّعي هذه الصناعة إلّا أنه على سيرة جميلة في بدنه وسياسة صالحة لنفسه؟ فإن اتّفق لهذا المدّعي أن يتغلّب ويتسلّط ويستدعي من الناس أن يتدبّروا بتدبيره فكيف لا يزداد الناس من النفور عنه والضحك منه؟ فهذا مثل صحيح مطابق للممثّل به فينبغي أن يُنظر فيه فإنّه كاف فيما سألت عنه إن شاء الله.

مسألة

لم صار من يطرب لغناء ويرتاح لسماع يمدّ يده ويحرّك رأسه وربّما قام وجال ورقص ١،١٥٥
ونعر وصرخ وربّما عدا وهام؟ وليس هكذا من يخاف فإنّه يقشعرّ ويتقبّض ويواري شخصه ويغيّب أثره ويخفض صوته ويقلّ حديثه.

to be governed by others and to be ruled by people who put him to order and set him straight. So could there be anything worse than for this situation to be inverted and to pursue the wrong course? Human nature loathes crookedness, so how could it fare otherwise when things are turned upside down and transposed from their proper places?

You remark that this is so even if the king acts with extreme oppression and much tyranny, shedding blood and profaning things that ought to be inviolable. This is something that detracts from, rather than adding to, the conditions of kingship, and such a king is more likely to fall in his subjects' regard, for it is a condition of kingship that these things be applied in the right manner and according to all the conditions we mentioned earlier. Isn't this like the case of a doctor who claims he can cure people of all ailments, and who pledges to sustain the health of bodies and preserve their balanced states whatever their various humoral mixtures, yet who, upon inquiry, is found to be prone to illness and to have an irregular humoral mixture as a result of his bad regime? When he is questioned and his condition is probed, he is found to have such poor insight and to be so defective in self-management that he could not be expected to rectify the humoral mixture of his own body. How could such a person avoid ridicule and mockery, and not be disdained by people who are not doctors and who do not pretend to be practitioners of this craft, yet who follow a fine bodily regime and govern themselves well? If this pretender should happen to gain ascendancy and power and demand that people submit to his regime, how could people not find him all the more repugnant and ridicule him all the more? This is a sound comparison adequate to its target, so it should be considered carefully, for it meets the purpose of your question, God willing. 154.3

On the physical reactions people exhibit when listening to music

Why do people in a transport at singing and delighted by a musical performance stretch out their hands, move their heads, and sometimes get up and drift about—dancing, making impassioned sounds, crying out, and sometimes even running and wandering here and there distractedly—whereas people who are afraid do not act like this; rather, they shudder and shrink, conceal their presence and obliterate their traces, lower their voices and say as little as possible? 155.1

الجواب

قال أبو عليّ مسكويه رحمه الله هذه المسألة قد تقدّم الجواب عنها عند كلامنا في سبب السرور والغمّ حيث قلنا إنّ النفس عند السرور تبسط الدم في العروق إلى ظاهر البدن وإنّها عند الغمّ تحصره وبانحصار الحرارة إلى عمق البدن وإلى منشئها[1] من القلب ما يكثر هناك البخار الدخانيّ ويبرّد[2] ظاهر البدن. واشتقاق اسم الغمّ يدلّ على معناه لأنّ القلب يلحقه ما يلحق الشيء الحارّ إذا غُمّ فيمنع ذلك الحرارة من الانتشار والظهور إلى سطح البدن ولذلك يتنفّس الإنسان عند الغمّ تنفّساً شديداً كثيراً لحاجة القلب إلى هواء يخرج عنه الفضلة الدخانيّة التي فيه ويجلب له هواء آخر صافياً ينمّي الحرارة ويروّحها كالحال في النار التي من خارج. ٢،١٥٥

وهاتان الحالتان متلازمتان أعني مزاج القلب وحركة النفس وذلك أنّه عرض للنفس انقباض غارت الحرارة من أقطار البدن إلى عمقه. وإن اتّفق لمزاج البدن غؤور من الحرارة وانحصار إلى ناحية القلب انقبضت النفس لأنّ أحدهما ملازم للآخر تابع له ولهذا ظنّ قوم أنّ النفس مزاج ما وظنّ آخرون أنّها حال تابعة لمزاج البدن. والخمر وما يجري مجراها من الأشربة والأدوية التي تبسط الحرارة بلطفها وتنمّيها وتنشرها إلى ظاهر البدن يعرض منها السرور والطرب والأدوية التي تبرّد البدن وتقبض الحرارة يعرض منها ضدّ ذلك والمزاج السوداويّ معه أبداً[3] الغمّ والمزاج الدمويّ معه أبداً السرور. وكما أنّ الأدوية والأغذية يعرض منها للمزاج هذا العارض وتتبعه حركة النفس فكذلك الحديث والألحان وصوت الآلات من الأوتار والمزامير تحرّك النفس أيضاً وتتبع ذلك حركة مزاج البدن لاتّصال المزاج بالنفس ولأنّهما متلازمان يؤثّر أحدهما في الآخر ويتبع فعل أحدهما فعل الآخر. ٣،١٥٥

١ الأصل: منشأه. ٢ ط: ويبرز. ٣ الأصل: السوداويّ ابدا.

Miskawayh's response

We answered this question in our earlier discussion of the causes of joy and grief, where we said that when the soul experiences joy it expands the blood in the veins toward the exterior of the body, and when it experiences grief it constricts it. The constriction of the heat into the interior of the body and into its point of origin in the heart makes the smoky vapor increase and cools the exterior of the body. The meaning of "grief" (*ghamm*) is revealed in its etymological derivation, for what happens to the heart is what happens to something hot when it is "covered" (*ghumma*), preventing the heat from spreading and reaching the surface of the body. That is why people breathe very heavily when they are aggrieved, on account of the heart's need for air to expel the smoky excess it contains and allow in pure air to increase and aerate the heat, as is the case with fire in the external world. 155.2

These two aspects—the mixture of the heart and the movement of the soul—are inseparably linked, for if the soul experiences a contraction, the heat sinks from the various regions of the body toward its interior; and if in the mixture of the body the heat happens to sink and constrict itself in the area of the heart, the soul undergoes contraction, because the one is inseparably linked to, and follows upon, the other. This is why some people have thought that the soul consists in a particular mixture, and why others have thought that it is a state that depends upon the mixture of the body. Wine and similar drinks, and medicines that expand the body's heat through their fine qualities, increasing it and spreading it toward the body's exterior, produce joy and delight, whereas medicines that make the body cold and contract the heat produce the opposite. A melancholic mixture is always accompanied by grief, whereas a sanguine mixture is always accompanied by joy. Just as medicines and foods produce this kind of effect in the mixture, which is followed by a movement of the soul, so too words, melodies, and the sound of instruments, such as strings and woodwinds, move the soul, and that is followed by a movement in the mixture of the body, since the mixture is connected to the soul. As the two are inseparably linked, one has an impact on the other, and the action of one is followed by the action of the other. 155.3

مسألة

لم صار الكذّاب يصدق كثيرًا والصادق يكذب نادرًا؟ وهل ينتقل إلف الصدق إلى الكذب؟ وهل يتحوّل إلف الكذب إلى الصدق أم يستحيل ذلك؟ ١٫١٥٦

الجواب

قال أبو عليّ مسكويه رحمه الله إنّ الصدق والكذب يجريان من النفس مجرى الصحّة ٢٫١٥٦ والمرض لأنّ الصدق لها صحّة ما والكذب مرض ما. وأيضاً فإنّ الصدق من الخبر يجري مجرى الصحّة والكذب منه يجري مجرى المرض. فكما أنّ الصحّة من الجسم أكثر من المرض لأنّ المرض إنّما يكون في عضو أو عضوين أو ثلاثة فكذلك الصحّة في النفس أكثر من المرض لأنّ المرض إنّما يكون منها في قوّة أو قوّتين وفي خُلق أو خلقين. فكما أنّ الجسم لو كثرت أمراض أعضائه أو لو توالت أمراض كثيرة على عضو منه لأبطلته وأعدمته فكذلك النفس لو كثرت أمراض قواها أو لو توالت أمراض كثيرة على قوّة واحدة لأهلكتها. وإنّما الاعتدال الموضوع لكلّ واحد من الجسم والنفس هو الذي يحفظ عليه وجوده فإن طرق واحداً منهما مرض في بعض الأحوال حتّى يخرجه عن اعتداله فإنّما يكون ذلك في جزء من الأجزاء وقوّة من القوى ثمّ يكون ذلك زماناً يسيرًا ويرجع بعد ذلك إلى الاعتدال الموضوع له. فأمّا إن توهّم متوهّم أنّ الأمراض تستولي على جميع أعضاء الجسم حتّى لا يبقى منه جزء صحيح أو تتوالى أمراض كثيرة في زمان طويل متّصل على عضو واحد فإنّ ذلك وهم باطل لأنّه لو صحّ وهمه لبطل ذلك الجسم أو ذلك العضو الذي توهّم فيه. والدليل على ذلك أنّ القلب لمّا كان مبدأ الحياة الذي منه تسري الحياة في جميع البدن صار محفوظاً غاية الحفظ من الأمراض لأنّه لو عرض له مرض لسرى ذلك المرض في جميع أجزاء البدن سريعاً وعرض منه التلف السريع والموت الوحيّ.

On why liars often tell the truth but not the reverse, and on whether habits can change

Why do liars often speak the truth, whereas truth tellers rarely lie? Can a habit of telling the truth change to a habit of lying? Can a habit of lying transform into a habit of telling the truth, or is that impossible? 156.1

Miskawayh's response

Telling the truth and lying are as health and illness to the soul, for telling the truth represents a form of health for the soul, whereas lying represents a form of illness. Furthermore, telling the truth relates to informative statements as to their state of health, and lying relates to them as representations of their illness. Just as health outweighs illness in the body—illness being confined to one or two or three bodily members—similarly, health outweighs illness in the soul, illness being confined to one or two powers or one or two character traits. And just as the body would be annihilated if the illnesses affecting its members became numerous or if a certain member was affected by numerous, successive illnesses, similarly the soul would perish if the illnesses affecting its powers became numerous or if a single power was affected by numerous, successive illnesses. The balanced state appointed for the body and the soul is that which preserves the existence of each. If in certain circumstances one of these is struck by an illness and dislodged from its balanced state, this is confined to one particular part and one particular power, and moreover it only lasts for a short amount of time, after which it returns to the balanced state appointed for it. The supposition that illnesses might take control over all members of the body so that not a single part remained healthy, or that a large number of successive illnesses might affect a single member without interruption over a long period of time, would be false, for were it true, the body in question or the member that formed the subject of the supposition would be destroyed. This is demonstrated by the fact that the heart, as the source of life from which life flows out to the entire body, enjoys the utmost degree of protection against illness, for were it to be affected by illness, that illness would quickly extend to all parts of the body, and this would soon lead to a speedy death. 156.2

وهذه حال النفس في اعتدالها ومرضها. ولمّا كان الكذب يعطيها صورة مشوّهة أي صورة الشيء على خلاف ما هو به صار المعطي والمعطى مريضين به ولذلك لا يتكلّف أحد ذلك ولا يتعمّده إلّا لضرورة داعية أو لأنّه يظنّ بذلك الكذب أنّه نافع له أيضاً كما ينفع السمّ الجسم في بعض الأحوال فيتجشّم هذه السماجة على استكراه من نفسه وربّما تكرّر منه ذلك فصار عادة كما تصير سائر القبائح أخلاقاً وعادات وكما تصير المآكل الضارّة عادة سيّئة لقوم. وأيضاً فإنّ المعتاد للكذب إنّما يتمّ له الكذب إذا خلطه بالصدق وإذا سُمع أيضاً منه الصدق وإلّا لم يتمّ له الكذب أيضاً لأنّ الباطل لا قوام له إلّا إذا امتزج بالحقّ. ٣،١٥٦

فأمّا قولك هل ينتقل من اعتاد الصدق إلى الكذب أو من ألف الكذب إلى الصدق؟ فلولا أنّ ذلك ممكن ومشاهد في الناس لما وضعت السنن ولا قوّم الأحداث ولا عني الناس بتأديب أولادهم ولا عاتب أحد أحداً ولكن هذه الأشياء شائعة في الناس ظاهرة فيهم وقد بُيّن ذلك في كتب الأخلاق فإن أردت استقصاءه فخذه من هناك إن شاء الله. ٤،١٥٦

مسـألة

ذكرت أيّدك الله مسائل لا تستحقّ الجواب من آراء العامّة وجهالات وقعت لهم مثل قولهم إذا دخل الذباب في ثياب أحدهم يمرض وقولهم دية نملة تمرة وإذا طنّت أذن أحدهم قالوا كيت وكيت. وهذه المسائل وأشباهها إنّما ينبغي أن يُهزأ بها ويُتملّح بإيرادها على طريق النادرة فأمّا أن تطلب لها أجوبة فما أظنّ عاقلاً يعترف بها فكيف نجيب عنها؟ والله يغفر لك ويصلحك. ١،١٥٧

This is how things stand with the soul as regards its balanced state or its illness. Since lying imparts a disfigured form to the soul—that is to say, a form of the object that conflicts with the way it really is—the one who imparts it and the one to whom it is imparted fall ill on its account. That is why nobody undertakes to lie or intentionally pursues lying unless he is driven by some necessity or unless he believes that act of lying is beneficial to him, the way poison might be beneficial to the body in certain circumstances, so that he brings himself to engage in this distasteful action despite the repugnance he feels toward it. He might do this a number of times, and it might then become a habit, the way all other foul deeds become traits of character and habits, and the way harmful foods become a bad habit for some people. Furthermore, the person who habitually lies can only lie with success if he mingles his lies with a bit of truth and if he is also heard to be telling the truth on other occasions. Otherwise, he would not be able to lie successfully, for falsehood can only stand if mixed with the truth. 156.3

You ask, can a person who habitually tells the truth change into a liar, or can a person accustomed to lying change into a teller of the truth. Were this not possible and attested among people, there would not be norms of behavior, the young would not be corrected, the education of children would not be a matter for concern, and there would be no censure. Yet these things are widespread and manifest among people. This matter has been clarified in books of ethics, so if you wish to probe it in depth you can consult such works, God willing. 156.4

On certain popular sayings

Here you mentioned—God grace you with His support—questions that merit no reply, questions that derive from opinions of the common people and from ignorant notions they have conceived, such as their saying, "When a fly enters a person's clothing he falls ill," "The blood money of an ant is a fruit," and "If a person's ears buzz, people are gossiping about him." These questions and their like should be viewed with derision and only brought up facetiously and in jest. But to solicit replies to them—I believe there is hardly an intelligent person who accepts them, so how could we possibly reply to them? May God grant you forgiveness and guide you to goodness. 157.1

مسألة

١٫١٥٨ ما الفرق بين العرافة والكهانة والتنجيم والطرق والعيافة والزجر؟[١] وهل تشارك العرب في هذه الأشياء أمّة أخرى أم لا؟

الجواب

٢٫١٥٨ قال أبو عليّ مسكويه رحمه الله أمّا الفرق بين العرافة والكهانة فهو أنّ العرّاف يخبر عن الأمور الماضية والكاهن يخبر بالأمور المستقبلة وذلك أنّ العرافة معرفة الآثار والاستدلال منها على مؤثّرها والكهانة هي قوّة في النفس تطالع الأمور الكائنة بتخلّيها عن الحواسّ ومرتبتها عالية على العرافة وقد تكلّمنا عليها في كتابنا الذي سمّيناه الفوز عند ذكرنا الفرق بين النبيّ والمتنبّي والقوّة[٢] التي يكون بها الوحي وكيفيّة ذلك فخذه من هناك.

٣٫١٥٨ وأمّا الفرق بين التنجيم وما يجري مجرى الفأل فظاهر لأنّ التنجيم صناعة تتعرّف بها حركات الأشخاص العالية وتأثيرها في الأشخاص السفليّة وهي صناعة طبيعيّة وإن كان قد حُمّل عليها أكثر من طاقتها أعني أنّ المنجّم ربّما تضمّن العلم من جزئيّات الأمور ودقائقها ما لا يوصل إليه بهذه الصناعة فيخبر بالكائنات على طريقة تأثير الشيء في مثله وذلك أنّ الشمس إذا تحرّكت في دورة واحدة من أدوارها أثّرت فيها ضروباً من التأثير في هذا العالم وكذلك كلّ كوكب من الكواكب له أثر بحركته ودورته وشعاعه الذي يصل إلى عالمنا هذا. فالمنجّم إنّما يقول مثلاً إنّ السنة الآتية تجتمع فيها دلائل الشمس وزحل فتؤثّر في عالمنا هذا أثراً مركّباً من طبيعتي هاتين الحركتين فتكون حال الهواء كيت وكيت وكذلك حال الاستقصّات الأربع. ولمّا كان الحيوان والنبات مركّبين من هذه الطبائع وجب أن يكون كلّ ما أثّر في بسائطها يؤثّر أيضاً في المركّبات منها. فتأثير النجوم في عالمنا تأثير طبيعيّ والمنجّم يخبر بحسب ما يحسب من حركاتها

---

١ الأصل: والجزو. ٢ الأصل وط: وفي.

On the distinction between different forms of divination

What is the distinction between the types of divination referred to as *ʿirāfah* and *kihānah*, divination by means of the stars, divination by means of pebbles, and the two types of divination by means of birds? Do the Arabs share these practices with any other nation or not? 158.1

Miskawayh's response

The distinction between the forms of divination termed *ʿirāfah* and *kihānah* consists in the fact that the practitioner of *ʿirāfah* gives information about things that lie in the past, whereas the practitioner of *kihānah* gives information about things that lie in the future. *ʿIrāfah* consists in the knowledge of physical traces and in their use for determining their cause, but *kihānah* is a power of the soul that, by abandoning the senses, discloses things that will be in the future. It occupies a higher rank than *ʿirāfah*. We discussed this in our book *The Triumph*, when considering the distinction between a prophet and someone who claims to be a prophet, the power through which inspiration is achieved, and how that happens, so you can consult that work for this purpose.[51] 158.2

The distinction between divination on the basis of the stars and that which resembles divination on the basis of random occurrence is plain. Astrology is a craft by means of which one acquires knowledge of the movements of the higher bodies and their effects on the lower bodies. It is a natural craft, even though more has been referred to it than it can accommodate; that is, astrologists sometimes claim to have knowledge of particulars and minutiae that cannot be gained through this craft. Astrologists thus give information about future events based on the effect something has on its like. When the sun carries out one of its rotations, it exercises a variety of effects on this world, as does every planet through its movement, its rotation, and the rays it emits, which reach the world we live in. What the astrologist might say, for example, is that in the coming year, the indicators of the sun and of Saturn will both be present, and they will have an effect on our world that will be a composite of the natures of these movements, so the condition of the air will be such and such, and likewise with the condition of the four elements. Since animals and plants are composed from these natures, everything that has an effect on their basic elements must also have an effect on the things composed from them. 158.3

وشعاعاتها الواصل إلينا آثارها حكمًا طبيعيًا وإن كان يغلط أحيانًا بحسب دقّة نظره وكثرة الحركات والمناسبات التي تجتمع من جملة الأفلاك والكواكب وقبول ما يقبل من أجزاء عالم الكون والفساد وتلك الآثار مع اختلافها.

٤،١٥٨ فأمّا أصحاب الفأل وزجر الطير وطرق الحصى وما أشبه ذلك فإنّها ظنون والصدق فيها إنّما يكون على طريق الاتّفاق وفي النادر وليس يستند إلى أصل ولا يقوم عليها دليل لأنّها ليست طبيعيّة ولا نفسانيّة ولا إلهيّة وإنّما هي اختيارات بحسب الأوهام والظنون وهي تكذب كثيرًا وتصدق قليلًا كما يعرض ذلك لمن أخبر أنّ غدًا يجيء المطر أو يركب الأمير بغير دليل ولا إقناع بل تكلّم بذلك وأرسل الحكم به إرسالًا فربّما صحّ ووافق أن يطابق الحقيقة وفي الأكثر يبطل ولا يصحّ والأمم تشارك العرب في هذه الأشياء إلّا أنّ العرب تختصّ من العرافة ومن زجر الطير بأكثر ممّا في الأمم الأخر.

مسألة

١،١٥٩ لم صارت[١] أبواب البحث عن كلّ شيء موجود أربعة وهي هل والثاني ما والثالث أيّ والرابع لِمَ؟

الجواب

٢،١٥٩ قال أبو عليّ مسكويه رحمه الله لأنّ هذه الأربعة الأشياء[٢] هي مبادئ جميع الموجودات وعللها الأولى والشكوك إنّما تعرض في هذه فإذا أحيط بها لم يبق وجه لدخول شكّ

١ الأصل: صار. ٢ ط: الأشياء الأربعة.

Thus, the effect the stars have on our world is a natural one. Astrologists give information based on the calculations they make concerning their movements and their rays, whose effects reach us through natural force, though astrologists might sometimes make mistakes, depending on how accurate their examination is, how large the aggregate of movements and relations yielded by the ensemble of celestial bodies and planets is, and how receptive the parts of the world of generation and corruption that receive those various effects are.

The practices of augury by means of animals, birds, pebbles, and the like 158.4
are all groundless speculations. They only happen to come true fortuitously and on rare occasions. They do not rest on any foundation, nor can any proof be given to support them, for they are neither natural, nor derived from the soul, nor divine. They are, rather, willful choices based on fancies and groundless speculations, and they often turn out to be false and seldom come true, as happens when someone without any proof or persuasive grounds for his claim states that tomorrow it will rain or the emir will ride out. He simply produces his statement and makes free with his judgment; occasionally it turns out to be correct and correspond with the truth, but most often it proves to be invalid and incorrect. Other nations share these practices with the Arabs, but, compared with other nations, Arabs have a greater number of forms of the kind of divination known as *ʿirāfah* and of bird augury exclusive to them.

On why there are four categories for inquiry: whether, what, which, and why

Why do the categories for inquiring about any existing object come down to 159.1
four—namely, whether, what, which, and why?

Miskawayh's response

These four aspects form the principles and first causes of all existents, and 159.2
any doubts that arise direct themselves to these; so once they have been fully grasped, all occasions for doubt have been removed. For the first principle regarding the existence of a given thing is that its being should be established—that is to say, the fact that it is, which we inquire about using the interrogative

وذلك أنّ المبدأ الأوّل في وجود الشيء هو ثبات ذاته أعني هويّته التي يُبحث عنها بهل فإذا شكّ إنسان في هويّة الشيء أي في وجود ذاته لم يبحث عن شيء آخر من أمره فإذا زال عنه الشكّ في وجوده وأثبت له ذاتاً وهويّة جاز بعد ذلك أن يبحث عن المبدأ الثاني من وجوده وهو صورته أعني نوعه الذي قوّمه[1] وصار به هو ما هو وهذا هو البحث بما لأنّ ما هي بحث عن النوع والصورة المقوّمة فإذا حصّل الإنسان في الشيء المحجوب عنه هذين[2] وهما الوجود الأوّل والهويّة التي بحث عنها بهل والوجود الثاني وهو النوعيّة أعني الصورة المقوّمة التي بحث عنها بما جاز أن يُبحث عن الشيء الذي يميّزه من غيره أعني الفصل وهذا هو المبدأ الثالث لأنّ الذي يميّزه من غيره هو الذي يبحث عنه بأيّ أعني الفصل الذاتيّ له.

فإذا حصل من الشيء المبحوث عنه هذه المبادئ الثلاثة لم يبق في أمره ما يعترضه ٣،١٥٩
شكّ وصحّ العلم به إلّا حال كماله والشيء الذي من أجله وجد وهذه العلّة الأخيرة التي تسمّى الكماليّة وهي أشرف العلل وأرسطوطالس هو أوّل من نبّه عليها واستخرجها وذاك أنّ العلل الثلاث هي كلّها خوادم وأسباب لهذه العلّة الأخيرة وكأنّها كلّها إنّما وجدت لها ولأجلها[3] وهذه التي يبحث عنها بلم فإذا عرف لم وجد وما غرضه الأخير أعني الذي وُجد من أجله انقطع البحث وحصل العلم التامّ بالشيء وزالت الشكوك كلّها في أمره ولم يبق وجه تتشوّقه النفس بالرويّة فيه والشوق إلى معرفته لأنّ الإحاطة بجميع علله ومبادئه واقعة حاصلة وليس للشكّ وجه يتطرّق إليه فلذلك صارت البحوث أربعة لا أقلّ ولا أكثر.

١ الأصل: قوم. ٢ الأصل: هذان. ٣ الأصل: له ولأجله.

"whether." If a person has doubts about the fact that something is—that is, that its being exists—he makes no further inquiries about it. Once his doubts about its existence have been eliminated and he has established that it has being and that it is, he may then inquire about the second principle of its existence, which is its form—that is, its species, which constitutes it and makes it what it is. This is the inquiry that uses the interrogative "what"; for "what" poses a question about the entity's species and its constitutive form. Once a person has determined these two aspects about the thing that is unclear to him—namely, the first existence, the fact that it is, which we inquire with the interrogative "whether"; and the second existence, which is its species, that is, its constitutive form, which we inquire about with the interrogative "what"—he may inquire about the aspect that distinguishes it from other entities, that is to say, its specific difference. That is the third principle; for what distinguishes it from other entities is what we inquire with the interrogative "which," that is to say, the specific difference essential to it.

Once these three principles have been determined regarding the object of inquiry, there is nothing left to arouse doubt, and sound knowledge of the object has been obtained except as regards the state that constitutes its perfection and that for the sake of which it exists. This is the final cause that is designated as "perfectional," the noblest of the causes. Aristotle was the first to call attention to it and expound upon it. For all the other three causes are subservient to and conducive to this final cause; it is as though they all existed on its account and for its sake. This is the cause that we inquire about using the interrogative "why." Inquiry comes to an end, once why the thing exists and what its final purpose is—that is, that for the sake of which it exists—have been understood: Complete knowledge of it has been achieved, every doubt eliminated, and no aspect remains that the soul yearns to attain through reflection and longs to know, for its causes and principles have been grasped fully and in their entirety, and there is no aspect to which doubt can adhere. This is why there are four forms of inquiry, no more and no less. 159.3

مســألة

١،١٦٠ مـا المعدوم؟ وكيف البحث عنه؟ وما فائدة الاختلاف فيه؟ وما الذي أطال المتكلّمون الكلام في اسمه ومعناه؟ وهل لقولهم[١] محصول؟ فإنّي ما رأيت مسألة لا تمكّن من نفسها غيرها.

الجواب

٢،١٦٠ قال أبو عليّ مسكويه رحمه الله إنّ المعدوم الذي يشير إليه المتكلّمون خاصّة هو موجود بوجه من الوجوه ولذلك صحّت الإشارة إليه والكلام عليه ومثال ذلك أنّ زيداً إذا تُوهّم معدوماً فإنّ صورته قائمة في وهم المتكلّم على عدمه وتلك الصورة له في الوهم هي[٢] وجود ما له وكذلك حال كلّ ما يتوهّمونه معدوماً من جسم أو عرض أو حال لا معدومة بل[٣] ملحوظة والدليل على ذلك أنّا[٤] لا نتوهّم شيئاً معدوماً إلّا ونتصوّر له حالاً قد وُجد فيها أو يوجد فيها وصورته تلك قائمة في وهمنا وهي وجود ما. فأمّا المعدوم المطلق الذي لا يستند إلى شخص ما ولا إلى عرض فيه وحال له فإنّه لا يُضبط بوهم ولا يُتكلّم عليه ولا تصحّ مسألة أحد عنه لأنّه لا شيء على الإطلاق. وإنّما تصحّ المسألة عن شيء[٥] تعرض له أحوال إمّا حاضرة فيه أو منتظرة له ولذلك زعم أكثر المتكلّمين أنّ المعدوم هو شيء وزعم بعضهم أنّه لا شيء أعني أنّهم لا يسمّونه بشيء. وإنّما عرض لهم هذا الخلاف لأنّ منهم من لحظه من حيث الوهم ومنهم من لحظه من حيث الحسّ فمن لحظه في وهمه أثبته شيئاً ومن لحظه من حسّه لم يثبته شيئاً.

٣،١٦٠ والدليل على أنّ المعدوم الذي يشيرون إليه هو ما ذكرناه وعلى الحال التي وصفناها أنّ القوم إذا تعاوروا مسألة المعدوم سألوا عن الجوهر هل هو جوهر في العدم؟ وعن السواد هل هو سواد في العدم؟ وكذلك جميع أمثلتهم إنّما هي من أمور محسوسة

١ الأصل: لقواهم. ٢ الأصل: هو. ٣ الأصل: إلى. ٤ الأصل: على أنّا. ٥ الأصل وط: شيء ثمّ.

On the nonexistent

What is the nonexistent, and how can it be investigated? What is the benefit of disputing about it? What has occupied the dialectical theologians to such an extent that they have gone on debating its name and meaning at length? Do their views deliver anything of value? It is the only question I have ever seen that grants the inquirer no leverage over itself. 160.1

Miskawayh's response

The nonexistent specifically referred to by dialectical theologians possesses existence of some kind; this is why it is possible to refer to it and speak about it. For example, if Zayd is imagined to be nonexistent, his form obtains in the imagination of the person speaking about his nonexistence, and this form found in the imagination constitutes a kind of existence for him. The same applies to everything else they imagine to be nonexistent, be it body, accident, or state: its state is not nonexistent; rather, it is an object of consideration. The proof of this is that whenever we imagine a nonexistent thing, we envisage a state in which it existed or in which it exists. That envisaged form obtains in our imagination, and constitutes a kind of existence. The imagination cannot grasp the absolute nonexistent—the one that cannot be referred to any individual entity, to any accident that inheres in it, or to any state that pertains to it—it cannot be discussed, and no one can possibly ask about it, for it is nothing in the absolute sense. We can only ask questions about things on which certain states either supervene at present or are expected to supervene. That is why the majority of dialectical theologians asserted that the nonexistent is a thing, whereas some asserted that it is not a thing, that is, that they do not designate it as a "thing." The reason they fell into this dispute is that some of them considered it from the perspective of the imagination, whereas others considered it from the perspective of the senses. Those who considered it with regard to the imagination affirmed it to be a thing, whereas those who considered it from the perspective of the senses did not affirm it to be a thing. 160.2

The proof that the nonexistent they refer to is what we have mentioned and as we have described is that when these people make their successive forays on the topic of the nonexistent, they ask, "Is an atom an atom when it is nonexistent?" and "Is black black when it is nonexistent?" In the same vein, all of their 160.3

إذا صارت غير محسوسة كيف تكون أحوالها؟ ثمّ يكون جوابهم عن ذلك بما يُتصوّر منه للنفس ويقوم في الوهم فيقولون في السواد الذي حقيقته[1] أنّه أثر في البصر من مؤثّر يعرض منه القبض إنّه في العدم أيضاً كذلك كأنّهم يتوهّمون أنّه يفعل بالبصر وهو معدوم ما يفعله وهو موجود وإنّما عرض لهم هذا الوهم لأنّ القوّة التي ترتقي إليها الحواسّ تقبل شبيهاً بالآثار التي تقبلها أي تحصل لها الصورة مجرّدة من المادّة وهذا هو العلم الحسّيّ. لو أمكنهم إثبات صورة عقليّة ونفيها لتكلّموا على الموجود العقليّ والمعدوم العقليّ ولو أمكنهم ذلك لجاز أن يسألوا أيضاً عن العدم المطلق هل يُشار إليه أم لا يُشار إليه؟ ولكن هذه[2] الأمور غابت عنهم[3] وإنّما سألت عن مذاهبهم وعمّا يسألون عنه وقد خرج الجواب ولاح لك بمشيئة الله.

مسـألة

١،١٦١ سمعت شيخاً من الأطبّاء يقول أنا أفرح ببرء العليل على تدبيري وأسرّ بذلك جدّاً قلت له فما تعرف علّة ذلك؟ قال لا فذكرت له ما يمرّ بك في الجواب إن شاء الله.

الجواب

٢،١٦١ قال أبو عليّ مسكويه رحمه الله إنّما فرح الطبيب بنفسه وصحّة علمه وذاك إنّه إذا شاهد عليلاً احتاج أن يتعرّف أوّلاً علّته حتّى يعلمها على الصحّة والحقيقة فإذا علمها قابلها بضدّها من الأدوية والأغذية فيكون ذلك سبباً لبرء العليل فالطبيب حينئذ يكون قد أصاب في معرفة العلّة ثمّ في مقابلتها بالدواء الذي هو ضدّها وهذه الإصابة والمعرفة هي الحال التي يلتمسها بعلمه ويسعى لها طول زمان درسه ورويّته ومن شأن

[1] الأصل: حقيقة. [2] الأصل: هذه هذه. [3] الأصل: غايتهم عنهم.

examples are drawn from sense-perceptible things, and the question asked is: What happens to them if they cease to be perceived by the senses? The answer they give to that question is then based on what can be envisaged by the soul and obtain in the imagination. Thus, they say about the color black—whose basic reality is that it is an effect produced on the visual sense by an object that creates a contraction—that it is the same when it is nonexistent. It is as though they imagined it to be acting upon vision when nonexistent in the same way it acted upon it while existent. The reason they were affected by this imaginary idea is that the power which the senses feed into receives effects that are similar to those of the senses; that is, the form occurs in it denuded of matter, which is what constitutes sensory knowledge. Had they been able to affirm and deny an intelligible form, they would have spoken about intelligible existents and intelligible nonexistents. And had they been able to do that, it would have been possible for them to also ask about the absolute nonexistent, "Can it be referred to, or can it not be referred to?" But these matters escaped their notice. However, you asked about their approaches and the questions they pose, and my answer has emerged and become plain, God willing.

On why a physician rejoices at the recovery of his patient

I heard an accomplished physician say: I rejoice when a sick person recovers under my stewardship; it makes me very happy. I asked him: Don't you know the cause of that? He replied: No. I shall mention to him what you say in reply, God willing. 161.1

Miskawayh's response

What the physician rejoices in is his soul and his sound understanding. When he sees a sick person, he first needs to ascertain the cause of his sickness and to gain a sound and correct understanding of it. Once he has gained an understanding of it, he addresses it using medicines and foods that oppose it, which brings about the sick person's recovery. When this happens, the physician has been successful in determining the cause and then addressing it using the medicine that opposes it. This success and right determination are what he seeks to achieve through his knowledge and what he strives for during the entire time he spends studying and reflecting. When the soul moves with vigor and ardent 161.2

النفس إذا تحرّكت نحو مطلوب حركة قويّة في زمان طويل بشوق شديد ثمّ ظفرت به فرحت له ولحقها انبساط وسرور عجيب.

مسألة

١،١٦٢ ثمّ قلت أيّدك الله سُئل ابن العميد لم لم يتّفق الناس في التعامل على المثامنة بالياقوت والجوهر أو بالنحاس والحديد والرصاص دون الفضّة والذهب؟ وما الذي قصرهم عليهما مع إمكان غيرهما أن يقوم مقامها ويجري مجراهما؟

الجواب

٢،١٦٢ قال أبو عليّ مسكويه رحمه الله قد تبيّن أنّ الإنسان لا تتمّ له الحياة بالتفرّد لحاجته إلى المعاونات الكثيرة ممّن يعدّ له الأغذية الموافقة والأدوية والكسوة والمنزل والكِنّ وغير ذلك من سائر الأسباب التي بعضها ضروريّة في المعيشة وبعضها نافعة في تحسين العيش وتفضيله حتّى يكون لذيذاً أو جميلاً أو فاضلاً. وليس يجري الإنسان مجرى سائر الحيوانات التي أزيحت علّتها في ضرورات عيشها وفيما تقوم به حياتها بالطبع كالاهتداء[١] إلى الغذاء والرياش وغيرهما من حاجات بدنه ولذلك أُمدّ بالعقل وأعين به ليستخدم به كلّ شيء ويتوصّل بمكانه إلى كلّ أرب.

٣،١٦٢ ولمّا كان التعاون واجباً بالضرورة والاجتماع الكثير طبيعيّاً في بقاء الواحد وجب لذلك أن يتمدّن الناس أي يجتمعوا ويتوزّعوا الأعمال والمهن ليتمّ من الجميع هذا الشيء المطلوب أعني البقاء والحياة على أفضل ما يمكن ولمّا فرضنا أنّ الاجتماع قد وقع والتعاون قد حصل عرض أنّ النجّار الذي يقطع الخشب ويهيّئه للحدّاد والحدّاد

١ الأصل وط: فالاهتداء.

desire toward a particular end over a long period of time and then obtains it, it rejoices in it and experiences an extraordinary feeling of happiness and delight.

On why money is made of silver and gold and not other substances

Then you said, may God grace you with His support: Ibn al-ʿAmīd was asked, Why didn't people agree to use sapphires and jewels, or copper, iron, and lead, instead of silver and gold, as the basis of value for their transactions? What made them restrict themselves to these two, even though it was possible to replace them with others to serve the same role? 162.1

Miskawayh's response

It has been shown that human beings are not capable of living in isolation owing to their need for great amounts of assistance from people who supply them with agreeable foods, medicines, clothing, housing and shelter, and other items, some of which are necessary for people to live, while others are beneficial for improving and enhancing life, so that it may be pleasant, fine, or excellent. Human beings are not like other animals, whose impediments were removed regarding what they need to live and what naturally sustains their life, such as being able to procure food, being protected by their bodily coverings, and other corporeal needs. That is why they were equipped with reason and provided with its assistance, so as to put everything to their service and attain every desire through its power. 162.2

Since cooperation constitutes an unavoidable necessity and since it is natural for large groups to be formed in order for single individuals to survive, people must necessarily enter into a civic state; that is, they must form groups and distribute the different kinds of labor and occupations among themselves so that everyone may achieve the desired end—namely, to survive and live in the most excellent way possible. Once people have formed groups and cooperation has been established, the following situation arises: The carpenter who cuts the wood and prepares it for the blacksmith, the blacksmith who shapes the iron and prepares it for the plowman, or any other person in the group 162.3

الذي يقطع الحديد ويهيّئه للحرّاث وكذلك كلّ واحد منهم إذا احتاج إلى صاحبه الذي عاونه قد يقع استغناء صاحبه عنه في ذلك الوقت فإنّ الحدّاد إذا احتاج إلى صناعة الحياكة وصاحب الثوب غير محتاج إلى صناعة الحدّاد وقف التعاون ولم تدر المعاملة وحصل كلّ واحد على عمله الذي لا يجدي عليه فيما يضطرّ إليه من حاجات بدنه التي من أجلها وقع التعاون واحتيج لذلك إلى قيّم للجماعة ووكيل مشرف على أعمالهم ومهنهم موثوق بأمانته وعدالته ليقبل الجميع أمره ويصير حكمه جائزًا وأمره نافذًا مصدّقًا وأمانته صحيحة ليأخذ من كلّ أحد ويستوفي عليه قدر ما عاون به ويعطيه من معاونة غيره بقسطه من غير حيف وإنّما يتمّ له ذلك بأن يقوّم عمل كلّ واحد منهم ويحصّله ثمّ يعطيه بمقدار تعبه وعمله من عمل الآخر الذي يلتمس معاونته.

وهذا الفعل أيضًا لا يتمّ لهذا القيّم المستوفي أعمال الناس إلّا بأن يأتيه كلّ من عمل عملًا فيعرضه عليه ويأخذ منه علامة من طابع أو غيره يكون في يده متى عرضه قُبل ولم ينس وعُرفت[1] صحّة دعواه وأعطى به من تعب غيره بمقدار. ثمّ لمّا نظر في هذا الشيء الذي يُحتمل أن يكون بهذه الصفة فلم يمكن أن يجعل من الأشياء الموجودة دائمًا وممّا يقدر كلّ أحد على تناوله ومدّ اليد إليه لئلّا يحصّله من لا يعمل عملًا ولا يعين أحدًا بكدّه ويتوصّل به إلى كدّ غيره وتعبه فيؤدّي إلى خلاف ما دبّر لإتمام المدنيّة والتعاون فوجب أن يكون هذا الطابع من جوهر عزيز الوجود ليمكن حفظه والاحتياط عليه ولا يصل إلّا من جهة ذلك القيّم إلى مستحقّه الذي يعرض عمله وكدّه ووجب مع ذلك أن يكون مع عزّة وجوده غير قابل للفساد من الماء والنار والهواء بنحو ما يمكن ذلك في عالمنا هذا فإنّه متى كان شيئًا ممّا يبتلّ بالماء أو يحترق بالنار أو تُفسد صورته بعض العناصر الأربع لم يأمن صاحب التعب ٤،١٦٢

[1] الأصل وط: وعرف.

may need something from his fellow to whom he provides help, yet his fellow may not need anything from him at that particular time. If the blacksmith has a need for the craft of weaving yet the person who makes garments has no need for the blacksmith's craft, cooperation comes to a standstill, exchange has ceased to flow, and every person can only obtain the product of his own labor, which is of no use to him for his bodily necessities, for the sake of which cooperation was established. That is why someone was needed to serve as a custodian for the group and as trustee capable of supervising their different kinds of labor and occupations—a person known for his honesty and fairness, so that his command might be accepted by everyone, his judgment stand, his orders be effective and enjoy credibility, and his trustworthiness be sound. His task was to exact in full and receive from every person the value of the help he has provided, and to give him his fair share of others' help. The way he was to accomplish this was by appraising and mustering the labor of every person, and then by giving him an amount of the labor of the other person whose help he seeks that corresponds to the amount of his own effort and labor.

Furthermore, the only way this action could be accomplished by the custodian who exacts the different kinds of labor carried out by people is by having everyone who has carried out some labor come to him, show it to him, and receive a mark from him, such as a stamp or some other such thing. The laborer would then hold on to this, and whenever he showed it to another, it would be accepted and its purport not forgotten, so his claim would be recognized as sound, and he would receive a corresponding amount of another person's effort in return. Upon consideration of the object that could satisfy this description, it was clear that the kind of objects that are always available and that anyone could get hold of could not be selected, for they could be acquired by people who do not carry out any labor or help anyone through their hard work, and they might then use them to gain access to the hard work and effort of others; thus, a measure designed to further political association and cooperation would have an effect contrary to that intended. Hence, it was necessary that the stamp in question be drawn from a rare and precious substance, so that it might be possible to preserve and protect it, and so that those who had a rightful claim to it and who could demonstrate their labor and effort should only be able to receive it from the custodian. At the same time, it was necessary that, in addition to being rare, it should not be susceptible to the kind of damage through water, fire, or air that is possible in our world. For were 162.4

الكثير أن يحصّله ثمّ يفسده عنده فيضيع عمله ولا يُصدّق فيما أعان به وكدّ فيه فوجب أن يكون هذا الطابع حافظاً لصورته خفيف المحمل مع ذلك مأموناً عليه الفساد مدّة طويلة من الطبائع الأربع ومن الفساد الذي يكون بالمهنة أيضاً كالكسر والرضّ وغيرهما.

٥،١٦٢ ولمّا تُصفّحت الموجودات لم يوجد شيء يجمع هذه الفضائل إلّا الأشياء المعدنيّة ومن بين الأشياء المعدنيّة الجواهر التي تذوب بالنار وتجمدّ بالهواء ومن بين هذه الذهب وحده فإنّه أبقاها وأعزّها وأحفظها لصورته وأسلمها على النار والهواء والماء والأرض وهو مع ذلك سليم على الكسر والقطع والرضّ يعيد صورة نفسه بالذوب ويحفظها من جميع عوارض الفساد زماناً طويلاً جدّاً فجعل مقوّماً للصنائع وعلامة لهذا القيّم ثمّ احتيط عليه بأن طبع بخاتمه وعلاماته كلّ ذلك خوفاً من توصّل الأشرار إليه ممّن يرتفق من عمل غيره ولا يرفق غيره فإنّ هذا الفعل هو الظلم الذي يرتفع به التعاون ويزول معه النظام ويبطل بسببه الاجتماع والتعايش. ثمّ لمّا وجد هذا الجوهر الذي جمع[1] هذه الفضائل واحتيط عليه ضروب الاحتياط من أن يصل إلى غير مستحقّه عرض فيه عارض آخر وهو أنّ[2] الذي عاون الناس بمعاونة استحقّ بها شيئاً منه ربّما احتاج إلى معاونة يسيرة لا تساوي تعبه الأوّل ولا تقرب منه. مثال أنه ربّما تعب الإنسان أيّاماً ليحصل لغيره عمل الرحى بمؤونة وكلفة وحكمة بليغة فإذا أعطي من هذا الجوهر قيمة عمله ثمّ احتاج إلى بقل أو خلال أو عرض يسير لا يستطيع أن يعطيه شيئاً من الجوهر الذي عنده ولا أقلّ القليل منه لأنّ الجزء اليسير جدّاً منه أكثر قيمة من العمل الذي يلتمسه من غيره فاحتيج لذلك إلى جوهر آخر تكون فضائله أنقص من الذهب ليصير خليفة له يعمل عمله وإن كان دونه فلم يوجد ما يجمع تلك الفضائل التي حكيناها في الذهب شيء[3] غير الفضّة فجُعلت[4]

١ الأصل: الجوهر جمع. ٢ الأصل: وهو. ٣ الأصل: لشيء. ٤ الأصل: فجعل نائبا.

it the type of thing that could be soaked in water or burnt by fire or whose form could be damaged by one of the four elements, the person who had toiled greatly would not be insured against the possibility that, having acquired it, it might subsequently be damaged while in his possession; this would result in the loss of his labor and there would be no means of verifying the help he had provided and the hard work he had contributed. Thus, it was necessary that this stamp be capable of preserving its form, be light enough to carry, and remain impervious to damage by the four elements as well as to damage from handling, such as by being broken, crushed, and so on.

When the different kinds of existents were inspected, the only objects found to unite these excellences were minerals, and among minerals only precious substances that melt in fire and solidify in air, and of these gold alone. For it is the most durable and rarest mineral, the most capable of retaining its form, and the most immune to the impact of fire, air, water, and earth. At the same time, it is impervious to breaking, cutting, and crushing, and can recover its form through smelting, preserving it from damage for a very long time. So it was chosen as a measure for the appraisal of crafts and as a distinguishing mark of the custodian, and was subsequently protected by having his seal and marks stamped upon it. All of this was done for fear that it might be obtained by evildoers, who help themselves to others' labor yet offer no help to others, for that is the type of injustice that nullifies cooperation, destroys order, and brings communal life and coexistence to ruin. Then, once the precious substance that combined all these excellences had been located and protected in a variety of ways against the prospect of falling into the hands of people with no rightful claim over it, another contingency arose—namely, that someone who had provided help to people and thereby acquired a rightful claim to a certain amount of it might happen to need some light help that was not equal to his original effort and did not come near its level. For example, a person might put in several days' effort in order to operate, with toil and hard work and considerable skill, a mill for another person. If he was given an amount of this precious substance equivalent to his labor and he subsequently needed a few herbs or a pin or some other minor commodity, he would not be able to exchange any of the precious substance in his possession for it, not even the smallest fraction, as even the smallest fraction of it would be worth more than the labor he was soliciting from another. That is why another precious substance was needed, one with fewer excellent qualities than gold, which despite its inferiority could 162.5

نائبة عنه ثمّ جُعل كلّ واحد من الذهب يساوي عشرة أضعافه من الفضّة لأنّ العشرة نهاية الآحاد فوجب لذلك أن تكون قيمة الواحد من ذلك الجوهر عشرة أمثاله من هذا الجوهر.

٦،١٦٢ فأمّا التفاوت الذي وقع بين صرف الدينار والدرهم أعني أن صار منه الواحد بخمسة عشر درهماً ونحوها وهي المسألة التي جعلتها تالية لهذه المسألة فإنّما ذلك لأجل التفاوت في الوزن بين المثقال والدرهم ثمّ لأجل الغشّ الذي يكون في أحدهما والأمر محفوظ مع ذلك في أنّ الواحد من الذهب بإزاء عشرة من الفضّة إذا كان كلّ واحد منهما غير مشوب ولا مغشوش.

مسألة

١،١٦٣ متى تتّصل النفس بالبدن؟ ومتى توجد فيه؟ أفي حال ما يكون جنيناً أم قبلها أم بعدها؟

الجواب

٢،١٦٣ قال أبو عليّ مسكويه رحمه الله إنّ اتّصال النفس بالبدن ووجودها فيه ألفاظ متّسع فيها والأولى أن يُقال ظهور أثر النفس في البدن على قدر استعداد البدن وقبوله إيّاه وإنّما تحرّزنا من تلك الألفاظ لأنّها توهم أنّ لها اتّصالاً عرضيّاً أو جسميّاً وكلا هذين غير مطلق على النفس والأشبه إذا عبّرنا عن هذا المعنى أن نقول إنّ النفس جوهر بسيط إذا حضر مزاج مستعدّ لأن يقبل له أثراً كان ظهور ذلك الأثر على حسب ذلك الاستعداد لنسلم بهذه العبارة مِن ظنّ مَن زعم أن النفس تتقلّب وتفعل أفعالها على سبيل القصد والاختيار أعني أنها تفعل في حال وتمنع في أخرى فإنّ هذا يجلب كثيرًا من الشكوك التي لا تليق بخصائص النفس وأفعالها.

act as its deputy and perform its function. Silver was the only object found to unite the excellences that we have said gold possesses, so it was appointed as its representative, and one part of gold was assigned the value of ten parts of silver. Single units stop at ten, and therefore it was necessary that one part of the former precious substance be valued at ten similar parts of the latter.

As for the disparity between the conversion rate of gold dinars and silver dirhams—that is, the fact that one dinar is equivalent to fifteen or so dirhams, which was the question you next posed—this is due to the disparity between the weight of dinars and dirhams and also due to the debasement undergone by one of the two. Nevertheless, the principle is preserved insofar as one part of gold is equal to ten parts of silver, so long as neither has been subjected to adulteration or debasement. 162.6

On the specific time when the soul attaches itself to the body

When does the soul attach itself to the body, and when does it come to be present in it? Is it when the body is a fetus, or before or after that? 163.1

Miskawayh's response

To talk of the soul as "attaching" itself to the body and "becoming present" in it involves a loose usage of words. It is preferable to say: The effect of the soul is manifested in the body in accordance with its preparedness for and receptivity to it. The reason we are wary of those words is that they give the impression that the soul has an accidental or physical attachment, and neither of these notions can be unqualifiedly predicated of the soul. If we wish to convey this meaning, it is more appropriate to say: The soul is a simple substance such that, when a certain humoral mixture arises that is prepared to receive a certain effect from it, that effect is manifested in the measure of that preparedness. This expression may preserve us from the notion of those who have claimed that the soul changes and performs its acts intentionally and by choice—that is, that it acts at one time and restrains at another, for this gives rise to a great number of doubts unbefitting to the characteristics and actions of the soul. 163.2

وإذ قد تحقّقت هذه العبارة فنقول إنّ النطفة التي يكون منها الجنين إذا حصلت في الرحم الموافق كان أوّل ما يظهر فيه من أثر الطبيعة ما يظهر مثله في الأشياء المعدنيّة أعني أنّ الحرارة اللطيفة تنضجه وتمخضه وتعطيه إذا امتزج بالماء الذي يوافقه من شهوة الأنثى صورة مركّبة كما يكون ذلك في اللبن إذا مُزج بالأنفحة أعني أنّه يثخن ويختثر ثمّ تلحّ عليه الحرارة حتّى يصير ملوّنًا بالحمرة فيصير مضغة ثمّ يستعدّ بعد ذلك لقبول أثر آخر أعني أنّ المضغة تستمدّ الغذاء وتتّصل بها عروق كعروق الشجر والنبات فيأخذ من رحم أمّه بتلك العروق ما تأخذه عروق الشجر من تربته فيظهر فيه أثر النفس النامية أعني النباتيّة ثمّ يقوى هذا الأثر فيه ويستحكم على الأيّام حتّى يكمل وينتهي بعد ذلك إلى أن يستعدّ لقبول الغذاء بغير العروق أعني أنّه ينتقل بحركته لتناول غذائه فيظهر فيه أثر الحيوان أوّلاً أوّلاً فإذا كمل استعداده لقبول هذا الأثر فارق موضعه وقبل أثر النفس الحيوانيّة ثمّ لا يزال في مرتبة البهائم من الحيوان إلى أن يصير فيه استعداد لقبول أثر النطق أعني التمييز والرويّة فحينئذ يظهر فيه أثر العقل ثمّ لا يزال يقوى هذا الأثر فيه على قدر استعداده وقبوله حتّى يبلغ نهاية درجته وكماله من الإنسانيّة ويشارف الدرجة التي تعلو درجة الإنسان فيستعدّ لقبول أثر الملك فحينئذ يجب أن ينشأ النشأة الآخرة بحال أقوى من الحالة الأولى المتقدّمة. ٣،١٦٣

وهذا الكلام ليس يقتضي أن يقال فيه متى تتّصل وتنفصل بل من شأن القائل له أن يقال فيه متى يستعدّ ويقبل وأمّا النفس فهي معطية بالذات لكلّ[1] ما قِبل أثرها بحسب قبوله واستعداده وتهيّئه وقد تبيّن أنّها تعطي البدن أحوالاً مختلفة وصورًا متباينة[2] قبل أن يكون جنينًا وبعد أن تتمّ الصورة الإنسانيّة ليس[3] ينقطع أثر النفس من البدن البتّة على ضروب أحواله إلى أن يدور ضروب أدواره وينتهي إلى غاية كماله ولا ينبغي أن يقال إنّه يخلو منها في حال من أحواله وإنّما يقوى الأثر ويضعف بحسب قبوله والسلام. ٤،١٦٣

---

١ الأصل وط: للذات كلّ ما. ٢ الأصل: متناسبة. ٣ الأصل: قبل ليس.

Having established the correct expression, we may now respond as follows: When the drop of semen from which the fetus is produced arrives in a suitable womb, the first effect of nature to manifest itself in it is of the kind manifested in mineral objects. That is, the delicate heat ripens and agitates it, and if it is mixed with suitable water produced by the female's desire, it gives it a composite form such as one sees in milk when mixed with rennet. That is to say, it curdles and coagulates, and then the heat persists with it so that it acquires a reddish tinge and becomes a lump of flesh. After that it prepares to receive another effect, which is when the embryo draws nourishment, developing roots like the roots of trees and plants by means of which it derives nourishment from its mother's womb, just as tree roots get this from soil. The growing—that is, the vegetative—soul manifests its effect in it, and this effect grows stronger in it and takes firm hold until it is perfected over time. The next step is that it prepares itself to receive nourishment without the roots, which means reaching for its nourishment through its own movement, and the animal effect manifests itself in it little by little. Once it has fully prepared itself to receive this effect, it leaves its location and receives the effect of the animal soul. It remains at the level of beasts until it develops the preparedness to receive the effect of rationality, that is, discrimination and reflection. At that point, the effect of the intellect manifests itself within us, and this effect continues to grow strong within us in the measure of our preparedness and receptivity, until we reach the highest grade and perfection possible for us with regard to humanity. We then come within view of the grade above the grade of human beings, and we prepare to receive the effect of the angels. At that point, we must rise up in the next realm in a stronger state than the earlier preceding state. 163.3

This form of words does not allow for the question, "When does the soul attach or detach itself?" The person who holds to that view should rather ask, "When is there preparedness and receptivity?" The soul essentially gives to everything that receives its effect in accordance with its receptivity, preparedness, and readiness. It has been established that it imparts a variety of states and disparate forms to the body before it becomes an embryo. Once the human form is complete, the soul never wholly ceases to exercise its effect on the body throughout its manifold states until it completes its manifold cycles and reaches its ultimate perfection. It must not be said that it is ever without it in any of its states; rather, the effect grows stronger and weaker depending on its receptivity. That is all there is to say. 163.4

مسألة

سئل بعضهم إذا فارقت النفس الجسد هل تذكر من علومها شيئاً أم لا؟ فأجاب بأنّها تذكر المعقول كلّه ولا تذكر المحسوس فزاد السائل بما يعرض للعليل من النسيان أي كيف تذكر النفس معقولها إذا فارقت البدن وهي لا تذكر شيئاً منه إذا اعتلّ البدن أو بعض أعضاء البدن؟ فأجاب بما سيمرّ بك. ١،١٦٤

الجواب

قال أبو عليّ مسكويه رحمه الله إنّما يظهر أثر النفس في البدن بحسب حاجة البدن وعلى قياس ما حكيناه من حالاته في الترقّي من حال إلى حال والتذكّر إنّما هو إحضار صور المحسوسات من قوّة الذكر إلى قوّة الخيال[1]. وهاتان القوّتان جميعاً إنّما تحصّلان[2] صور المحسوسات من الحواسّ أوّلاً في حواملها[3] من الأجسام الطبيعيّة ثمّ تحصّلانها بسيطاً في غير حامل جسميّ بل في قوّة النفس المسمّاة[4] ذكراً. وإنّما احتيج إلى هذه القوّة لأغراض البدن وحاجته إلى الشيء بعد الشيء فإذا استحال البدن وزالت الحاجة إلى الحواسّ سقطت الحاجة إلى الذكر أيضاً وصارت النفس مستغنية بذاتها وما فيها من صور العقل أعني التي تسمّى أوائل لأنّ تلك هي ذات العقل غير محتاجة إلى مادّة ولا إلى جسم توجد بوجوده أعني أنّ الأمور الموجودة في العقل هي العقل وهي التي نسمّيها الآن أوائل وليست في مادّة ولا محتاجة إليها. وجميع قوى النفس التي تتمّ بالبدن وبآلات جسميّة فإنّها تبطل ببطلان البدن أي تستغني عنها النفس بما هي نفس وجوهر بسيط وإنّما احتاجت إليه لأجل حاجات البدن المشارك للنفس المستمدّ منها البقاء الملائم لها إذا كان نباتاً أو حيواناً أو إنساناً. ٢،١٦٤

١ الأصل: الحمال. ٢ الأصل: إنها ويحصلان. ٣ الأصل: أولا إن في حواملها. ٤ الأصل: المسمّى.

On whether souls can recollect what they used to know after leaving the body

A thinker was asked: When the soul leaves the body, does it recollect any of the things it used to know, or not? He answered that it recollects all intelligible but not sensible things. The questioner followed up by pointing to the forgetfulness that ill people are prone to. That is, how can the soul recollect intelligible things when it leaves the body, when it does not recollect any of them when the body, or some parts of the body, fall ill? He gave the reply that you shall see. 164.1

Miskawayh's response

The effect of the soul manifests itself in the body in accordance with the body's need and relative to its progression from one state to the next, as we have explained above. Recollection consists in summoning the forms of sensible objects from the power of memory to the power of imagination. Both these powers first acquire the forms of sensible objects from the senses out of the natural bodies that bear them, and then acquire them simply, not in a corporeal carrier but in the power of the soul that is called memory. This power is needed because of the purposes of the body and its successive needs for different things. When the body is transformed and the need for the senses is eliminated, the need for memory also falls away, and the soul comes to require nothing outside itself and outside the forms of the intellect it contains, that is, outside those that are termed first principles. For those constitute the intellect itself and in order to exist do not need any matter or any body. That is, the things found in the intellect are what the intellect consists in, and they are the ones we now term first principles, which are not found in matter nor need it. All of the powers of the soul that are realized through the body and physical organs cease with the cessation of the body, that is, the soul ceases to require them insofar as it is a soul and simple substance. It needed them on account of the needs of the body that was partnered to the soul and that used them to derive the continued existence that was suitable to it, depending on whether it was plant, animal, or human. 164.2

فأمّا النفس بما هي جوهر بسيط فغير محتاجة إلى شيء من هذه الآلات الجسميّة ٣،١٦٤
وإنّما عرضت لك هذه الحيرة لأنّك سألت عن أمر بسيط مع توهّمك إيّاه مركّبًا وحال المركّب غير حال البسيط أعني إنّ الآلات البدنيّة كلّها هي أيضاً مركّبة نحو تمامات لها ليكمل بها أيضاً شيء مركّب. والحواسّ الخمس والقوى التي[1] تناسبها من التخيّل والوهم والفكر لا تتمّ إلّا بآلات وأمزجة مناسبة تتمّ بها أفعال مركّبة. فإذا عادت الجواهر إلى بسائطها بطل الفعل المركّب أيضاً ببطلان الآلات المركّبة واستغنى الجوهر البسيط القائم بذاته عن حاجات البدن وضروراته التي تمّ وجوده بها من حيث هو مركّب لأجلها.

مسألة

سئل عن الحكمة في كون الجبال. ١،١٦٥

الجواب

قال أبو عليّ مسكويه رحمه الله إنّ منافع الجبال ووضعها على بسيط الأرض كثيرة ٢،١٦٥
جدّاً ولولا هي[2] ما وُجد نبات ولا حيوان على بسيط الأرض وذلك أن سبب وجود النبات والحيوان وبقائهما بعد هو الماء العذب السائح على وجه الأرض. وسبب الماء العذب السائح هو انعقاد البخار في الجوّ أعني السحاب وما يعرض له من الانحصار بالبرد حتّى يعود منه إمّا مطر وإمّا ثلج وإمّا بَرَد. ولو أنّك توهّمت الجبال مرتفعة عن وجه الأرض وتخيّلت الأرض كرة مستديرة لا نتوء ولا غور[3] فيها لكان البخار المرتفع من هذه الكرة لا ينعقد في الجوّ ولا ينحصر ولا يعود منه ماء عذب بل كان غاية ذلك البخار أن يتحلّل ويستحيل هواء قبل أن يتمّ منه ما هو سبب عمارة وجه الأرض وذلك لأجل أنّ البخار المرتفع من الأرض يحصل بين أغوار الأرض وبين الجبال التي

١ الأصل: الخمس التي. ٢ ط: ولولاها. ٣ الأصل: غوور.

Insofar as it is a simple substance, by contrast, the soul needs none of these physical organs. The reason you succumbed to this confusion was that you inquired about a simple entity while fancying it to be composite, and composite entities do not have the same qualities as simple ones. That is, all bodily organs also have a composite character oriented to particular ends, in order that something composite be in turn perfected through them. The five senses and the powers that fall in with them—such as imagination, fancy, and thought—are realized through appropriate organs and humoral mixtures, through which composite acts are accomplished. When substances revert to their simple elements, the composite acts also cease to exist with the cessation of the composite organs, and the self-subsisting simple substance dispenses with the needs and necessities of the body, through which its existence was realized insofar as it was composite on account of them. 164.3

On why mountains exist

Here a question was posed about the purpose served by the existence of mountains. 165.1

Miskawayh's response

There are very many benefits to mountains and to their presence on the surface of the earth. Were it not for mountains, there would be no plants or animals on the surface of the earth. For what enables plants and animals to come into existence and to continue in existence thereafter is the fresh water that flows over the face of the earth. Fresh, running water is caused by the thickening of vapor in the air—I am referring to clouds and to the compression they undergo through cold, producing rain, snow, or hail. Were we to suppose that mountains were removed from the face of the earth and to imagine the earth as a round sphere with no protuberances or cavities, the vapor that rises from this sphere would not thicken in the air or become compressed, nor would fresh water be produced by it. All that would come of the vapor is that it would dissolve and turn into air before it had the chance to bring about that which causes the face of the earth to be filled with life. The vapor that rises from the earth accumulates in the cavities of the earth and among the mountains, 165.2

تمنعه السيلان ومطاوعة حركة الفلك وأسباب الريح[1] التي هي حركة الهواء أعني أنّ قلل الجبال الشاهقة تحفظ الهواء المحتقن بين أغوارها من الحركة التي يوجبها الفلك بأسره والكواكب فيها وشعاعاتها المؤثّرة الملطّفة التي توجب له[2] السيلان. فإذا حصل الهواء بين الجبال كذلك كان البخار المرتفع فيه أيضاً محفوظاً من التبدّد والحركة بتحرّك الهواء ولحق هذا البخار من برد الجبال التي تحفظه في زمان الشتاء على أنفسها ما يجمّده ويعقده ثمّ يعصره فيعود ماء مستحيلاً أو غيره ممّا يجري مجراه.

٣،١٦٥ ولولا الجبال لكانت هذه المياه المدبّرة بهذا التدبير مع ما ذكرناه لا تجري على وجه الأرض إلّا ريثما يهطل[3] المطر ثمّ تنشّفه الأرض فكان يعرض من ذلك أن يكون النبات والحيوان يعدمه في صميم الصيف وعند الحاجة الشديدة إليه في بقائهما[4] حتّى كان لا يوصل إليه إلّا كما يوصل في البوادي البعيدة من الجبال أعني باحتفار الآبار التي يبلغ عمقها مائة ومائتين من الذرعان. فأمّا الآن مع وجود الجبال فإنّ الأمطار والثلوج تبقى عليها فإذا نشفتها في الوقت أو بعد زمان نشأت من أسافلها العيون وسالت منها الأنهار والأودية وساحت على وجه الأرض منصبّة إلى البحار جارية من الشمال إلى الجنوب فإذا فني ما استفادته من الأمطار في الصيف لحقتها نوبة الشتاء والأمطار فعادت الحال.

٤،١٦٥ والدليل على أنّ العيون والأنهار والأودية كلّها من الجبال أنك لا ترتقي في نهر ولا واد إلّا أفضى بك إلى جبل فأمّا العيون فإنّها لا توجد إلّا بالقرب من الجبال البتّة وكذلك ما يُستنبط من القنى وما يجري مجراها. فالجبال تجري من الأرض في إساحة الماء عليها من الأمطار مجرى إسفنجة أو صوفة تُبلّ بالماء فتحمل منه شيئاً كثيراً ثمّ توضع على مكان يسيل منه الماء قليلاً قليلاً حتّى إذا جفّت أعيد بلّها وسقيها من الماء لتدوم الرطوبة السائلة منها على وجه الأرض ويصير هذا التدبير سبباً لعمارة العالم ووجود النبات والحيوان فيه. وللجبال منافع كثيرة إلّا أنّ ما ذكرناه من أعظم منافعها

١ الأصل: الريحة؛ ط: الرجة. ٢ الأصل وط: لها. ٣ الأصل وط: يهدأ. ٤ الأصل: بقائه.

which prevent it from drifting and from submitting to the movement of the celestial sphere and to the factors that produce the wind, which constitutes the movement of the air. That is, the high summits of mountains preserve the air that has concentrated itself among their cavities from the movement necessarily caused in it by the whole of the celestial sphere, along with its stars and their effective, emollient rays, which necessarily cause it to drift. If the air finds itself among the mountains, likewise, the vapor that rises in it is also preserved against dispersion and against movement produced by the motion of the air; the cold of the mountains the vapor is exposed to—retained during wintertime—causes it to freeze and thicken and then be pressed out, transformed into water or suchlike.

Were it not for mountains, the water produced in this manner with the 165.3
characteristics we have mentioned would only run on the face of the earth while rains are falling, and the earth would absorb it. The result would be that plants and animals would not have access to it at the height of summer and at times when they urgently need it to survive, so that access to it would only be gained as happens in desert areas located far from mountains, that is, by digging wells that run one hundred or two hundred cubits deep. Under current circumstances, by contrast—with mountains in existence—the rains and the snow remain there, and if they absorb them straightaway or after some time, springs of water well up at the feet of the mountains and streams and rivers gush forth and run over the face of the earth in the direction of the seas, from north to south. When the rains they have collected are depleted in the course of the summer, the next bout of wintry weather and rainfall comes along and restores things to their former state.

The proof that springs of water, streams, and rivers all stem from mountains 165.4
is that when we follow a stream or a river to its source, it always leads us to a mountain. Springs of water are only ever found close to mountains. The same applies to the water canals we come upon and the like. Thus, in causing water to flow over the earth, mountains relate to the earth like sponges or pieces of wool that are soaked in water and take in a large amount of it, and are then placed in a position where the water can seep out of them bit by bit. When dry, they are soaked and filled with water anew, so that the moisture may continue to seep out of them over the face of the earth. This arrangement makes it possible for life to flourish in the world and for plants and animals to exist in it. Mountains provide many benefits, but what we have mentioned is one of their

فليُقتصر عليه ولثابت مقالة في منافع الجبال من أحبّ أن يستقصي هذا الباب قرأه من تلك المقالة إن شاء الله.

مسـألة

١،١٦٦ لِمَ صارت الأنفس ثلاثًا[١] في العدد؟ وهل يجوز أن تكون اثنتين؟ أو هل يستحيل أن تكون أربعًا؟

الجواب

٢،١٦٦ قال أبو عليّ مسكويه رحمه الله النفس في الحقيقة واحدة وإنّما يظهر أثرها كما قلنا فيها فيما تقدّم بحسب قبول القابل وإنّما قيل إنّها ثلاث[٢] لأنّ من شأن الشيء الذي يبدأ أثره ضعيفاً ثمّ يقوى غاية القوّة أن ينقسم ثلاثة[٣] أقسام أعني الابتداء والتوسّط والنهاية. ولمّا كان مبدأ أثر النفس في النبات أعني أنّه يظهر فيه معنى يقبل الغذاء الموافق وينفض الفضلة وما ليس بموافق ويحفظ صورته بالنوع سمّي هذا الطرف الأوّل نفساً نباتيّة. ثمّ لمّا قوي هذا الأمر حتّى صار ينتقل المتنفّس لتناول غذائه وصارت له حواسّ وإرادة سُمّيت هذه المرتبة المتوسّطة والحيوانيّة. ولمّا قوي هذا الأثر حتّى صار مع هذه الأحوال يرتئي ويفكّر ويستعمل التمييز بتقديم المقدّمات واستنتاج النتائج ثمّ يعمل أعماله بحسبها سمّي ناطقاً وعاقلاً وما أشبه ذلك.

٣،١٦٦ ولكلّ واحدة من هذه المراتب لو قُسّمت مراتب كثيرة إلّا أنّ الأولى في كلّ ما جرى هذا المجرى أن يُقسم إلى المبدأ والوسط والنهاية كما فُعل ذلك بقوى الطبيعة فإنّ الحرارة والبرودة وما جرى مجراها إنّما تقسم إلى ثلاث[٤] مراتب أعني الابتداء والوسط والنهاية وإن كانت كلّ واحد من هذه المراتب تنقسم أيضاً وإذا ما تأمّلت جميع القوى

١ الأصل: ثلثا. ٢ الأصل: ثلث. ٣ الأصل: ثلثة. ٤ الأصل: ثلاثة.

greatest benefits, so that is enough. Thābit[52] wrote a treatise about the benefits of mountains, and whoever wishes to probe this topic in depth may read about it there, God willing.

On why there are three souls

Why are the souls three in number? Is it possible that they be two? Or is it impossible that they be four? 166.1

Miskawayh's response

In reality the soul is one, but as we said earlier, its effect is manifested according to the receptivity of that which receives it. The reason it has been described as threefold is that it is natural for something whose effect is initially weak and then reaches its fullest strength to divide into three parts—namely, beginning, middle, and end. As the effect of the soul first arises in plants—which is to say that a certain element manifests itself in them that accepts suitable nourishment, expels what is superfluous and unsuitable, and preserves the form of their species—this first stage was called the vegetative soul. When this aspect grew stronger and the ensouled being began to move in order to take its nourishment and acquired senses and a will, this level was called the intermediate or the animal soul. When this effect grew stronger, and along with these conditions it began to judge, think, and exercise discrimination by laying down premises and deriving conclusions and then acting on the basis of the latter, it was called rational, intelligent, and the like. 166.2

Each of these levels could be divided into a large number of further levels, yet the most proper approach with everything of this sort is to divide it into beginning, middle, and end, as has been done with the powers of nature. For heat, cold, and the like are divided into three levels—namely, beginning, middle, and end, even though each of these levels is in turn subject to further division. If you dwell on all of the different powers, you will find that they answer to the same pattern. You ask, "Is it possible that they be two?" 166.3

وجدت الأمر فيها جارياً هذا المجرى. فأمّا قولك هل يجوز أن تكون اثنتين فهي إنّما تكون واحدة أوّلاً ثمّ اثنتين ثمّ تُستكمل فتصير ثلاثاً وقد شُرح هذا.

مسـألة

لِمَ صار البحر في جانب من الأرض؟ ١،١٦٧

الجواب

قال أبو عليّ مسكويه رحمه الله لولا حكمة عظيمة اقتضت أن ينحسر الماء عن وجه الأرض لكان الأمر الطبيعيّ يوجب أن يكون الماء لابساً وجه الأرض أجمعه حتّى تصير الأرض في وسطه شبيهة[1] بمحّ البيض والماء حولها شبيهاً بالبياض والهواء محيط بهما على ما هو موجود الآن والنار محيطة بالجميع ليكون الأثقل الأولى[2] بالمركز وهو الأرض في موضعه الخاصّ من المركز ويليه الماء الذي هو أخفّ من الأرض وأثقل من الهواء ويليه الهواء ثمّ النار على سوم الطباع. ولكن لو تُركت هذه الأشياء وسومها الطبيعيّ لم تكن على وجه الأرض عمارة من نبات وحيوان وبشر وبهيمة وطائر وبطلت هذه الحكمة العجيبة والنظام الحسن فلأجل ذلك خولف بين مركز الشمس ومركز الفلك الأعلى فتبع هذا الفعل[3] أن صارت الشمس تدور على مركز لها خاصّ بها غير الأرض أعني أنّ مركزها خارج من الأرض. ٢،١٦٧

ولمّا دارت على مركزها قربت من ناحية من الأرض[4] وبعدت من أخرى وصارت الناحية التي تقرب منها تحمى بها ومن شأن الماء إذا حمي أن ينجذب إلى الجهة التي يحمى فيها بالبخار وإذا انجذب إلى هناك انحسر عن وجه الأرض الذي يقابله من الشقّ الذي تبعد عنه الشمس وإذا انحسر عن وجه[5] الأرض حدث من الجميع كرة واحدة أعني من الماء والأرض إلّا أنّ شقّ الكرة الجنوبيّ الذي يقرب الشمس فيه من الأرض مكان ٣،١٦٧

١ الأصل: شبيها. ٢ ط: الأوّل. ٣ ط: فتبع هذا. ٤ الأصل: ناحية الأرض. ٥ الأصل: انحسر وجه.

It is first one, then two, and then it is perfected and becomes three; this has been explained.

On why the sea is located on a particular side of the earth

Why is the sea located on one particular side of the earth?[53] 167.1

Miskawayh's response

Were it not for the momentous wisdom that demanded water be withdrawn 167.2
from the face of the earth, the natural course of things would necessarily be that water cover the entire face of the earth, such that the earth would stand in the middle like the yolk of an egg, water would encircle it like the white of an egg, air would surround the two as it does now, and fire would surround the whole ensemble. The heaviest object, which is the one closest to the center—namely, the earth—would thus stand at its proper place relative to the center, followed by water, which is lighter than earth and heavier than air, followed by air and then by fire, according to the natural inclination of the elements. Yet, had these things been left to their natural inclinations, no life would have flourished on the face of the earth, such as plants, animals, human beings, beasts, and birds, and this wonderful wisdom and good order would have been thwarted. That is the reason why the center of the sun's orbit and the center of the highest celestial sphere were made to diverge. As a consequence, the sun rotates around a distinctive orbital center of its own other than the earth. In other words, the center of its orbit lies outside the earth.

When the sun follows its orbit, it approaches closer to one side of the earth 167.3
and draws farther away from the other, and as a consequence the side it is near to becomes heated. When water is heated, it tends to be drawn in the direction in which it is being heated by vapor. When drawn up, it withdraws from the surface of the opposite end of the earth, the half from which the sun is distant. When withdrawn from the surface of the earth, the two combined—that is, the water and the earth—form a single sphere, yet the southern part of the sphere, the one close to the sun, is where water is located—that is, the sea—whereas

الماء وهو البحر وشقّ الكرة الشماليّ الذي يبعد عنه الشمس من الأرض يابس تظهر فيه الأرض ثمّ وجب بعد ذلك أن تنصب عليها الجبال لتستقيم الحكمة وينتظم أمر العالم على ما هو به موجود. عزّ مبدئ الجميع ومنشئه وناظمه ومقدّره وتبارك اسمه وجلّ جلاله وتقدّست أسماؤه وتعالى عمّا يقول الظالمون علوّاً كبيراً.

مسـألة

لم صارت مياه البحر ملحاً؟ ١،١٦٨

الجواب

قال أبو عليّ مسكويه رحمه الله إنّما ذلك لأجل قرب الشمس من سطح الماء وتمكّنها من ٢،١٦٨
طبخه ومن طبيعة الماء إذا ألحّت عليه الحرارة بالطبخ أن يتحلّل لطيفه إلى البخار ويقبل الباقي أثراً من الملوحة فإن زادت الحرارة ودامت صار ذلك الماء شديد الملوحة ثمّ انتهى في آخر الأمر إلى المرارة. وأصحاب الصنعة يدبّرون ماء لهم بالنار ويدبّرونه حتّى يكثر تردّده على النار فيصير بذلك الماء حارّاً يضرب إلى المرارة.

مسـألة

إذا كان المرئيّ لا يُدرك إلّا بآلة وتلك هي الحسّ فما تقول فيما يراه النائم؟ ألم يدركه من ١،١٦٩
غير حسّ ولا انبثاث شعاع ولا إعمال آلة؟

الجواب

قال أبو عليّ مسكويه رحمه الله قد كنّا بيّنّا في مسألة الرؤيا وما أجبنا به عنها ما فيه ٢،١٦٩
غنى عن تكلّف الجواب عن هذه المسألة ولكنّا نذكر جملة وهو أنّ الحواسّ كلّها ترتقي

the northern half of the sphere, the one distant from the sun, is dry, and land is visible. Then it was necessary that mountains be erected, so that the wise purpose should be properly executed and the state of the world be ordered as its existence requires. Mighty is the one who originated and created all of this, who ordered and determined it. May His name be blessed, His glory extolled, and His names be sanctified, and may He be exalted far above the claims of the iniquitous.

On why seawater is salty

Why is seawater salty? 168.1

Miskawayh's response

This is because the sun, being close to the surface of the water, is able to cook 168.2
it. The nature of water is such that, when heat is applied to it through cooking, its finer parts dissolve into vapor and the remainder receives an effect of saltiness. If the heat increases and is sustained for a long time, the water becomes extremely salty, and eventually turns bitter. Alchemists prepare with fire a particular sort of water they use, repeatedly exposing it to fire, so that the water becomes hot and salty with a touch of bitterness.

On how we can see things in our sleep without an organ of sense perception

If the only way to perceive objects of sight is by means of an organ, and it—that 169.1
is, the eye—is the relevant sense, then what can one say about what we see in our sleep? Do we perceive this without employing a sense, without the emission of rays, and without the use of an organ?

Miskawayh's response

The exposition we provided to the question about dreams and the response 169.2
there make it unnecessary for us to undertake a response to this question,

إلى قوّة يقال لها الحسّ المشترك وهذا الحسّ يقبل الآثار من الحواسّ ويحفظها عليها في القوّة التي تُعرف بالوهم فإذا غاب المحسوس أحضرت هذه القوّة صورة ذلك المحسوس من الوهم سواء كان مرئيًّا أو مسموعًا أو غيرهما من الصور المحسوسات وليس يمكن أن يحصل في هذه القوّة شيء من الصور إلّا ما قبلته[1] وأخذته من الحواسّ وقد مرّ هذا الكلام في الموضع الذي أذكرنا به مستقصى مع الكلام في حدّ المرئيّ وما يتبعه.

مسألة

١،١٧٠ لا يخلو في طلبنا لعلم شيء من أن يكون قد علمنا ذلك المطلوب أو لم نعلمه فإن كنّا قد علمناه فلا وجه لطلبنا له والدأب من ورائه وإن كنّا لا نعلمه فمحال أن نطلب ما لا نعلمه وعاد أمرنا فيه مثل الذي أبق له عبد لا يعرفه وهو يطلبه.

الجواب

٢،١٧٠ قال أبو عليّ مسكويه رحمه الله لو كان طلبنا للشيء إنّما هو من وجه واحد وذلك الوجه مجهول لكان الأمر على ما ذكرت لكنّا قد تقدّمنا قبل فشرحنا أنّ كلّ مطلوب يمكن أن يبحث من أمره عن أربعة مطالب أحدها أنّيّته وهذا البحث بهل ثمّ بما ثمّ بأيّ ثمّ بلم وهذه جهات لكلّ مطلوب فإذا عرفت جهة جُهلت أخرى وليس يغني العلم بأحدها عن الأخرى مثال ذلك أنّك إن بحثت عن جرم الفلك التاسع هل له وجود فتبيّن هذا المطلب بقيت الجهة الأخرى وهي جهة ما هو لأنّك قد عرفت جهة هل وجهلت جهة ما فإذا عرفت هذه الجهة بقيت الجهة الثالثة وهي جهة أيّ. وقد شرحنا هذه الجهات فيما مضى فإذا حصلت هذه بقيت جهة العلّة القصوى أعني لم وهي البحث عن الشيء الذي من أجله وُجد على ما وُجد عليه من المائيّة والكيفيّة فإذا عرفت هذه

[1] الأصل: قبله.

yet we will outline some general points.[54] All of the senses feed into a power called the common sense, which receives different effects from the senses and preserves them in the power known as the imagination. If the sensible object is absent, this power produces the form of that object from the imagination, regardless of whether it is an object of sight or hearing or some other sensible form. No forms can arise in this power unless it has received them and taken them from the senses. These matters were discussed in detail in the place we mentioned, along with a definition of the objects of sight and subsidiary topics.

On a puzzle concerning the possibility of seeking something we do not know

When we seek to know something, one of two possibilities obtain: either we know the object we seek, or we do not. If we know it, there is no reason for us to seek it and to apply ourselves to pursuing it. If we do not know it, it is impossible to seek something we do not know. In that case we resemble a person looking for a runaway slave whom he does not know. 170.1

Miskawayh's response

Matters would be as you describe if we only ever sought something from a single aspect and that aspect was unknown, yet we have already explained that one can inquire into any given object under four concerns: first, its existence—that is, the inquiry conducted through the interrogative "whether," then through "what," then through "which," and then through "why."[55] These considerations pertain to every object. One may be familiar with one consideration but ignorant of another, and knowledge of one does not relieve us of the need to know another. For example, if we inquire whether the existence of the body of the ninth celestial sphere exists and reach a clear view on this topic, the other consideration persists, namely, what it is; for we have established "whether," yet remain ignorant of "what." If we establish this consideration, the third persists, namely, "which." These considerations were explained earlier in the discussion. Once this has been secured, the consideration of the ultimate cause remains open, namely, "why": this involves inquiring why it exists in its specific nature and modality. If we establish this consideration, 170.2

الجهة لم يبق من أمره شيء مجهول إلّا جزئيّات الأمور التي لا نهاية لها وليس يُبحث عن تلك لقلّة الفائدة فيها أعني أن تطلب مساحتها ومبلغ عدد الأجزاء التي تمسحها ونسبة كلّ جزء إلى غيره ووضعه وما أشبه ذلك وهذه المطالب هي بحث مطلب كيف وغيره من المقولات في أنواعها وأشخاصها وإذا عرفت الجنس العالي لم تطلب أجزاءه لحصول الجهة العليا فقد صحّ أنّ المطلوب إنّما هو الجهة المجهولة لا الجهة المعلومة وأنّ الشيء الواحد قد يُعلم من جهة ويُجهل من جهة أخرى وزال موضع الشكّ إن شاء الله.

مسألة

لم لا يجيء الثلج في الصيف كما قد يجيء المطر فيه؟ ١،١٧١

الجواب

قال أبو عليّ مسكويه رحمه الله الفرق بين حالي الثلج والمطر أنّ البخار إذا ارتفع من ٢،١٧١ الأرض حمل معه جزءاً أرضيّاً ويكون مقدار هذا الجزء الأرضيّ ما يخفّ مع البخار ويتحرّك معه ويصعد بصعوده كالهباءة التي تراها أبداً في الهواء فإنّ ذلك القدر من أجزاء الأرض لخفّته يتحرّك بحركة الهواء ويصعد مع بخار الماء فإذا اتّفق وقت صعود هذا البخار أن يصيبه في الهواء برد شديد حتّى يجمد جمد معه الجزءُ الأرضيّ وثقل بما يكتسبه من انضمام البعض إلى البعض بالبرد فارجحنّ إلى أسفل وهو الثلج وإن اتّفق أن يكون البرد الذي يلحقه يسيراً لا يبلغ أن يجمّده عصر البخار عصراً فخرج منه الماء الذي يقطر وهو المطر. والدليل على أنّ في الثلج جزءاً أرضيّاً القبض الذي فيه الثلج وسلامة المطر منه وأيضاً فإنّ في الثلج جرم البخار بعينه أعني الحالة التي ليست ماءً ولا هواءً فإذا جمدت تلك الحالة ردّت طبيعة البخار فأمّا المطر فلا طبيعة للبخار فيه وهو ماء بعينه ولذلك يصيب آكل الثلج من النفخ والأسباب العارضة من البخار ما لا

the only thing about the object that we are ignorant of is the particulars, which are infinite in number. These yield little advantage, so we do not inquire into them, that is, by seeking to know their extent, the total number of parts they extend over, the relation of each part to every other part, its position, and the like. These concerns constitute the inquiry into "how" and other categories pertaining to their species and individuals. If we have established the high-level genus, then we do not seek its parts, for we have secured the highest consideration. Thus, it has been established that what we seek is not the known but the unknown consideration, and that a single thing may both be known from one consideration and unknown from another; so the point of doubt has been removed, God willing.

On why it does not snow in the summer

Why doesn't snow come during summer, as rain sometimes does? 171.1

Miskawayh's response

The difference between snow and rain is as follows. When vapor rises from the earth, it carries an earthly part with it. The quantity of this earthly part is such that it grows light with the vapor, moves with it, and ascends along with it, like the motes we always see in the air, for it is so light that it moves with the air and ascends with the water's vapor. If it so happens that while this vapor is ascending, it is exposed in the air to severe cold so that it freezes, the earthly part freezes along with it and becomes heavier because of how the different elements aggregate together through the cold, and it inclines downward. This is snow. If it happens that the cold is slight and not severe enough to freeze it, the vapor is pressed out and water comes out in drops. This is rain. The fact that we are able to hold snow in our hands proves that it contains an earthly part, whereas rain is not amenable to that. Moreover, snow contains the body of vapor itself, that is, the condition that is neither water nor air. If this condition freezes, the nature of vapor is established. Rain, by contrast, does not contain any of the nature of vapor, and it is water itself. This is why a person who eats snow experiences bloating and the kinds of effects produced 171.2

يصيب شارب ماء المطر. وإذ قد وضح الفرق بين المطر والثلج فإنّا نقول في جواب مسألتك إنّ الشتاء يشتدّ فيه برد الهواء حتّى يجمد البخار الصاعد إليه من الأرض فيردّ ثلجًا فأمّا الصيف فليس يشتدّ فيه برد الهواء ولكن بقدر ما عرض فيه من البرد ينعقد[1] البخار ثمّ ينعصر فيجيء منه مطر.

مسألة

ما الدليل على وجود الملائكة؟ ١،١٧٢

الجواب

قال أبو عليّ مسكويه رحمه الله أمّا الكتاب والسنّة فمملوءان من ذكر الملائكة وأنّها خلق شريف لله تعالى ولها مراتب متفاضلة. فأمّا العقل فإنّه يوجب وجودها[2] من طريق أنّ العقل إذا قسم شيئًا وُجد لا محالة إلّا أن يمنع منه محال وذلك أنّ قسمة العقل هي الوجود الأوّل والحقّ المحض الذي لا يعترضه مانع ولا تعوق عنه مادّة فإذا قُسم فقد وجد الوجود العقليّ وإذا حصل هذا[3] الوجود تبعه الوجود النفسانيّ والوجود الطبيعيّ لأنّ هذين متشبّهان بالعقل مقتديان به تابعان له غير مقصّرين ولا وانيين ولكنّ الطبيعة تحتاج في هذا الاقتداء إلى حركة لقصورها عن الإيجاد التامّ ولذلك قيل في حدّ الطبيعة إنّها مبدأ حركة ولأنّ العقل إذا قسم الجوهر إلى الحيّ وغير الحيّ قسم الحيّ منه إلى الناطق وغير الناطق وقسم الناطق منه إلى المائت وغير المائت فيحصل من القسمة أربعة وهي حيّ ناطق مائت وحيّ غير ناطق غير مائت وحيّ ناطق غير مائت وحيّ غير ناطق مائت. ٢،١٧٢

١ الأصل وط: ولكن بما عرض فيه من البرد بقدر ما. ٢ الأصل: وجوده. ٣ الأصل: في هذا.

by vapor, but a person who drinks rainwater does not. Now that the difference between rain and snow has become clear, we respond to your question as follows. During winter, the coldness of the air intensifies, with the result that the vapor ascending to it from the earth freezes and turns into snow. In summer, by contrast, the coldness of the air does not intensify, but, depending on the amount of cold that affects it, the vapor thickens and is then pressed out, and rain is produced from it.

On the proof for the existence of angels

What is the proof that angels exist? 172.1

Miskawayh's response

The Qur'an and prophetic practice are filled with references to the angels, noting that they are noble beings created by God and occupy ranks of varying excellence. Reason also judges their existence to be necessary, based on the fact that when the intellect produces a division in something, that thing must necessarily exist unless something renders it impossible. For the divisions produced by the intellect represent the first existence and the pure truth, which is not affected by any impediments or thwarted by matter. So, if the intellect produces a division, it possesses an intelligible existence, and if this existence is realized, it is followed by existence in the soul and by natural existence; for these two emulate the intellect, imitate it, and follow it, without wearying or falling short. Yet nature needs movement for this imitation owing to its inability to effect existence completely. That is why nature has been defined as the principle of movement. When the intellect divides substance into living and nonliving, subdividing the living into rational and nonrational and subdividing the rational into mortal and non-mortal, the result of this division is fourfold: living, rational, mortal; living, nonrational, non-mortal; living, rational, non-mortal; and living, nonrational, mortal. 172.2

والقسم الثالث هم المسمّون ملائكة وهي مشتركة في أنّها غير مائتة ومتفاضلة في النطق وبهذا التفاضل صار بعضها أقرب إلى الله تعالى من بعض وبه أيضاً صرنا نحن معاشر البشر متفاضلين في التقرّب إلى الله تعالى والبعد منه ولأجله قيل فلان شبيه بملك وفلان شبيه بشيطان وبسببه قيل فلان عدوّ الله وبسببه قيل فلان وليّ الله وفي السبّ يقال بعّد الله فلاناً ولعنه وقرّب الله فلاناً وأدناه. وقد يمكن أن يثبت وجود الملائكة من طريق آثارها وأفعالها الظاهرة في هذا العالم ولكنّي لمّا احتجت في ذلك إلى مقدّمات كثيرة وبسط للكلام أخرج به عن الشرط الذي شرطته في أوّل هذه المسائل اقتصرت على ما ذكرته وهو كاف إن شاء الله. ٣،١٧٢

مسألة

وسألت أيّدك الله عن آلام الأطفال ومن لا عقل له من الحيوان وعن وجه الحكمة فيه. ١،١٧٣

الجواب

قال أبو عليّ مسكويه رحمه الله أمّا هذه المسألة فإنّها تتوجّه إلى من أثبت جميع الأفعال التي ليست للناس منسوبة إلى الله تعالى ولم يعترف بأفعال الطبيعة ولا بأفعال الأشياء التي هي وسائط بيننا وبين الله تعالى فإنّ المتكلّمين كالمجمعين على أنّ الحرارة والإحراق وسائر أفعال الطبائع وما ننسبه نحن إلى الوسائط التي فوّض الله إليها تدبير عالمنا من الأفلاك والكواكب كلّها أفعال الله تعالى بلا واسطة بل هو يتولّاها بذاته. وفي مناقضة هؤلاء القوم[1] طول فإن أحببت أن أفرد له مقالة أو كتاباً فعلت. فأمّا من زعم أنّ النار إذا جاورت النفط ألهبته وإذا جاورت الماء أسخنته وكذلك كلّ عنصر ٢،١٧٣

[1] الأصل: مناقضة القوم.

The third subdivision represents the beings designated as angels, which have in common the fact that they are not mortal and have varying degrees of excellence with regard to rationality. This variance is what makes some of them closer to God than others, and also what makes us human beings vary with respect to how close we come to God and how distant we are from Him. This is why we say, "He's like an angel" and "He's like a devil," and also, "He's an enemy of God" and "He's a friend of God." As abuse we say, "May God drive him far away and damn him," and then there's "May God draw him close and bring him near." We could also establish the existence of angels on the basis of the acts and effects they manifest in this world, but in order to do that I would need to lay down a number of premises and to expand on the topic in such a way that I would breach the terms you set at the start of your questions, so I have restricted myself to these points. That is sufficient, God willing. 172.3

On what justifies the suffering of children and non-rational animals

You asked—may God grace you with his support—about the pains suffered by children and animals lacking reason, and about the wise purpose behind this. 173.1

Miskawayh's response

This question addresses itself to those who affirm that all acts not performed by people are to be ascribed to God, and who do not acknowledge the acts of nature or the acts of the things that serve as intermediaries between us and God. For dialectical theologians appear to be united in believing that heat and burning and all the other acts of the elements and the things that we ourselves ascribe to the intermediaries to which God has delegated the governance of our world—such as the celestial spheres and the stars—are all acts of God, which He performs without intermediary and undertakes in His own person. Refuting these people is a lengthy task; if you wish me to devote a separate treatise or book to the topic I will be happy to do so. Now, there are those who have asserted that when fire approaches naphtha it makes it burst into flame, and when it approaches water it heats it, and similarly with every element 173.2

وركن وكلّ شعاع وأثر ممتدّ من العلوّ إلى أسفل فإنّه يؤثّر في جميع ما يقابله آثاراً مختلفة إمّا لاختلاف الفواعل وإمّا لاختلاف القوابل فإنّ هذه المسألة غير لازمة له وإنّما ينبغي أن يُسأل من وجه آخر لم تسأل عنه فلذلك لم أتكلّف جوابه وقد ظهر من مقدار ما أومأت إليه جواب مسألتك إن شاء الله.

مسألة

لم كان صوت الرعد إلى آذاننا أبطأ وأبعد من رؤية البرق إلى أبصارنا؟ ١،١٧٤

الجواب

قال أبو عليّ مسكويه رحمه الله أمّا البرق فإنّه من استحالة الهواء إلى الإضاءة ولمّا كان الهواء سريع القبول للضوء بل يستضيء في غير زمان وذاك أنّ الشمس حين تطلع من المشرق يضيء منها الهواء في المغرب بلا زمان وكذلك الحال في كلّ مضيء كالنار وما أشبهها إذا قابل الهواء قبل منه[1] الإضاءة بلا زمان وكان الهواء متّصلاً بأبصارنا لا واسطة بيننا وبينه وجب أن يكون إدراكنا له[2] أيضاً بلا زمان ولذلك صرنا أيضاً ساعة نفتح أبصارنا ندرك زحل وسائر الكواكب الثابتة المضيئة إذا لم يعترض في الهواء عارض يستر أو يحجب. فأمّا الرعد فلمّا كان أثره في الهواء بطريق الحركة والتموّج لا بطريق[3] الاستحالة وجب أن يكون وصوله إلى أسماعنا بحسب حركته في السرعة والإبطاء وذاك أنّ الصوت الذي هو اقتراع في الهواء يموّج ما يليه من الهواء كما يموّج الحجر الجزء الذي يليه من الماء إذا صكّ به ثمّ يتبع ذلك أن يموّج أيضاً بعض الماء بعضاً وبعض الهواء بعضاً على طريق المدافعة بين الأجزاء إذا كانت متّصلة. ٢،١٧٤

١ الأصل: الهواء منه. ٢ ط: إدراكنا. ٣ الأصل: بلا طريق.

and principle and every ray and effect extending from the higher to the lower region—for it produces different effects in everything it encounters, either because of differences in the acting elements or because of differences in the receiving elements—however, these topics are not necessarily connected to the question you have asked. The question would have had to be posed under a different aspect, which you did not inquire about, so I have not gone to the trouble of responding to it. The indications I have provided make the response to your question clear, God willing.

On why it takes us longer to hear thunder than to see lightning

Why does it take longer for us to hear the sound of thunder than to see lightning, and why is it farther away? 174.1

Miskawayh's response

Lightning arises when air changes into a state of luminance. Air is quick to receive light—indeed, it becomes illuminated in no time, for when the sun rises in the east, the air in the west is illuminated in no time. The same applies to everything that illuminates, such as fire and the like; when it meets air it receives illumination in no time. Moreover, air is connected to our eyes with no intermediary. Consequently, our perception of it must also happen in no time. This is also why the moment we open our eyes we perceive Saturn and the rest of the luminous fixed stars, so long as there is nothing in the air to screen or conceal them. The effect of thunder on the air, by contrast, occurs through motion and undulation rather than through a change of state, so how it reaches our ears must depend on the speed or slowness with which it moves. For sound, which consists in an impaction in the air, causes the air adjoining it to undulate, just as a stone causes that part of the water adjoining it to undulate if it strikes it. This results in different parts of the water and different parts of the air causing each other to undulate, by way of mutual propulsion among the parts if connected. 174.2

٣،١٧٤ فكما أنّ جانب الغدير إذا تموّج حرّك ما يليه في زمان ثمّ ما يلي ما يليه إلى أن ينتهي إلى الجانب الأقصى منه حتّى تصير بينهما مدّة وزمان على قدر اتّساع سطح الماء فكذلك حال الهواء إذا اقترع فيه الجسم الصلب حرّك ما يليه من الهواء وتموّج به ثمّ حرّك هذا الجزء ما يليه في زمان بعد زمان حتّى ينتهي إلى الجزء الذي يلي آذاننا فنحسّ به ولذلك صار صوت وقع الحجر على الحجر إذا لمح الإنسان محرّكه من بعيد يصل إلى أسماعنا بعد زمان من رؤيتنا إيّاه وكذلك حالنا إذا رأينا القصّار من بعيد على طرف واد فإنّا نرى حركة يده وإلاحته بالثوب حين رفعه وضربه الحجر قبل أن نسمع صوت ذلك الوقع بزمان فهذه بعينها حال البرق والرعد لأنّ السحاب يصطكّ بعضه ببعض فينقدح من ذلك الاصطكاك ما ينقدح من كلّ جسمين إذا اصطكّا بقوّة شديدة ويخرج أيضاً من بينهما صوت وهما جميعاً أعني البرق والرعد يحدثان معاً في حال واحدة إذ كان سببهما جميعاً الصكّ والقرع أعني حركة الجسم الصلب وقرع[١] بعضه ببعض كحال المقدحة والحجر إلّا أنّ البرق يضيء منه الهواء بالاستحالة التي تكون بلا زمان فنحسّه في الوقت. فأمّا الرعد فيتموّج منه الهواء الذي يلي السحاب المصطكّ ثمّ يتموّج أيضاً ما يليه ويسري في الجزء بعد الجزء إلى أن ينتهي إلى الهواء الذي يلي أسماعنا في زمان فنحسّ به حينئذ.

مسـألة

١،١٧٥ إذا كان الإنسان على مذهب من المذاهب ثمّ ينتقل عنه لخطأ يتبيّنه فما تنكر أن ينتقل عن المذهب الثاني مثل انتقاله عن الأوّل ويستمرّ ذلك به جميع المذاهب حتّى لا يصحّ له مذهب ولا يتّضح[٢] له حقّ؟

١ الأصل: الصلب قرع. ٢ ط: يضح.

When one side of a pond undulates, it moves the part next to it within a certain interval of time, then the next part moves the part next to it, until it finally reaches the far side; the two sides are separated by an amount and interval of time commensurate to the extent of the water's surface. It is similar with air; when a firm body is impacted in it, it moves the adjoining air and causes it to undulate, and this part then moves the air that adjoins it over successive moments in time, until it finally reaches the part that adjoins our ears and we sense it. This is why the sound of a stone falling on another stone, when we glimpse the agent producing this movement from a distance, reaches our ears some time after our seeing it. Something similar happens when we see a clothes washer on a riverbank from a distance, for we see the movement of his hand and the way he waves the garment about as he raises it and beats it against the stone some time before we hear the sound of the blow. This is exactly what happens with lightning and thunder; for clouds clash against each other, and the clashing sparks off the same thing that is sparked off whenever two bodies clash against each other with great force, and sound also emerges from them. Both of these—I mean lightning and thunder—occur together at a single time, as the cause of both is clashing and striking, that is, the movement of the firm body and the way part of it strikes against the other, as happens with a fire steel and flint. Air is illuminated by lightning through a change of state, which occurs in no time and which we thus sense immediately. Thunder, by contrast, causes the air that adjoins the cloud where the clashing happens to undulate, and then the air adjoining it undulates, and this moves from one part to the next until over a certain interval of time it reaches the air that adjoins our ears, and only then do we sense it. 174.3

On the possibility that a person may abandon every belief he adopts ad infinitum

If a person adheres to a certain doctrine and then abandons it after noticing that it contains an error, can you deny the possibility that he might abandon the second doctrine as he did the first and do the same with all doctrines, so that he ends up considering no doctrine to be sound and reaching no conclusions about what is true? 175.1

الجواب

٢،١٧٥ قال أبو عليّ مسكويه رحمه الله لو كانت الإقناعات ومراتبها متساوية في جميع الآراء لما أنكرت ما ذكرته ولكنّي وجدت مراتب الأدلّة والإقناعات فيها متفاوتة فمنها ما يسمّى يقيناً ومنها ما يسمّى دليلاً وقياساً إقناعياً بحسب مقدّمات ذلك القياس ومنها ما يسمّى ظنّاً وتخيّلاً وما أشبه ذلك فأنكرت أن تستوي الأحوال في الآراء مع تفاوت القياسات الموضوعة فيها. فمن ذلك أنّ القياس إذا كان برهانيّاً وهو أن تكون مقدّماته مأخوذة من أمور ضروريّة وكان تركيبها صحيحاً حدثت منه نتيجة يقينيّة لا يعترضها شكّ ولا يجوز أن ينتقل عنه ولا يسوغ فيه خطأ. وكذلك . . . . التي امتدّت بها فأثر الحرارة في المبدأ يكون ضعيفاً لكثرة المادّة ومقاومتها فإذا قويت الحرارة بالتدريج وانتهت إلى غاية أمرها كان زمان الشباب وكأنّه صعود وحال نشأ حتّى ينتهي ثمّ يقف وقفة كما يعرض في جميع الحركات الطبيعيّة ثمّ ينحطّ وهو زمان التكهّل فلا يزال إلى نقصان حتّى يفنى فناء طبيعيّاً كما وصفنا وهو زمان الشيخوخة والهرم وقد كان في زمان جالينوس من ظنّ ما ظننته حتّى حكاه عنه وذكر أنّه بلي بمرض طويل أضحك منه من كان حفظ عليه مذهبه.

١،١٧٦ هـذا آخر مـا سـألت في الهوامل. وقد سلكت في الجواب عن جميعها المسلك الذي اخترته واقترحته من الاختصار والإيماء إلى النكت والإحالة فيما يحتاج إلى شرح إلى مظانّه من الكتب نفعك الله بها وعلّمك ما فيه خير الدارين بمنّه ولطفه الحمـد لله ربّ العالمين وصلواته على رسوله محمّد وآله أجمعـين.

Miskawayh's response

If the different forms and levels of persuasion involved in all views were equal, I would not deny the possibility that what you mention should happen. Yet I have found the levels of proofs and persuasions involved to be subject to variation. They include that which is termed certainty, that which is termed a persuasive proof and syllogism in accordance with the premises of that syllogism, that which is termed supposition and imagination, and the like. Thus, I deny the possibility that different views should be equal despite the variation in the syllogisms used to support them. For example, if a syllogism is demonstrative—which means that its premises derive from necessary matters and are soundly combined—it produces a conclusion that is insusceptible to doubt, impossible to abandon, and impervious to error. Likewise . . . .[56] through which it is extended, so heat has a weak effect in the beginning because there is an abundance of matter that presents resistance. When the heat grows progressively stronger and reaches its highest level, this is the time of youth. It is as though it were an ascent and a state that develops until it reaches its end point, upon which it pauses—as happens with all natural movements—and then enters decline, this being the time of middle age. It continues to diminish until it naturally succumbs to destruction, as we have described; this is the time of old age and decrepitude. There was a person in Galen's time who entertained the same notion as you and whose view Galen reported, mentioning that he was afflicted with a long illness that provoked laughter among those who remembered his view. 175.2

This was the last question you posed in your "Wandering Herd." In responding to them, I have followed the course chosen and recommended by you, keeping my exposition concise and allusively indicating subtler points, and, for anything that requires explanation, referring to the books where proper discussions can be found. May God make you profit from them and may He, through His bounty and grace, teach you that in which is vested the happiness of both abodes. Praise be to God, Lord of all being, and His blessings be upon His messenger Muḥammad and all his family. 176.1

Notes

1 Miskawayh has in mind Aristotle's remarks in *De Anima* Book III.4, 429a27–29.

2 The verse is by the sixth-century Christian Arab poet ʿAdī ibn Zayd. See *Dīwān ʿAdī ibn Zayd*, 106, using variant wording.

3 This is a loose reference to Aristotle's remarks in *Nicomachean Ethics* 1115b7–9.

4 This example is discussed by Galen, as Miskawayh goes on to mention. See Galen, "The Diagnosis and Treatment of the Affections and Errors Peculiar to Each Person's Soul," in *Psychological Writings*, 252, 257. Miskawayh brings it up again in *Tahdhīb*, 203.

5 Miskawayh is referring here to §24.1.

6 The term "materialists" refers loosely to different groups with irreligious views, including the denial of a future life. They often featured in theological discussions about the nature of ethical value and moral motivation, and in arguments against the dependence of ethical value on revealed scripture.

7 Abū Dāwūd, *Sunan Abī Dāwūd*, 6:586 (#4530); Aḥmad ibn Ḥanbal, *Musnad al-Imām Aḥmad ibn Ḥanbal*, 2:286 (#993).

8 Abū Dāwūd, *Sunan Abī Dāwūd*, 6:59 (#3916); Aḥmad ibn Ḥanbal, *Musnad al-Imām Aḥmad ibn Ḥanbal*, 8:392–93 (#4775).

9 Miskawayh is evidently omitting part of the text of al-Tawḥīdī's original question here. It is unclear what story this is a reference to.

10 This hadith doesn't appear in the main collections, but see for example Ibn Abī Shaybah, *al-Muṣannaf*, 17:521 (#33679).

11 The Arab terms are respectively: *ghurāb*, *ghurbah*, *bān*, *bayn*, *nawan* ("date pits" and "distance"), and *buʿd*.

12 The verse is by the pre-Islamic poet Zabbān ibn Sayyār al-Fazārī, who was related by marriage to the renowned poet al-Nābighah al-Dhubyānī—the poem's "Ziyād."

13 The verse is by Ibn al-Rūmī: see *Dīwān Ibn al-Rūmī*, 1:335 (#237).

14 The term translated as "fair skinned" is *aḥmar*, which also means "red," giving an extra lexicographical context for this point.

15 A broad reference to a constellation of heterodox religious groups, which most notably included the Manicheans. They featured prominently in theological polemics as challengers of key tenets of the Muslim faith.

16 Q Zumar 39:15.

17 See §§33.1–34.17, especially the response at §§34.11–15.

18 Miskawayh touches on both these points at various stages of his responses: see, e.g., §§63.1–11, especially §63.8; §§71.1–2; and §§93.1–4, especially §93.4.

19 The verse is by the poet and anthologist Abū Tammām (d. 231/845 or 232/846).

20 Miskawayh no doubt has Galen's work in mind here, particularly his immensely influential *De usu partium* (*Fī manāfiʿ al-aʿḍāʾ*).

21 A reference to Q Muʾminūn 23:14: «. . . then We created of the drop a clot then We created of the clot a tissue then We created of the tissue bones then We garmented the bones in flesh; thereafter We produced him as another creature.»

22 It is not completely clear which response Miskawayh refers to here. Perhaps he means §22.2 in Volume 1?

23 It is difficult to determine who is speaking here because the comment seems opaque: How could al-Tawḥīdī be telling Miskawayh "you will hear your own response"? Some odd editing hand seems to have been at work in the text at this point.

24 The poet is Isḥāq al-Mawṣilī (d. 235/850).

25 Abū Bishr Mattā was at the heart of a culturally important controversy regarding the claims of philosophical logic, which found its best-known expression in an exchange between him and the grammarian Abū Saʿīd al-Sīrāfī reported by al-Tawḥīdī in his *Imtāʿ* (1:107–28). The question posed is: "Isn't *manṭiq*, 'logic,' simply a derivation from the term 'speech,' *nuṭq*, on the morphological pattern *mafʿil*?"

26 "Abū Ḥafṣ" was the patronymic of the second caliph, ʿUmar, whom Shiʿah have historically regarded with animosity for having undermined the claims of ʿAlī and the House of the Prophet.

27 The former view had been expressed by several Ashʿarite theologians, among others, and fiercely opposed by Muʿtazilite thinkers. The latter view found a number of expressions in the Greek philosophical tradition, notably in Plato's *Cratylus*, as contrasted with Aristotle's conventionalist approach to language. In Islamic theological circles it is perhaps most strongly associated with the Muʿtazilite ʿAbbād ibn Sulaymān (d. 250/864).

28 See, e.g., §§3.1–7 and §§93.1–4.

29 The reference is to the Muʿtazilites, and to the distinctive doctrine about God's attributes that divided them from Ashʿarites and other theologians, as outlined in the continuation.

30 The text is clearly corrupt.

31 The discussion of God's existence and attributes takes up the entire first question in the *Fawz*. See *Fawz*, 3–32, and especially the programmatic remarks at 25–27.

32 The term *muwalladūn* is a loose category that can indicate more broadly poets who belong to the post-Umayyad, early Abbasid era.

33 The translation of these lines draws in part on Jones, *Early Arabic Poetry*, 2:114. See *Mufaḍḍaliyyāt*, 247 (#57), with slightly altered wording.

34 That is, effecting changes in the syllables, e.g., by reducing a long syllable to a short one, or two short syllables to one. For further detail, see Stoetzer, "Ziḥāf."

35 This line has been attributed to different poets, including al-Shanfarā and Ta'abbaṭa Sharran. See Ibn Manẓūr, *Lisān al-ʿarab*, 8:161 (s.v. *s-l-ʿ*).

36 The distinction between types of argument—demonstrative, dialectical, rhetorical, sophistical, and poetic—carrying different epistemic credentials is key to Aristotle's *Organon* as a whole. See al-Fārābī, "Kitāb al-Burhān," in *Al-Manṭiq ʿinda al-Fārābī*, 20–22, for a discussion that provides some context for Miskawayh's remarks.

37 The term *Kānūn* could strictly refer to either December (Kānūn I) or January (Kānūn II).

38 Al-Tawḥīdī's term here is *al-shawāmil*, which is the second half of the book's title.

39 Miskawayh has in mind Aristotle's discussion of future contingents in *De Interpretatione* Chapter 9, though his ensuing remarks also draw on ideas developed by later commentators in both the ancient and Arabic tradition. See Adamson, "The Arabic Sea Battle," for some helpful context. Miskawayh's remarks echo the terminology used by al-Fārābī in his related discussion in "Kitāb Bārī Armīniyās ay al-ʿIbārah," *Al-Manṭiq ʿinda al-Fārābī*, 1:160–162; cf. at greater length, *Al-Fārābī's Commentary*, trans. Zimmermann, 76–96.

40 Q Furqān 25:23.

41 The reference is to the fifth caliph, Hārūn al-Rashīd (d. 193/809) and to the two brothers, al-Faḍl (d. 193/808) and Jaʿfar (d. 190/805), members of the influential Barmakid family.

42 The reference is probably to ʿAbd Allāh Muḥammad ibn Sālim al-Baṣrī (d. 297/909), the disciple of the Sufi Sahl al-Tustarī.

43 Our translation of this obscure passage is tentative. One would have expected the opposite: "what is unknown is as good as nonexistent/might as well not exist."

44 Miskawayh makes this point in the course of his response to question §101.1: see §101.2.

45 Peter Adamson, in a private communication, suggests that *aʿrāḍ* (accidents) should be read for *amrāḍ* (illnesses).

46 As mentioned in the Introduction, Aḥmad ibn ʿAbd al-Wahhāb was the addressee of al-Jāḥiẓ's *Kitāb al-Tarbīʿ wa-l-tadwīr*, whose objective was partly to lampoon him and expose his ignorance through a fusillade of challenging questions. The phrasing of both the present question and Question 152 seems to suggest that al-Jāḥiẓ's victim responded in kind by issuing his own counter-fusillade of questions (in this regard, responding to al-Jāḥiẓ's apparent invitation in *Tarbīʿ*, 88, §166). Yet, perplexingly, the topic of Question 152 is brought up by al-Jāḥiẓ himself on p. 38, §67.

47 Al-Kindī's works included an *Epistle on the Deceptions of the Alchemists* (*Risāla fī-l-tanbīh ʿalā khudaʿ al-kīmiyāʾiyyīn*) according to Ibn al-Nadīm, *Fihrist*, 320. Al-Rāzī's response is mentioned by al-Masʿūdī, *Murūj al-dhahab*, 5:159–60 (#3312). Neither work has survived. Note that in the Arabic Miskawayh gives al-Kindī's name as Yūsuf ibn Isḥāq rather than Abū Yūsuf ibn Isḥāq.

48 It is unclear whether Miskawayh went on to compose the promised epistle, though a broad reference in the overview of his output in the *Muntakhab Ṣīwān al-ḥikmah* allows us to speculate that he may have: al-Sijistānī, *Muntakhab Ṣīwān al-ḥikmah*, 347. In any case, no such work has come down to us.

49 The Arabic terms are *mustabham* and *mustaghlaq*, respectively. As Miskawayh goes on to explain, the latter term derives from *ghalaqa*, meaning "to close a door," and the former from *abhama*, to close a door in such a way as "to block" it.

50 A reference to Q An'ām 6:59.

51 The discussion of prophecy, which touches on the themes just mentioned, takes up the whole of the third question in the *Fawz*: see *Fawz*, 85–120.

52 The reference must be to a treatise titled *Kitāb fī sabab kawn al-jibāl*, which is mentioned by the biographer Ibn Abī Uṣaybiʿah, *ʿUyūn al-anbāʾ*, 1:218.

53 This may be a reference to the common assumption that the inhabitable landmass was encompassed on all sides by an "Encircling Sea" (*al-baḥr al-muḥīṭ*).

54 See §§48.1–5.

55 See §§159.1–3.

56 Here there is a lacuna in the manuscript, and when the text resumes it is clear that Miskawayh has moved on to a new question. It seems difficult to speculate about the exact question al-Tawḥīdī had posed.

Glossary

Abū Ayyūb al-Anṣārī (d. ca. 52/672) companion of the Prophet and participant in many of the military operations of the early Islamic period.

Abū Bakr (r. 11–13/632–34) the first caliph and Muḥammad's father-in-law.

Abū Bakr Muḥammad ibn Zakariyyā al-Rāzī (d. ca. 313/925 or 323/935) prominent philosopher, physician, and alchemist. His best-known philosophical works include *Spiritual Medicine* (*Kitāb al-ṭibb al-rūḥānī*) and *The Philosophical Life* (*Kitāb al-Sīrah al-falsafiyyah*).

Abū Bishr Mattā ibn Yūnus (d. 328/940) Nestorian Christian who translated and commented on Aristotle's works and played an important role in the translation of Peripatetic philosophy from Syriac into Arabic.

Abū l-Fatḥ ibn al-ʿAmīd (d. 366/976) son of Abū l-Faḍl ibn al-ʿAmīd and one-time vizier of the Buyid emir Rukn al-Dawlah.

Abū Ḥanīfah (d. 150/767) theologian and jurist who founded an eponymous school of law.

Abū Hāshim al-Jubbāʾī (d. 321/933) theologian who was one of the foundational figures of the school of Baṣran Muʿtazilites, best known for his theory of modes or *aḥwāl*.

Abū l-ʿIbar (d. 252/866) a poet and relative of the Abbasid caliphs who was known for composing humorous and frivolous verse.

Abū ʿĪsā l-Warrāq independent Shiʿi thinker and religious skeptic of the third/ninth century, said to have been Ibn al-Rāwandī's teacher, author of well-informed reports and refutations of non-Muslim religions, including Christianity.

Abū Saʿīd al-Ḥaṣīrī Sufi theologian and heresiographer with skeptic tendencies, also referred to in other sources as al-Ḥuṣrī, al-Ḥaḍrī, or even al-Ḥaḍramī.

Abū Tammām (d. 231/845 or 232/846) poet and anthologist who achieved fame during the rule of the caliph al-Muʿtaṣim.

Abū ʿUthmān al-Jāḥiẓ (d. 255/868–69) eminent Muʿtazilite theologian and belletrist from Baṣra whose works inspired many generations of prose writers, including al-Tawḥīdī.

Abū ʿUthmān al-Nahdī (d. ca. 95/714) first-century transmitter of prophetic traditions.

Abū Yūsuf al-Kindī (d. after 256/870) philosopher and scholar who played a paramount role in the reception, translation, and dissemination of Greek philosophical thought and authored multiple works across a broad range of philosophical sciences.

Abū Zayd al-Balkhī (d. 322/934) prolific author of philosophical, scientific, and religious works in the Kindian tradition, possibly a teacher of the philosopher Abū Bakr al-Rāzī.

ʿAlī ibn Abī Ṭālib (d. 41/661) the Prophet's son-in-law and fourth caliph, and the first Imam of the Shiʿah.

Allāt the name of a pre-Islamic goddess, given to many goddesses worshipped in the ancient Near East.

ʿAlwah name given to the beloved in many poems by al-Buḥturī.

ʿĀmir ibn al-Ẓarib sage of the pre-Islamic era.

Aristotle (d. 322) Greek philosopher who authored an influential series of works on logic, ethics, metaphysics, and scientific and other subjects. Many of these works, including the *Organon* and the *Nicomachean Ethics* to which Miskawayh refers in this book, were translated into Arabic during the Abbasid era. Reflecting his stature, many writers refer to him simply as "the Philosopher."

Baghdad capital city of the Abbasid caliphate, founded along the Tigris river in 762 by the second Abbasid caliph, al-Manṣūr. In Tawḥīdī and Miskawayh's day, the capital of the Buyid principality of Iraq, with Rayy (now a suburb of present-day Tehran) being the capital of the principality of the Jibal and Shiraz the capital of Fars.

Bāqil a figure proverbial for a lack of eloquence, often mentioned in the same breath as Saḥbān Wā'il.

Bashshār ibn Burd (d. ca. 167/783) renowned poet of Persian origin of the late Umayyad and early Abbasid period.

Bryson (fl. before the second century CE) obscure neo-Pythagorean philosopher who authored the treatise *Management of the Estate*, which was highly influential for Arabic approaches to economics.

al-Buḥturī (d. 284/897) prominent court poet of the Abbasid era.

Da'd woman's name, given to the beloved in some Arabic poems.

al-Faḍl ibn Yaḥyā (d. 193/808) member of the powerful Barmakid family and eldest son of Yaḥyā ibn Khālid al-Barmakī. He served as vizier to Hārūn al-Rashīd.

Farghānah valley in present-day eastern Uzbekistan and parts of Kyrgyzstan and Tajikistan, surrounded on three sides by the Tianshan Mountains and traversed by the Syr Darya river, which flows out of the western end of the valley to the Aral Sea. In the third/tenth century, it represented a remote eastern outpost of the Muslim world.

Fartanā woman's name, given to the beloved in some Arabic poems.

Galen (d. ca. AD 216) medical writer and physician from Pergamon whose translated works played a critical role for the development of the medical tradition in the Islamic world. Though more limited in extent, his ethical writings (notably the *Peri Ethon*) were also highly influential.

Hārūn al-Rashīd (d. 193/809) fifth ʿAbbasid caliph, whose rule was enmeshed with the Barmakid family and whose court formed a lodestone of poets, scholars, and entertainers.

Hind woman's name, given to the beloved in many Arabic poems.

Ibn al-Khalīl unidentified individual.

Ibn Mujāhid (d. 324/936) religious scholar best known for his role in establishing the seven canonical variants or readings of the Qurʾan.

Ibn al-Rāwandī prominent heterodox figure of the third/ninth century, notorious for his polemics against religious (including Muslim) belief, and his attacks on prophecy, the credibility of miracles, and the compatibility of religious claims with reason.

Ibn Sālim al-Baṣrī, ʿAbd Allāh Muḥammad (d. 297/909) Sufi thinker who was a disciple and companion of Sahl al-Tustarī.

Imruʾ al-Qays (fl. sixth century) renowned pre-Islamic poet who was the author of one of the most famous of the pre-Islamic poems known as the *Suspended Odes* (*al-Muʿallaqāt*).

Isḥāq al-Mawṣilī (d. 235/850) musician, poet, and composer associated with the court of several Abbasid caliphs.

Jābir ibn Ḥayyān (d. ca. 193/812) linchpin figure in the early development of alchemy in the Islamic world and putative (though disputed) author of a vast corpus of alchemical writings.

Jaʿfar ibn Yaḥyā (d. 190/805) member of the powerful Barmakid family and youngest son of Yaḥyā ibn Khālid al-Barmakī, vizier to Hārūn al-Rashīd.

Khālid ibn Yazīd (d. ca. 85/704) Umayyad prince who, according to a disputed tradition, commissioned translations that first introduced alchemy into Arabic culture.

al-Khalīl (d. ca. 175/791) celebrated Baṣran grammarian and lexicographer who laid the foundations for Arabic phonetics and prosody.

Kharijites hardline Islamic sect that arose in the first Islamic century in connection with a dispute about the caliphate and that remained a source of political and theological unrest during the Umayyad period.

Khurasan region comprising present-day northeastern Iran, Afghanistan, and parts of Central Asia.

Luqmān ibn ʿĀd a figure from pre-Islamic times, proverbial for his wisdom.

Mālik ibn Anas (d. 179/796) Medinan jurist who founded an eponymous school of law.

al-Maʾmūn (d. 218/833) seventh Abbasid caliph, whose rule was punctuated by theological upheavals but also by a flowering of intellectual activity, including the large-scale translation of Greek philosophical and scientific texts.

Maʿrūf al-Karkhī (d. 200/815–16) prominent early ascetic and mystic of the Baghdad school.

al-Muraqqish al-aṣghar (fl. sixth century CE) poet from the predominantly Christian town of Ḥīrah in southwestern Iraq.

al-Mutanabbī (d. 354/965) renowned poet and panegyrist who flourished under the patronage of the ruler of Syria, Sayf al-Dawlah.

Muʿtazilites theological school that emerged in the second/eighth century, distinguished by its rationalistic methods and austere emphasis on theological tenets relating to divine unity and justice.

al-Nābighah (fl. sixth century CE) celebrated poet of the pre-Islamic era famous for his panegyrics of the rulers of the predominantly Christian town of Ḥīrah in southwestern Iraq.

The Philosopher *See* Aristotle.

Plato (d. 347) Greek thinker who played a seminal role in the development of ancient philosophy and whose ethical and metaphysical views, especially in their Neoplatonic reworkings, were highly influential in the Islamic world.

Polemon of Laodicea (d. ca. AD 144) politician and intellectual who authored an influential treatise on physiognomy, the science of discerning character from external appearance. The work was translated into Arabic in Abbasid times.

al-Rūdakī (d. ca. 329/940–41) prominent Persian poet who flourished in the first half of the fourth/tenth century.

Saḥbān Wāʾil a figure of proverbial eloquence, often mentioned in the same breath as Bāqil.

Salmā woman's name, given to the beloved in many Arabic poems.

al-Shāfiʿī (d. 204/820) jurist and legal theoretician who founded an eponymous school of law.

Tāhart city in northwest Algeria founded by the Rustamid dynasty in the late second/eighth century.

al-Ṭarmī an obscure poet about whom little is known.

Thābit ibn Qurrah (d. 288/901) eminent mathematician and scientist known both for his original scientific work and his translations of Greek texts.

Bibliography

Abū Dāwūd Sulaymān ibn al-Ash'ath. *Sunan Abī Dāwūd*. Edited by Shu'ayb al-Arna'ūṭ et al. 7 vols. Damascus: Dār al-Risālah al-'Ālamiyyah, 2009.

Adamson, Peter. "The Arabic Sea Battle: Al-Fārābī on the Problem of Future Contingents." *Archiv für Geschichte der Philosophie*, 88 (2006): 163–88.

———. *Al-Kindī*. Oxford: Oxford University Press, 2007.

'Adī ibn Zayd. *Dīwān 'Adī ibn Zayd al-'Ibādī*. Edited by Muḥammad Jabbār al-Mu'aybid. Baghdad: Sharikat Dār al-Jumhūriyyah li-l-Nashr wa-l-Ṭab', 1965.

Amīn, Aḥmad. *Fajr al-Islām*. 3 vols. Cairo: Lajnat al-Ta'līf wa-l-Tarjamah wa-l-Nashr, 1928.

———. *Ḍuḥā al-Islām*. 3 vols. Cairo: Lajnat al-Ta'līf wa-l-Tarjamah wa-l-Nashr, 1936.

———. *Ẓuhr al-Islām*. 4 vols. Cairo: Lajnat al-Ta'līf wa-l-Tarjamah wa-l-Nashr, 1955.

Aristotle. *Manṭiq Arisṭū*. Edited by 'Abd al-Raḥmān Badawī. 3 vols. Kuwait: Wakālat al-Maṭbū'āt; Beirut: Dār al-Qalam, 1980.

———. *Aristotle's Ars Rhetorica: The Arabic Version*. Edited by M. C. Lyons. Cambridge: Pembroke Arabic Texts, 1982.

Arkoun, Mohammed. "Deux épîtres de Miskawayh (mort en 421/1030)." *Bulletin d'études orientales*, 17 (1961–62): 7–74.

———. "L'humanisme arabe au IVe/Xe siècle, d'après le *Kitâb al-Hawâmil wal-Šawâmil*." *Studia Islamica*, 14 (1961): 73–108, and 15 (1961): 63–87.

———. *L'humanisme arabe au IVe/Xe siècle: Miskawayh, philosophe et historien*. Paris: Vrin, 1982.

Daiber, Hans. "Masā'il wa-Adjwiba." *Encyclopaedia of Islam, Second Edition*. Edited by P. Bearman, Th. Bianquis, C. E. Bosworth, E. van Donzel, and W. P. Heinrichs. Brill Online.

El-Bizri, Nader. "Time, Concepts of." In *Medieval Islamic Civilization: An Encyclopedia*, vol. 2, edited by Josef W. Meri, 810–12. New York: Routledge, 2006.

Al-Fārābī, Abū Naṣr. *Kitāb al-Mūsīqā al-kabīr*. Edited by Ghaṭṭās 'Abd al-Malik Khashabah. Cairo: Dār al-Kātib al-'Arabī li-l-Ṭibā'ah wa-l-Nashr, 1967.

———. *Al-Fārābī's Commentary and Short Treatise on Aristotle's De Interpretatione*. Translated by Franz W. Zimmermann. London: Published for the British Academy by Oxford University Press, 1981.

———. *Al-Manṭiq 'inda al-Fārābī*. Edited by Rafīq al-'Ajam. 3 vols. Beirut: Dār al-Mashriq, 1985–87.

———. *Al-Manṭiq 'inda al-Fārābī*. Edited by Mājid Fakhrī. Beirut: Dār al-Mashriq, 1987.

———. *Kitāb al-Ḥurūf*. Edited by Muḥsin Mahdī. 2nd ed. Beirut: Dār al-Mashriq, 1990.

Filius, Lou S. "The Genre *Problemata* in Arabic: Its Motions and Changes." In *Aristotle's* Problemata *in Different Times and Tongues*, edited by Pieter De Leemans and Michèle Goyens, 33–54. Leuven: Leuven University Press, 2006.

———. *La tradition orientale des Problemata Physica.* In *Dictionnaire des philosophes antiques, Supplément*, edited by Richard Goulet with Jean-Marie Flamand and Maroun Aouad, 593–98. Paris: CNRS, 2003.

Galen. *Psychological Writings.* Edited by P. N. Singer and translated by Vivian Nutton, Daniel Davies, and P. N. Singer. Cambridge: Cambridge University Press, 2013.

Ghersetti, Antonella. "The Semiotic Paradigm: Physiognomy and Medicine in Islamic Culture." In *Seeing the Face, Seeing the Soul: Polemon's Physiognomy from Classical Antiquity to Medieval Islam*, edited by Simon Swain, 281–308. Oxford: Oxford University Press, 2007.

Gutas, Dimitri. *Greek Wisdom Literature in Arabic Translation.* New Haven: American Oriental Society, 1975.

Hoyland, Robert. "The Islamic Background to Polemon's Treatise." In *Seeing the Face, Seeing the Soul: Polemon's Physiognomy from Classical Antiquity to Medieval Islam*, edited by Simon Swain, 227–80. Oxford: Oxford University Press, 2007.

Ibn Abī Shaybah, ʿAbd Allāh ibn Muḥammad. *Al-Muṣannaf.* Edited by Muḥammad ʿAwwāmah. 26 vols. Jeddah: Dār al-Qiblah li-l-Thaqāfah al-Islāmiyyah; Damascus: Muʾassasat ʿUlūm al-Qurʾān, 2006.

Ibn Abī Uṣaybiʿah, Aḥmad ibn Qāsim. *ʿUyūn al-anbāʾ fī ṭabaqāt al-aṭibbāʾ.* Edited by August Müller. 2 vols. Frankfurt: Institute for the History of Arabic-Islamic Science, Johann Wolfgang Goethe University. Reprint of 1882 Cairo edition.

Ibn Ḥanbal, Aḥmad ibn Muḥammad. *Musnad al-Imām Aḥmad ibn Ḥanbal.* Edited by Shuʿayb al-Arnaʾūṭ et al. 50 vols. Beirut: Muʾassasat al-Risālah, 1993–2001.

Ibn Manẓūr, Muḥammad ibn Mukarram. *Lisān al-ʿarab.* 15 vols. Beirut: Dār Ṣādir, 1997.

Ibn al-Nadīm, Muḥammad ibn Isḥāq. *Al-Fihrist.* Edited by Riḍā Tajaddud. Tehran: Maṭbaʿat Dānishgāh, 1971.

Ibn al-Rūmī, Abū-l-Ḥusayn ʿAlī. *Dīwān Ibn al-Rūmī.* Edited by Ḥusayn Naṣṣār. 6 vols. 3rd ed. Cairo: Maṭbaʿat Dār al-Kutub wa-l-Wathāʾiq al-Qawmiyyah, 2003.

Irwin, Robert. *The Penguin Anthology of Classical Arabic Literature.* London: Penguin, 2006.

Al-Iṣfahānī, Abū l-Faraj. *Maqātil al-ṭālibiyyīn.* Edited by Aḥmad Ṣaqr. Cairo: Dār Iḥyāʾ al-Kutub al-ʿArabiyyah, 1949.

———. *Kitāb al-Aghānī.* Edited by Iḥsān ʿAbbās, Ibrāhīm al-Saʿāfīn, and Bakr ʿAbbās. 25 vols. 3rd ed. Beirut: Dār Ṣādir, 2008.

Al-Jāḥiẓ, Abū ʿUthmān. *Al-Tarbīʿ wa-l-tadwīr.* Edited by Charles Pellat. Damascus: Institut Français de Damas, 1955.

Jarīr ibn ʿAṭiyyah. *Dīwān Jarīr*. Edited by Nuʿmān Muḥammad Amīn Ṭāhā. 2 vols. Cairo: Dār al-Maʿārif, 1969–71.

Jones, Alan. *Early Arabic Poetry*. 2 vols. Reading: Ithaca Press, 1992–96.

Al-Kindi, Abū Isḥāq. *Risālat al-Kindī fī l-luḥūn wa-l-nagham*. Edited by Zakariyyā Yūsuf. Baghdad: Maṭbaʿat Shafīq, 1965.

Kraemer, Joel L. *Humanism in the Renaissance of Islam: The Cultural Revival during the Buyid Age*. Leiden: Brill, 1992.

Al-Masʿūdī, Abū-l-Ḥasan. *Murūj al-dhahab wa-maʿādin al-jawhar*. Edited by Charles Pellat. 7 vols. Beirut: al-Jāmiʿah al-Lubnāniyyah, 1966–79.

Al-Maydānī, Aḥmad ibn Muḥammad. *Majmaʿ al-amthāl*. Edited by Muḥammad Muḥyī l-Dīn ʿAbd al-Ḥamīd. 2 vols. Cairo: Maṭbaʿat al-Sunnah al-Muḥammadiyyah, 1955.

Mez, Adam. *Die Renaissance des Islams*. Heidelberg: Carl Winter, 1922.

Miskawayh, Abū ʿAlī. *Tahdhīb al-akhlāq*. Edited by Constantine Zurayk. Beirut: American University of Beirut, 1966.

———. *Al-Fawz al-aṣghar*. Beirut: n.p., 1319 AH [1901].

———. *An Unpublished Treatise of Miskawaih on Justice*. Edited by M. S. Khan. Leiden: Brill, 1964.

Montgomery, James E. "Al-Ǧāḥiẓ and Hellenizing Philosophy." In *The Libraries of the Neoplatonists*, edited by Cristina d'Ancona, 443–56. Leiden: Brill, 2007.

Mufaḍḍal ibn Muḥammad. *Al-Mufaḍḍaliyyāt*. Edited by Aḥmad Muḥammad Shākir and ʿAbd al-Salām Muḥammad Hārūn. 6th ed. Cairo: Dār al-Maʿārif, 1979.

Muhanna, Elias. "The Scattered and the Gathered: Abū Ḥayyān al-Tawḥīdī's Infrequently Asked Questions." In *Essays in Islamic Philology, History, and Philosophy*, edited by Alireza Korangy, Wheeler M. Thackston, Roy P. Mottahedeh, and William Granara, 248–80. Berlin: De Gruyter, 2016.

Al-Mutanabbī, Abū l-Ṭayyib. *Dīwān al-Mutanabbī*. Beirut: Dār Bayrūt, 1983.

Naaman, Erez. *Literature and the Islamic Court: Cultural Life under al-Ṣāḥib Ibn ʿAbbād*. London; New York: Routledge, 2016.

Pines, Shlomo. "A Tenth Century Philosophical Correspondence." *Proceedings of the American Academy for Jewish Research*, 24 (1955): 103–36.

Pomerantz, Maurice A. "An Epic Hero in the *Maqāmāt*?: Popular and Elite Literature in the 8th/14th Century," *Annales Islamologiques* 49 (2015): 99–114.

Al-Rāzī, Abū Bakr. *Rasāʾil falsafiyya*. Edited by Paul Kraus. Cairo: Jāmiʿat Fuʾād al-Awwal, Kullīyyat al-Ādāb, 1939.

Al-Ṣafadī, Ṣalāḥ al-Dīn ibn Aybak. *Al-Wāfī bi-l-wafayāt*. 30 vols. Beirut; Wiesbaden; Berlin: Franz Steiner; Klaus Schwarz, 1931–2010.

Ṣaqr, Sayyid Aḥmad. *Sharḥ dīwān ʿAlqamat al-faḥl*. Cairo: al-Maṭbaʿah al-Maḥmūdiyyah, 1935.

Sayyid, Ayman Fu'ād. "Les marques de possession sur les manuscrits et la reconstitution des anciens fonds de manuscrits arabes." *Manuscripta Orientalia* 9 (2003): 14–23.

Al-Sijistānī, Abū Sulaymān. *Muntakhab Ṣiwān al-ḥikmah wa-thalāth rasā'il.* Edited by ʿAbd al-Raḥmān Badawī. Tehran: Bunyād-i Farhang-i Īrān, 1974.

Simplicius. *On Aristotle Categories 1–4.* Translated by Michael Chase. Ithaca, NY: Cornell University Press, 2003.

Stoetzer, W. "Ziḥāf." In *Encyclopedia of Islam, Second Edition.* Edited by P. Bearman, Th. Bianquis, C. E. Bosworth, E. van Donzel, W. P. Heinrichs. Brill Online.

Al-Suyūṭī, Jalāl al-Dīn. *Al-Muzhir fī ʿulūm al-lughah wa-anwāʿihā.* Edited by Muḥammad Aḥmad Jād al-Mawlā, Muḥammad Abū l-Faḍl Ibrāhīm, and ʿAlī Muḥammad al-Bajāwī. 2 vols. Saida: al-Maktabah al-ʿAṣrīyyah, 1986.

Swain, Simon, ed. *Seeing the Face, Seeing the Soul: Polemon's Physiognomy from Classical Antiquity to Medieval Islam.* Oxford: Oxford University Press, 2007.

Swain, Simon. *Economy, Family, and Society from Rome to Islam: A Critical Edition, English Translation, and Study of Bryson's Management of the Estate.* Cambridge: Cambridge University Press, 2013.

Swanton, Christine. *Virtue Ethics: A Pluralistic View.* Oxford: Oxford University Press, 2003.

Talib, Adam. "Caricature and Obscenity in *Mujūn* Poetry and African-American Women's Hip Hop." In *The Rude, the Bad and the Bawdy : Essays in Honour of Professor Geert Jan van Gelder.* Edited by Adam Talib, Marlé Hammond, and Arie Schippers, 276–98. Cambridge: E. J. W. Gibb Memorial Trust, 2014.

Al-Tawḥīdī, Abū Ḥayyan. *Al-Imtāʿ wa-l-mu'ānasah.* Edited by Aḥmad Amīn and Aḥmad al-Zayn. 3 vols. Cairo: Lajnat al-Ta'līf wa-l-Tarjamah wa-l-Nashr, 1939–44.

———. *Al-Baṣā'ir wa-l-dhakhā'ir.* Edited by Wadād al-Qāḍī. 10 vols. Beirut: Dār Ṣādir, 1988.

Al-Tawḥīdī, Abū Ḥayyan, and Abū ʿAlī Miskawayh. *Al-Hawāmil wa-l-shawāmil.* Edited by Aḥmad Amīn and al-Sayyid Aḥmad Ṣaqr. Cairo: Lajnat al-Ta'līf wa-l-Tarjamah wa-l-Nashr, 1951.

———. *Il libro dei cammelli errabondi e di quelli che li radunano.* Translated by Lidia Bettini. Venice: Ca' Foscari, 2017.

Wakelnig, Elvira, ed. and trans. *A Philosophy Reader from the Circle of Miskawayh.* Cambridge: Cambridge University Press, 2014.

Yāqūt ibn ʿAbd Allāh al-Ḥamawī. *Muʿjam al-udabā': Irshād al-arīb ilā maʿrifat al-adīb.* Edited by Iḥsān ʿAbbās. 7 vols. Beirut: Dār al-Gharb al-Islāmī, 1993.

Further Reading

ʿAbbās, Iḥsān. *Abū Ḥayyān al-Tawḥīdī.* Beirut: Dār Bayrūt, 1956.

Bergé, Marc. *Pour un humanisme vécu: Essai sur la personnalité morale et intellectuelle d'Abū Ḥayyān al-Tawḥīdī.* Damascus: Institut francais de Damas, 1979.

———. "Abū Ḥayyān al-Tawḥīdī." In *ʿAbbāsid Belles-Lettres*, edited by Julia Ashtiany, T. M. Johnstone, J. D. Latham, R. B. Serjeant, and G. Rex Smith, 112–24. Cambridge: Cambridge University Press, 1990.

Endress, Gerhard. "The Integration of Philosophical Traditions in Islamic Society in the 4th/10th Century: Tawḥīdī and al-Siǧistānī." In *Philosophy in the Islamic World, Vol. 1: 8th–10th Centuries*, translated by Rotraud Hansberger, edited by Ulrich Rudolph, Rotraud Hansberger, and Peter Adamson, 272–304. Leiden: Brill, 2017.

———. "Ancient Ethical Traditions for Islamic Society: Abū ʿAlī Miskawayh." In *Philosophy in the Islamic World, Vol. 1: 8th–10th Centuries*, translated by Rotraud Hansberger, edited by Ulrich Rudolph, Rotraud Hansberger, and Peter Adamson, 304–44. Leiden: Brill, 2017.

Fakhry, Majid. "Aḥmad ibn Muḥammad Miskawayh (d. 1030), Chief Moral Philosopher of Islam." In *Ethical Theories in Islam.* 2nd ed. Leiden: Brill, 1994.

Al-Kīlānī, Ibrāhīm. *Abū Ḥayyān al-Tawḥīdī.* Cairo: Dār al-Maʿārif, 1957.

Kraemer, Joel L. *Philosophy in the Renaissance of Islam.* Leiden: Brill, 1986.

Leaman, Oliver. "Islamic Humanism in the Fourth/Tenth Century." In *History of Islamic Philosophy*, edited by Seyyed Hossein Nasr and Oliver Leaman, 155–61. London: Routledge, 1996.

———. "Ibn Miskawayh." In *History of Islamic Philosophy*, edited by Seyyed Hossein Nasr and Oliver Leaman, 252–57. London: Routledge, 1996.

Rowson, Everett K. "The Philosopher as Litterateur: Al-Tawḥīdī and His Predecessors." *Zeitschrift für Geschichte der arabisch-islamischen Wissenschaften*, 6 (1990): 50–92.

Stern, Samuel M. "Abū Ḥayyān al-Tawḥīdī." In *Encyclopaedia of Islam, Second Edition.* Edited by P. Bearman, Th. Bianquis, C. E. Bosworth, E. van Donzel, and W. P. Heinrichs. Brill Online.

ʿUmar, Fāʾiz Ṭāhā. *Al-Ẓamaʾ: Dirāsah fī asʾilat al-Tawḥīdī, al-Ḥawāmil.* Baghdad: Dār al-Shuʾūn al-Thaqāfiyyah al-ʿĀmmah, 2007.

Index

ʿAbbād ibn Sulaymān, 296n27
Abū ʿAlī Miskawayh. *See* Miskawayh
Abū Ayyūb al-Anṣārī, §83.1
Abū Bakr, §83.1
Abū Bakr Muḥammad ibn Zakariyyā al-Rāzī. *See* Muḥammad ibn Zakariyyā al-Rāzī
Abū Bishr Mattā ibn Yūnus, §114.1, 296n25
Abū Ḥanīfah, §153.5
Abū Ḥayyān al-Tawḥīdī, §121.1, 295n8, 296n23, 296n25, 297n38, 298n56
Abū l-ʿIbar, §123.1
Abū ʿĪsā al-Warrāq, §88.1
Abū Saʿīd al-Ḥaṣīrī, §88.1
Abū Sulaymān al-Sijistānī, 298n48
Abū Tammām, §123.2, §142.2, 296n19
Abū ʿUthmān al-Jāḥiẓ. *See* al-Jāḥiẓ
Abū ʿUthmān al-Nahdī, §94.1
Abū Yūsuf al-Kindī. *See* al-Kindī
Abū Zayd al-Balkhī, §127.1, §149.1
ʿādah. *See* custom, habit
affectation, §67.2
age, §75.3, §91.1, §96.1, §135.1, §175.2
Aḥmad ibn ʿAbd al-Wahhāb, §§148.1–2, §150.1, §152.1, 297n46
alchemy, §§151.1–3
ʿĀmir ibn al-Ẓarib, §113.1
anatomy, §100.2
angels, §90.2, §92.3, §163.3; proof of existence, §§172.1–3
anger (*ghaḍab*), §71.2, §84.2, §85.2, §93.4, §§95.2–3, §107.2, §§117.1–2, §134.1, §136.1
anxiety, §§70.1–2, §85.2; reason why people with shameful secrets experience, §104.1; reason why people respond differently to, §121.1
apparition (*ṭayf*), §§140.1–2
appetite(s) (*shahwah*), §71.2, §79.2, §79.4, §85.2, §88.7, §92.4, §95.2, §95.4, §96.3, §138.1, §143.2, §151.2, §153.1, §154.1
Arabs, §83.4, §86.1, §107.1, §113.1, §§115.1–2, §§124.2–3, §134.1, §158.1, §158.4
Aristotle, §66.4, §70.2, §131.2, §159.3, 295n1, 295n3, 296n27, 297n36, 297n39
arithmetic, §147.4, §153.5
arrogance, §134.1; why the devout are susceptible to, §136.2
ascetics, §103.2, §103.4
astrology, §158.3
augury, §83.1, §83.4, §158.4
avarice, §137.3

beauty, §75.1, §75.3, §103.5; reason why the imagination cannot represent the highest, §§98.1–3
black bile (*sawdāʾ*), §87.2, §121.3
black people, §87.1
blind desire(s), §78.2, §84.2, §128.3, §143.2, §151.4, §153.1
brain, §§72.1–2, §79.2, §86.3, §100.2, §139.2, §140.2
al-Buḥturī, §123.1
buildings, reason why they fall to ruin when uninhabited, §§110.1–2
Byzantines, §81.2, §86.1

cause, §67.2, §70.2, §71.2, §80.2, §81.2, §82.2, §83.3, §§85.2–3, §87.2, §90.2, §90.4, §90.9, §91.1, §93.2, §93.4, §94.1, §96.2, §98.2, §104.2, §§110.1–2, §112.1, §112.3, §113.1, §§115.1–2, §119.1, §129.2, §130.1, §130.3, §131.1, §134.2, §136.1, §§145.1–2, §147.2, §155.2, §158.2, §§159.2–3, §§161.1–2, §165.2, §170.2, §§174.2–3; whether God created the world for a, §122.2, §§133.1–2
celestial sphere (*falak*), §68.2, §86.3, §91.1, §118.2, §158.3, §165.2, §167.2, §170.2, §173.2
certainty, §83.1, §§128.1–2, §130.3, §131.1, §145.3, §151.1, §175.2
character trait(s) (*khuluq*), §78.2, §85.2, §86.3, §111.2, §141.2, §156.2, §78.2
character, §71.2, §75.2, §78.2, §§86.2–3, §153.1, §156.3, §164.3; influence of companions on, §66.1–4
chess, §88.3, §§119.1–2, §121.2
choice (*ikhtiyār*), §67.1, §73.2, §74.1, §74.3, §§88.8–9, §§90.1–3, §§90.6–10, §94.3, §104.2, §126.2, §134.1, §154.2, §158.4, §163.2
coincidence, §89.1; and the concept of possibility, §131.1
common sense (*al-ḥiss al-mushtarak*), §169.2
compulsion (*jabr*), §83.1, §§90.1–2, §§90.7–9
constitutive difference (*faṣl muqawwim*), §133.2
courage, §70.2, §80.1, §§87.3–4, §95.3, §107.3, §119.2
cowardice, §70.2
craft(s) (*ṣināʿah*), §83.2, §93.3, §103.5, §116.2, §116.4, §119.2, §124.3, §132.2, §148.2, §151.3, §§154.2–3, §158.3, §162.3, §162.5
custom (*ʿādah*), §67.2, §81.2, §120.3, §§147.2–3, §§147.6–8, §153.4

death, §74.1, §74.3, §85.3, §93.4, §§96.1–2, §99.2, §107.1, §109.2, §147.3, §147.5, §147.7, §153.1, §156.2
declarations of pedigree, purpose of, §107.1, §107.3
defect(s) (*radhīlah*), §70.2, §83.4, §95.4, §124.3, §136.2
definition (*ḥadd*), §169.2
delegation (divine) (*tafwīḍ*), §90.9
deliberation (*rawiyyah*), §90.6, §90.10, §94.3, §126.2, §153.5
demonstration (*burhān*), §130.3, §132.2
description (*rasm*), §162.4
dialectical theologian, §69.1, §§114.1–2, §130.1, §131.1, §151.3, §153.2, §§160.1–2, §173.2
disposition (*hay'ah*), §70.1, §77.2, §80.2, §81.2, §83.4, §111.2, §123.1, §124.3, §136.2, §141.2, §143.2, §§147.2–3, §147.8, §151.1, §153.5
divination, §§83.1–2, §§158.1–4
dreams, §140.2, §169.2

East Africans, §87.3
elemental mixture (*mīzāj*), §73.2, §78.2, §80.2
elements, natural (*arkān*, *ʿanāṣir*, *usṭuqusāt*), §66.2, §§68.1–2, §68.4, §74.2, §82.2, §§86.2–3, §90.3, §§90.7–10, §91.2, §92.3, §93.1, §§96.3–4, §98.3,

elements, natural (cont.), §103.3, §108.2, §112.2, §113.2, §116.2, §117.2, §122.2, §124.3, §133.2, §134.1, §143.1, §150.3, §158.3, §162.4, §164.3, §166.2, §167.2, §171.2, §173.2
eloquence, §88.2, §§126.1–2
embarrassment, §144.1, §§145.2–3
eminence, §75.2, §78.1, §105.2; reason for human love of, §§79.1–4
envy, §75.2
ethical trait or characteristic (*khuluq*), §85.2, §§95.2–3, §107.1
ethically good, 295n6; nature of and relation to religious Law, §§147.1–3, §§147.5–8; reason for unbelievers' performance of what is, §§77.1–2; reason why people heed preachers acting so, §105.2
excellence (*faḍīlah*), §67.1, §68.2, §81.2, §82.2, §88.2, §106.1, §124.1, §137.3, §153.2, §154.2, §162.5, §§172.2–3. *See also* virtue

facial hair, as an indication of character, §§73.1–2
al-Faḍl ibn Yaḥyā, §137.1
fame, §67.2
familiarity, §97.2
fancy (*wahm*), §140.2, §146.2, §164.3
fear, §77.1, §98.1, §99.2, §100.0, §103.4, §136.2, §138.2, §144.2, §§145.2–3, §162.5; of death, §74.3; why it is experienced in the absence of anything fearful, §§70.1–2
form(s) (*ṣūrah*), §§66.2–4, §§68.2–4, §71.2, §§75.2–3, §81.2, §83.1, §84.2, §85.3, §86.3, §88.1, §§88.5–10, §§90.3–4,
forms (cont.), §90.8, §91.3, §§92.2–4, §93.2, §97.3, §§98.1–3, §101.2, §102.2, §103.5, §§108.2–3, §114.2, §§116.1–2, §121.4, §123.2, §124.3, §§130.2–3, §132.2, §§135.1–2, §137.3, §139.3, §§140.1–2, §141.1, §142.2, §145.2, §150.2, §154.2, §§156.2–3, §158.2, §158.4, §§159.2–3, §§162.4–5, §§163.3–4, §164.2, §166.2, §169.2, §175.2; to acquire a (*taṣawwara*), §67.2, §§160.2–3
friend(s), §74.3, §88.3, §90.4, §113.1, §120.3, §172.3; reason for difficulty of forming, §§76.1–2
friendship, §113.1
future, §83.2, §153.3, §§158.2–3, 295n6, 297n39; truth value of statements concerning the, §131.2

Galen, §71.2, §86.2, §87.2, §116.2, §175.2, 295n4, 296n20
generosity, §88.9, §§122.2–3, §137.3
genus (*jins*), §133.2, §142.2, §170.2
geometry, §75.3, §144.2, §147.4, §153.5
gluttony, §91.4
God, §71.2, §§77.1–2, §§88.1–2, §88.9, §§90.9–10, §92.3, §94.1, §94.4, §102.2, §115.2, §134.1, §136.1, §150.2, §151.3, §153.1, §§153.3–4, §§172.2–3, §173.2; application of attributes and linguistic terms to, §§122.1–3, 296n29, 296n31; God-fearing, §81.1, §153.1; law handed down by, §§147.1–2; names and attributes of, §69.1; whether He perceived the world during its non-existence, §139.1, §139.3; whether He created the world for a cause, §122.2, §§133.1–2

grammar, §124.3, §144.2; analogical reasoning and, §114.2, §132.1
great-spirited, §141.2
greed, §91.4; greedy, §137.3
grief, §85.2, §93.4, §§99.1–2, §121.1, §§155.2–3; reason why intelligent people experience greater, §§87.1–2

habit (*ʿādah*), §71.2, §79.3, §86.3, §§120.3–4, §121.4, §123.1, §156.1, §156.3
Hārūn al-Rashīd. *See* al-Rashīd
heart, §70.1, §71.2, §72.2, §74.1, §79.2, §86.3, §§87.3–4, §88.1, §93.4, §98.1, §99.2, §§105.1–2, §112.1, §115.1, §121.1, §128.2, §140.1, §147.7, §§155.2–3, §156.2, 296n25
home(s), §91.1, §91.4, §95.1 §137.1; reason for intensification of longing for upon approach of, §112.1
honor, §75.1, §79.2, §79.4, §81.2, §84.2, §92.4, §106.1, §107.2, §137.3, §138.2, §154.2; love of, §136.2, §§137.3–5; reason why all people do not command the same degree of, §§82.1–2; reason why it derives from forebears rather than offspring, §80.1; why some people eschew, §§141.1–2
hope, §76.1, §82.2, §§83.3–4, §88.3, §107.3, §137.2, §147.1, §151.1, §151.4; relation to wishing and anticipation, §§94.1–4
human beings, §66.2, §70.2, §71.2, §74.2, §85.2, §90.2, §90.4, §90.7, §90.10, §93.2, §95.4, §96.3, §98.1, §104.2, §116.1, §§118.1–2, §125.2, §150.2, §153.3, §163.3, §167.2, §172.3; nature of, §68.1, §68.4, §77.2, §§79.3–4, §§83.2–3, §95.2, §§102.1–2, §103.2, §107.2, §117.2, §123.2,
human being(s), nature of (cont.), §141.2, §§143.1–2, §144.2, §147.2, §162.2; reasons for upright posture of, §127.1; specific perfection of, §§88.5–10, §91.3, §§92.2–4, §150.2
humoral mixture (*mīzāj*), §70.2, §74.1, §§87.1–2, §91.2, §93.4, §94.2, §96.2, §98.2, §99.2, §111.2, §121.3, §154.3, §163.2, §164.3

Ibn al-ʿAmīd, §162.1
Ibn al-Khalīl, §99.1
Ibn Mujāhid, §88.2
Ibn al-Rāwandī, §88.1
Ibn Sālim al-Baṣrī, ʿAbd Allāh Muḥammad, §139.1, 297n42
Ibn Sīnā. *See* Avicenna
imagination (*khayāl, wahm*), §97.3, §§98.1–3, §119.2, §120.1, §122.2, §139.2, §140.2, §146.2, §§160.2–3, §§164.2–3, §169.2, §175.2
Imruʾ al-Qays, §88.10
Indians, §81.2, §86.1
injustice, §74.3, §75.2, §81.2, §162.5
innate heat (*ḥarārah gharīziyyah*), §86.2, §§87.3–4, §96.4
intellect(s) (*ʿaql*), §66.4, §68.3, §98.1, §§113.1–2, §139.2, §145.1, §163.3, §164.2, §172.2
intermediaries, §173.2
interpretive effort (*ijtihād*), §§153.3–6
Isḥāq al-Mawṣilī, §§137.1–3, 296n24

Jābir ibn Ḥayyān, §151.1
Jaʿfar ibn Yaḥyā, §§137.1–3, 297n41
al-Jāḥiẓ, §86.1, §148.1, §150.1, §152.1, 297n46
jealousy, §85.2, §§95.1–4

joy, §§87.1–2, §93.4, §100.1, §112.1, §137.4, §§155.2–3; reason for violent effect of sudden, §§99.1–2

jurists, §130.1; reason for disagreements among, §§153.1–3, §153.5

justice, §88.2, §98.1, §103.2, §151.4, §153.4, §154.2

Khālid ibn Yazīd, §151.1

al-Kindī, Abū Yūsuf, §151.3, 298n47

king(s), §121.3, §§138.1–2; reason why people respond to moral character of, §154.1, §154.3

knowledge, §§75.2–3, §79.2, §83.2, §88.8, §90.10, §91.3, §95.1, §97.2, §98.1, §102.3, §103.5, §105.2, §107.1, §§114.1–2, §115.1, §119.2, §121.1, §121.4, §122.1, §122.3, §124.2, §125.2, §128.2, §§130.2–3, §139.3, §146.2, §147.1, §153.2, §153.6, §154.1, §§158.2–3, §160.3, §161.2; benefit of and reason for human desire of, §§92.1–2, §92.4; four aspects of, §159.3, §170.2; possibility of human beings encompassing all forms of, §§116.1–3

language, §83.3, §88.1, §115.1, §§116.1–2, §120.2, §152.2, 296n27

laughter, §107.2, §175.2, §136.1; reason for contagiousness of, §101.1; reason for intensity when not exhibited by the one who provokes it, §§129.1–2; reason why some people become a standing object of, §78.1

letters of the alphabet, §83.4, §93.2, §120.2, §120.4

lightning, §§174.1–3

likenesses, reason for human love of, §§97.1–3

liver, §79.2, §86.3

logic, §114.1, §131.2, §131.2, 296n25; Book on, §128.2

luck, §85.3

Luqmān ibn ʿĀd, §83.4

lying, §67.2, §147.7, §§156.1–4

Mālik ibn Anas, §153.5

al-Maʾmūn, §119.1

matter, prime (*hayūlā*, *māddah*), §§66.2–4, §68.4, §90.3, §90.7, §90.9, §93.2, §§98.2–3, §§102.2–3, §107.3, §§108.2–3, §113.2, §127.2, §131.2, §140.2, §144.2, §146.2, §150.3, §160.3, §164.2, §170.2, §172.2, §175.2

medicine, §68.4, §116.2, §155.3, §161.2, §162.2

melancholy (*mīlākhūliyyā*), §87.2, §120.3

memory (*dhikr*, *tadhakkur*), §164.2

merit, §67.2, §88.7, §88.9, §137.4, §§141.1–2, §154.1. *See also* virtue

meter (poetic), §§124.1–3, §142.2

misfortune, §147.7, §151.2; reason for comforting effect of others' sharing in one's, §85.1, §85.3

Miskawayh, Abū ʿAlī, 295n1, 295n4, 295n9, 296n20, 296n23, 297n36, 297n39, 298n47, 298n48, 298n49, 298n56

mixture (*mizāj*), §68.2, §78.2, §§79.2–3, §83.4, §§86.2–3, §§87.3–4, §93.3, §94.2, §96.2, §98.3, §100.2, §§108.2–3, §155.3; melancholy (*sawdāwī*), §87.2, §155.3; sanguine (*damawī*), §87.2, §155.3. *See also* elemental mixture; humoral mixture

mīzāj. *See* elemental mixture, humoral mixture, mixture
money, §92.4, §109.1, §137.4, §153.1; blood money, §147.1, §147.8, §157.1; evolution of, §§162.1–6
mountains, §124.2, §167.3; purpose of, §§165.1–4
Muḥammad, §82.1, §83.1, §83.3, §176.1, 296n26
Muḥammad ibn Zakariyyā al-Rāzī, §68.2, §151.3, 298n47
al-Muraqqish al-aṣghar, §124.2
music, §§93.3–4, §124.2; reason for human response to, §155.1
Muʿtazilites, 296n29

al-Nābighah al-Dhubyānī, 295n12
names, §68.4, §69.1, §§83.3–4, §91.4, §95.4, §114.2, §§115.1–2, §122.1, §141.1, §152.2, §160.1, §167.3; reason for people's attachment to their own, §§120.1–2, §120.4; reason why people like some and hate other, §93.2
nations, §83.4, §87.2, §158.4; relative excellence of different, §86.1, §86.3
natural constitution (*fiṭrah*), §77.2, §123.2
natural disposition (*ṭabʿ*), §82.1, §83.4, §124.3, §141.2, §143.2, §§147.2–3, §148.2
natural elements (*ṭabāʾiʿ*), §96.3
nature (ṭabīʿah), §§66.2–3, §§68.2–3, §70.2, §71.2, §78.2, §§79.1–2, §§83.2–3, §85.3, §90.2, §90.6, §92.1, §94.2, §§98.1–2, §102.3, §103.2, §104.2, §111.1, §112.2, §113.2, §118.2, §§120.1–3, §121.1, §§124.1–3, §128.3, §131.2, §141.2, §§147.2–4, §150.3, §§151.2–4, §153.2, §154.2, §158.3, §163.3, §166.3, §168.2, §170.2, §171.2,
nature (cont.), §172.2, §173.2, 295n5
nerves, §§100.2–3, §139.2
nonexistent, §§74.1–2, §139.1, §141.1, §§160.1–3, 297n43

old, §96.1; why some things are better when they are, §135.1
old people, §91.1, §96.1, §175.2; reason for greater propensity to hope, §§94.1–2, §94.4; reason for people's varying reactions when addressed as, §§84.1–2
orphan, role of fathers versus mothers in becoming an, §§118.1–2

pain, §84.1, §109.2, §§134.1–2, §141.2, §143.2, §150.2; justification of children's and animals', §173.1; reason why well-being is experienced less acutely than, §§100.1–3
passion (*infiʿāl*), §70.2, §§102.1–3, §107.3, §§113.1–2, §§140.1–2
passive effect (*infiʿāl*), §93.2, §139.3
past, §107.1, §158.2
patronymics, 296n26; reason for people's attachment to their own, §120.1
perception, §83.4, §90.1, §97.3, §169.1, §174.2; intellectual versus sensory, §§139.2–3
Persians, §81.2, §86.1, §130.2
philosophy, §68.3, §74.2, §100.4, §116.2, §116.4
physiognomy, §73.2, §78.2
place, §66.4, §112.2, §129.2, §167.2
pleasure, §79.2, §84.2, §§88.6–9, §92.4, §109.2, §§137.3–4, §151.2, §154.1; malicious, §134.1; nature of, §134.2

plants, §§88.6–7, §90.2, §§92.2–3, §102.2, §127.2, §137.4, §158.3, §163.3, §§165.2–4, §166.2, §167.2; reason why they are not generated inside animals, §§150.1–3

Plato, §66.4, §79.4, 296n27

poetry, §121.4, §§124.1–3, §142.2, §144.2; Early Arabic, 296n33

political association (*madaniyyah*), §103.2, §162.4

power (*quwwah*), §70.2, §71.2, §78.2, §79.3, §81.1, §90.4, §§90.9–10, §92.4, §93.3, §§96.3–4, §103.2, §106.1, §107.2, §108.2, §113.2, §119.1, §122.1, §122.3, §141.2, §145.3, §147.6, §150.2, §151.3, §154.3, §156.2, §158.2, §160.3, §164.3, §166.3, §169.2; appetitive (*quwwah shahwiyyah*), §90.4, §95.4, §154.2; beastly, §79.2, §79.4; deliberative, §119.2; desiderative (*quwwah nizāʿiyyah*), §91.2, §91.4; "divine," §79.2, §79.4, §123.2, §139.2, §162.2; of imagination, imaginative (*quwwat al-khayāl, al-quwwah al-mutakhayyilah*), §98.1, §140.2, §§164.2–3, §169.2; irascible (*quwwah ghaḍabiyyah*), §79.2, §79.4, §90.4, §95.3, §§107.2–3, §154.2; of memory (*quwwat al-dhikr, al-quwwah al-dhākirah*), §164.2; rational (*quwwa nāṭiqah*), §79.2, §90.4, §92.2, §94.2

praise, §75.1, §95.1, §95.4

preachers, reason why we are more likely to heed those who practice what they preach, §§105.1–2; reason why they become tongue-tied, §144.1; reason why one shares their embarrassment, §§145.1–3

pride, §79.2, §81.2, §107.1, §107.3, §136.1, §137.3

prohibitions, §121.1; reason for oppressiveness of, §§143.1–2

prophet(s), prophecy, §67.2, §81.2, §102.3, §128.3, §134.1, §151.3, §158.2

proportional relation (*nisbah*), §§93.2–3, §124.2

prose, merit compared with poetry, §§142.1–2

prosody (*ʿarūḍ*), §124.1, §124.3

Qur'an, §153.3, §153.6, §172.2

al-Rashīd, Hārūn, §137.1, 297n41

reason (*ʿaql*), §71.2, §74.1, §74.3, §79.4, §80.2, §82.1, §88.5, §§88.7–9, §90.1, §90.10, §91.3, §97.3, §103.4, §§121.2–3, §122.3, §123.2, §128.3, §130.2, §139.2, §141.2, §172.2, §173.1; ethical principles and content of, §§77.1–2, §§147.1–8; people possessed of, §67.1, §136.2, §139.3, §154.1, §162.2. *See also* power, "divine"

religious Law, §74.3, §78.2, §83.1, §121.2, §122.3, §153.2, §154.2; possibility of conflicting with reason, §§147.1–8; relation to natural disposition, §77.2; relation of reason-based moral principles to religious commands, §§77.1–2

reticence, reason for prevalence in king's entourage, §§138.1–2

rhetoric, §124.3; rhetorical, §86.2, §113.2, 297n36

ruling, §95.2, §145.1, §§147.3–5; whether rare instances attract a, §§130.1–3, §132.2; reason for conflicts between legal rulings, §153.1, §§153.3–6

sea, §70.2, §79.4, §103.3, §115.1, §137.2, §165.3, 297n39; reason for its location, §167.1, §167.3, 298n53; reason for saltiness of its water, §168.1
secret(s), §67.1, §77.1, §85.1, §92.1, §99.1, §118.1, §125.1, §130.1, §134.1, §135.1, §141.1, §145.1; divulgence of, §138.2
self-love, §75.2
sensory perception, visual versus imaginary, §139.2
shame, §94.1, §104.1, §§145.1–3
al-Shāfiʿī, §153.5
short people, character of, §73.1
singing, §78.1, §155.1
sleep, §101.2, §121.2, §§140.1–2, §169.1
small-headed people, §72.1
snow, §110.2, §§165.2–3; why it does not come in summer, §§171.1–2
soul (*nafs*), §§66.1–2, §77.1, §78.2, §§85.1–2, §92.1, §93.2, §94.2, §98.1, §103.5, §109.2, §§112.1–2, §120.1, §121.2, §121.4, §124.2, §125.2, §136.2, §140.2, §145.2, §149.1, §151.2, §151.4, §153.5, §154.1, §§156.2–3, §158.2, §158.4, §160.3, §161.2, 295n4; animal, §150.2, §163.3, §166.2; beastly (*nafs bahīmiyyah*), §71.2, §79.4, §90.2, §137.4; essential motion of, § 149.2, §155.3; essential oneness of, §101.2, §145.2, §166.2; growing (*nafs nāmiyah*), §163.3; irascible (*nafs ghaḍabiyyah*), §79.4, §137.4; love of one's own, §70.2, §§75.2–3;
soul (cont.), nature of, §§66.2–4, §§83.3–4, §86.2, §§93.2–4, §94.2, §97.3, §99.2, §104.2, §§107.2–3, §111.2, §118.2, §144.2, §145.3, §146.2, §154.2, §155.2, §172.2; objective of, §§68.1–4, §111.1, §159.3, §161.2; rational (*nafs nāṭiqah*), §68.4, §74.2, §79.2, §86.2, §104.2, §§137.4–5, §150.2, §154.2; recollection of knowledge after disembodiment, §§164.1–3; reason for distinction between three souls, §§166.1–3; time of attachment to body, §§163.1–4; vegetative (*nafs nabātiyyah*), §163.3, §166.2
species (*nawʿ*), §88.5, §§91.3–4, §92.3, §103.3, §108.2, §133.2, §142.2, §159.2, §166.2, §170.2
speech, §66.4, §67.1, §83.3, §114.1, §123.1, §126.2, §142.2, §148.2, 296n25
stable state (*malakah*), §66.2, §86.2
substance (*jawhar*), §72.2, §74.2, §83.1, §88.6, §102.3, §120.1, §137.2, §140.2, §144.2, §147.3, §§150.2–3, §151.1, §151.3, §§162.4–5, §163.2, §§164.2–3, §172.2
Sufi, 297n42
suicide, §74.3

tall people, character of, §73.1
al-Ṭarmī, §123.1
al-Tawḥīdī. *See* Abū Ḥayyān al-Tawḥīdī
temperance, §154.2
Thābit ibn Qurrah, §165.4, 298n52
thunder, §§174.1–3
time, §90.3, §101.2, §121.2, §122.2, §144.2, §147.2, §147.4, §147.6, §153.4, §§174.2–3, §175.2

travel, reason for people's differential longing for, §91.1
treachery, §117.2
Turks, §86.1

virtue, §67.2, §70.2, §84.2, §§86.1–3, §131.2, §136.2, §§137.4–5, §141.2, §142.2. *See also* excellence
well-being, reason why it is oppressive, §134.1; reason why we do not sense it as acutely as pain, §§100.1–2
wisdom, §68.3, §79.2, §§82.1–2, §83.4, §88.1, §102.3, §105.1, §106.1, §114.1, §147.1, §150.2, §167.2
wonder, §83.1, §86.2, §96.2, §98.1, §107.1, §119.1, §145.1
world, §67.2, §§68.1–3, §82.1, §83.2, §86.3, §88.4, §88.8, §90.1, §91.1, §92.3, §93.1, §105.2, §113.2, §116.1, §131.1, §§133.1–2, §135.2, §139.1, §143.1, §151.2, §153.3, §155.2, §158.3, §162.4, §165.4, §167.3, §172.3, §173.2; causes of flourishing or ruin of the, §§103.1–5; reason for human love of the, §§102.1–3
worldly goods, §87.1, §105.2, §134.2, §147.6; reason why merit does not coincide with, §§88.1–10
wounds, §85.3

young people, §66.4, §§84.1–2, §156.4; reason why their rate of death is higher than old people, §96.1

volatility of temper, §136.1

About the NYU Abu Dhabi Institute

NYU ABU DHABI INSTITUTE

The Library of Arabic Literature is supported by a grant from the NYU Abu Dhabi Institute, a major hub of intellectual and creative activity and advanced research. The Institute hosts academic conferences, workshops, lectures, film series, performances, and other public programs directed both to audiences within the UAE and to the worldwide academic and research community. It is a center of the scholarly community for Abu Dhabi, bringing together faculty and researchers from institutions of higher learning throughout the region.

NYU Abu Dhabi, through the NYU Abu Dhabi Institute, is a world-class center of cutting-edge research, scholarship, and cultural activity. The Institute creates singular opportunities for leading researchers from across the arts, humanities, social sciences, sciences, engineering, and the professions to carry out creative scholarship and conduct research on issues of major disciplinary, multidisciplinary, and global significance.

About the Typefaces

The Arabic body text is set in DecoType Naskh, designed by Thomas Milo and Mirjam Somers, based on an analysis of five centuries of Ottoman manuscript practice. The exceptionally legible result is the first and only typeface in a style that fully implements the principles of script grammar (*qawāʿid al-khaṭṭ*).

The Arabic footnote text is set in DecoType Emiri, drawn by Mirjam Somers, based on the metal typeface in the naskh style that was cut for the 1924 Cairo edition of the Qurʾan.

Both Arabic typefaces in this series are controlled by a dedicated font layout engine. ACE, the Arabic Calligraphic Engine, invented by Peter Somers, Thomas Milo, and Mirjam Somers of DecoType, first operational in 1985, pioneered the principle followed by later smart font layout technologies such as OpenType, which is used for all other typefaces in this series.

The Arabic text was set with WinSoft Tasmeem, a sophisticated user interface for DecoType ACE inside Adobe InDesign. Tasmeem was conceived and created by Thomas Milo (DecoType) and Pascal Rubini (WinSoft) in 2005.

The English text is set in Adobe Text, a new and versatile text typeface family designed by Robert Slimbach for Western (Latin, Greek, Cyrillic) typesetting. Its workhorse qualities make it perfect for a wide variety of applications, especially for longer passages of text where legibility and economy are important. Adobe Text bridges the gap between calligraphic Renaissance types of the 15th and 16th centuries and high-contrast Modern styles of the 18th century, taking many of its design cues from early post-Renaissance Baroque transitional types cut by designers such as Christoffel van Dijck, Nicolaus Kis, and William Caslon. While grounded in classical form, Adobe Text is also a statement of contemporary utilitarian design, well suited to a wide variety of print and on-screen applications.

Titles Published by the Library of Arabic Literature

For more details on individual titles, visit www.libraryofarabicliterature.org

Classical Arabic Literature: A Library of Arabic Literature Anthology
Selected and translated by Geert Jan van Gelder (**2012**)

A Treasury of Virtues: Sayings, Sermons, and Teachings of ʿAlī, by al-Qāḍī al-Quḍāʿī, with the **One Hundred Proverbs** attributed to al-Jāḥiẓ
Edited and translated by Tahera Qutbuddin (**2013**)

The Epistle on Legal Theory, by al-Shāfiʿī
Edited and translated by Joseph E. Lowry (**2013**)

Leg over Leg, by Aḥmad Fāris al-Shidyāq
Edited and translated by Humphrey Davies (**4 volumes; 2013–14**)

Virtues of the Imām Aḥmad ibn Ḥanbal, by Ibn al-Jawzī
Edited and translated by Michael Cooperson (**2 volumes; 2013–15**)

The Epistle of Forgiveness, by Abū l-ʿAlāʾ al-Maʿarrī
Edited and translated by Geert Jan van Gelder and Gregor Schoeler (**2 volumes; 2013–14**)

The Principles of Sufism, by ʿĀʾishah al-Bāʿūniyyah
Edited and translated by Th. Emil Homerin (**2014**)

The Expeditions: An Early Biography of Muḥammad, by Maʿmar ibn Rāshid
Edited and translated by Sean W. Anthony (**2014**)

Two Arabic Travel Books
Accounts of China and India, by Abū Zayd al-Sīrāfī
Edited and translated by Tim Mackintosh-Smith (**2014**)
Mission to the Volga, by Aḥmad ibn Faḍlān
Edited and translated by James Montgomery (**2014**)

Disagreements of the Jurists: A Manual of Islamic Legal Theory, by al-Qāḍī al-Nuʿmān
Edited and translated by Devin J. Stewart (**2015**)

Consorts of the Caliphs: Women and the Court of Baghdad, by Ibn al-Sāʿī
Edited by Shawkat M. Toorawa and translated by the Editors of the Library of Arabic Literature **(2015)**

What ʿĪsā ibn Hishām Told Us, by Muḥammad al-Muwayliḥī
Edited and translated by Roger Allen **(2 volumes; 2015)**

The Life and Times of Abū Tammām, by Abū Bakr Muḥammad ibn Yaḥyā al-Ṣūlī
Edited and translated by Beatrice Gruendler **(2015)**

The Sword of Ambition: Bureaucratic Rivalry in Medieval Egypt, by ʿUthmān ibn Ibrāhīm al-Nābulusī
Edited and translated by Luke Yarbrough **(2016)**

Brains Confounded by the Ode of Abū Shādūf Expounded, by Yūsuf al-Shirbīnī
Edited and translated by Humphrey Davies **(2 volumes; 2016)**

Light in the Heavens: Sayings of the Prophet Muḥammad, by al-Qāḍī al-Quḍāʿī
Edited and translated by Tahera Qutbuddin **(2016)**

Risible Rhymes, by Muḥammad ibn Maḥfūẓ al-Sanhūrī
Edited and translated by Humphrey Davies **(2016)**

A Hundred and One Nights
Edited and translated by Bruce Fudge **(2016)**

The Excellence of the Arabs, by Ibn Qutaybah
Edited by James E. Montgomery and Peter Webb
Translated by Sarah Bowen Savant and Peter Webb **(2017)**

Scents and Flavors: A Syrian Cookbook
Edited and translated by Charles Perry **(2017)**

Arabian Satire: Poetry from 18th-Century Najd, by Ḥmēdān al-Shwēʿir
Edited and translated by Marcel Kurpershoek **(2017)**

In Darfur: An Account of the Sultanate and Its People, by Muḥammad ibn ʿUmar al-Tūnisī
Edited and translated by Humphrey Davies **(2 volumes; 2018)**

War Songs, by ʿAntarah ibn Shaddād
Edited by James E. Montgomery
Translated by James E. Montgomery with Richard Sieburth (2018)

Arabian Romantic: Poems on Bedouin Life and Love, by ʿAbdallah ibn Sbayyil
Edited and translated by Marcel Kurpershoek (2018)

Dīwān ʿAntarah ibn Shaddād: A Literary-Historical Study
By James E. Montgomery (2018)

Stories of Piety and Prayer: Deliverance Follows Adversity, by Muḥassin ibn ʿAlī al-Tanūkhī
Edited and translated by Julia Bray (2019)

Tajrīd sayf al-himmah li-strikhrāj mā fī dhimmat al-dhimmah: A Scholarly Edition of ʿUthmān ibn Ibrāhīm al-Nābulusī's Text
by Luke Yarbrough (2019)

The Philosopher Responds: An Intellectual Correspondence from the Tenth Century, by Abū Ḥayyān al-Tawḥīdī and Abū ʿAlī Miskawayh
Edited by Bilal Orfali and Maurice A. Pomerantz
Translated by Sophia Vasalou and James E. Montgomery (2 volumes; 2019)

The Discourses: Reflections on History, Sufism, Theology, and Literature—Volume One, by al-Ḥasan al-Yūsī
Edited and translated by Justin Stearns (2020)

English-only Paperbacks

Leg over Leg, by Aḥmad Fāris al-Shidyāq (2 volumes; 2015)
The Expeditions: An Early Biography of Muḥammad, by Maʿmar ibn Rāshid (2015)
The Epistle on Legal Theory: A Translation of al-Shāfiʿī's *Risālah*, by al-Shāfiʿī (2015)
The Epistle of Forgiveness, by Abū l-ʿAlāʾ al-Maʿarrī (2016)
The Principles of Sufism, by ʿĀʾishah al-Bāʿūniyyah (2016)
A Treasury of Virtues: Sayings, Sermons, and Teachings of ʿAlī, by al-Qāḍī al-Quḍāʿī with the **One Hundred Proverbs**, attributed to al-Jāḥiẓ (2016)
The Life of Ibn Ḥanbal, by Ibn al-Jawzī (2016)

Mission to the Volga, by Ibn Faḍlān (2017)

Accounts of China and India, by Abū Zayd al-Sīrāfī (2017)

A Hundred and One Nights (2017)

Disagreements of the Jurists: A Manual of Islamic Legal Theory, by al-Qāḍī al-Nuʿmān (2017)

What ʿĪsā ibn Hishām Told Us, by Muḥammad al-Muwayliḥī (2018)

War Songs, by ʿAntarah ibn Shaddād (2018)

The Life and Times of Abū Tammām, by Abū Bakr Muḥammad ibn Yaḥyā al-Ṣūlī (2018)

The Sword of Ambition, by ʿUthmān ibn Ibrāhīm al-Nābulusī (2019)

Brains Confounded by the Ode of Abū Shādūf Expounded: Volume One, by Yūsuf al-Shirbīnī (2019)

Brains Confounded by the Ode of Abū Shādūf Expounded: Volume Two, by Yūsuf al-Shirbīnī and **Risible Rhymes**, by Muḥammad ibn Maḥfūẓ al-Sanhūrī (2019)

The Excellence of the Arabs, by Ibn Qutaybah (2019)

Light in the Heavens: Sayings of the Prophet Muḥammad, by al-Qāḍī al-Quḍāʿī (2019)

About the Editor–Translators

Bilal Orfali is Associate Professor of Arabic Studies at the American University of Beirut. He co-edits *al-Abhath Journal* and Brill's series *Texts and Studies on the Qurʾan*, and he is the author and editor of more than twenty books on Arabic Studies. His recent publications include *The Anthologist's Art*, *The Book of Noble Character*, *The Comfort of the Mystics*, *In the Shadow of Arabic*, and *Sufism, Black and White*.

Maurice A. Pomerantz is Associate Professor of Literature at New York University Abu Dhabi. He is the author of *Licit Magic: The Life and Letters of al-Ṣāḥib b. ʿAbbād*.

Sophia Vasalou is Senior Lecturer and Birmingham Fellow in Philosophical Theology at the University of Birmingham. Her books include *Moral Agents and their Deserts: The Character of Mu'tazilite Ethics*, *Wonder: A Grammar*, and *Ibn Taymiyya's Theological Ethics*.

James E. Montgomery is Sir Thomas Adams's Professor of Arabic, Fellow of Trinity Hall at the University of Cambridge, and an Executive Editor of the Library of Arabic Literature. His latest publications are *Loss Sings*, a collaboration with the celebrated Scottish artist Alison Watt, and *Dīwān ʿAntarah ibn Shaddād: A Literary-Historical Study*. He is preparing a translation of poems by al-Mutanabbī for Archipelago Books.